Ginger and Salt

WOMEN IN CROSS-CULTURAL PERSPECTIVE
Sue-Ellen Jacobs, Series Editor

This series presents ethnographic case studies that address theoretical, methodological, and practical issues in basic and applied fieldwork; it also includes cross-cultural studies based on secondary sources. Edited by Sue-Ellen Jacobs, the series aims to broaden our knowledge about the varieties and commonalities of women's experiences. One important focus of the series is on women in development and the effects of the development process on women's roles and status. By considering women in the full context of their cultures, this series offers new insights on sociocultural, political, and economic change cross-culturally.

Ginger and Salt

Yemeni Jewish Women in an Israeli Town

Lisa Gilad

Westview Press
BOULDER, SAN FRANCISCO, & LONDON

Women in Cross-Cultural Perspective

The poems excerpted from *Daughters of Yemen* by Mishael Caspi (copyright © 1985 by Mishael Caspi and published by the University of California Press) are reprinted by permission. The interview with "Esther" in Chapter 5 appeared in full in "A Jewish Yemeni Woman's Explanation of the Family Purity Rituals," by Lisa Gilad, in *Cambridge Anthropology, Vol. 7, no. 3* (Copyright © 1982 by Lisa Gilad). Reprinted by permission. The excerpts "Coping with Sexual Conduct" in Chapter 7 are reproduced from "Contrasting Notions of Proper Conduct: Yemeni Jewish Women in an Israeli Town," by Lisa Gilad, in *Jewish Social Studies*, Volume 45, Winter 1983. Reproduced by permission.

This Westview softcover edition is printed on acid-free paper and bound in softcovers that carry the highest rating of the National Association of State Textbook Administrators, in consultation with the Association of American Publishers and the Book Manufacturers' Institute.

All rights reserved. No part of this publication may be reproduced or transmitted in any form or by any means, electronic or mechanical, including photocopy, recording, or any information storage and retrieval system, without permission in writing from the publisher.

Copyright © 1989 by Westview Press, Inc.

Published in 1989 in the United States of America by Westview Press, Inc., 5500 Central Avenue, Boulder, Colorado 80301, and in the United Kingdom by Westview Press, Inc., 13 Brunswick Centre, London WC1N 1AF, England

Library of Congress Cataloging-in-Publication Data
Gilad, Lisa.
 Ginger and salt: Yemeni Jewish women in an Israeli town / Lisa Gilad.
   p.   cm.—(Women in cross-cultural perspective)
Bibliography: p.
Includes index.
ISBN 0-8133-7686-6
 1. Women—Israel—Social conditions. 2. Jews, Yemenite—Israel—
Social conditions. 3. Immigrants—Israel—Social conditions.
4. Yemen—Emigration and immigration. 5. Israel—Emigration and
immigration. 6. Israel—Ethnic relations. I. Title. II. Series.
HQ1728.5.G55 1989
305.4'2'095694—dc19   88-28063
                                                                        CIP

Printed and bound in the United States of America

∞ The paper used in this publication meets the requirements of the American National Standard for Permanence of Paper for Printed Library Materials Z39.48-1984.

10 9 8 7 6 5 4 3 2 1

For my grandmother
Sarah Zychick

Contents

List of Tables and Photos   x
Acknowledgments   xi
Author's Note   xiii

1 Introducing Ginger and Salt   1

Choosing the Field, 3
Women and the Immigrant Experience, 6
Questions and Issues, 9
Notes, 10

2 From Yemen to Israel   13

From Child to Bride to Woman:
   The Life Cycle in Yemen, 16
"On the Wings of Eagles":
   Immigration to Israel, 23
Notes, 26

3 Introducing Gadot and Israeli Ethnicities   29

Introducing Gadot, 29
The Yemenis of Gadot, 34
Doing Field Work, 38
Ethnic Issues in Israeli Society, 43
Notes, 50

4 The Immigrant Generation   53

The Noble Brother, 54
Marriages of the Immigrant Generation, 60
"My Friend Is My Sister," 81
Images of the Ashkenazi Employer, 85
Overview, 88
Notes, 91

5 Being Female in Transition — 105

The Immigrant Generation as Daughters, 107
Purification of the Family, 114
Conjugal Duty: Sexual Intercourse, 121
Being Female Is Being a Mother, 124
Overview, 128
Notes, 131

6 The Israeli-born Generation: Unmarried Women — 135

Going to School—New Opportunities, 138
The Army, 143
Work, 145
The Residential Choice: Living at Home
  or Moving Out, 146
Changing Notions of Proper Conduct:
  New Codes of Honour, 151
Overview, 158
Notes, 162

7 Proper Conduct and Social Reality: The Immigrant and Israeli-born Generations — 169

Derekh Erets and Interes, 172
Housework: Perennial Problems, 173
Leisure Time, 175
Coping with Sexual Conduct, 182
Mothers and Sons, 189
Fears of Old Age, 194
Sibling Relationships, 196
Overview, 202
Notes, 204

8 The Immigrant Experience — 211

Israel as a Receiving Society, 212
Yemeni Jewish Ethnicity
  and the Israeli State, 216
Issues in the Anthropological Study
  of the Immigrant Experience, 226

Epilogue, 238
Notes, 239

Glossary 243
Bibliography 247
Index 270

Tables and Photos

Tables

4.1	Domestic and public domains in Yemen	64
4.2	Domestic and public domains in Israel	82
7.1	Daughter's self-defined religious affiliation and relationship to her mother	180

Photos

A Yemeni Jewish youth	100
The traditional wedding outfit	100
An old mother and grandmother prepare henna	101
The ritual separation of the bride from her family	101
A grandfather born in Yemen chooses the palm branch for his *lulav*	102
Men dancing at a Bar Mitzvah celebration	102
One of Gadot's first apartment buildings	103
New "*vilot*" in Gadot	103

Acknowledgments

I like to make acknowledgments because it is one of the few ways to say thank you. First there are the three generations of my own family whose financial and emotional support enabled the research and writing-up of this study. They include my grandparents, Sarah and Julius Zychick; my parents, Charlotte and Larry Gould; and my siblings Tammy and Marc Gould. My late brother, Brian, helped in ways he will never know. He died shortly before I began field work; he spent a number of Sabbaths with the Yemenis of Gadot, who grew to love him and he them. When I arrived in the field, people who knew him opened their doors to his sister, a *miskena* (wretched one) because she was grieving. In this way, the Yemenis also helped me to adjust to my loss.

During field work, the Jerusalem Centre for Anthropological Research and the William Wyse Fund of Trinity College, Cambridge, generously provided financial assistance. The New Hall Travel Fund enabled me to make a return trip to Israel to tie up loose ends. The Wyse Fund also provided a maintenance grant during the final stage of the writing of my Ph.D., on which this book is based. The Fortes Fund generously provided funds to that effect, as well.

In Israel, the most credit goes, of course, to the Yemeni Jews of Gadot and to other residents, who were very hospitable and generous with their time. I thank them for accepting me as *bat bayit*, a daughter of the house. A special thanks goes to my research assistant and friend, who is called in this book Amalia, for her remarkable work habits, for completing a follow-up questionnaire after I left the field, for always making time for me, and for her patience and understanding.

A number of anthropologists helped me in Israel, particularly in choosing a place of research and identifying key issues. They include Don Handelman, Alex Weingrod, Yael Katzir, Yedida Stillman, Henry Abramovitch, and the sociologist Lea Handelman. My debt to Phyllis Palgi for her help throughout all stages of my Ph.D. cannot be repaid. Her work experience among Yemenis for over thirty years was generously shared with me. The late Eileen Basker made invaluable suggestions for understanding my material, and I valued her encouragement. Yosef Tobi, a Yemeni Jewish historian, made criticisms on the chapter on Yemen; without his help inaccuracies would have appeared.

In Cambridge, Martha Mundy added considerably to my knowledge of Muslim Yemeni society. The late Meyer Fortes, who was my supervisor during pre-field work and field work, always asked provocative questions. Esther Goody, my supervisor during the initial writing-up of this study, was wonderful at making sense out of a lot of hard data. Sue Benson, friend and teacher, provided emotional support and academic criticism throughout; my gratitude to her for this and for reading several earlier drafts of this study cannot be expressed in words.

The Department of Social Anthropology, Cambridge, and the Queen Elizabeth II Library of Memorial University kindly provided me with the office space to write this book. Pat Little and Jeannette Gleeson patiently typed the manuscripts, and Helen Peters swiftly performed as copy editor. Also in St. John's, Judy Adler and Cecilia Benoit made fruitful comments.

A special thank you to Unni Wikan in Oslo for sharing with me her 1982 slides of Yemeni Jews in Yemen, a rare treasure, and for permitting me to use them freely.

Five people read the final versions of this manuscript (besides the anonymous readers to whom I am extremely grateful). Three specialists on women and society, Ziba Mir Husseini, Deirdre Meintel, and Sue-Ellen Jacobs, helped considerably, as did Nigel Rapport. And last, but foremost, my husband, Robert Paine, has been following my progress with Yemeni Jewish women for seven years. Not only did he read and comment on two drafts of the manuscript, but he heard about it over numerous lunches and helped me to arrange my thoughts. He believed in me, and I would not have written this book without him.

And, my thanks to Jessica Erin, for putting up with an absentee mother even if she didn't know any better.

Lisa Gilad

Author's Note

Gadot and Asher, the two towns mentioned in *Ginger and Salt,* are pseudonyms. All names of persons in the study are also pseudonyms and certain details have been changed in order to protect people's privacy.

The first time a Hebrew or Arabic word is used, it is italicized; in subsequent appearances it is not. All Hebrew and Arabic words appear in the Glossary.

Throughout the book I have kept the text largely ethnographic and analytical. Readers wishing to understand more about my analyses or to receive more information, particularly of a cross-cultural nature, are advised to read the notes as they go along. Readers wishing to read primarily for ethnographic content, can skip the notes until the end of the chapter.

L. G.

1

Introducing Ginger and Salt

It was a quiet autumn morning in Gadot, Israel; everyone was at work or at school. I was at my typewriter, trying to remember some of the events of the previous evening. Suddenly, through my open windows I heard a woman's sobs. I ran out to the square to see what the problem was. There was Adina—a Yemeni Jewish woman, forty-nine years old, mother of ten children—sobbing. She was moving from side to side, extending her arms to the sky as if asking God to help her. Since we knew each other well, I asked what troubled her so; she replied that it was too awful to speak about. I insisted that she come to my flat for a cup of coffee, and finally, after an hour of tears, she poured out her heart. The night before her husband had defiled her; instead of waiting until fifteen days after the onset of menses and her immersion in the *mikveh* (ritual bath) as required by religious law, her husband forcibly had sexual intercourse with her. She could not understand his behavior because he had not done so in thirty years of marriage. More important, and this was the reason for her tears, she feared that the evil eye would destroy her whole family because they did not adhere to the family purity rituals (*taharat hamishpahah*).

I asked Adina if she knew that in Yemen, Jewish women had a cure for this type of pollution: her reply was negative. Without hesitation I suggested that she seek the advice of a Yemeni healer who had told me the cure consists of a ginger and salt paste which is spread on the vagina. After reciting several blessings, the defiled woman would then be purified. Adina left immediately to learn the appropriate blessings used during the purification ritual. The next day she rewarded me with a dozen roses, thanking me profusely for having saved her family. She wanted to know how I knew about the ritual; I replied that learning such things was part of my research.

The point of this story is not simply that when working in immigrant societies, the anthropologist often ends up filling in aspects of "lost" culture, but that women with whom I spent a lot of time continue to practice ancient rituals from their Yemeni Jewish heritage, even when they no longer have the knowledge to cope with calamities in the new context of Israeli society. This episode in Adina's life took place thirty-two years after she immigrated to Israel. If she had still been in Yemen, undoubtedly she would have known the cure. It is also possible that if she had lived in an ethnically segregated Yemeni community in Israel, other women could have informed her of the cure. Gadot, an Israeli immigrant settlement and the setting for this study, was far from homogeneous; Yemenis were dispersed among Jews who had emigrated from seventy other countries. I chose Gadot precisely because of its cultural diversity, allowing a unique opportunity to study Israeli values of "integration" and to see how one particular *eidah* (ethnic community), the Yemeni Jews, interacted with others from all around the globe.[1] I wanted to understand why being "Yemeni" was still an important identity to people thirty-two years after the group immigrated to Israel and to learn what it meant to their children.

The title of this book was chosen for the symbolic significance of those ingredients used in the purification ritual undergone by Adina: ginger, a spice used daily in Yemen for both flavour and healing, and salt, the mineral evoking the bitterness and troubles of the Jewish people. Ginger and salt, then, bring together two of the socially important identities and cultures of the Yemeni Jews in Israel. While I studied Yemeni Jews of all ages, the people in this book are two generations of women.[2] One generation is the women who immigrated from Yemen shortly after the creation of the state of Israel; the other is their daughters, who were born in Israel. *Ginger and Salt* is about starting afresh in an "old-new" country, about radical changes in the self-images and actions of the immigrant generation, and particularly interesting, the "invention" for the younger generation of a period of life as *unmarried women*.

Both generations of women experience conflicting imperatives placed upon them and created by them in Israeli society. The immigrant generation believes in the traditionally Yemeni Jewish model of women solely committed to managing their households. Yet in Israel mothers find they must work in paid employment in order to provide their children with a good education and to "supplement" their husbands' low incomes. Outside work, in turn, is often seen to interfere with good mothering because it takes away from the time a mother spends with her children and affects her ability to manage her household efficiently. At the same time, women's experiences in paid employment are seen to threaten and re-arrange the family authority structure. Nevertheless, work outside the home and involvement in a wide variety of extra-domestic activities has enabled immigrant women to gain more authority in the home, to gain more independence from the family unit, even to engage in politics. In sum, they achieve an understanding that their lives as women in Israel are considerably "liberated" from what they now view as enslaving constraints on Jewish women's lives in Yemen.

Daughters, by contrast, do not suffer from the problems—for example, illiteracy or confronting a Western medical system—their mothers faced upon arrival to Israel. They find themselves filling a social status previously unknown to Jewish women in Yemen: unmarried adulthood. In Yemen, a girl went from child to bride to become a complete "woman" only upon the birth of her children. In Israel, as in the West in general, childhood is followed by prolonged "adolescence." The majority of these women spend two years in the army, several years in university, and finally, years in the work force and often travel abroad. Thus they postpone marriage, in many cases, until their late twenties, having passed through at least ten years during which their parents wished for nothing more than the successful marriages of their daughters—even though they are pleased that their daughters achieve university degrees. The conflicting imperatives of unmarried women's lives revolve around their desire to experience the world around them and meeting the expectations of their "primitive" (a word learned in Israel) and religious parents demanding early marriage. This pocket of time—unmarried adulthood—is without precedence in traditional Yemeni Jewish culture. Nor do they really have a welcome place in the wider Israeli society, once they reach their mid-twenties, because by this age Israeli women—even the secular—are expected to marry, "to be fruitful and multiply."

What is striking is how the two generations constantly seek to accommodate the conflicting imperatives that invade their lives. Particularly notable is how some of the immigrant generation continue to believe in the practices of the past while accepting the social realities of the present. In fact, at the level of belief unmarried women are faced with making considerable changes in notions of honour and shame. Here there is the contrast between the imperative of pre-marital chastity in Yemeni Jewish society and the practice of pre-marital sex in secular Israeli society. Not surprisingly, such differences and contradictions, especially between the two generations, are often at the root of bitter and inflamed arguments, particularly in those cases where unmarried women continue to live in their parents' homes. This book, then, looks at the creation of new cultural patterns in the family, and in society, according to the perceptions of the women themselves.

Choosing the Field

There were personal and intellectual reasons why I chose Gadot for a research site, and I should also explain my interest in the Yemeni Jews.

Before I began field work in April 1980, I had already lived in Israel intermittently for three years, dividing my time between a *kibbutz* in Southern Galilee and university studies. I met several women soldiers who were working on the kibbutz as part of their service in the agricultural core of the army. I became close friends with two sisters who are daughters of Yemeni immigrants and who grew up in Gadot. I used to visit them in their parents' home when they were there on leave and it was through this family that I became interested in mother-daughter relationships among the Yemenis. After some months of visiting, I was invited to spend Passover with their uncle's family; the Passover service among this large extended family (some forty persons) was very different from that which I knew growing up in an American Jewish home. Though the story of the exodus from Egypt was the same, the rituals and melodies accompanying the story were very different. I felt out of place, and I wanted to know why. How was it that these Yemeni Jews were so different—what was their history, and why was the "old country" still a part of the new?

In the summer of 1978, after my third year of university in Israel, I left with one of the sisters for the United States. She had finished her army service and wanted to travel; I arranged for her to be a guest in my parents' home in Cleveland, Ohio, for a year. I did not know at the time that her stay with my parents would later help me as a field worker. At that time I had no clear research plans. But one reason why I eventually decided on Gadot was because her family and their friends wanted to reciprocate: my parents had given her a home for a year, they wanted to give me one. I had heard that Yemenis were quick to distrust outsiders, so it seemed obvious that if I wanted to study Yemenis, I should go to Gadot where I would be welcome. This indeed was the case; from the moment I arrived in Gadot I was able to begin field work.[3]

I was also attracted to Gadot for reasons which were intertwined with my understanding of Israeli society at that time. During my first summer in Israel as a sixteen year-old tourist, I had the opportunity to live for one week with a Kurdistani Jewish family on a *moshav* (co-operative farm). I never knew that there were Jews from Kurdistan (where was Kurdistan anyway? Certainly not anywhere on my Jewish map). I also never knew that there were Jews in Israel who lived in poverty. The moshav was located in an area which was difficult to farm because of its extremely hot climate and bad soil; nonetheless, the families who lived there made the best of a bad situation.[4] I stayed with a family of fifteen (a mother, father and thirteen children) who lived in a small dwelling consisting of three and a half rooms. Needless to say, coming from my middle-class background, I was shocked by these cramped quarters. Although I could not speak Hebrew at the time and could not get used to the crowded conditions, this experience did lead me to become interested in Jews who were very different from those I knew growing up in Ohio. I spent the next six years learning all that I could about Middle Eastern and North African Jews.

The books which I had read as an undergraduate, almost all written by sociologists and anthropologists, tended to give me an unbalanced view of Israel. Most researchers had been funded by various development agencies who contracted research largely concerned with why certain new settlements or particular *eidot* (ethnic communities) faced difficulties in Israeli society. As a result, these studies focused on social problems, whether in moshavim or development towns, in criminal activities, or as expressed by protest groups (such as the Black Panthers).[5] The relationship of social class and country-of-origin in Israel became readily apparent: immigrants from Europe and America (*Ashkenazim*) and their children invariably had more years of education, better paying jobs, more political representatives, and lived in more prestigious areas than did the immigrants from North Africa and the Middle East.[6] Certainly there were studies explaining the relationship between ethnic origin and class status and underdevelopment in Israel, but I felt the balance needed some correcting. It eventually became clear to me that the "normal" side of Israel was not represented in such studies and I do not mean only the *Ashkenazi* middle class, but also Eastern immigrants who had done well for themselves. Like several others, then, I decided to study a place in Israel which was neither unsuccessful nor of an entirely Middle Eastern Jewish population.[7]

Beginning with my first visit to Gadot in the spring of 1978 I became curious about the town. On the basis of my social science reading, I pictured almost all new towns in Israel as ridden with problems of ethnic strife, political immaturity, unemployment, and so on. But other than a dilapidated, run-down central market, Gadot was clearly thriving and I learned very quickly that it had virtually no unemployment or unoccupied youth, or out-migration. Contrary to many other new towns in Israel, young couples from Gadot remained there, the school system was good, most of the houses were in excellent condition, and it had a vibrant political life. Also, its population was at least 30 percent Ashkenazi. Why was the town different, why had Gadot discovered a successful development path without the utilization of, even more surprisingly, a selective absorption policy like other new towns?[8] I also felt that to work in a place such as Gadot, I would be able to learn about issues that were not central to the prevailing sociological concerns in Israel. For me, Gadot seemed like an ideal place to do research, and so it proved.

While I learned a great deal about council politics, urban development, and the educational system in Gadot, most of my time I spent with

Yemeni Jewish women. I was able to speak with and observe men in the household or the synagogue, but it would have been inappropriate for me as an unmarried woman to try to become close with married men of the immigrant generation, largely because of the concern over the possibility of illicit affairs and religiously-inspired taboos. In fact, it took me about eight months to get up the nerve to greet men at the all-male tables found at celebrations where they debated religious questions, told stories, and drank brandy.

Nor, clearly, could I study people from seventy different ethnic groups in Gadot. For one thing their identity as "Israelis" was not really of interest to them or to me—not in the local context, that is. I was not interested in immigrants from Hungary, Germany or Russia because they were too familiar to me; like most anthropologists I wanted to study "the other." Nor did I want to study Moroccans or Tunisians because they were already the subjects of extensive social research; I was interested in the large Turkish population, but husbands would not let me get close to their wives who would always be shooed out to the kitchen when I came to visit. I chose the Yemenis because, as I said above, I knew several families who would help me get started with research—"connections" are important in any complex society. More importantly, perhaps, in Israeli society Yemenis represented an Oriental (*Mizrahi*) ethnic community that maintained a prestigious ethnic profile. I wanted to know why they differed from the other immigrants from the East, or at least why Israelis in general held such a (relatively) high opinion of Yemenis. And, although Yemeni Jews were the subject of previous anthropological studies, no one had worked with Yemenis who did not think of themselves as a cohesive ethnic community.[9]

Women and the Immigrant Experience

There are features of Yemeni Jewish society which are somewhat unique, both in the Yemen and as immigrants. In the Yemen, Jews lived as an encapsulated minority in an isolated Muslim environment, but Jewish women shared similar life conditions and self-images with Muslim women.[10] As immigrants, the transplanted community of Yemeni Jews find themselves in a Jewish society, in which they could make immediate claims as Zionists and as Jews. This differentiates them (along with other Jewish immigrants to Israel) from immigrants to other countries where a sense of belonging is more difficult to achieve, and even once achieved has different implications. Nonetheless, Yemeni Jews, men and women alike, are involved in the continual emotional and social adjustments felt by immigrants everywhere. Here I briefly discuss several important issues found in the study of immigrant women's lives generally and which have specific relevance to Yemeni Jewish women.

The sociological study of women and migration is a recent phenomenon even though that of immigrant (ethnic) cultures is not—in such studies (conducted largely by men) women feature in discussions of the family. The new focus on women as immigrants (people who leave their home countries permanently) and as migrants (those who leave their homes usually for economic reasons but intend to return) is probably due to three factors: (1) the opening up of Western societies as legitimate places of anthropological enquiry; immigrants are a target for research because they are so obviously of the anthropological "other"; (2) the constraints of the job market whereby trained anthropologists are hired by governments or private foundations to conduct "applied" projects in respect to the work, health, and educational needs of immigrant women; and (3) the concerns of feminist debate in which immigrant women are seen to be "oppressed" on several levels—sex, work, and minority status. Aside from these reasons, there is also personal involvement together with the need to break stereotypical images through the medium of scholarly discourse: several writers about immigrant women belong to the cultures in which they conducted research.[11]

In earlier studies, "women" were usually seen as "dependents" upon men; these studies also tended to be pre-occupied with each immigrant group's ability to amalgamate, assimilate, acculturate, and integrate into their host societies.[12] Any study of immigrant people—including this one—can draw benefit from insights thrown up by such concepts, but, on the whole, the subtleties and nuances of life in a new society escape them. I avoid the use of such language in *Ginger and Salt* in the interests of a more intimate portrait of the immigrant experience.

Feminist studies have undoubtedly contributed the most to our understanding of the life conditions of immigrant women. Some of that work has focused on the broad structural implications of the exploitation of immigrant women in the labour market and their hidden contribution to the development and maintenance of industrial capitalism.[13] On the micro level, most of the anthropological research on immigrant women has dealt with the effects of migration on sex roles, gender relations, family patterns and women's status. While the major focus is often expressed as the "effects of migration," it is not the physical move itself, from one country to another, that is of interest. Rather, the significant questions pertain to the effects of a woman's entry into wage labour—or into wage labour that brings in a greater economic contribution than that known in the old country—on her authority in the family, on the necessity for her husband to help in the home, on her own self-image and so on. For many immigrant women—even if, objectively, they work harder in and out of the home—bringing in an income, and controlling its use, is liberating. However, some feminist writers maintain that the severe exploitation of women's labour is even more oppressive than was the case in the old country. To some extent, this is because it appears, to the external eye, that immigrant women's wage labour is an extension of the duties of wife and mother, and not an intrinsic value.[14] Moreover, in cases where women do not work in paid employment, migration might further isolate them from the outside world and women themselves might very well become the guardians of the traditions and values of the old country, whether they like it or not.[15]

It would be unwise to argue with the fact that immigrant women are, in many cases, exploited in the labour market because they are forced to take low-paying and low status jobs. This is particularly likely where the women face language and educational barriers, but we have to take note that this exploitation does not necessarily mirror their domestic relations. Women themselves may view their new situation in a different light: they often believe they are better off, financially and socially, than they were in their countries-of-origin. At the same time, account must be taken of the position of men in the labour market, and their immigrant experience as it relates to conjugal and parental relations. Much of Chapter 4 pertains to the social and economic repercussions of immigration on both women and men, separately and together. We will see that many Yemeni Jewish women have benefited more from immigration than men.

Immigrant peoples display an enormous variety of responses to living in a new society. The crude facts of women's labour force participation and position are the least problematic to document and to compare across different cultures. By contrast, the daily habits, family relationships, sentiments and frustrations experienced by immigrants take considerable time and sensitivity for the outside observer to comprehend. *Ginger and Salt* is concerned with Yemeni Jewish women of the immigrant generation and their Israeli-born daughters, but we can readily see their troubles and joys in accounts of immigrant family lives elsewhere in the world.[16] However, caution should be exercised before generalizing about immigrant women as a group. At all events, no study of immigrant lives is complete without an appreciation of the cultural contexts from which they have come; of the journey to the new society, its immigration policies, the type of place in which they settle, the constraints of the local labour market; and of the racial and cultural attitudes they confront. These and other factors together shape the process of becoming a member of the host society: a process that may be complete in months if one is (say) a white English-speaking immigrant to another English-speaking country of the West; but more likely it takes years. Later in *Ginger and Salt* I address the question of when one ceases to be an immigrant.

Questions and Issues

Ginger and Salt begins in Yemen where we learn about the social and political environment in which Jews had lived for 2,000 years prior to their immigration to Israel. This cultural and historical overview provides the wider context in which to understand Yemeni Jewish women of both generations in Israel. I then describe the physical movement of 55,000 people, straight out of a medieval technology in Yemen, who were guided into Skyhawk airplanes and transported to Israel. This is a notable migration in that with the airlift, an entire people was transplanted from its home of exile to its home of redemption. We then come to Gadot and to its Yemeni Jewish population, but we also locate Yemenis in the complex mosaic of ethnic groups and images in Israeli society. In Chapter 2, we begin to find answers to the question of why Yemeni identity is still important to the immigrant generation and why it is potentially important to their children even though over thirty years have passed since they immigrated to Israel. Remaining Yemeni has enormous implications for the family and community life of the immigrant generation.

"Time" has various dimensions in anthropological usage. In the study of immigrants it is particularly important to learn how people remember their past and incorporate it into their present understandings and how they use their past in conceptualizing their future.[17] The past-present-future orientation is also integral to the study of relationships between generations. After the introduction to Yemen's Jews in Chapter 2, the immigrant generation's memories and accounts of the past in Yemen are referred to throughout *Ginger and Salt*. This is not simply further to inform or remind the reader of the many contrasts between life in Yemen and in Israel; rather this constant recall belongs to the daily conversations and psychology of Yemeni Jews in Israel. Not all immigrant people draw upon their recollections of a glorious—or a not so glorious—past in the old country. That Yemenis in Gadot do, reflects upon who they are in Israeli society. I shall clarify this in the course of the book.

Inevitably, this study of immigrants and their children raises a range of questions concerning perceptions and meanings. Each chapter is associated with specific issues, although there is some overlap. They include:

1. Under what circumstances do people use old rituals, beliefs, and models in new contexts?
    - Is it dangerous to do so?

- Is it inappropriate to do so?
- Is it necessary?
2. What makes for the ability to accommodate conflicting imperatives—those dictated by the past and those that belong to the present?
   - How is it that some people do so successfully while in the case of others there is a great deal of confusion?
   - Does the maintenance of an intact belief system aid or hinder the process of (a long-term) social and psychological adjustment?
3. Are these conceptual and practical challenges to personal integrity and self-images experienced differently by women and men?
   - If so, how are different responses within a family handled?
   - How does a spouse's place in public life affect the conjugal relationship?
4. How do ideas associated with being female change?
5. Do children born in Israel, whose lives are situated in its realities, complete the process of their parents' immigration?
6. But how does the immigrant (parental) generation perceive the lives of their children, for which there is no cultural precedent in the Yemeni Jewish past?
   - How do parents' places in public life affect relationships with their children?

Notes

1. On inter-ethnic relations among Jewish groups in Israel see: Y. Amir 1973; Avineri 1973; P. Cohen 1967, 1968; Curtis and Chertoff 1973; Eisenstadt 1954, 1967; Friendly 1972; Klaff 1973, 1977; Krausz 1972; Lipset 1973; Mars 1980; Peres 1971; Peres and Schrift 1978; Rejwan 1968; Smooha 1978; Smooha and Peres 1975; Toledano 1973; Weingrod 1975; Weller 1974; and Willner 1979.

2. See the section "Doing Field Work" in Chapter 3 for how the research sets were created.

3. I believe that if I had gone to another Yemeni community, I could have successfully conducted field work, but it might have taken several more months to gain entry and to establish rapport and trust.

4. On moshavim in Israel see: Baldwin 1972; Deshen 1966; Deshen and Shokeid 1974; Goldberg 1972; Mars 1980; Shapiro 1971; Shokeid 1971; Weingrod 1962, 1966, 1971; and Weintraub 1971.

5. On development towns in Israel see: Aronoff 1973a, 1973b, 1973c, 1974a, 1974b; Berler 1970; Berler and Shaked 1966; E. Cohen 1970; Comay and Kirschenbaum 1973; Deshen 1965, 1970, 1974; E. Marx 1976; Matras 1973; Spiegel 1968; and Spilerman and Habib 1974.

On crime and drug abuse in Israel see: Amir 1973; Miller 1971; Shoham 1970a, 1970b, 1973a and 1973b.

Introducing Ginger and Salt

On Jewish protest groups in Israel see: Bernstein 1976; E. Cohen 1972; Elon 1973; Rejwan 1971; and Shama and Iris 1977.

6. The reasons for the class differences within Israeli society are rather complicated and I touch on them briefly in Chapter 3.

7. Cf. Aronoff; and Mars.

8. For example, the towns of Arad, Carmiel and Kiryat Gat maintained selective absorption policies.

9. Studies published in English on Yemeni Jews in Israel include: Ben-Rafael 1982; Berdichevsky 1980; Caspi 1985; P. Cohen 1961; Jiggets 1957; Katzir 1976; H. Lewis 1980, 1982, 1985; and Palgi 1975, 1978, and 1983.

10. On Jewish life in Yemen, refer to Chapter 2.

11. For example, Bhachu 1985; Kramer and Masur 1976; and Wilson 1978.

12. For example, see the studies in Mindel and Habenstein 1976, and for a theoretically influential study Eisenstadt 1954.

13. Boyd 1986; Gannage 1985; Kudat 1982; Lamphere 1986a, 1986b; Morokvasic 1984; Safa 1984; Simon and Delay 1984.

14. Boone 1980; Foner 1986; Gilad and Meintel 1985; and Pessar 1984.

15. Andezian 1985; Andezian and Streiff 1982; Baum *et al.* 1981; Saifullah-Khan 1976.

16. In particular, I am thinking of similarities in experience and perception of Boone's (1980) study of Cuban women in the U.S.; Saifullah-Khan's (1977) description of inter-generational conflict among Pakistanis in Britain; Ballard and Ballard (1977) on second generations Sikhs in Britain; Elkholy (1976) on Arab families in the U.S.; Fitzpatrick (1976) on Puerto Rican women in the U.S.; and Haddad (1981) on Syrian women in Chicago.

17. I am indebted to Meyer Fortes for pointing out this time dimension before I went to the field.

2

From Yemen to Israel

The Yemen Arab Republic, commonly known as North Yemen, is the country-of-origin for the Jews of the immigrant generation; they refer to it simply as *Teman* (Yemen). Yemen is located in the south-western corner of Arabia and has a varied climate: the coastal plain along the Red Sea is largely desert, while the large central plateau and mountainous regions where three-quarters of its population of 6,000,000 live, is green and fertile. It is one of the most isolated areas of the Arab world and has a distinct personality—particularly its architecture of mud skyscrapers built into mountainsides. Once famous for its coffee, amongst other crops, Yemenis now farm large quantities of *qat,* a leafy green plant with a slight valium content.[1] While the present government is trying to bring modern technology to Yemen, its character remains feudal and fraught with tribal tensions. This chapter, however, does not present an historical overview of Yemen.[2] Rather it is concerned with the place of Jews in Muslim society, and the life of women as recalled by Yemeni Jews now living in Gadot.

Accounts of the origin of Jewish settlement in Yemen vary considerably, but all historians agree that it is of considerable antiquity.[3] Legend has it that Jews settled in Yemen during the time of King Solomon when ancient Israel was involved in long-distance trade with the Far East. In all events, archaeological evidence of burial sites of Yemeni Jewish rabbis at Bet Sha'arim, near Haifa, date from 70 C.E.,[4] so it is certain that there was a Jewish community in Yemen at least from the beginning of the Common Era.[5] Other Jewish communities in the Arabian peninsula disappeared, but the Yemeni diaspora population, despite the impact of plague, economic adversity, persecution and forced conversions to Islam, is distinguished by its tenacious survival and its strict adherence to Judaism until the return to Israel *en masse* in 1948.[6]

By the fifth century, the Jewish community was a well-established segment of the Himyar Kingdom of Southern Arabia. With the victory of Islam in the area (*circa* 628 C.E.), however, the Jews became a subjugated people and later a persecuted minority under the legal status of *d'himmi*. Islamic attitudes towards Jews are ambiguous: Jews are respected as a People of the Book who received divine revelation in the Scriptures, but they are subjected to hostile attitudes and actions because they do not believe in Islam.[7] Apart from two periods of relative freedom during Ottoman rule over Yemen (mid-fifteenth to mid-sixteenth centuries and 1872–1918), severe restrictions were imposed on Jews. For example, Jews were forbidden to raise their houses above those of Muslims, to raise their voices in prayer, to sit on donkeys when Muslims walked by, and to wear the same clothes as Muslims.[8] Jews also paid property tax as well as a poll-tax (the *jizya*) which was levied on non-Muslims. Yet, despite the historical record of pogroms against Jews, the people with whom I worked remember their Muslim neighbours as friends; they do not often recall inter-communal strife.[9] Only those from the Jewish quarter on the outskirts of the capital city of San'a recall their fears of Muslim soldiers and religious leaders.

It is estimated that Jews lived in more than 1,000 towns and villages throughout the Yemen;[10] only a minority, approximately 20 percent, lived in the cities of San'a, Dhamar, Rada, and Manakha. The vast majority lived in small villages, in clusters of ten to forty Jewish households in each.[11] Few villages were entirely Jewish; each Jewish community was involved in a patronage system with local tribal chiefs or *shaykhs* who protected Jews in return for the products of Jewish labour. Each Jewish community had a headman, called *aqil* (wise man) who was either wealthy or had connections to the local shaykh. He was responsible for collecting taxes, keeping peace in the Jewish community, mediating disputes, and protecting Jewish interests to the government and belligerent groups.

In Jewish settlements, there was communal property, such as synagogues, hostels for the poor, ritual baths, cemeteries, some fields, water supplies, and a house for widows.[12] The religious functionaries, who were paid in kind, consisted of the local rabbi who was responsible for performing marriage and decreeing divorce, circumcision of male babies, and teaching; the *mori*, teacher of religious texts; and the butcher who slaughtered in adherence to the Jewish dietary laws. Yemeni Jews strongly valued literacy, and it is said that every Jewish male knew how to read and write in Hebrew if not in Arabic, and for this they were respected by their Muslim rulers.

An emphasis on the study of holy texts helped preserve the Jewish rabbinical tradition, and Jews were also strongly influenced by Jewish spiritualist movements outside of Yemen.[13] North and South Yemen adhered to Sephardic (Spanish Jewish tradition) influence, while Central Yemen had Jewish traditions peculiar to itself. It has been suggested that this literary tradition, combined with influences from other Jewish sources, and the Yemeni experience of coping with continual tribal strife, facilitated the process of adaptation for Yemeni Jews in Israel.[14]

For Jewish men, spiritual life concentrated on the study of the Torah and other religious texts which guided Jews in their daily routine. Although men usually studied in small groups, prayers were recited communally, as were the readings of the Torah portions (unlike in Ashkenazi and Sephardi synagogues where the Torah is read by a special reader).[15] Every Sabbath, however, a different man would read the main Torah portion, and for this honour he paid a fee to the keeper of the synagogue for its maintenance, a custom still practised in Yemeni synagogues in Israel. Women, by contrast, were usually illiterate in biblical Hebrew and only attended the synagogue on Sabbath and holidays. They knew the prayers and rituals specifically oriented to women and saw their role in keeping the dietary laws as integral to the maintenance of the Jewish family.

Yemeni Jews also maintain that important for the continuation of their families and communities was their belief in and practice of *Derekh Erets* (proper conduct). While this is a primary value in Judaism generally, Yemenis believe that the first most important prescript of Derekh Erets is that certain religious practices such as daily prayer, dietary laws and family purity rituals be followed. Secondly, it demands honour and respect of parents, kin and neighbours before consideration of oneself. It is ultimately the guide for behaviour for *Adam v'Hevrato* (collective responsibility) and thus Derekh Erets represents a notion of self that is oriented towards relevant "others." A person who has Derekh Erets is admired and trusted; by contrast, a person who lacks it, such as a woman who has lost her virginity before marriage, is often physically or verbally chastised.

While Derekh Erets represents Yemeni ideas of collective responsibility and formal etiquette, the extent to which this guide for proper behaviour was constantly implemented in Yemen is questionable. For example, the largely individualistic ethic espoused by Jews in Yemen, particularly in the realm of economic activity, seems antithetical to Derekh Erets. Proverbs—here seeming to reflect reality—were related to me, and showed the extent to which the person was concerned with oneself before relevant others. One such Sanani proverb was: *fummi agdam min ummi* (my mouth before my mother's).

Yet it is probably true that Jewish children had little opportunity to acquire the habits of disrespect towards their parents. Given the nature of Muslim domination and the close-knit communities in which Jews lived, children also had no other standards of judgement other than those learned in their families. If a person deviated from social conventions, it was only because a *shed* (evil spirit) entered the soul. Thus, if one did not conform to the principles of Derekh Erets it was not the result of calculated choice but of supernatural intervention.

Every household—comprised of a man, his wife, his married sons and their wives and children, and his unmarried children—depended on itself for economic survival, although during crises it could usually rely on kin for help. Occupations were usually passed down from father to son and were often the exclusive domain of *patronymic* groups, which consisted of families who shared a patronym if nothing else. During periods of extensive international trade, Jewish men in port towns were extremely active in large-scale commerce. For the most part, however, they worked as craftsmen and artisans, particularly in weaving, leatherwork, jewellery-making, carpentry, and gold- and silversmithing. Some also worked as long-distance peddlers, merchants and money-lenders. Islam did not allow its believers to work in gold and silver because it saw these occupations as acts of usury, so Jews filled this economic niche, thus playing a vital role in the Yemeni economy.[16] Jewish men were forbidden to farm—although some did—but in the village Jewish women were engaged in vegetable farming for their own consumption, but not on the scale that Muslims farmed. To a large extent, then, Jews and Muslims were economically inter-dependent. In fact, before the 1948 exodus to Israel every Jewish man was required to teach a Muslim man his trade; nonetheless, the country suffered economically when the Jews left.

From Child to Bride to Woman: The Life Cycle in Yemen

One Saturday afternoon in Gadot, I overheard several men reminiscing about the position of women in Yemen; they said that in Yemen a woman was respected like a precious candle for she was the light of the home. This was the reason for her seclusion in it, for like a precious candle, a woman had to be protected. Moreover, *halakhah* (religious law) provided the basis for the separation of female and male activities. Since in Yemen only men were literate, they had considerable control over women and, accordingly, delegated them solely to domestic duties on the pretence that only men knew, and could interpret, religious law. Moreover, this gender dichotomy was found in the wider Muslim society. Women, for their part, regard their past in Yemen with ambivalence. They lament the lack of simplicity in their present lifestyle in Israel, but they believe that in Yemen there were "slaves" (rather than "candles") and lacked "cultured" learning.

The collective memory of Jewish women in Yemen is surprisingly consistent, considering that on almost every other topic there is significant variation depending upon where Jews lived: whether in the North or South, in the mountains or on the plateau, in the city or the village. I have chosen, therefore, to describe the life of women through the use of a generalized biography of a person I call Rumia Khayat.

Rumia was born in 1896 in the city of Dembt in Central Yemen. Her father was a tailor. After finishing the chores, her mother would embroider the pants' legs of women's trousers which were worn underneath their long black dresses, an occupation of many women after finishing their household chores. In their large household lived the families of three brothers—the other two were weavers. Rumia's mother, Rahmia, was the senior of her father's two wives and Rahmia was also the female head of the household because she was eldest of the four women. (Rahmia's mother-in-law, who formerly held that position, had died when Rumia was three years old). In all there were eleven children in the household; three others died in infancy. One boy had been with them since the age of four when both of his parents died in a cholera epidemic; for some time he was hidden in the cellar because of the law prescribing that only Muslims could adopt Jewish orphans to ensure a forced conversion to Islam.

The house was large enough for all three families, containing seven rooms. One served as a salon and kitchen, another was the workshop, a third was for menstruating women to sleep in, and four bedrooms— one for each wife, her husband, and her children. In the cellar was a large storage room for grains; in the yard there were goats and chickens which the women and children tended. The yard was overgrown with weeds, and other than the *mezuzah*—the parchment scroll in a silver container attached to the doorpost—there were no adornments on the outside of the white-washed house. The reason for this was that the evil eye would not be attracted to a house that looked unkempt or that displayed little wealth. Inside, however, the house was spotless, even around the hearth.

Rumia was the younger of Rahmia's two daughters; for reasons which Rumia did not understand her mother could bear no more children, and her father, Zekhariah, who was not a poor man, had decided to take a second wife. A Jew was allowed more than one wife only if his first wife had not given him a son within ten years of marriage and if he could treat all of his wives equally.[17] Zekhariah's second wife gave birth to two boys. He was an honest and generous man, who was known for his good deeds. For example, Rumia remembered how he would feed several Arab farming families who were suffering from drought. They would come to her father and say, "Zekhariah, we have had no rain this summer so our harvest was not good. Can we please have some grain?" Zekhariah would invite them in for dinner and take them down to the storage cellar and give them grain which he had purchased and stored. Rumia felt sorry for such families. If there were no rain the farmers had little food; by contrast, the Jews seemed better off because they had professions for which there were always abundant materials, and from whose products they could buy grain.[18]

As a little girl Rumia often played with her father, but as she grew up she was taught to respect him and even to fear him. Her mother, who had originally been permissive with her, taunted her with, "Honour your father lest he make a bad match for you!" By the time she was five, Rumia was considered to have "received her common sense," so from this age she learned housekeeping skills and how to embroider and make baskets. She always wanted to read; when she asked why girls were not taught like the boys, she was told that religious law did not permit it, that, if girls spent their time learning to read, rain would pour for days on end, and that crime would flourish. More to the point: if a woman was taught to read and write, she might become more knowledgeable than her husband.

Rumia's mother was responsible for teaching her to be a good and efficient housekeeper. She did not tell Rumia about menstruation or about sexual intercourse because mother and daughter did not discuss intimate topics such as these. When Rumia was twelve years old she bled for the first time. Very frightened by the experience, she ran and told her favourite aunt who explained to her that this was part of womanhood. The next day, Rumia learned that she was engaged to be married; it seemed to her that her aunt must have told her father that she was ready to become a woman and leave her girlhood behind. Like all girls and boys, Rumia had no control over whom she was to marry.[19]

Rumia's father arranged her marriage, and if he had not been alive, her oldest uncle would have done so. Zekhariah arranged a good match for her; she was to marry his father's brother's son. He would have preferred that she marry one of his own brothers' sons, but this was impossible because they were still young boys.[20] Like most girls, Rumia would have to leave her family to go live in her husband's household, but at least he also lived in the Jewish quarter of Dembt. Zekhariah and his uncle (the groom's father) negotiated the *ketuba,* the marriage contract required in all Jewish marriages.[21] Most importantly, the ketuba stipulated the amount to be paid to a wife from the husband's or his family's estate in case of divorce or death of the husband. More often than not the sum stipulated was small; a woman usually received a cow upon the death of her husband.

Rumia was considered a good catch: she knew how to embroider beautiful leggings and thus had some economic worth; she was pretty and obedient; and she came from a respected and well-to-do family.

Thus her father was able to demand a high *mohar* (bridewealth). This was a payment by the bridegroom to Zekhariah *without* the transference of any form of payment to Rumia; she went to her husband with a new dress, a pair of candle holders for the Sabbath eve, and some gold jewellery. While the women of the household joked that Rumia was being "bought," she learned that the mohar payment to her kin meant that if she needed a home in case of divorce, she had some residual rights in her family.[22] It also meant that her father or his brothers would help to mediate if she had marital troubles (for if she did divorce her husband, they would have to return the mohar which would have, inevitably, been already invested by them in a new loom).

The day that Rumia learned of her engagement the preparations for her wedding began. A wedding was no small affair; it meant the joining of two families and the investment of property. After one month of preparation, the festivities began with the Sabbath of the Bride. On that day Rumia's family hosted the family of her bridegroom, Sa'adia Khayat, aged eighteen, also a tailor, and other friends and relatives, some from far distant towns and villages. A large meal was prepared; for the entire Sabbath the men and women sat separately telling stories, gossiping, and singing. For Rumia, the Sabbath of the Bride ushered in a week of excitement and trepidation in which she was the central figure in the ceremony of the *hinna,* the lengthy ritual that marked the separation of the bride from her natal family.[23] Through the use of songs and stories, the young bride was instructed on how to be a wife, how to keep house, how to co-operate with her mother-in-law who would hold authority over her, how to rear her children, and how to maintain taharat hamishpahah, the family purity rituals. Rumia had much to learn and she paid close attention to the wisdom of the older women. Other events took place during the ceremony, particularly on the night before the wedding when the female guests were called up one by one to put henna on Rumia's hands. The henna symbolized fertility and also protected the young bride against the evil eye. Oh, that evil eye! She learned a lot about it that week, particularly the sayings she was to use to protect her children from receiving it. At the end of the week she felt quite exhausted, as did the other women who attended the ceremony; the men spent the week working, and studying the Torah.

Shortly before the wedding ceremony, the bridegroom signed the ketuba in front of two male witnesses and then he presented it to the bride. It was the first time since Rumia's engagement that she had seen her fiancé, and after the wedding ceremony, she was nervous during the half-hour walk to his parents' house, to the new room which had been built on for the couple. In that room their marriage was consummated; after their first sexual intercourse, the groom handed out the blood-stained sheet to his mother who was waiting outside for it. Rumia was a *bona fide* virgin; had she not been she would have been returned to her family who would all live in shame. She remembered that first sexual experience with distaste for it was frightening and painful, and she wondered why she was not told of this during the hinna. For her, sex was related only to bearing children, and in fact she began to look forward to practising the family purity rituals so that for fourteen days she would not have to sleep with her husband.

The week after the wedding until the Sabbath of the Groom the festivities continued, but this time at Rumia's new home. The men and women celebrated separately as was the custom, but Rumia did get acquainted with the youth who was her husband in the evenings in their room. Sa'adia was clearly a fair and kind man, and as a talented tailor he could support her. What worried her was getting to know her mother-in-law and two sisters-in-law with whom she would spend her days. She did not meet another sister-in-law who had moved to a distant town to live in her husband's household, nor another brother-in-law who moved away because he could not get enough work as a tailor in Dembt, which was full of tailors! This was not unusual, however, for Jews often had to move because they could not make a living where they grew up.[24] Rumia prayed that they would not have to move so that she could continue to visit her family.

Two days after the Sabbath of the Groom, Rumia began to menstruate and like all married women, she started to practise the family purity rituals. Every Jewish woman conformed strictly to the rules of taharat hamishpahah, which involves observance of *niddut* (segregation of husband and wife) and mikveh (ritual bathing). During niddut, which lasts for fourteen days from the onset of menses, a woman did not touch a utensil her husband used; nor did she share their bed. She was ritually unclean and dangerous until she purified herself in the mikveh on the fourteenth day. Her husband would not touch her until she went to the mikveh. Someone, even a small girl, must accompany her to be sure that she did not catch sight of her husband on that day. At the mikveh she scrubbed herself, and then she dipped herself three times in the ritual bath to bless and welcome the imperative of sexual relations with her husband and to ensure the good health of her family. Then she dressed in clean clothes and left, still not looking at anyone until she arrived home. She then went to her husband, coming to him like a bride, with polished nails and covered in jewellery. This, at least, was the custom, and while women might not relish it, they strictly followed the ritual for fear that the evil eye might strike their families. Rumia practised these rituals only five times before she became pregnant.

During her first year of marriage, much of which was spent in pregnancy, Rumia learned the ways and routine of her husband's household. She felt comfortable only with the young children, but she clearly was not one of them. She learned to collect firewood outside of the city, and to help farm the family's two fields. She met other married women at the well from where they drew water and often went to the mikveh simply to bathe and visit her newly married friends. Like most young brides, she felt tormented by her mother-in-law who expected her as the youngest to do more housework that the other daughters-in-law. But in time she became used to her work load and, perhaps because of her strict upbringing, was an obedient wife. When the time came to give birth she happily went to her mother's house; and Rahmia was becoming an experienced midwife. The first childbirth was a major accomplishment for a Yemeni Jewish woman; it completed the process of becoming a "woman." Like all other women, Rumia wished for a son to care for her in old age; in fact she wanted only sons since daughters left to live with their husbands. She did have a son, and this meant that she was considered ritually unclean for thirty-three days (sixty-six for a girl) and slept in the room for menstruating women.[25] Another woman or girl always had to be with her, however, for to be alone with the child at this time invited *shedim*, evil spirits.

With the birth of her son, Rumia was not expected to perform as many household chores. In fact, by the time her daughter was born two years later, Sa'adia's mother told her to spend more time embroidering pants' legs because she had great talent and was able to bring a better price for the trousers she herself embroidered. Of course, Rumia had no control over any income earned through her own talents: all of the income went to the household head, Sa'adia's older brother. Rumia was generally unhappy; she hated her mother-in-law and longed to be free of her. At least her husband was good to her and even supported her, sometimes, when she argued with her mother-in-law. However, when her son reached his third birthday she became especially depressed because he began to attend the *ma'almeh* (the boy's school) and to learn his father's trade. He no longer seemed like her child, but this was normal: all young boys spent their days in school and with their fathers. At least he was healthy, blessed be the Lord, what more could she ask for?

Rumia's life with Sa'adia's family did not last for many years. Shortly after her son turned five, Sa'adia was killed while taking clothes to a village across the mountain: his cart overturned and took the mule and Sa'adia down the mountains with it. His mother blamed Rumia for his death, saying that she had not been a good enough wife for him and so the Lord took him for other purposes. While Rumia grieved, she realized that she could now return to her father's household, and that gave her cause for relief. So she took her two children and left seven days after his death. But she was not to be a widow for long. One year after her husband's death, at the completion of the period of ritual mourning, her father asked her if she was willing to remarry.

To some extent this was simply a formality—as a married women, now widowed, she should have some say in who her next husband would be. At the same time, she knew that if her father had a match in mind, she should respect his wishes. After all, she could not go to the coffee house and look for a groom herself! As a woman she was forbidden even to go to the market. A goldsmith had moved to town with three young children; his wife had died of cholera and he wished to leave her memory behind in the village where they grew up. But he needed a housekeeper, and this meant a wife. They were introduced and quickly Rumia realized that he was a man she could respect and honour—and what is more, she would be in charge of her own household. It is true that her housework would double because his children were so small, and she would have little time to embroider, but she would have no mother-in-law looking over her shoulder. So they married and built a house near her father's; her new husband seemed to become a part of her father's family and she felt herself very lucky indeed. They had three children together, two of whom died in infancy. Although Rumia was sad about their death, she accepted it as fate. Her luck, otherwise, had turned and she liked her new husband—by this time most of her friends had already divorced once or twice.[26]

The older Rumia became the more freedom she acquired to leave the house: an old woman—one beyond child-bearing years—was unlikely to be suspected of improper sexual conduct. She gained security with her old age, in her home and with her sons, and like most older women, she was regarded as sly and cunning, a manipulator of her husband. While she spent much of her day preparing flour, soup and dough, collecting firewood and fetching water, she had some free time to sit and gossip with friends, to smoke *nargila* (water pipe), to chew qat, and to tell tales.[27] The women spoke in the Yemeni Jewish dialect of Arabic, the language of the home, and they created a rich variety of folklore and songs in Arabic which portrayed the harshness of their daily lives, the security of old age, love for their sons, moral lessons, and their desire to move to the Promised Land. In fact, Rumia's children eventually moved to the Promised Land, but she herself died, in 1948, after a long illness, shortly after Imam Ahmed's decree that Jews could move to the new state of Israel. Rumia told her eldest son that she was dying as a happy and fulfilled woman because she knew that they would live a better life in Jerusalem.

* * *

Yemeni Jewish women had more informal power than their memory of female servitude generally indicates as is illustrated in many studies of Middle Eastern women.[28] However, I agree with the conclusions of Phyllis Palgi who worked with Yemeni Jews in Israel for thirty years:[29]

> To sum up the situation, her correct sexual behaviour was controlled through family structure, sanctified by religious legal code and re-enforced by fear of supernatural powers, such as evil spirits, ghosts, and the evil eye. In Yemen there was no difficulty in perpetuating this family structure and rigid relationships. While the Jews suffered serious disabilities as a minority group, in this area there was complete harmony between them and the ruling community.

As we next see, this situation changed dramatically upon the move to Israel.

"On the Wings of Eagles": Immigration to Israel

But they that wait for the Lord shall renew their strength;
They shall mount up with wings as eagles;
They shall run and not be weary.
They shall walk, and not faint.

—Isaiah 40:31

Yes, in Yemen we had to work hard, but we didn't feel it. If there were weddings we would work and cook, but not feel tired—not like here . . . but here, blessed be the Lord, this is our city, this is our Land. Here. There are those who have come from Rumania, Turkey and America who want to return there. But we, the Yemenis, no. We live here and we will die here. That is to say that we will never return to Yemen. We left property there—in Yemen. We left houses of three stories, we left our stores, we left our villages, we left many things. I am telling you that we gave it all to the Arabs like a gift. On my life, we gave it all to them. We left the gold business, the jewellery, thousands [money]. . . . We were told that we did not need anything to come to Israel. We accepted this in good faith, all our leaders had to say to us was "Aliyah" [immigration to Israel] and nothing else mattered. We left behind everything so that we could come to the Land.

Within two months everyone from the Jewish quarter of Dembt was on the road to Aden. We went along one path, by camel or horse, or simply on foot. Nothing else mattered except Aliyah. They sold the fields and the houses and the businesses for pennies. If a law came into being today that we should get our property back for what it is worth, we Yemenis would be rich. . . . I do not know if it was worth it, but the truth is that this is our Land and we Yemenis will never leave her.

—Shulamith, an older woman in Gadot

Like most Diaspora Jews, the Yemenis longed for their return to the Promised Land. The Yemeni hymn and song book, the *Diwan,* is filled with songs relating to the event of their return to Zion—about their desire to go, and their deep faith that a Jewish nation would be formed— and this undoubtedly helped them to survive their precarious existence in Yemen.[30] Like Jews elsewhere, the Yemenis believed that they would return to Zion when the Messiah came; in fact, there was a score of false Messiahs in the Yemen for whom many Jews sold their property and started to walk to the Holy Land, only to be disappointed and turn back. Given this background, it is not surprising that when the Jews were permitted to leave Yemen in 1948 many truly believed that David Ben Gurion, then the Prime Minister, was the real Messiah.

From 1882 until 1918 the Ottoman Empire controlled the Yemen, having taken power from the Zaydis, a moderate sect of Shi'a Islam which had been established by the Imam al Hadi Yehya in 901 C.E. (today, the Zaydis are once again in power, ruling over North Yemen).[31] Coincident with this period of Turkish rule over Yemen, the Ottomans also controlled Palestine, so the gateway was open for Jewish immigration. The emigration of Jews from Yemen began in 1881 with a trickle, but numbers picked up until the time of the British Mandate in 1917 when some Jews illegally left Yemen and entered Palestine. In all, between 1881 and 1947, approximately 25,000 Yemenis had arrived in Israel.

In 1882, rumour had it that a wealthy Jew (Rothschild) had bought land in Israel for the Yemenis. A small number of Jews, all from San'a, and financially able, decided to leave for Palestine; having spent all of their money on the passage, they arrived there penniless. They soon learned that the wealthy Jew had not bought land specifically for the Yemenis; those who arrived eventually settled in the poorer quarter of the old city of Jerusalem. Later immigrants also settled in the *moshavot* (farming colonies) of Rehovot, Petah Tikva and Zikhron Ya'acov, and in the city of Jaffa. Unable to earn a living by their traditional trades for which there was little place in Palestine, Yemeni men filled positions in unskilled labour, largely in construction, in road building and in agriculture. Although they were physically small and totally unequipped for such work, they laboured without complaining about their difficult work conditions and substandard housing. Leaders of the *Yishuv* (Jewish settlement in Palestine) were quick to recognize Yemeni industriousness, so in 1911 the Palestine Office, an agency responsible for Jewish immigration to Palestine, decided that encouraging more Yemeni Jews to immigrate would facilitate building up a Jewish state while supplying an answer to the labour needs of the time. Zionist ideology required an indigenous Jewish working class—but, other than in agricultural communities, there were few Jews prepared to engaged in manual labour. The historical record suggests that the first Jewish delegates sent to Yemen under the guise of urging immigration for religious purposes had, in fact, a more specific and material aim in mind: the importing of a working class.[32]

The Yemeni Jews who arrived before the creation of the State of Israel did become active in the labour federations of Palestine and in the underground paramilitary organizations. There was a Yemeni political party, but it received only one seat in the first Knesset; in fact, the majority of Yemenis voted for Labour or for the religious parties. There was (and is) an organization of Yemenis for cultural purposes and once it consolidated, it also provided material aid to immigrants. Thus when the 55,000 immigrants in Operation Magic Carpet arrived between 1948–1950, there was a pre-existing Yemeni community: kin looked up their newly-arrived relatives and found them places to live and work. Thus not all Yemenis were entirely subjected to the plans of the Settlement Authorities to place them in development towns and moshavim, although there were thousands who lived for months in *ma'abarot* (temporary immigrant camps) where housing and working conditions were dreadful.[33]

It is said that Imam Ahmed, ruler of Yemen, permitted most Jews to emigrate in 1948 because he feared that the Israelis would otherwise come to fetch them,[34] but his motivation is yet unknown.[35] A small minority (estimated between 3–5,000) did not leave Yemen, either because their economic services were deemed irreplaceable or because they believed that David Ben Gurion was another false Messiah.

By October 1948, 7,000 Yemeni Jews had arrived in the Hashed refugee camp in Aden from which they would emigrate to the new state of Israel. However, conditions in the camp were wretched and overcrowded—some people had been there for several years—and it was clear to the Israeli authorities in the camp, and in Israel, that a major effort had to be made quickly to evacuate the Jews. The American Joint Distribution Committee, a philanthropic foundation financed by Diaspora Jews and concerned at that time with the immigration of Jewish refugees to Israel, financed and organized Operation Magic Carpet. This unprecedented airlift operation was under contract with the American Alaska Airlines, and later with the Near East Transport Company. During the time that Israel and her Arab neighbours were at war, the airlift had to be run in secret. The entire operation involved 430 flights and it came to an end in September 1950.[36]

The journey to Israel was not an easy one; it is said that nearly one-third of the emigrants died *en route* and many suffered from trachoma, malnutrition and other diseases. There were hospitals in the Adeni camps and in the ma'abarot in Israel once they arrived, so many were saved from early death. The first Yemenis in Gadot had lived in ma'abarot; in fact, they were recruited by a group of Gadot's first settlers who had gone to the camps to choose suitable residents for the new town. From then on, other Yemenis from neighbouring moshavim and from areas as far away as Jerusalem and Tiberias were attracted to Gadot because of their Yemeni brethren.

Notes

1. On qat see Kennedy *et al.* 1980 and Weir 1985.
2. For ethnographic and historical sources on Yemen see: Ahroni 1986; Brauer 1934; Dorsky 1986; Gerholm 1977; Makhlouf 1979; Mundy 1979, 1981; Schmidt 1968; Scott 1942; Stevenson 1985; and Weir 1985.
3. Ratzhabi 1978:209.
4. To my knowledge, the only reason such rabbis were buried in the Holy Land is so that their souls would ascend quickly to heaven; when the Messiah comes, those buried in the Holy Land would be the first to be resurrected.
5. Jews and many historians call C.E. the Common Era and not the Christian Era.
6. Abir 1974:1.
7. Goitein 1964.
8. H. Cohen 1973:62–63.
9. Stevenson (1985:45) found in 1979 in a northern Yemeni town that Muslims remember good and harmonious relations with Jews, often attributed to the good offices of the shaykh who ensured that Jews would be protected.
10. Goitein in Ratzhabi 1978:238.
11. P. Cohen 1961:233.
12. Goitein 1955:18.
13. Goitein 1969:230–233; Tobi 1974.
14. Goitein 1953:1; 1969:233. It is clear, however, that material factors were also important as we see later in this chapter.
15. Ratzhabi 1978:242–245.
16. Tobi personal communication; *Encyclopedia Judaica 1971:744*.
17. Polygyny was not common, but did exist among Jews in Yemen. It was forbidden in most areas of the Jewish diaspora. A man and his wives were seen as one family. A husband usually rotated between the bedroom of each wife. There were three polygynous Yemeni families in Gadot even though it was no longer legal practice when Jews moved to Israel.
18. In fact most Jews, too, were miserably poor and not much better off than farmers. When farmers reaped a poor harvest, Jews were adversely affected since demand for their work dropped proportionately. However, some Yemeni

Jews in contemporary Israel claim that Jews were more economically secure than farmers because they were not dependent on the will of God to bring rain.

19. Here my data depart from Caspi 1985 who claims that girls could refuse a betrothal. The Yemenis with whom I worked claim that this was impossible.

20. In Yemen, 60 percent of marriages among Jews were between patrilineal kin (P. Cohen 1961:236).

21. See Peres *et al.* 1978.

22. de Vaux's (1965:27) interpretation concerning the ancient Israelite marriages seems to be applicable to the Yemeni Jews: "This obligation to pay a sum of money, or its equivalent, to the girl's family obviously gives the Israelite marriage the outward appearance of a purchase. But the mohar seems to be not so much the price paid for the woman as a compensation given to the family, and, in spite of the apparent resemblance, thereby acquires a right over the woman, but the woman herself is not bought and sold."

23. See Spector 1960 and Caspi 1985 on the hinna rituals.

24. For economic reasons, particularly when an area was over supplied with one type of artisan, there was considerable internal migration of Jews in Yemen.

25. This is Yemeni Jewish custom; it is not halakhic.

26. Divorce was very common among Jews in Yemen. While in accordance with Jewish law only men could grant a *get* (a writ of divorce), women were remembered for successfully manipulating their husbands into divorce.

27. Women's visiting sessions are a very important part of daily life in Yemeni Muslim society (Dorsky 1986; Makhlouf 1979). In a totally female milieu, women readily exchange information—which enables them to influence male decision-making—male activities are criticized and female strengths admired (Dorsky: 20–21). Jewish women did not partake in extensive daily visiting because of their duties in craft production, but the conversational and dramatic content (in terms of telling tales and acting out skits) during visiting sessions was virtually the same as among Muslim women. Among the oldest women in Gadot, visiting sessions are still the focal point of Sabbath afternoons.

28. Dorksy 1986; Dwyer 1978; Fernea 1969, 1976; Katzir 1976; Lancaster 1981; Maher 1974; Makhlouf 1979; Mernissi 1975; Nelson 1974; and Wikan 1980.

29. Palgi 1975:2.

30. Schectman (1961:46), a historian, says: "The least educated (men) knew large portions of the Bible by heart, and the more oppressed they were, the more ardently did they cling to and cultivate the exalted spiritual vision of their people. They found in it refuge and solace from their abject existence, keeping alive and intense their dream of the Holy Land, fervently longing for the Messiah who would deliver them from exile. It was this dream of redemption that, more than anything gave the Jews of Yemen the strength to survive millennia of servitude and persecution." Women, too, expressed their love for Zion in their songs (Gamlieli 1971:207–240).

31. Most Yemeni Arabs are Sunni Muslims.

32. Patai 1970b:187–88; and Schechtman 1961:47. Patai (187–88) notes of the Yemenis who came *circa* 1908–1915: "This second Yemenite Aliyah and the

rapid adjustments of its members to agricultural work in Palestine made Dr. Arthur Ruppin aware of the possibilities of building up a Yemenite-Jewish agricultural labour force in Palestine to replace the Arab workers who were then commonly employed in the Jewish agricultural settlements. . . . Samuel Yavnieli, one of the first members of the Second (Russian) aliyah, was entrusted in 1911 with the delicate and difficult task of going to Yemen in the guise of a religious emissary to spread there the idea of immigration to Palestine. . . . In one of his lectures Yavnieli epitomized the argument he used vis-à-vis the Yemeni Jews: 'I called upon them to bend the yoke. Enough of your standing aside and taking no part in the upbuilding of Palestine. For hundreds of years you have been sitting here on this land, and have only received. You received the Talmud from there. . . . Where are the stones which you have contributed to the building of the nation? Now you must send your strength to Palestine, the best of your sons. . . . He who takes part in the suffering of the community will have the merit to see its consolation. Go up to Palestine to take your share, go up to work, go up to watch!'"

33. Other Middle Eastern and North African groups were not so fortunate because they did not have large numbers of relatives already in the Yishuv. For example, less than 1000 Jews had arrived from Morocco, Algeria, and Tunisia between 1919–1948 (Schechtman:366). By 1919 there were 4,234 Yemeni Jews in Palestine, 7.6 percent of the total Jewish population. The majority were agricultural labourers. By 1943, there were twenty Yemeni settlements (Schechtman 48–49). In 1961 Schechtman (360–361) claimed, with some justification and a bit of exaggeration, that the Yemeni Jews were the most "thoroughly integrated Jewish community in Israel, firmly rooted in the land. . . . This is due in the main to the Yemenites *(sic)* own qualities, first and foremost to their boundless love for and attachment to the Holy Land . . . they are imbued with a deep-seated and genuine pioneering spirit. They never spurn any kind of work and possess that rare quality of being satisfied with their lot. . . . "

34. Tobi, personal communication.

35. Schechtman: 60.

36. Schechtman 1952:209. See Barer 1953 for a complete account of Operation Magic Carpet.

3

Introducing Gadot and Israeli Ethnicities

Absorbing immigrants in Israel was easier than in the United States because religion brought people together. However, the first generation of immigrants was full of antagonism. For example, in Gadot's local council there were three major groups: 1. Ashkenazim, 2. Sephardim (Turks, Bulgarians), and 3. Easterners (Yemenis, Algerians, Tunisians, Moroccans, etc.). Everyone was concerned with their own ethnic group and tried to make sure that they were represented in the council. That is one reason why Gadot grew; there is growth if there is heterogeneity. One group learns from the other as well as competes with the other. Where there is only one major ethnic group, like in Ma'alot or Bet She'an (predominantly Moroccan), there is rarely development. Gadot, by contrast, was lucky not to have one group as a majority. It was because of their antagonism that there was competition, and because of their competition, this place developed.

Now it is different with the second generation, especially because of successful intermarriage. Even though it may take 100 years elsewhere in Israel, there will be integration in Gadot because of the high rate of intermarriage.

—Simon, a sixty-two-year-old
Czechoslovakian Jewish paramedic in Gadot

Introducing Gadot

It takes only a little imagination to picture Gadot in the early 1950s because there are remnants of the original Arab village which comprised the foundation of the town. Scattered throughout the centre of Gadot are old Arab houses of one and two storeys, with faded pink and blue walls, usually in a state of disrepair. The people who live in these houses are not poor, as the scene would suggest, but are waiting for the local council to offer them plots of land on to which they can build private homes. While such houses, and the vibrant market, exist in the centre of town, Gadot will continue to have a distinctly Middle Eastern character. The market boasts wonderful open-air fruit and vegetable stalls, Turkish cafes, and clothing stores whose goods hang outside to attract the shopper. During working hours the market is bustling with activity, not only with Gadot residents, but with shoppers from four neighbouring moshavim and towns, including that of Asher, one of Israel's wealthiest areas. People cannot be in a rush when they go to the centre of Gadot, for it is one of several places to meet friends and neighbours, to learn of local events, and to make purchases as well as to take care of business in the local council building which is located at the very heart of the market. While Gadot has its tranquil areas of one- and two-family homes, the market area is somewhat illustrative of the surrounding neighbourhoods of two- to eight-storey apartment buildings, where the streets and squares are always teeming with life from the elderly and housewives in the morning, and the children, teenagers, and workers in the afternoons and until late in the evening during the long, hot summer. The only quiet day in the week is the Sabbath, but even then the summer afternoon quiet is broken by the shouting of local soccer fans cheering on their team at the Gadot stadium. While the street life of Gadot is probably typical of many small towns in Israel, it differs significantly from the majority of development towns in that there are few unemployed men on the street or in the coffee houses during working hours, nor are there unoccupied youth. The story of the successful development of Gadot should be told in detail elsewhere, but a brief description is in order here.

The Arab village on which Gadot now rests was captured by the Israeli Defence Forces in 1948. Since there were two main roads near the village, it was designated a suitable place for the settlement of new immigrants arriving at Israel's open ports of entry by the thousands. The first thirteen settlers, all Turkish Jews, arrived during September and October 1948, and moved into abandoned Arab housing. By June 1950 there were 3,200 residents, many living in tents and cabins until permanent housing was constructed. Most of the original residents were Turks, followed by Yemenis, Poles and Rumanians—all of whom, had been settled in Gadot soon after their arrival in Israel. The Turks, who continue to comprise the largest eidah in Gadot, were merchants in Turkey, so many opened small shops in the abandoned Arab village; others worked as street peddlers from house to house (several still do), and textiles and rugs were sold on sidewalk carpets as in the so-called Persian market. Until the 1953 influx of Polish Jews into a neighbourhood constructed specifically for Holocaust survivors, Gadot was nicknamed "Little Turkey."

During the early years, there were plans to turn Gadot into an agricultural settlement; several dunams of farmland adjoined most housing and functioned to supplement family income. By 1960, however, the supplementary farms were no longer worked because everyone had employment in road works, construction and industry. Although the population grew steadily during the first decade, many families left because of bad school facilities and shortage of jobs. Beginning in 1961, however, there was a significant upward swing in population growth due to the construction of schools, industrial developments (particularly the aircraft industries), adequate transportation to Tel Aviv and Petah Tikva and inexpensive housing. Thus native-born Israelis were attracted to living in Gadot. Gadot's population continues to grow steadily (in 1981 there were 14,000 residents); young people from Gadot often settle there after marriage because it offers them near-by employment, family, and good schools; in short, what Israelis deem to be a good "quality of life." In fact, the lack of migration from Gadot is one indicator of its successful development: of the young couples who now settle in Gadot, approximately 80 percent contain at least one spouse who grew up in the town.[1]

There are Jews in Gadot from seventy countries-of-origin, which is a source of pride for most residents who see Gadot as *kibbutz hagaluyot* (ingathering of the exiles), that is, as a model of cultural integration. Middle Eastern and North African Jews, including the large Turkish population, comprise 70 percent of its population, while the rest are from Europe. There is no firm ethnic segregation in Gadot, but there are some areas which have concentrations of people from one country. Particularly notable is the neighbourhood built for Holocaust survivors, but it now has residents from countries other than Poland. There are eight apartment buildings of four- to eight-storeys which house newly arrived Russian immigrants, and there are several streets of private and semi-private housing which are almost entirely Yemeni. One long street on one border of the town, houses some of the managerial staff of the aircraft industry, and is viewed locally as the "elite" area of the town even though there are several Yemeni families who also live on this street. Gadot thus differs from other new towns in Israel because of its extremely mixed population.[2] Significantly, it has not followed any particular recruitment programmes such as those employed by other successful new towns such as Arad, Carmiel and Kiryat Gat.[3]

Gadot is administered by the town council which has eleven members who chair various committees that are responsible for utilities, local taxes, education, cultural activities—including naming streets, and so on. I was impressed by the fact that it seems decisions are never made during council meetings; meetings rather serve as a forum for gaining political influence, and for the Yemeni-born former mayor, who had been in this position since 1951, exercising authority. This is not to say that issues on the agenda are not seriously discussed, because they are. Discussions and arguments are always chaotic, and entail a good deal of screaming and yelling because of differences of opinion, personal vendettas, and cultural style. I never once observed a vote on any particular issue, and council members would end the meeting in time for the televised weekly basketball game.

Despite the fact that the council does not appear to be a decision-making body, Gadot is remarkably well-organized. The mayor and his deputy work full-time for the council, but it is my feeling that the public clerk, who by 1980 had held this position for thirty years, is actually responsible for the smooth running of the town. It is clear, too, that local politicians are fully committed to continuing the successful development of Gadot and they spare no effort to this effect. The former mayor, in particular, although of dubious reputation, was renowned for his ability to badger federal officials into providing more funding and programming for the town. He was known to pound on the desks of bureaucrats, demanding only the best for his town; he certainly played a large part in Gadot's growth from its inception.

Like most towns and cities in Israel, Gadot has a social welfare office (not often in use—only fifty-eight families received welfare assistance in 1980),[4] *Histadrut* office, workers' council, pedagogical centre, community centre, and religious council. Of these, the last two are particularly important. The community centre is full of people from morning to evening; it offers adult education courses, exercise classes, ceramics, choir training, folk dancing, and numerous other activities; it also brings either a national orchestra or a theatre group to Gadot once a month.

The religious council, in one way or another, touches all residents of Gadot at some time in their lives. Like the local council, it has eleven elected members who are responsible for chairing many committees. The religious council and particularly its head, who is a Yemeni teacher, directs the building of synagogues, supervises *kashrut* (dietary law procedures) for restaurants, issues marriage certificates, operates the mikveh (ritual baths), organizes funerals, provides a *mohel* (circumcisor) for infant boys, holds classes on the Torah, supports the local branch of the national religious youth group (*B'nei Akiva*), offers an informal mediation service for families with problems, and directs a guidance service for people with religious problems.

There are twenty-eight synagogues in Gadot which are supported by the Ministry of Religious Affairs, the Histadrut and the synagogue members themselves. Perhaps the number of synagogues seems large for Gadot's population, but it reflects the need to cater for the wide variety of cultural differences in prayer exhibited by the eidot. Almost all of the synagogues are distinguished by the eidah of their membership, particularly Ashkenazi (3), Turkish (2), North African (6), Georgian (1), Indian (1), Bulgarian (2), and Yemeni (12).[5] However, some synagogues have mixed memberships; for example, the Yemeni synagogue which I regularly attended has two Moroccan members. The synagogue provides study sessions and offers an intimate atmosphere and a circle of friendship to its members, especially for men of the immigrant generation who find that in the synagogue they are free to express themselves as they did in the "old country." Indeed, Yemenis are free to express their Judaism in a way in which they could not in Yemen where they were forbidden to raise their voices in prayer. In Israel, they chant loudly— almost shouting—forever remembering their subjugation as Jews in a Muslim society. Unlike members of the Yemeni immigrant generation, Gadot could hardly be called a "religious" town—only one third of the male population attend services weekly.

There are seven schools in Gadot, five of which are elementary schools; as a reflection overcrowding in the existing schools, a sixth is under construction. Three schools are in the secular educational system run by the central government (450 pupils per school), one is a religious school supported by the government (450 pupils of which approximately 60 percent are children of Yemeni parents), and the last is a small school of 100 pupils which is supported by the ultra-religious Agudat Yisrael political party. In addition, a small school for handicapped children operated until 1981 when it was closed because of shortage of pupils. The local high school has 1,200 pupils, half of whom come from twenty-five towns and agricultural villages. The high school enjoys an excellent reputation, and like Gadot, is considered a model of successful integration. This is a somewhat idealistic viewpoint, however, as is suggested in our discussion of the educational background of the unmarried Yemeni daughters who were raised in Gadot (see Chapter 6). Lastly, there is a local *yeshiva*, a centre for the study of religious texts, but it does not enjoy a good reputation so no one from Gadot attends.[6]

Gadot has an industrial area specializing in crafts, textiles and metal works and many auto mechanic shops which employ people from the town and surrounding settlements, as well as an active market. However, the residents also go to the near-by larger urban centres for employment, shopping and cultural activities. Frequent bus service gives easy access and at least one-third of all households own cars. The importance of the participation of many Gadot residents in the labour market of metropolitan Tel Aviv-Petah Tikva cannot be underestimated. Since there is almost full employment in the town—is a major reason for Gadot's successful development—its residents do not feel that they are disadvantaged by living in a small town.

Most men work in largely "blue collar" jobs, especially in transportation, industry, construction, auto mechanics and electronics. The younger generation, educated in Israel, tend to work in the more prestigious skilled industries, in clerical work, in the regular army and in managerial positions. According to the public clerk, at least 70 percent of all women in Gadot are employed part-time or full-time.[7] Excellent day care facilities, both private and public, provide most mothers with the opportunity to work, and a large number of grandmothers also act as childminders. The uneducated women in the labour force work primarily as domestic labourers, office cleaners, and childminders. The more educated women are usually found in commerce, in clerical jobs, and as nursery and elementary school teachers.

There is some ethnic differentiation in the Gadot labour market as in the country-at-large. In particular, most Ashkenazim work as skilled technicians, in local administration, in the professions (particularly law and insurance), and in managerial positions in the aircraft industries. By contrast, most stores in Gadot are owned by Turks and Yemenis, the latter also owning most of the auto mechanic and metal workshops. The two large banks employ large numbers of Yemeni and Turkish employees: this is not by accident, but is a reflection of ethnic preference in hiring practices.

Gadot has succeeded as an immigrant settlement both according to the federal government's statistical portrait of the town and, more importantly, according to the people who live there. The reasons for this are many, but the most important ones have been outlined here. They include its strategic location on main roads near two urban centres, its close proximity to employment for all sectors of the population, its reputation for good schools and cultural programmes, its continuity of effective political leadership, and not least its diverse population which discouraged stagnation. Of the various eidot, the Yemenis have made an important contribution to the town, particularly in small local industries. They also maintain a high profile because of the large numbers of Yemenis in managerial and administrative positions. This results, in part, from apparently nepotistic appointments made through the good offices of the now deceased Yemeni mayor and his colleagues. Yet, even though Yemenis often choose other Yemenis for jobs, they do not regard themselves as a "community," rather they view Gadot as their community. Perhaps this is because they are residentially dispersed throughout the town and thus interact with people from a variety of eidot. It may also be because their lifestyle in Gadot affirms their general success as immigrants in Israel and so Gadot is a town of which they can be proud.

The Yemenis of Gadot

During the years 1948–1950 a group of Gadot's first settlers went to the ma'abarot in the Tel Aviv and Haifa areas to choose suitable residents for the town; these people brought the first Yemeni Jews to Gadot. From then on, other Yemenis from the surrounding moshavim and from areas as far away as Jerusalem and Tiberias were attracted to Gadot because of their Yemeni brethren. Today, Yemenis comprise a significant percentage of Gadot's population—approximately 1,500 persons in at least 600 households are of Yemeni origin or descent.[8]

Many Yemenis in Gadot live in private or two-family houses ranging anywhere from three to seven rooms, each having large backyards. Yard space is used for a small fruit orchard, chickens and goats, a workshop, a second house for married children, and more recently for flower gardening. The appearance of the latter provokes considerable comment from both fellow Yemenis and Ashkenazim who contend that Yemenis who plant gardens are trying to be like their Ashkenazi neighbours. The remaining Yemenis live in apartment complexes which surround large public squares; each flat usually has three or four rooms often housing up to a dozen people.

There is some tendency for people to try and live near their relatives and this is seen in at least eight streets that have a predominance of Yemeni families with the same surname. In other neighbourhoods, particularly in the two predominantly Ashkenazi ones, Yemeni households are in a minority. There is no strict ethnic segregation. An older Yemeni woman may have a Moroccan, Turkish, Bulgarian or Rumanian friend or neighbour even though most of her friends are Yemeni. Thus she learns about the habits outside her own culture, different foods and different ways of behaving. Some of these features she introduces into her own home, and it is this interaction with people of other cultures which forms a critical difference when comparing the Yemenis of Gadot and those from homogeneous moshavim or urban neighbourhoods. The cultural diversity which characterizes Gadot also has important implications for the maintenance of Yemeni values and customs as we will see.

There is one place *outside* the home where Yemenis are free to express their ancient heritage and that is in the synagogue. Of the twelve Yemeni synagogues in Gadot, six were formed by what is now known in the vernacular as *hamulot* (large family groups or "patronymic groups"); the other six are known as "public" synagogues because they were formed by friends from different hamulot and regions in the Yemen. Each synagogue individually portrays its own style of prayer—Jews from North Yemen have prayer styles known as Shami and those from South Yemen have styles known as Baladi. In Yemen, the synagogue was regarded as a place of prayer and as a place for strangers to go for aid. In Israel, it is also a social meeting place, particularly for men. The synagogue, therefore, plays an important role in maintaining links among the dispersed Yemeni population of Gadot.

The typical Yemeni synagogue is built on two floors, the top for women who can look down on the men. Women do not go on weekdays but some attend on the Sabbath, and for rites of passage and the holidays. Very religious and recently widowed women will go daily for eleven months to say the mourning prayers for their late husbands. However, it is not incorrect to say the synagogue is exclusively a men's club. The ark holding the Torah scrolls is at the front of the synagogue and the pulpit is placed two feet above the centre. Men sit around the pulpit, usually with members of their extended families. They take turns leading daily services and the small fee paid each time they read from the Torah contributes to the upkeep of the synagogue. On holidays the privilege of reading from the Torah is usually auctioned off—and in this women engage as well, yelling down from the top floor how much they will pay for a son to read from the Torah. Success in "buying" a portion reflects well on their self-esteem.

For the immigrant generation, extensive participation in synagogue affairs—in prayer and in the study of religious texts—may be seen as a continuation of the most beloved activity of Jewish men in Yemen. Many men have also recreated the afternoon qat sessions where they sit for hours in a friend's home chewing qat and conversing. Women, for their part, engage in entirely new pastimes in Gadot, activities which simply did not exist in Yemen either for women or for men. While the significant implications of women's extra-domestic involvements are discussed later, they include: adult education courses, religious training, working women's association, Parent-Teacher Association, discussion groups on child-rearing and parenting methods, exercise classes, sewing, choir, and others.

* * *

This work studies thirty-five women of the immigrant generation who are 35–55 years old and thirty-three unmarried women born in Israel, aged 18–32. In all cases members of the household are related through ties of blood or marriage.[9] The vast majority of these households are comprised of the nuclear family: husband and wife and all or some of their unmarried children. Eleven families have children already married and living elsewhere. In several households, the husband's mother is also present. In Israeli terms, these Yemeni families are "blessed with many children": in this study, the average number of children per family is 4.71. (Between them, the thirty-five married women have 165 children.)

Most of the wives and husbands in this study work outside of Gadot in the metropolitan area. Only five men work in white collar professions, particularly in municipal administration; a larger number, eight in all, work as skilled labourers, while the rest work in unskilled labour, particularly in road and building maintenance. Only one man is chronically unemployed. Men's occupations reflect their formal educational achievements. The unskilled labourers received only religious education in Yemen or less than eight years of elementary school in Israel. The skilled workers had eight to eleven years of schooling in Israel, while the professionals completed secondary school or vocational training in Israel.

Nearly all the women in our research set work outside of the home in domestic work, childminding, and factory work and (as with the men) this is a reflection of their educational backgrounds. A minority of women, ten in all, are illiterate but are trying to rectify this situation by attending adult education courses. Twenty women attended school in Israel for eight years or less, having entered the labour force as adolescents. Only five women attended secondary school and this achievement is seen in their occupations as a secretary, restaurant owner, cosmetician, health educator, and nursery school teacher. Work in unskilled labour belongs entirely to the immigrant generation. Their daughters and sons, born and educated in Israel, work in either skilled labour or the professions.

During intensive interviews with women of the immigrant generation, I asked them to describe the extent of their religious observances, using the vernacular terms: (1) *dati* (religious), meaning that most if not all religious practices prescribed by Jewish law are followed; (2) *mesorati* (traditional), meaning that some religious practices are observed but not others; and (3) *hiloni* (secular), meaning that few religious rituals, if any, are practised. The wide majority of the women define themselves as religious, although they also say that their parents are (or were) even more religious than themselves. Eight women see themselves as traditional and only one as secular. The overwhelming majority of husbands attend the synagogue either daily or every Sabbath and on all holidays.

We shall see in the course of *Ginger and Salt* how the native categories of religious, traditional, and secular sum up different lifestyles. In particular, they point to the contrast between the life of the past (in Yemen), where Jewish law defined and regulated all forms of social relations among Jews, and life in contemporary Israel. (I frequently use "secular" to refer to the wider Israeli society because this is how Yemeni women of the immigrant generation refer to their non-religious surroundings.) For Yemeni Jews, "secular" means more than the non-observance of religious rituals; it refers to a world revolving around them which, bypassing ritual, has an entirely different constellation of values. These values are seen as non-Jewish, even "pagan" (their word) and as belonging to the Western world where there is not only a loss of religious ways, but also the postponement of marriage and family, unchastity before marriage, the desire to limit children in marriage to two or three, and (in many ways the most disturbing trait), the nerve to question parental authority. At the same time, extensive formal education for women, as well as for men, belongs to the secular world, and this is something which immigrant women appreciate for their children so that they might be upwardly mobile in Israeli society. While education can belong to the religious world, in religious schools, few Israeli-born children in Gadot go to such schools after elementary education. The reader will also notice the equation of secular with Ashkenazi (Western Jews). In the Yemeni Jewish mind, as well as my own, this identification is true only of non-religious Ashkenazim.

Doing Field Work

Undoubtedly my experience as an anthropologist in the field differed significantly from that of many of my peers. I was not going to a strange and unfamiliar place; rather for me, going to the field was more like returning to an old-new home—old in the sense that I had lived in Israel as a student and a *kibbutznik* for nearly three years on five previous trips to the country. I knew Hebrew and had learned how to conduct myself in a variety of milieux in Israeli society. However, I was new in the sense that, although I had frequently visited Gadot, it was the first time that I was to live there. And, to be honest, Gadot appeared to me as a possible *permanent* home. I went to the field to do doctoral research but I had come to identify myself as a potential Israeli with a high level of political and emotional commitment. Thus, to some extent, going to the field was a homecoming.

While I was very much "at home" in Gadot, I had to assume a religious identity. Even before I went there, I realized that I would have to "pretend" I was more religious than I was if I wanted to work with religious Jews. A non-Jewish researcher, while respecting the religious traditions, simply would not have had to meet the expectation that I did of practising the religious rituals. I was able to play the part of a fairly observant Jew quite successfully because I had been raised in a traditional Jewish home (approximately mesorati) and because I had learned a good deal about Jews more religious than my parents. What did "being religious" mean in this context? It meant that for fifteen months I did not drive on the Sabbath—aside from a couple of very discreet exceptions later on in the field work; it meant I kept the dietary laws, attended the synagogue frequently on the Sabbath and on all holidays, dressed modestly, and took on the habits of a young religious Yemeni woman. I did not feel hypocritical. First of all, it was not too strange (or difficult) for me; moreover I was, after all, participating in the lifestyle of the immigrant generation that I chose to study. Secondly, I identified very strongly with these people and felt myself spiritually uplifted by my experiences in the often ecstatic world of the Yemeni

Jewish synagogue. I am certain that this strategy of engaging in some religious practices helped my acceptance as a researcher: the immigrant women in particular were able to relate to me. I was their daughter's peer, *and* I was behaving as their daughters should—that is as a girl imbued with Derekh Erets (proper conduct). With their daughters on the other hand, I was able to be myself and they respected my necessity of their being discreet about who I "really" was—a young woman more like themselves than like their mothers. I explain more about my relationships in Chapter 6.

During my first three weeks in Gadot I lived with my original contacts in their flat. I was a welcome guest, because as I have said, one of the daughters had lived with my parents for a year. Within days I was treated as a daughter of the house and this meant helping with the chores and getting involved in daily celebrations and quarrels. Two days after arriving there, I began to look for an apartment, to set myself up as soon as possible. Although this family generously asked me to stay with them, I knew that I could not live in three small rooms with five other people. Perhaps, more importantly, I felt that living with one family would prevent me from getting to know many others. However, my three weeks living with this family considerably smoothed my entry into the field. I met many of their friends and relatives who came to visit during that time and thus had new addresses to visit right away.

Finding a flat required extensive use of people's networks. There were no advertised flats for rent in Gadot when I arrived, so I quickly had to learn who knew about possible rental accommodation. I was sent by one of my friend's brothers to visit Simon, the local paramedic, in his office in the health clinic. My first encounter with Simon was typical of that with other town officials—as an American I was given special treatment, for reasons which I never really understood, but which seemed to be related to the prestige associated with knowing Americans. For example, Simon greeted me in between seeing patients; after the next patient went out of the room, he invited me into his office—thus I jumped the queue by some fifteen people. (I felt embarrassed by this, but I learned to jump the queue as a matter of course.) Simon told me whom to ask about flats, and then invited me to visit his home. He proved to be a goldmine of information on Gadot since he had been intimately involved in its development for over thirty years, during which time he had always been a member of the local council. Although his impressions were sometimes ethnocentric, he was knowledgeable about Yemenis since he seemed to know each and every one through his office at the clinic. Simon was also somewhat of a lay sociologist, as evidenced by his analysis of Gadot's development at the beginning of this chapter. He always sent me home with ideas to follow up.

At the end of my second-day's hunt for a flat, one of my host family's sons came home to tell me that he had heard of a Tunisian shopkeeper with a flat to rent. I asked him why he told me she was Tunisian, and he quickly replied that they always identified people with where they originally came from. Later that night I rented the small three-room flat belonging to the shopkeeper which was in a heavily populated apartment complex. My porch looked out on the central square where adults met to gossip and children played. It was in an ideal location, set in the middle of the main boulevard. There were four Yemeni families in the complex of three buildings, but among the forty-eight families living there, people came from some twenty countries-of-origin. Thus the cultural diversity of the complex mirrored that of Gadot as a whole. I lived in this flat for the next fifteen months; it slowly became a centre of activity of unmarried women and men whenever I was at home (particularly in the late evenings after their parents had gone to sleep).

During my first few weeks in the field I realized that there were two places I had to learn about quickly, Gadot *and* Yemen. Concerning Gadot, I interviewed the administrators and the mayor and received permission from the local council to sit in on all council meetings. I also interviewed a number of residents who had lived in Gadot from the early days, and read as much material as was then available on the development of the town. Like all anthropologists, I spent a good deal of time just hanging around, often sitting in the council building to see how business there was conducted and spending hours in the busy market eavesdropping and observing the daily tempo of Gadot. After writing up field notes from the previous day, my mornings were devoted to my interests in Gadot as an immigrant settlement, and so nearly every day I visited either the bank, the market or the council, three places always teeming with people.

Information on Yemen was obtained in a rather different manner. Before I went to the field I read whatever was available in English on the Jews in Yemen. Such material is scanty on the family, in general, and the life of women, in particular: so it seemed clear that I had to conduct formal interviews (chiefly with women) about Yemen. Looking back at these interviews and my daily journal, however, I see that I learned most about Yemen simply through listening to the conversations of the immigrant generation. Life in Yemen is constantly referred to— either as a point of reference or in comparison to life in contemporary Israel. I conducted fifteen interviews on life in Yemen with women and men over the age of sixty who remembered the nitty-gritty details of life with a clarity which would suggest that they had moved to Israel just yesterday. Gaining an early knowledge of life in Yemen also enabled me to demonstrate to others a real interest in their culture and history.

This encouraged people to open up. I gathered intensive case studies of twenty families, fourteen of the immigrant generation.[10] I visited some families three or more times a week and others less frequently, perhaps once every week or fortnight. With time, I managed to fit into the daily routine of the women after they came home from work. By two in the afternoon I was always off to someone's house for lunch and then to help with the chores, and often to nap with the families; usually I would go to visit someone else before dinner in the early evening or after dinner. The later part of the day I usually spent with unmarried women either in their homes or mine, or going out to movies and cafes in Tel Aviv. I also observed families outside of their own homes, with their relatives at rites of passage and other major celebrations, or with their friends in town. I rarely arrived back at my flat before midnight.

Thirty-five women of the immigrant generation participated in intensive interviews on Yemeni Jewish life in Israel. Almost all of these were recruited *via* contacts made in the first place, through the two families (my friend's and her uncle's families) I knew before going to the field, and later, through the networks of those already interviewed. I rejected random sampling techniques because of the impossibility of gaining a list of all Yemenis in Gadot from the population registry. More importantly, when working with a set of people who generally mistrust outsiders, it was more sensible to meet people through the two families I knew in Gadot upon my arrival than to try to initiate contacts with complete strangers. Through observing many families, moreover, questions of typicality became less relevant as situations were replicated in many families.

I was well acquainted with some women before interviewing them and became close to others afterwards. Each interview took, on average, three hours; I was struck by the fact that women whom I met for the first time in the interview seemed to be as forthcoming about their personal lives as women whom I knew quite well. Almost all seemed pleased to tell their story to an interested outsider, even if this meant considerable psychological trauma for some of them who told tales of troubles with their families, and with life in Israel, which they had not repeated in years.

Early on in the field work I realized that there were important differences in life experiences and in attitudes of mothers born in Yemen and those born in Israel. Therefore I decided to have two "research sets," one aged 35–55 and the other 20–34. Thirty-five became the lower age limit and fifty-five as the upper age limit for the older group because: (1) almost all women had lived at least five years in the Yemen, and therefore, it was assumed that their childhood experiences would be meaningful in their present social circumstances and interpretations; (2) with the exception of one household, all children were over the age of five and hence attending school; and (3) most of the children of women over fifty-five were married. Women within this age group, then should have much in common and they were found, in fact, to be broadly comparable to the younger age group. Since I am not concerned in *Ginger and Salt* with mothers in the Israeli-born generation, when I refer to mothers or to wives, I mean specifically those women over the age of thirty-five who were the subjects of intensive case studies and interviews and who were born in Yemen.[11]

While I was in the field I was able to hire as a research assistant for one month Amalia, an Israeli-born Yemeni and a trained sociologist: she conducted most of the interviews with younger mothers of the Israeli-born generation. Together, after I had been in the field for four months, by which time I had learned of important areas of enquiry critical to daily life in Gadot, we formulated the intensive interview. We aimed to ask questions which would illuminate attitudes towards Israeli society, Yemeni identity and the role of women. In all, seventy questions were asked concerning: (1) demographic data (for example, date of emigration to Israel of the wife and the spouse, date of birth of all family members, the educational and occupational backgrounds of all family members, and the number of children in families of birth and marriage); (2) religious practices (including ideas about evil spirits and the evil eye); (3) ethnic and social opinions (including choice of friends); (4) social life inside and outside the home; (5) the division of labour in the home of all household members; (6) relationships with members of families of birth and marriage and with wider kin groups; (7) ideas about the upbringing of children; and (8) attitudes towards sex and sexuality. Throughout *Ginger and Salt* when I refer to "the interview," unless otherwise stated, this is the interview which I personally conducted with the thirty-five mothers of the immigrant generation.

When I began to do the research in Gadot I was interested in learning about the relationships between mothers and their adult unmarried daughters, and as it became clear that women in Yemen had married at a very young age (usually thirteen), I began to get seriously intrigued by the new social category of unmarried women (*ravakot*), in Israel, for which there was no precedent in Yemeni Jewish culture. Therefore, I began to learn systematically about unmarried women themselves and not only in relationship to their mothers. The chapters on unmarried women and mother-daughter relationships discuss thirty-three unmarried women and their mothers, coming from twenty-three families; in eighteen of these families mothers were involved in the intensive interview. Again it was decided to limit recruitment by age. Eighteen was chosen as the lower age limit of the "status group" of unmarried adults because many

Israeli women leave school at this age and then entertain the possibility of marriage. This is also an important age for many women because they leave home to do their National Service, thus becoming the full responsibility of the state. Once free to leave the home, they are freer to change their lifestyles. However, most of the women with whom I worked closely had already completed army service and thus were over the age of twenty-one. At the time I did not know of unmarried Yemeni women in Gadot who were over the age of thirty-two, so that became the upper age limit for this research set of the unmarried women. It seems that there were "never-married" Jewish women in Yemen—although the women of the immigrant generation would not admit to that—but among the Yemenis in Gadot, all older women known to me were married, or had been, at least once. Of women in Israel in general, only 2.5 percent have not married by the age of forty, and 4.7 percent of the men have not married by this age.[12] Israel, then, is a very married society. I became interested in the specific problems of those who did not choose to marry at a young age—the average age of marriage for women in Israel is 21.5.[13]

Ethnic Issues in Israeli Society[14]

Israel is a state composed of two nations, Jews and Arabs, the Jewish nation being politically dominant. Through the central government, it defines how other minorities (Druze, Christians, and Arabs) operate. The state extends judicial rights to Christian, Druze, Muslim, and Jewish courts as well as to national courts. The Jewish population itself is internally differentiated and this plays a critical role in social, economic and political life.

Two broad distinctions among Israeli Jews have constant symbolic significance; on the one hand, Ashkenazim—who came from Western and Eastern Europe and North America—and on the other, Mizrahim—who are associated by origin or descent with the Asian and African continents, particularly the North African and Middle Eastern countries. A specific country-of-origin such as Canada, Germany, Poland, Libya, Iraq, or Yemen may be mentioned if this is deemed important in context. However, within the general category of Ashkenazim, Jews from English-speaking countries are usually referred to as *Anglo-Saxim*.[15] Although the two broad categories share some attributes in common, but are generally differentiated by different historical pasts, and by different religious, educational and political backgrounds. The Ashkenazim were the founders of the modern Israeli state, dominating the political and economic apparatus in 1948.[16] At that time, there were just over 700,000 Jews in Israel, most of whom were foreign born. Of the foreign-born population, 85 percent was of European-American origin, while the remaining 15 percent was of Asian-African origin. Nearly a third of the Mizrahi category were Yemenis.[17]

With the proclamation of statehood, the Law of Return was enacted, permitting unrestricted immigration for all Jews of the world to Israel. Immediately after the creation of this law, the country saw her greatest influx of immigrants, and within two decades the population quadrupled in size. At this time, Jews had to flee the Arab nations and, as a result, came *en masse* to Israel. Practically all the Jews of Yemen, Libya, Syria and Iraq came; Jews from Morocco and Tunisia followed in significant numbers during the 1950s and 1960s.[18]

People who arrived after 1948 came to be referred to as "immigrants" by the settlement authorities, while the pre-1948 settlers, even if foreign-born, became known as the "veterans." Today, veterans, largely Ashkenazim, still enjoy considerable prestige because of their association with the values of political Zionism and the founding of the State. Moreover, they have consistently enjoyed considerable power as the ruling and economic elite of the country.[19]

The most urgent dilemma facing the new Israeli government in respect to immigrants, was housing. Some people moved in with relatives who were already settled; a few were accepted into existing kibbutzim and moshavim; a larger number (125,000, including several sent to Gadot) settled in abandoned Arab houses, many of which were in slum areas; and many others occupied transit camps. The inhabitants of these camps were primarily Mizrahi immigrants, since the Europeans—mostly Holocaust survivors—had already been absorbed into the dominant culture and found homes there, because they shared common cultural, educational and occupational characteristics with the veteran Ashkenazi society. The settlement authorities soon realized that the immigrants were growing increasingly dependent upon the protective atmosphere of the transit camps, many lacking the knowledge of how to look for work outside. To remedy this situation, ma'abarot (temporary immigrant settlements) were set up near urban areas where employment could more easily be secured.[20] Ma'abarot soon turned into slum suburbs of shacks, tents and canvas huts, which defeated their original purpose of providing an economic transition into the social and cultural life of the country.[21] By 1956 the country had caught up with the need for housing, and apartments were assigned on arrival. Physical planning was unspeakably poor, however, and families were often found living in extremely crowded conditions—a situation which still has not been rectified for many families.

After 1956 most immigrants came to Israel out of choice, not having to flee their countries-of-origin. Westerners usually came because of Zionist ideals. Eastern Jews, it is said, did not have a modern Zionist ideology; they came out of political and economic motivations. By 1961 there was a spectacular growth in the number of settlements. Newcomers, mostly from Asia and Africa, were directed into areas in need of development. At least twenty-five development towns were built, comprising one quarter of the Israeli Jewish population; 80 percent of their residents were Jews of Eastern origin or descent.[22] Gadot was one of these towns, even though it was originally ear-marked to be a large agricultural village. The moshav was considered to be the most suitable form of settlement by those involved with the residential placement of immigrants; these authorities were keenly concerned with the successful absorption of immigrants into the agricultural sector for ideological and economic reasons. Like the development towns, the new moshavim were predominantly comprised of Eastern Jews, including large numbers of Yemenis.

In 1948 mainstream Zionist ideology envisioned a new society, essentially socialist in nature, with a fair division of labour and relative economic equality. Prior to independence, however, the somewhat egalitarian society began to change with the development of large urban centres, occupational and ethnic ranking, and class crystallization. This was not due primarily to the influx of Eastern immigrants; rather, other segments of the population, particularly the Israeli-born children of pioneers and professionals and technicians of varied backgrounds, were resisting the socialist claims of Labour Zionism. The managerial staff of public agencies and, indeed, all enterprise, had been drawn from these segments of the population.[23] By contrast, most of the politicians remained committed to Labour Zionism, and thus the government rhetoric was strongly egalitarian, but the social and economic realities were not.[24]

The formation of the State of Israel was (and is) based upon the fundamental assumption of the essential unity of the Jewish nation. This ideal created the basis of kibbutz hagaluyot (ingathering of the exiles) and *mizug hagaluyot* (the melting pot policy, the mixing of the exiles).[25] The term mizug hagaluyot is a problematic one, culturally somewhat arbitrary and ill-conceived, as well as overcharged with emotion.[26] What was the "new Jew" suppose to be? According to its critics, mizug hagaluyot denoted "little more than the 'remolding' of the Oriental immigrant, 'bringing him up to our own level,' and making him something that he is not. The result has been de-culturalization, marginalization, and educational and cultural deprivation."[27] The Eastern immigrants were pressured to Westernize and conform to the social norms and cultural model of the dominant political and economic forces, those of Western Jewry.[28] In a sense, the ideology of mizug hagaluyot is similar to what has been characterized as the philosophy of Anglo-conformity in the United States.[29] Yet the official melting pot policy should be understood within the framework of nation-building. At independence, the Israeli politic and the new Israeli people were critically concerned with legitimizing the existence of a *Jewish* nation.

There is an implicit questioning of the notion of common descent among Jews when Israelis speak of the "social gap" or the "ethnic problem," phrases used by government, media, and academe—as well as by members of the general public—to refer to socio-economic disparities which have their origins in the different cultural and economic baggage brought by various eidot from the Diaspora to Israel. Harsh realities were brought to the fore by the riots, in 1959, at Wadi Salib (a slum in Haifa): a group of North African immigrants demonstrated against ethnic prejudice and job discrimination. Some years later, the Black Panthers, a largely Moroccan youth protest movement, caught the headlines (1971). The dominant Ashkenazi society (which includes top government circles) was forced to recognize "cultural pluralism" in Israel; this has since become the official ideology. The melting pot concept has lost its political attraction or, at least, its realization has been postponed for a few generations.[30]

In the daily round of personal contacts, public images, and economic realities, ethnic origin remains a critical part of social life in Israel. On one level, ethnicity is an important component in personal identity. Eidah is the term used by Israelis when they ask one another from which country they or their parents came. Such identities are not value free. Researchers have found—what is a recurrent theme in the media—that each eidah is severely stereotyped, many eidot have been given derogatory names, and that prejudice has increased between the two broad categories of Ashkenazi and Mizrahi since statehood.[31] Ashkenazim are often ethnocentric, looking down upon the dress, language, and physical characteristics of Eidot HaMizrah.[32] Stereotypical imagery is at work in both directions, however; certainly the people of *Ginger and Salt* bring into sharp focus how they perceive Ashkenazim, and we will see how they use their ideas about Ashkenazim when facing, for example, their own Israeli-born children, some of whom have joined the world of the "other"—the Ashkenazi.

Ethnicity among Israelis is also highly "situational" because people are involved in wider national or religious identifications: they are also Israeli and Jewish, particularly heart-felt during times of war or during holidays.[33] Among Yemenis in Gadot, ethnic allegiance works in several ways: within the course of conversation many people refer to themselves as Yemeni, as members of Eidot HaMizrah, or at the wider level as Israeli, thus shifting from the particular to the general usage of ethnicity and back again.[34] Here a person has a choice of ethnic reference in any given situation. The wider context of Israeli society indicates, however, that Yemenis, like others, are also in a situation of 'no choice' in that their identity is also defined by other Israelis—friends, employers, politicians, and strangers—who act as reference groups for them, and who in subtle ways influence their life chances, choices and behaviour.

While in this book I am primarily concerned with self-defined identity and culture, the group (political and economic) dimensions of ethnic identity are very important. There are, for example, many voluntary associations, such as the Association of Americans and Canadians in Israel, the Yemeni Cultural Association (to which many Gadot Yemenis belong), the Association for North African Immigrants, the United Sephardi Federation, amongst many others. These associations are usually exclusive, have communal activities, weekend retreats and frequent meetings. Members must be able to claim origin or descent from the relevant geographical location. Such associations are now often supported by government grants, as well as by members' contributions.[35]

Concerning the economics of ethnicity, discussion of income differentials makes little sense without taking into account factors like differences in the length of time of various immigrant populations.[36] For example, the average income of Ashkenazim (those born in Europe and North America) is higher than that which many people newly arrived from North America or Europe actually enjoy, because the "veterans" have always earned consistently high income. Mizrahim who arrived before 1948 (many of whom attended schools in Israel) have had consistently higher incomes than immigrants from the Asian and African continents who arrived after 1955.[37] Even so there are exceptions to this and one should be cautious about accepting black and white statements about the association of income and ethnic background. However, even though factors such as education, occupation, sources of income abroad and so on, are not "ethnic" *per se*, they are in fact seen as ethnic factors—and generalized as such—in folk conceptualizations about class development in Israel.

In 1980, of the broad ethnic categories of people who have not attended school at all, the North African and Middle Eastern born Jewish population has the highest percentage (19.8 percent as compared to 2.4 percent of Europeans/North Americans and 0.4 percent of Israeli-born). They also have the lowest percentage of those who obtained post-secondary and academic training (7 percent as compared to 24 percent of the Europeans and Americans and 21.2 percent of the Israel-born).[38] It is easy to understand, then, how it is that Eidot HaMizrah Jews are severely under-represented in the professions, managerial and administrative spheres while they are over-represented among farmers and blue-collar workers.[39] The new state simply did not have the resources to educate formally and retrain all the new immigrants. And, at that time, Zionist ideology saw a Jewish manual and agricultural labour sector as essential to a Jewish state and did not regard such work as demeaning. However, manual and agricultural labour (except on kibbutzim) was delegated primarily to the Mizrahi immigrants and, Zionist ideology notwithstanding, manual labour became despised.

Although the educational levels of children born in Israel to parents from Eidot HaMizrah are much higher than those obtained by their parents, they still lag behind children of the other origins. For example, in 1979, 8.7 percent of children born to fathers born in Asian and African countries had gone on to post-secondary and academic education as compared to 36.4 percent of those whose fathers were born in Europe or North America, and 21.2 percent of those whose fathers were born in Israel.[40] There are several reasons for this. Firstly, even allowing for the generally lower income of Mizrahi families, the outlay of Ashkenazi families on education and culture has been twice as high as that of the Mizrahim.[41] Secondly, there are regional disparities in the standard of education: those schools in development towns and slums, populated largely by Asian/African Jews, are inferior to schools in established towns and relatively prosperous suburbs.[42] Thirdly, teachers also partake in ethnic stereotyping, tending to send Mizrahi children to learn vocations and Ashkenazi children to learn professions[43] thus perpetuating the ethnic composition in the labour force.

Income differentials between ethnic categories, although showing signs of diminishing over time, particularly for the Israeli-born children of Mizrahi parents, are significant indicators of the "social gap."[44] In 1979, Asian/Africans as a category (there were internal differences according to the time of immigration) were making 81 percent of that earned by the European/North American category. One must remember that Mizrahi households (average 4.6 persons per household) are significantly larger than the Ashkenazi households (3.7 persons per household), so income is shared among more persons in those households earning less income.[45] Approximately 8 percent (250,000) of Israeli Jews were living in slum conditions in 1978 and 90 percent of the poor were of Mizrahi extraction at that time.[46] This evidence indicates that ethnic identity, obviously important at the level of personal relations, is also associated with a system of structured and acknowledged inequality. It is necessary to note, however, that the overall standard of living for Israelis has risen significantly since the beginning of the state, and that only a relatively small minority is living in poverty stricken conditions.[47] Given the economic problems and defence expenditures that face the state, however, it is unlikely that the "social gap" will close significantly in the next few years.

The Israeli-born generation of Mizrahim, even when they themselves have not personally felt discrimination, are, as I have hinted, quite articulate about the relationship between ethnic origin and social class and between ethnic origin and place of residence. Their opinions are now integral to local and federal politics in Israel, on all sides of the political spectrum. They are likely to vote for political parties claiming to represent their specific ethnic interests, for parties which express their disillusionment with Labour Zionism, for parties which—like themselves—espouse a free enterprise vision, and for parties which are very hawkish in respect to the situation of the occupied territories. Even so, a minority among them—such as those intellectuals in the East for Peace movement, a Mizrahi counterpart to Peace Now—espouse other ideological positions. I think the salient fact is that the Israeli-born Mizrahim are no longer prepared—as their parents were—to be patronized, culturally or politically, by Ashkenazi Israel.

Gadot proved to be an interesting—and, in a way, unusual—place to conduct research because, as a rule, its population does not concern itself with polemical inter-ethnic relations within the town itself. As a place where all residents have achieved a degree of middle class economic security, regardless of ethnic origin, and where there is no firm residential segregation, people do not, on the whole, relate to each other through jealousy, envy and antagonism. While the immigrant generation generally chooses friends among fellow ethnics, the Israeli-born generation—in the schools, in its social life, and particularly, in many cases in choice of spouse—is living more up to the image of an integrated Israel. However, people remain concerned about the social gap which afflicts the wider Israel, and the town's suburban neighbour next door reflects this situation. Yet Gadot residents are often misled by Asher, one of the wealthiest settlements in the country. While almost everyone in Gadot thinks Asher is simply a wealthy Ashkenazi suburb, in fact almost 25 percent of its population is of Moroccan and Iraqi origin. Of course, there are some people who realize this, particularly the vendors of fruit and vegetable stands who can tell you exactly from whence their clientele have come: "You see that well-dressed madam from Asher, fair-skinned and sophisticated? Well, she comes from Baghdad, from a family of bankers and her husband is a doctor at Hadassah!" Fair-skinned . . . ! Some Mizrahim simply do not meet the stereotypes which Israelis hold of them.

Ginger and Salt is about one eidah in Israel, the Yemenis, some of whom differ significantly from their brethren in ethnically homogeneous settlements. Due to the cultural diversity of Gadot, their identity and expectations must pay the price of constantly having to accommodate a complex situation, but this has its positive side as well, particularly for women, as we now see.

Notes

1. I would emphasise that this high resettlement rate among the newly married is somewhat atypical for Israeli immigrant settlements (Cf. Berler 1970; Comay and Kirschenbaum 1973; Marx 1976; and Spiegel 1968).

2. Klaff 1973, 1977. The following information will give the reader some background on the population of Gadot by continent of origin.

	1961		1972	
	No.	%	No.	%
Born In Israel	2261	34	4182	47
Born elsewhere:				
Asia (Turkey, Yemen, Iraq)	2408	36	2263	25
North Africa	357	5	738	8
Europe/America	1265	19	1395	16
Others	395	6	400	4
Total population	6686	100	8978	100

(Source: Central Bureau of Statistics 1961 and 1972)

3. Aronoff 1973c, 1974b; Berler 1970; Berler and Shaked 1966; E. Cohen 1970; and Matras 1973.

4. CBS 1980a:99.

5. Given the large Turkish population in Gadot, one might expect more synagogues. The two Turkish synagogues are considered to be large with over one hundred families each, but, on the whole, in Israel the Turks are not as religiously observant as they were in Turkey. I am not certain of the reason for this, but it may be because most Gadot Turks originating from urban Turkey were already somewhat cosmopolitan, and less inclined to remain religious in Israel. Such failing to maintain religious observances after immigration is not peculiar to Turks.

6. The yeshiva students travel daily to Gadot from an ultra-orthodox suburb of Tel Aviv. I never learned their reasons for studying at the sub-standard yeshiva in Gadot.

7. The public clerk was an excellent source of information on these matters because he was well-acquainted with the occupational composition of Gadot through his participation in forming local tax brackets.

8. The Yemeni head of the local Religious Council and I drew up this estimate by counting the surnames in the population registry that were definitely of Yemeni origin. He then added on 150 families for those who changed their names. The number may be higher than 600 households, but certainly is not lower.

9. For the purposes of this book, I shall define a "household" as a residential group, that is, persons who share a particular dwelling, on a temporary or permanent basis.

10. Six families came from the Israeli-born generation, mothers aged 20–34. Along with forty-four other mothers of this age group, these women were the subjects of intensive interviewing conducted (only for this age group) mostly by my Yemeni research assistant. The lifestyles of these younger families warrants a discussion but is outside the scope of this book (see Gilad 1982).

11. Many of the changes endured by the immigrant generation in this study are not specific to them but shared with other immigrants in Israel, particularly those from the Yemen. On the other hand, one must be careful about generalizing these data to *all Yemeni Jews in Israel* since, as I have noted, Yemenis in Gadot do not maintain a homogeneous ethnic community like most Yemenis of the immigrant generation elsewhere in Israel.

12. Hazleton 1977:165.

13. I did not conduct formal interviews with unmarried women for reasons which I explain in Chapter 6. I learned about them through spending time with them and gaining their trust as a friend.

14. This section is written largely for the reader who knows little of the background of Israeli ethnic composition.

15. For the origins of the terms Ashkenazi and Sephardi see Zimmels (1958:8–9). Sephardim are people who usually can claim their origins to the Jewish community in Spain prior to its expulsion in 1492, and who continue to utilize a variant of the customs and liturgical traditions of Spanish Jewish culture. A somewhat elite Sephardic community lived in Palestine for generations prior to Israeli statehood. Large communities of Sephardim were to be found in Bulgaria, Turkey, Holland, Russia, and, more recently, in North America. The Jews of South Yemen adhered to some forms of Sephardic tradition that filtered through to Yemen, but themselves are not Sephardim. It is common in Israel to hear Eidot HaMizrah referred to as Sephardim as well as Mizrahim. Since Yemeni Jews in Gadot almost always used the term Mizrahi to refer to North African and Middle Eastern Jews, I do as well.

16. See Ben-Rafael (1982:13–20) on "dominant culture" in Israel.

17. CBS 1980b:57.

18. It should be noted that the leaders and cadres of the Moroccan group usually emigrated elsewhere.

19. Eisenstadt 1954, 1967; Etzioni-Halevy 1977; Fein 1968; Peleg and Peleg 1977; and Willner 1969.

20. Shama and Iris 1977:48–50.

21. Weller 1974:21.

22. Weller:4.

23. Willner 1965:65.

24. Heller 1973:318.

25. E. Cohen 1972:95.

26. Rejwan 1971:19.

27. Rejwan:19.

28. Toledano 1973:333.

29. Heller:317.

30. Lissak 1973:364.

31. P. Cohen 1967, 1968; Heller 1973; Krausz 1972; Peres 1971; Smooha 1978; Smooha and Peres 1975; Weingrod 1965; and Weller 1974.
32. Krausz:4; Heller:321; Rejwan 1968; and Toledano 1973.
33. See Nagata (1974:333) on situational ethnicity.
34. Cf. Mars 1980:68.
35. In my opinion, the financial support of ethnic associations is to demonstrate that the government itself is not discriminatory against Mizrahim. Moreover, it is easier to support "cultural" activities than to really come to grips with the "ethnic-class" troubles of Israeli society.
36. Remba 1973:36.
37. CBS 1980b:275.
38. CBS 1980b:580.
39. CBS 1980b:314–15; Weller 1974:87–96.
40. CBS 1980b:580.
41. Remba:208.
42. Remba:208.
43. Horowitz 1980.
44. Smooha and Peres 1975.
45. CBS 1980b:275.
46. Bellos 1978:12.
47. Pack 1973.

4

The Immigrant Generation

In Yemen, a woman was a daughter, wife or mother. Her life was determined primarily by her female identities in relation to members of her families of origin and of marriage. By contrast, in Israel, other relationships are of critical significance: those of girlfriends, of employee-employer, and even of student to teacher. Links with people outside of the family sphere both influence a woman's place in her family and how she acts within it and towards herself. This chapter looks at the pivotal personal relationships of women of the immigrant generation, and how these shape and are shaped by the social concerns of the women and their continual adjustments to Israeli society. Through examining women as sisters, as wives, as friends and as employees, (as well as daughters in the next chapter), we see how profoundly affected they are by the immigrant experience, even thirty years after they left Yemen. The changes which women have endured are all-pervasive, touching every sphere of life.

Like all Israeli Jews, Yemenis use the term *mishpahah* for the family.[1] It can mean "family" at its largest: *krovei mishpahah* (relatives) including all those people related by blood or marriage; it can mean *b'nei mishpahah* (sons of the family); or it can mean the nuclear family, that is, a husband, a wife and their children. The context indicates the level at which mishpahah is being used.[2] Mishpahah is also a critical concept among Israeli Jews because it refers to the Jewish people as one family, intertwined by ties which are seen to be socially, morally, and historically united. Undoubtedly, the family—in terms of nationhood too, but more importantly in respect to close kin—is the focus of Yemeni Jewish women's lives.

However, and this separates them from their former lives in Yemen, social roles in Israel are allocated not only on the basis of kinship ties but also on other foundations. As a result of having a range of social networks in which to participate, the meaning and importance of family ties vary with each individual's experience.[3] Let us consider first the adult sibling bond: for a woman born in Yemen, of her relationships in her natal family that with her brother is second in importance only to that with her mother.

The Noble Brother

Men could repudiate their wives and often did so, but a sister was a lifelong responsibility. The noble brother was the rock on which the security of a woman rested. A Jewish woman from Yemen explained to me her situation by using these words: "A husband—I can get; children—I can bear; but a noble brother—from where can I get him?"

—Shlomo Goitein[4]

In Yemen, the relationship of a sister to her "noble brother" was an enduring aspect of most Jewish women's lives. This bond was nurtured from childhood; mothers encouraged warm relationships between siblings since they knew that the brother would be his sister's only recourse if her marriage failed and her parents died. During childhood, a boy was told that he was his sister's protector; similarly, a girl was always told to respect her brothers. If—as often happened—a girl's father died before she reached puberty, her eldest brother as head of the household arranged her marriage. After she married, a woman could turn to her brother for help with marital problems; he was sometimes asked to intercede if she felt mistreated by her mother-in-law, and he could be asked to act on her behalf in divorce proceedings. Equally, a brother had a keen interest in the stability of his sister's marriage, because the family had probably invested the mohar in their business or in property and would not want to return it in the case of divorce. In short, brother and sister were related by social obligations which women of the immigrant generation remembered as being indestructible.

Even if the ideal behaviour of the "noble" brother were not always practised, it provided a powerful model through which women defined and judged the behaviour of their brothers, and which continues in Israel today. When women are helped by their brothers, for example, they may refer to the "excellent upbringing" the generation reared in Yemen had received, arguing that brothers simply continue to provide for them as they had been taught. By contrast, if brothers do not help their sisters, or fail to resolve their family problems satisfactorily, women contrast their behaviour with that remembered in Yemen.

In Israel, women believe that the relationship of brother and sister should be guided by mutual respect. When a brother and sister who still adhere to Yemeni forms of greeting meet each other, each takes the other's hand, kisses it, then turns the hand over and kisses the palm.

The younger sister or brother first greets the older sibling in this way, and then the older returns the greeting; in this way mutual respect is symbolized. However, there is an element of hierarchy in the sibling relationship, sometimes based on gender: "As is written in the Torah, 'respect your brother like he is your father,'" says a mother of the immigrant generation to her Israeli-born children; or on relative age: when a sister is older than a brother, he is expected to respect her wishes—and an older sister is likely to receive more visits from her younger brothers than her younger sisters will.

The oldest brother becomes the head of the extended family on the death of the father. He hosts his brothers and their families, his sisters and their families, and his married children and their children on holidays and occasionally on the Sabbath. A man considers the home of his brothers to be his home—ideally a woman does, too. Therefore, brothers do not incur debts as a result of hosting each other, as brothers-in-law do, and for this reason men do not often visit their sisters. To do so is also to go to another hamula: men claim they are more comfortable with their own kin.

Sisterhood, for women born in Yemen, is the relationship they speak of least. Sisters tend to live some distance from each other and hence visit less often, but they always try to attend major celebrations. This is as might be expected on account of the traditional residence pattern of women going to live in their husbands' households, and hence seeing little of their sisters in adulthood. The enduring base for a woman was in the house of her father, and after his death, her brothers. Undoubtedly, women speak more often of their brothers because of the instrumental character of the brother–sister bond and the feeling that a brother's status in the community reflects well on her own.

A sister hopes that her brother will practise the Yemeni tradition and intervene in her marital troubles, but it is extremely unlikely nowadays that a brother will offer his sister a home in the case of divorce as he would have done in Yemen. Women who wished to live with their brothers, at least during times of serious argument with their husbands, were often refused because their sister-in-law would not allow it. In several cases, I spoke to the brother and his wife about their unwillingness to take in a desperate sister and her children. They felt unable to because of lack of space, their desire for privacy, and, most importantly, their conviction that in "modern" times it was impossible for two women to live under one roof.[5]

These reasons indicate changes in cultural conceptions of the use of space in the home as well as in power relations. In Yemen, a mother and her husband and children required one room in which to sleep, but in Israel, parents and children have their own bedrooms; nor does a wife share the kitchen with another woman. Related to these changes, is the "desire for privacy"—a need never expressed in recollections of life in Yemen. Perhaps the underlying reason that a brother no longer takes in a desperate sister, though one not stated directly, is that a wife's ability to refuse refuge to her husband's sister is a strong statement that she is now the boss of her own household. When it was still the cultural norm that sons lived with their aged parents who were the household heads, the mother had the authority to give refuge to her daughter, regardless of the wishes of her son's wife. With the mother absent the wife has the ability to decide on matters which will affect her own children and living arrangements. A woman thus vetoes the possibility of giving her husband's sister a temporary or permanent home. Here one woman's power to make decisions is another's inability to find relief from an impossible marital situation.[6]

Brothers will, however, try to intervene in marital troubles on their sisters' behalf. One case illustrates well the intricacies involved in these matters when a woman's brothers were able to effect a marked change in their brother-in-law's behaviour. One of Rachel's brothers, called here Daniel, lived four doors away from them and the other two brothers involved in this story lived in a town an hour's drive from Gadot. Rachel and her brothers were blood relations of her husband Sa'adia as well as being related by marriage because their fathers were brothers. This dual relationship bears directly on the brothers' ability to influence Sa'adia. The following description is taken directly from my journal (late August 1980) as it was reported it to me, shortly before the marriage of Rachel and Sa'adia's son, Ami:

> This incident began two years ago. Rachel's brother's son was married in Pardes Hanna, so they were going to the Sabbath of the Groom. Sa'adia should have been home from work by 4:00 p.m. on Friday afternoon but he was late so Rachel decided to go with her brother, Daniel. . . . Sa'adia hates Daniel because he did not want Sa'adia to marry Rachel, and they have not spoken for nearly thirty years. This probably contributed to Sa'adia's anger that his wife left for the celebration without him.
>
> Sa'adia arrived home five minutes after they left. . . . He tried to catch up with them in the car, but he arrived after they did at Rachel's brother's house. He was so angry when he saw his wife that he hit her, and then screamed at her in front of her three brothers and three sisters. The brothers took him by force and locked him in a room where he broke all the windows. The police were called in . . .
>
> The Sunday morning (two days later) Sa'adia and Rachel returned to Gadot. Rachel went directly to the religious court to file for divorce. Eventually,

right before the court proceedings, after they had not talked to each other for two months, he apologized . . .

Ami, the only son in this family, refused to get married unless his father, Sa'adia, made peace with Rachel's brothers. So in June, three months before the wedding, with the mediation of the head of the local religious council and the town mayor (two Yemeni men whom Sa'adia respects), they all had a meeting to settle up. After the peace was made, they returned to the house for a meal, where they slaughtered a calf, as was the custom in Yemen, and they celebrated together.

Other parts of this story were filled in at a later date. When the brothers called the police, they told Sa'adia that they would not prosecute if he promised never to hit their sister again. He agreed to this. During the peace-making efforts, Sa'adia was reprimanded for losing his temper. On the whole, he was more affectionate to his wife after this incident, despite a few outbursts of ill temper. So in this case, the woman's brothers were able to effect a marked change in the behaviour of a husband towards his wife.

I can only speculate about why Rachel's brothers were able to elicit a change in Sa'adia's behaviour, but it seems safe to suggest that a number of factors were at work. Perhaps most important, two of the brothers concerned were older than Sa'adia, and sons of his father's older brother. Because of the Yemeni prescript that one treats cousins as if they are brothers, Sa'adia would therefore be expected to respect the two brothers as his elders and "classificatory" brothers. Sa'adia was actually a firm believer in traditional Yemeni values which guided him in his own extended family relations, if not in those with his wife. Not to comply with his wife's brothers' wishes would have been a serious breach of Derekh Erets, and could have jeopardized his authority over his own eight younger brothers. Secondly, there was concern for family reputation. The brothers did not prosecute Sa'adia for damaging their property and for hitting his wife in return for his treating Rachel with more kindness and respect. If Sa'adia had not complied, he ran the risk of their carrying out their threat to prosecute him. Such prosecution would have damaged his authority and family name. Thirdly, the mediators were wisely chosen because they were good friends of Sa'adia. In this situation, he had no choice but to comply with their reasonable requests and the incident was simply not worth more embarrassment. Although Sa'adia felt that he "owned" his wife, he agreed that it was wrong to hit her. Fourthly, although it is possible that Rachel's threat of divorce really elicited the husband's change of behaviour, this was not the first time she had filed for divorce. His markedly different behaviour may have been due to her brother's influence. Finally, Sa'adia was willing to go through with peace-making procedures because he wanted to see his first-born and only son married. Thus the son as well as his wife and her brothers probably influenced his father's choices.

There were, by contrast, several cases known to me of brothers who were not able to elicit a change in the husband's behaviour; and it may be because these brothers were relatives only by marriage. In one case, the brother, a respected mediator in Yemeni affairs, was not able to bring about a change in his brother-in-law's unacceptable behaviour (inebriation, disturbances at celebrations, and, most importantly, wife- and child-beating). The brother-in-law was not interested in changing and, moreover, had no respected position in his own family to protect. In this case, the brother apparently tried to change the behaviour of his brother-in-law more because of his concern for the reputation of his extended family than because of concern for the welfare of his sister. He did not, for example, offer his sister the use of his large home when she ran away from her husband; this was a source of anger with her, even ten years after the event. Nor did her brother offer her financial aid when she desperately required it, which she resented greatly.

For women of the immigrant generation there are three types of financial aid which members of their families of origin and more specifically their brothers, might be expected to extend. First, there are financial contributions to help pay for the rental of halls, and cooking, cleaning, and serving during celebrations. It appears that brothers and sisters contribute more money to their brothers' celebrations than to their sisters', but women do not complain when their families contribute less than their husbands' family do, accepting the system which dictates this pattern probably because they expect significant input from their husband's siblings.

The second type of financial aid provides loans during times of economic trouble. Very few women say directly that they would ask their parents or brothers for such help, some recognizing that neither are financially able. A few say that if they were to ask their brother for a loan, his wife would surely not agree to it. Several women contend that if their mothers were still alive, they would be able to exert pressure on their brothers to extend aid when requested. In reality, however, in those few families where mothers are still alive, they are themselves subject to the goodwill of their sons, particularly if they are living with them. Thus they are not really in a position to pressure their sons to lend money to their daughters.[7]

The main reasons women say that in Israel they would not ask their brothers for financial aid are that family relationships are now guided by "self-interest" and not by Derekh Erets; everyone has his own business; and it is best not to get involved in the financial affairs of one's natal family because one might be obliged to extend aid in return. However, in fact, a number of women had asked their brothers for aid, and related to me the disappointments they endured when their brothers refused, particularly early in their marriages when they needed loans to buy apartments. Women said that their brothers failed to fulfil Yemeni obligations of helping their sisters financially. However, several very old Yemenis (over age seventy) told me that a woman's brothers never extended financial aid to her in Yemen. This seems to be a case of women "remembering" obligations that simply did not exist in Yemen—there a man helped his own brothers or paternal relatives, but not his sister or her family in an *economic* way. Here, then, such women distort the past through making false claims which affirm perceived inadequacies of their brothers in contemporary Israel. This brings us to the third type of financial exchange, and one which has been shaped by the Israeli experience: *nedunia* (dowry).

In Yemen, new brides received gifts such as jewellery (given during the week of hinna), new clothes, and, if they were fortunate, a cow. Nedunia was given when a bride was not desirable—if she was not a virgin, was reputed to be a poor housekeeper, was suspected of sorcery, or was slow-witted.[8]

Some women in Gadot claim that they expected to receive nedunia when they married in Israel. This new expectation, which had almost no cultural precedent in Yemen, may be explained as follows: Women seem to have thought nedunia would recompense them for all the economic contributions they made to their families before marrying. Because these women had helped to pay for the education of their brothers through wage labour, they felt that their brothers should help them in return. Their brothers and parents, however, have not shared their view, and women have not been given in marriage with a dowry. This is another way in which sons are given preference over daughters—sons are helped to set up their new households. As one woman said,

> Yes, there are preferences for sons over daughters in Yemeni families! And how! I felt this when I married and my parents gave me nothing, but they gave money to my brothers. When my brothers married, my parents helped them to buy apartments. Even though I worked for them as a girl, they did not think I needed help. They said, 'That is it, you are married, go!'

It is possible that the expectation—or need—for a dowry was influenced by the Ashkenazi practice of the bride's family helping the new couple to set up in a new household. Indeed, several Yemeni women told me that Ashkenazi women received dowries, while Yemenis were so "primitive" that they believed women were meant to be slaves to their families, not to be recompensed for their toils.⁹

Brothers, for their part, maintain that they should not be expected to give nedunia. They no longer receive mohar—gifts from the groom's family—upon the marriages of their sisters! There is a certain irony here: in Yemen, Jewish women joked about being "bought" upon marriage because of the institution of bridewealth. Although Yemeni women in Israel are no longer "purchased" by their husbands, women are not necessarily better off simply because they go to their husbands as free agents. On the contrary, mohar protected a woman—it gave her residual rights in her natal family, particularly so vis-à-vis her brothers, who received the mohar and invested it and thus were obligated to help with a sister's marital troubles or to offer a sister a home in the case of divorce. However, unlike in Yemen where women invariably had to have the protection of a man—if not her husband, then her brother—in Israel, a really determined woman could in fact set up her own household, if necessary.

In Yemen a girl joined the family of her husband, who expected to provide for her; this expectation endured in Israel—for men, anyway. Yet, in the case of many young couples, such support was not available because the parents of the groom simply could not afford to provide for the young couple. It seems that aid was extended to older sons upon their marriages, with nothing left for younger sons. Hence, many couples found themselves poverty-stricken upon marrying—and this is a source of some women's resentment towards their own families. Thus the cultural model of providing financial help to sons was not yet seen as inappropriate by women who continued to expect aid from their husbands' fathers or brothers. Women's resentment is compounded by the fact that brothers extend aid to brothers but not to sisters. Women find this incomprehensible when they have worked hard in their youth to help their brothers. For such women, the term "noble brother" has been lost in Israel. In Israel, the Yemeni situation is reversed: in Yemen one could repudiate one's husband but not one's brother; in Israel one can repudiate one's brother but not one's husband. Whereas in Yemen a woman's relationship with her brother represented her most stable male-female relationship, in Israel a woman must form a more interdependent relationship with her spouse.

Marriages of the Immigrant Generation

Marriage in Israel brings about new experiences for Yemeni Jewish women. No longer subjected to the mother-in-law, because the new couple lives alone, husband and wife have had to learn to depend on each other for maintaining their households. Women have more options in Israeli society, particularly in paid employment, and this fact has had considerable repercussions on their families. Their husbands also have had to learn to cope with their new position in Israel. I argue here that it is impossible to understand the status of wives vis-à-vis their husbands without understanding what has happened to their husbands—and themselves—as immigrants in Israel.[10]

The contemporary marital relationship is a complicated one, coloured with ideas from the past in Yemen and constrained by the realities of Israel. In virtually all marriages there is considerable contradiction, although the precise form it takes varies. While a wife might feel she makes an equal contribution to family welfare, her husband might consider her to be subordinate to him. Another wife might feel that she is overburdened, doing more than her share on account of working both in and out of the home; yet she probably recognizes that she has more authority over her children and is more able to guide her own life than was previously the case in Yemen.

In order to interpret the changes in marital relations, and in husbands' and wives' activities, I have found it useful to contrast life in Yemen and Israel through the use of the domestic/public distinction.[11] Since this analytical device has become the source of considerable debate in recent years, it is necessary to clarify Yemeni Jewish conceptions of domestic and public.[12] *Bayti* (domestic) refers to the residential unit, to almost all activities that take place in the home—such as food processing, child-rearing and housework—and to kin-based relationships. Work in paid employment belongs to the public domain, as do activities in the synagogue, adult education and local politics. In some instances, domestic and public are not characterized by spatial references. For example, Yemenis consider marketing for household goods as a domestic activity, but when information is exchanged with the merchant which does not pertain to household maintenance, marketing is a public activity. Or, when a political meeting takes place in the household, the residential unit is no longer solely domestic, but concurrently a public place. Thus domestic and public refer not only to the residential unit and what lies outside it, but to any particular activity and social relationship regardless of the usual definition of the space in which they occur. Lastly, I agree with Janet Bujra that if locating gender-based activities in domestic and public realms is to have any explanatory value, "what must be investigated is the *relationship,* the character of articulation, between domestic and non-domestic spheres of action."[13]

These data, however, challenge aspects of the domestic/public distinction proposed by the trend of feminist analysis which claims that women in capitalist society are almost universally confined to domestic spheres, while the public domain belongs to men.[14] Another claim is that because of the privatization of domestic labour in capitalist society, housewives are physically isolated from each other; this privatization encourages women's alienation and inability to organize themselves.[15] As will be illustrated, Yemeni Jewish wives in this study have not been confined to domestic spheres in contemporary Israel—in fact, the opposite has happened—and they have come to appreciate the privatization of domestic labour as a significant improvement over their entrenchment in mother-in-law dominated households which women endured in Yemen. The point that I wish to make is that some feminist interpretations claim to be universal, ignoring cultural diversity.[16]

Before moving on to Israel, Table 4.1 (see page 64) clearly shows the domestic and public domains of the Jewish family in Yemen.

Early Years of Marriage in Israel

In Israel, the immigrant generation has endured many pitfalls and setbacks in the road to achieving self-esteem and economic security. Many difficulties were encountered because, as immigrants in Israel, they had few ways of coping with the expectations and responsibilities of what they themselves term "modern marriage." In Yemen the most often repeated complaints about marriage involved domineering mothers- and sisters-in-law. In Israel, it is the husband with whom the young bride must build a life. There are several definitive criteria of "modern marriage": it is contracted by "free choice"; the emphasis on the marital bond is strong. The couple forms its own household, and the wife has a crucial economic role.

A minority of women were married by arrangement in Yemen between the ages of seven and fifteen; thus their marriages reflected traditional Yemeni Jewish practice.[18] The majority of women married in Israel by "free choice" between the years 1948–1962, with one exception—the local rabbi's wife who married her husband through the negotiation of a hired match-maker. Some married close relatives, while the others married non-relatives, all of whom are Yemeni-born; for women of this generation marriage to a fellow Yemeni was the rule.[19] Women who have married by free choice feel that they have contracted modern marriages.

One might ask why the institution of arranged marriage did not survive in Israel for the Yemeni immigrant generation.[20] First, it should be said that, as an institution, it *does* survive among the ultra-Orthodox (non-Yemeni) sectors of Israeli society; secondly, arranged marriage did not survive among other Jewish immigrant groups in Israel or elsewhere (although there are formal matchmaking services for non-religious people who have difficulty meeting an appropriate spouse). I imagine that arranged marriage among Yemenis did survive during the first few years after immigration in some settlements which were ethnically homogeneous, but this is not a feature remarked upon by Yemeni Jews in Gadot, some of whom had actually lived in such communities before moving to Gadot: in fact, it is one Yemeni feature of social relations which quickly lost its place in the new society.

In Yemen, marriages among Jews were arranged for the following reasons: (1) to ensure the early betrothal of Jewish children in case they should become orphans and thus be subjected to forced conversion to Islam; (2) to protect young girls' chastity–it was highly improper for a young woman to speak to men; the woman or man who did so might fall prey to dangerous sexual impulses–thus, arranged marriages were related to family honour; and (3) to make family alliances–marriage in Yemen entailed the bringing together of two families, not two individuals. (Jews did not fear inter-marriage with Muslims; it is said that neither side would permit that.)

In Israel, Yemeni immigrants were confronted with a dramatically different set of gender identities and relations, and expectations concerning marriage. The most immediately obvious of these in the immigrant camps in Aden or Israel, was the sight of Jewish women serving as nurses, doctors, teachers, translators, administrators, and so on, and who, clearly, were not secluded into some sort of domestic compound. At this point, then, the nascent seeds of women's ability to choose for themselves were planted. Secondly, child-marriages were forbidden by law, and thus children had to be at least sixteen in order to marry; by this time they invariably had learned the new attitudes about modern marriage among Jews in Israel. Thirdly, there was no fear of forced conversion to Islam, which leads us into the fourth and most important ideological reason, which, ironically happened in a secular framework: the policy of mizug ha'galuyot called for intermarriage among various Jewish groups—this had already become a hot national issue in the 1950s. Hence, arranged marriage was ideologically unsound and strongly discouraged by the state. If this "Jewish" state, as a whole, had been religiously devout, then presumably arranged marriages might have endured in Israel.

In respect to some women, however, we have to be a little skeptical about how "modern" their ideas about marriage really were: those who married close relatives, for example, invariably met their spouses in acceptable circumstances and were likely to be chaperoned. And in Gadot, virtually all women of the immigrant generation married fellow Yemenis, they were all under the control of their fathers or brothers while growing up in Israel—and they had all incorporated Yemeni Jewish notions of proper sexual conduct. While they say they chose their spouses, they chose spouses who met with parental and cultural approval. Their own

TABLE 4.1 Domestic and Public Domains in Yemen

	DOMESTIC DOMAIN	
	Women	Men
Socialization of Children	Women were responsible for the socialization of girls until they married and of boys until age of three when they went to school and spent more time with their father.	Men did not participate in basic child-rearing, although they had ultimate authority over their children. They were the the primary teachers of their sons in matters of ritual and occupation.
Household Chores	Women were responsible for all domestic labour. Women were active in some food production, including limited agricultural production outside the household. They were responsible for the care of livestock which were tended solely for domestic use. Women engaged in craft production when time permitted; income derived from this labour was controlled by men.	Men did not participate in food processing or in housework. Men did not partake in food production, except for the ritual slaughter. They did not partake in agriculture or in animal husbandry. Craft workshops were usually located in the household.
Leisure	Leisure time was spent with other women either in the household or in ritual baths where women congregated.	Leisure time was spent with other men either in the household or in the coffee houses.

PUBLIC DOMAIN

	Women	Men
Economic Roles[17]	Women had no economic roles. Women were forbidden to go to the market.	Some men were merchants or long-distance traders. Men engaged in the marketing and trading of goods.
Religious Roles	Women were denied participation in organized prayer, but on the Sabbath and on holidays they attended the synagogue.	Men attended the synagogue three times daily for prayer.
Political Roles	Women were excluded from representation in courts and could not enter government offices.	Men represented the family and the patronymic group in courts and government offices. Inter-family disputes were settled in the household. The Jewish code of practice provided the primary form of jural norms governing Jewish relations while contact with non-Jews was controlled by Muslim governors. The state controlled the spatial dimensions of their communities.

parents, then, did not face the threat of inappropriate matches for their children in Israel, but the immigrant generation, *as parents,* face a number of fears on all these accounts in respect to their Israeli-born children.

In Israel, once of age a woman searched for a spouse whenever possible, particularly at weddings or parties, and was often prepared to marry the first man who seemed appropriate. Marriage was the only honourable way to leave the parental home, and the desire to escape the control of the father and the older brothers was often expressed. Many women claim that they were "subordinated" (their term) by their natal families; they say that they resented the pressure extend on them to work during or after elementary or secondary school rather than continue to study. It seems that the early "emancipation" of women into the labour market in Israel was really a form of exploitation by the traditional family structure which prevented their further education by putting them to work as wage earners for their brothers' education.

Courtship seems to have been brief, and "love" seems to have been based on physical attraction rather than on any deeper assessment of personality or common interests. Several women blame their subsequent marital difficulties on such attitudes; one woman in a particularly strained marriage said that she and her husband curse the distant town where they met and she believes that an evil spirit must have entered her head to make her blind to the animal behind his handsome face. A minority of women, however, said that they were concerned that a prospective spouse came from a respected family; these women all enjoy good marriages. They stress, however, that if they had not been physically attracted to their husbands, they would not have married merely because of their family background.

Newly married women found themselves confronting circumstances quite different from those which had faced their mothers in Yemen. The changes are clearly evident if we consider the songs and stories that comprise an important element in the ceremony of the hinna in Yemen which marked the separation of the bride from her natal family. The values and expected behaviour patterns of the young bride are presented in dramatic form by experienced wives and mothers. While in Yemen these tales seemed to reflect accurately the most important areas of female concern, the songs and tales of the hinna have lost their significance in Israel.

In Yemen women typically moved into the house of their husband's extended family upon marriage, so in the hinna the bride was instructed first and foremost in how to co-operate with her mother-in-law, who was expected to exercise authority over her in married life. Young brides, typically between the ages of seven and fifteen, only gradually took on domestic responsibility in the form of household chores. After immigration to Israel, most women had moved directly to Gadot or other urban areas, where available housing was in apartment buildings, rather than in detached houses onto which rooms could be added at will as was the case in Yemen. The extended family household broke up immediately upon immigration and the nuclear family household took its place. Those families who did move into detached housing units after immigration often had to plant vegetable gardens in their yards in order to supplement household income; nor did parents have money to build on extra rooms for married children and their potential families. So newly-married couples were forced to find their own lodgings. In most cases, new couples set up housekeeping in one-room flats, and new brides were expected to manage the household. Even if new couples wished to settle near relatives, the choice of housing was logistical, depending on either the availability and location of cheap flats or proximity to employment. Despite ideas of "modern" marriage, that is, living apart from natal families, being separated from their families was remembered as a great hardship.[21] However, once these women became experienced housekeepers, they realized how fortunate they were not to have to cope with their mothers- or sisters-in-law as was the case in Yemen.

In the hinna the bride was instructed primarily about relationships with her husband's female relatives rather than her relationship with the husband himself. In Israel, however, a woman's relationship with her husband is much more important than those with relatives by marriage. Upon setting up independent households in Israel, sons stopped contributing to their fathers' household income because they needed their earnings to support their own families. Women said that their fathers-in-law were not upset to lose their sons' incomes because they understood that new couples had to be self-supporting. However, sons are still expected to support parents in their old age.

Lastly, during the week of the hinna, the new bride was instructed about the family purity rituals during and immediately following menstruation. In Yemen these rules were strictly followed; in Israel they are often found to be inconvenient and time-consuming. And since an older, more religious woman is not on the scene to see to their enforcement, the rules are not as strictly observed.[22]

Many older women remember their early years of marriage as a period of great suffering. Women who had married in Yemen recall fewer difficulties in Israel because they were already adjusted to life with a spouse and had some experience with housekeeping. These women were thankful to have been freed of their mothers-in-law and enjoyed their new-found independence in Israel after making initial adjustments. In spite of what seemed to be insurmountable obstacles, particularly poverty, in creating a secure family life, women's contributions to family welfare through income derived from wage labour provided them with more power in the household than their mothers had enjoyed in Yemen. Increased power and autonomy were also related to other factors such as the residential isolation of the couple from the husband's family. Wives' self-esteem increased—a side effect coupled with their husbands' loss of status and prestige after immigration to Israel.

Repercussions of the Move to Israel

In Yemen, as discussed above, women were not regarded as having any economic value. When they worked in craft production during their spare time, thus contributing to family income, husbands marketed the goods and controlled the disposal of all income. It was a man's greatest shame if his wife was forced to work for wages outside the home; and older Yemenis remember that many families would suffer extreme poverty rather than allow their women to work in paid employment.

In Israel, there was little need for the "backward" technology Jewish craftsmen employed in Yemen, so only a small proportion of Yemeni immigrants, most of them jewelers, were able to continue in their traditional occupations. Yemeni rabbis and teachers usually could not find jobs in Israel, finding themselves at a distinct disadvantage because of the pronounced differences between the religious educational system in Yemen and the secular and religious system in Israel. In Yemen, Jewish men in the Muslim community had enjoyed high prestige for achieving basic literacy;[23] in Israel they found that they were illiterate in modern Hebrew and had virtually no knowledge of how to compete in a modern capitalist economy. They were thus compelled to enter the unskilled labour market and helped to fulfill the new state's needs for manual labour. In this way, men lost control over their labour power and their sense of self-esteem was radically altered by having to sell their labour in the market place.[24] Although their roles in construction and road building were initially greatly appreciated by the wider society, soon after the creation of the state with the formation of social classes and the re-emergence of bourgeois attitudes, "nation-building" on the ground lost much of its original prestige. In these ways, Yemeni men found that they no longer enjoyed the high status they had formerly held.

In Gadot there are notable exceptions to this pattern. There are, for example, older Yemeni men who attended high school or university in Israel and subsequently engaged in skilled labour or occupied managerial positions, particularly in banking and administration. Several important local office holders in Gadot are Yemeni, including the heads of the religious council and the workers' council, and the mayor who had held office from 1951 to 1985.

For most Yemeni men, however, just as they found their occupational status altered in Israel, so they found their position within the family had changed, with regard to their wives and children. Men no longer controlled the productive labour of their sons, who entered the labour market as independent agents. An important aspect of patriarchal authority was thus undermined; and evidence suggests that this loss of authority, together with other changes, has had a profound and lasting effect on many men of the immigrant generation.[25] The prevalence of pathological responses to resettlement, such as alcoholism, extreme apathy, depression, and crime, have been associated predominantly with Middle Eastern Jewish immigrant men in Israel.[26] Although in popular Israeli opinion, the industrious Yemenis are exempt from difficult adjustments to Israeli society, in my experience this is not always the case.

* * *

After moving to Israel, in the early 1950s, Yemeni women in this study soon began to enter the paid labour force. We can understand the large-scale entry into paid labour of Yemeni immigrant women of the Magic Carpet generation (immigrants who arrived during 1948–50) only by looking at the activities of those who had arrived during the pre-state years (1882–1947).[27] During the pre-state years, Ashkenazi women entered the labour force in a variety of ways—in industry, bureaucracy, teaching, and commerce—and there thus arose a demand for paid domestic workers to clean their homes or to mind their children in their absence. Arab women were slow to enter such occupations, but Yemeni women were not and they provided most of the domestic labour. It is possible that the example of Ashkenazi women working outside their homes encouraged Yemeni that they, too, could leave their homes to engage in paid labour.

The other factor which pushed Yemeni women into the labour force was their desire to raise the standard of living of their dismally poor families. Husbands, as we have noted, worked in road construction, in agriculture, and in building—earning but meager incomes; they could not support their families, let alone pay for their children's secondary education. Without the earnings of the wife, children would have to work in agricultural jobs to help the family to survive. These early immigrants seemed to realize that if their children were pulled out of school to work, then they, too, would be left with the shame of feeling inferior to the better educated sectors of the new Jewish society; and they also knew that low education could mean a life of chronic poverty. Women entered the labour force to prevent their children from meeting this fate; although one or more children, usually girls, had to leave school to help provide, for their brothers' education.

Yemeni Jewish women's economic contributions helped to consolidate the pre-state Yemeni community, which, in turn as we have seen, provided a basis enabling immigrants of the Magic Carpet generation to find jobs and homes. These newer immigrants learned from the veteran sisterhood that women could leave home to work without causing the disintegration of the family.[28] One Yemeni woman in Gadot recalled the day her mother, who had eight children, went out to work two years after their arrival in Israel:

> Late one evening, our cousin Brakha who had come to Israel as a child in 1925, visited and she saw for herself the misery of our surroundings—the lack of heat, no refrigerator, four children in each bed. . . . She berated my father for not allowing mother to work outside. He talked of his honour and a woman's shame. . . . 'This is Israel,' Brakha replied. 'Tomorrow your wife comes to work with me. No one will judge you harshly.'

> After much discussion, my mother went to work the next day as a helper and cleaner in Brakha's day care centre. She came back tired, but proud and saw for herself that her children looked after each other and did their homework, and that grandma had once again felt useful in looking after the two babies. It was decided that my sister, aged twelve, could leave the fields and go to school, but that didn't last long because even her measly income was also necessary.

> You know, no one judged us harshly. Soon my mothers' relatives and friends also joined *dor ha'sponga* (the floor mop generation).

In the Magic Carpet generation, as with earlier generations, many Yemeni daughters, often as young as ten years old, were sent out to work in order to contribute to the support of the family, handing over their earnings to their fathers.[29] Women recall that their fathers were ashamed of sending their daughters out to work for pay because this confirmed that their income alone was insufficient for family needs. But, at the same time, as in Yemen, family prestige was associated with the formal education of sons. In Israel, many years of Western formal education are necessary to enter upwardly mobile occupations. Thus sons raised and formally educated in Israel would not repeat their fathers' immigrant experiences, and once sons achieved a measure of success, their fathers' loss of prestige would be redeemed.

After women married, most of them continued to work because of their stringent economic circumstances.[30] Moreover, unlike their parents, they wanted to ensure a good education for their *daughters* as well as their sons. Now that the major source of prestige in traditional Yemeni Jewish culture, formal education, had become accessible to women, these women placed tremendous value on it. Furthermore, both immigrant women and men undoubtedly realized that many years of formal education were necessary to be upwardly mobile in Israel. Their Israeli-born children would not be relegated to the unskilled labour sector as they themselves were.

Since women of the immigrant generation are illiterate or poorly educated at best, they continue to find jobs in the ever-growing market for domestics, childminders, and office cleaners. Although on a bourgeois scale of measurement the status of these working women is low, the women themselves are usually not perturbed by this fact. On the contrary (and in contrast to how their husbands viewed the change in their situation), the women viewed their entering the labour market as a rise in status and individual freedom compared with their seclusion in the domestic realm in Yemen, where they had lived, as women put it, as "ignorant slaves."[31] They feel that they are "liberated" (their term) as compared with the large numbers of other Middle Eastern Jewish and non-Jewish women in Israel who do not work in paid employment. At the same time there is an expressed ambivalence in their attitudes towards work. Although women's earnings are vital for the family's well-being, the women of the immigrant generation do not view themselves as the primary economic supporters of their households. They work in order to help their husbands provide.[32] As one woman told me, "I work because it helps him and if I help him, he will help me. I do not work because I enjoy it." In an ideal world, they would prefer to be full-time housewives and have their husbands support them, as husbands did in Yemen, because they dislike the drudgery which their work entails. They do not want, however, the whole Yemeni package because they want formal education, and they certainly do not wish to return to a preindustrial technology. They also do not want their daughters to repeat their own life careers; virtually all women want their daughters to be well-educated but they hope that once daughters marry, they will not have to earn money and can concentrate on the full-time duties of housewives and mothers.

Only four women view themselves as primary supporters of their families, all in different circumstances. One woman, a secretary in the local high school, has a chronically unemployed husband. The second is a successful cosmetician whose husband works as a poorly-paid bell-boy in the local hotel. The third woman holds down two cleaning jobs in order to finance her daughters' university fees; she would rather that her husband "moonlight," but, in her opinion, he is too lazy. The fourth woman wanted to be a full-time housewife, but her husband simply did not earn enough money in road maintenance to enable her to stop working. She owns and manages a restaurant which provides a good income. Six months after I left the field her husband died; when I went to visit her on a later trip to Gadot she told me that she thanked God that she had always been self-reliant.

Husbands' attitudes towards their wives working in paid employment are also ambivalent.[33] Although almost all husbands feel ashamed at being unable to provide for a "middle class" standard of living solely on their incomes, they appreciate their wives' economic contributions and their carrying the double burden of working inside and outside of the home. Women for their part usually recognize their husbands' feelings of inadequacy, and as a result, often try to play down their financial contributions to the household. Nor do they push husbands to help more in the house because they do not wish to threaten their feelings of masculinity.[34] While women "pay" for their double work day with exhaustion, they believe strongly in their own cultural attitudes about masculinity and male integrity. They would rather be tired, on the whole, than insult their husbands. Several women said that when a wife complains about having to work, she sticks a knife into her husband's back and reinforces his feelings of inadequacy. This encourages him to drink and may lead him to alcoholism. Only in strained marriages did I hear wives complain about working outside of the home. Most women do complain about their general state of exhaustion, but not about their double work day, perhaps because they are protecting both their husbands and their right to work.[35]

In many cases women's relationships with their husbands and children have taken on a new structure, one unknown to women in Yemen. For example, most men who have not been able to earn a decent wage dislike their jobs and have not achieved a position of prestige in local religious or political spheres.[36] Such men eventually become uninterested in trying to exert authority over their children, and unmarried and married children alike often disrespect their fathers' wishes. When husbands are unable to discipline their children and their wives successfully—a situation in which men are defined as dismal failures in their wives' opinion—women often become *de facto* the sole authority over children in the home.[37] Thus women's new position in the family and their power in the marital relationship in part results from the repercussions of their husbands failing to achieve a position of respect or economic success in the wider society.[38]

One detailed example is in order here: Shoshana, a childminder, moved to Israel in 1935 at the age of two. She attended elementary school for four years, then took employment in domestic work and later in a factory in order to help support her family and pay for her brothers' education. Shoshana is known for her independent spirit and is only one of two women of the immigrant generation (in this study) to have served in the army; a photograph of her in uniform, eyes shining, graces a shelf in their salon. After her discharge from the army, at age twenty, she attended a women's vocational training centre to learn to be a nursery school teacher, but she did not finish the course because at the age of twenty-one she married Menakhem who insisted that she go to work to bring home a wage packet. Already then, Shoshana says, she should have realized that Menakhem wished to subordinate her.

Shoshana claims that she is more "modern" and "open-minded" than other women of her age. She smokes cigarettes in the company of male visitors: smoking and sitting with male company are unheard of in traditional Yemeni circles. On the other hand, she admits to being "primitive" because her attitudes concerning sex and marriage are totally consistent with other women of her age. Also, despite having arrived in Israel at the age of two, her idealizations of the Yemen (for they cannot be memories) loom large in her mind, and are evident not only in how she views her daughters' conduct, but also in her claim to prestigious standing as a Yemeni in Israel.

Upon their marriage, Shoshana and Menakhem occupied a room in her parents' house since neither her family nor his—Menakhem was one of nine children—was financially able to loan the new couple money to set up their own household. For Menakhem, as an extremely custom-bound Yemeni man, this might have been the first serious setback in his life. In Yemen, Shoshana would have come to live in his parents' household; his moving to hers was an indication of his parents' low economic standing and his own as a low-salaried road worker. They lived with her parents for seven years, during which four of their five children were born, and then moved to Gadot because an inexpensive three-room apartment became available there.

Menakhem, like other men of similar standing in the immigrant generation, expressed—sometimes in jest, sometimes in earnest—that he should never have left Yemen. There, he argues, his wife and children would have obeyed him. Menakhem's desire to return to Yemen stems from his feelings of failure in Israel, as a worker, a husband, a father, and a member of his community. People in Gadot who know him well claim that he has adjusted poorly to Israeli society and he is particularly distressed that his wife is as formally educated and more experienced than he is in the ways of contemporary Israel. Shoshana has demonstrated considerable skill in making a place for herself in the community-at-large, as she has served on the executive committee of the Parent-Teacher Association (PTA) of the local religious elementary school, on the secretariat of *Na'amat,* as a leader in the successful lobby for adult education courses for women, amongst other appointments. Menakhem has ignored such *Israeli* activities; he immerses himself—or so he claims—in the study of Yemeni Jewish texts and, almost daily, spends long afternoons with several friends of similar standing drinking cognac, chewing qat, and smoking cigarettes. These habits—and addictions—deplete the household income and this, of course, finds no favour in the eyes of his family. To some extent, then, husband and wife lead separate lives, in "public" domains, of a very different sort.

Menakhem has no control over his six grown children. They pity their father, believing that his unpleasant behaviour resulted from his poor adjustment to Israeli society.[39] Although they occasionally are kind to him, they never defer to his attempts to exert parental authority. In the absence of a husband who can maintain domestic order, Shoshana has been primarily responsible for disciplining her children—a task whose difficulty has increased since they entered the army.

Among Shoshana's explanations for her bad marriage, for Menakhem's own failures, and for her chronic troubles with her children is the evil eye. She believes the evil eye struck both her father and Menakhem's sister and has been passed on to herself and Menakhem. Menakhem's sister was struck by the evil eye while they were still in Yemen: one day while drawing water from the well, several Arabs exclaimed on her beauty, forgetting to add the appropriate saying to ward off the evil eye. By the time she arrived home, the water had turned to rust and she fell seriously ill. Menakhem tended to her and prayed for her day and night. She recovered but suffered from bad headaches and eventually Menakhem did too. The local healer purged the evil eye by putting hot iron rails on Menakhem's head and at the base of his neck; he still bears the red scars. His headaches became less severe. However, Shoshana claims, the branding was the root of his mental imbalance—something he successfully hid from her during their courtship. If she had known about it, she says, she would never have married him.

Shoshana's father, a renowned healer, became blind in Aden (probably from trachoma) when they were in transit to what was then Palestine. When she was a little girl, she asked her father why God let him be blind. He replied that he was blinded by God who loved him and wished to spare him the despair he would otherwise feel were he to see pagan Jews in Israel breaking the Sabbath and Jewish women who dressed immodestly. However, Shoshana learned from her brother that the real reason for his blindness was the evil eye: he had headaches after a woman told him, to his face, that he was a fine man—and eventually blindness. When Shoshana confronted her father with what she had learned, he denied it. The next day she fell ill with smallpox—the scars still show on her face. Because she is so ugly, she claims, only an idiot like Menakhem would marry her. Thus the evil eye designed their fate, and Shoshana found this explanation for their maladies easy to believe. After relating these two stories, she quickly recited several incantations to protect us from the evil eye. Shoshana thus had supernatural reasons with which to explain her bad marriage, but it is clear that some earthly factors, drawn from her own experiences in Israeli society may have something to do with it. These reasons are not due only to Menakhem's low status job and his engagement in Yemeni male activities which are divorced from the social reality of his Israeli home and children. Shoshana herself is somewhat threatening to a Yemeni male ego, having achieved the same level of formal education as her husband, served in the army, made for herself a position of respect in Gadot through her participation, and even leadership, in community activities; she also earns a better income than her husband. For any custom-bound Yemeni Jewish man, this is difficult to handle.

Most women have more power in the home in Israel than in Yemen, and this is due not only to their husbands' difficulties in adjusting to Israeli society, but because of the material factor of their financial contributions to the maintenance and economic security of their families.[40] Few women hand over their incomes from work outside the home to their husbands; most bank it, either individually or in joint accounts. Women say that their income is usually spent on food, children's clothing and school supplies. Their income also allows them to go to the cinema and theatre, to pay for adult education classes, to attend weekend "ethnic retreats," to visit relatives in distant towns and, for some women, even to take tours around Israel with other female friends. Husbands' earnings are usually spent on major expenditures, such as paying utility bills and children's university tuition fees. Most husbands and wives decide together on major purchases, yet there is some secrecy involved in spending money when spouses have separate bank accounts. For example, women often loan their closest friends money (thus replacing brothers in some instances) either when the need is desperate or when a bargain—such as a stereo unit "on sale"—cannot be passed by. Women are unlikely to tell their husbands about these loans to their friends: in fact, women spend most of their income on their own families, so they see it as their prerogative to give help when they deem it necessary. On the whole, the "resource theory" of conjugal power—the more resources a person has, the greater power he or she has—holds true for most Yemeni women in the labour force in respect to decisions on how to spend money: husbands usually do not make purchases without consulting working wives even though they may claim to with other men.

In this immigrant context, it is noteworthy that women who do not work for income are not necessarily at a great disadvantage. These women are usually married to more educated men with higher paying jobs than the husbands of working women. The wives enjoy their husbands' respected position and their husbands, while somewhat more dictatorial than the less fortunate ones, respect their wives. Housewives also report that they manage their households, have access to husbands' bank accounts, and have a voice—even if more limited than working women—in deciding on major purchases. While they defer to their husbands' authority more regularly than the working women, this is not usually viewed as a sign of subordination but of their success as immigrants in Israeli society, and as evidence of a solid marriage. Most housewives are much envied by women who also work outside the home. For them, their "resource" in their marriage is related to their husbands' enjoyment of respect and prestige in the community. It seems, then, that for many women, whether they work in paid employment or not, they have become more assertive about their personal needs and in defining the needs of their families than they remember being the case for their mothers in Yemen.

I often heard men praising their wives for being wonderful mothers, but rarely for being wonderful workers. Both husbands and wives regard the idea of mothers finding equal satisfaction in work and in family roles as extremely strange and unwomanly. Women do not want to be *feministi* in this way (this is not to say that they do not want "equal rights," for they do), nor do their husbands want them to be.

The Division of Labour in the Household

In Yemen there was a strict division of labour in the household and a strict physical segregation of men and women in public spheres. In Gadot there continues to be a segregation of men and women in the synagogue in accordance with orthodox Jewish custom. At some traditional ceremonies, such as the Sabbath of the Groom, the Sabbath of the *brit* (circumcision) and at traditional weddings, men and women eat, sit, and celebrate separately. In general, however, there is little physical segregation of men and women in public spheres among Yemeni Jews in Gadot. Nevertheless, in the domestic sphere there is still accepted wisdom about the proper duties of men and women, which is not only a carry-over from everyday practice in Yemen, but is legitimated in halakhah.[41] There remains a general belief in the role of the man as provider for his family and in the role of the women as the manager of her household, devoted first and foremost to the upbringing of her children.

Women who are in paid employment work double-shifts, typically working seven hours a day as their husbands do, and an additional three to five hours a day in housework.[42] Typically, Friday is a day off, but the women put in a full day of cleaning to welcome in the Sabbath, while their husbands read, relax, or, at the most, sometimes do errands. Husbands perhaps devote an hour a day (no more) to managing the household, usually in the form of marketing or banking, which they did in Yemen; but women also go to the market and the bank in Israel.

There are many household tasks which men of the immigrant generation simply will not do: washing clothes, washing floors and cooking are "women's work." There are some men who never enter the kitchen except prior to major celebrations for which thousands of nuts must be roasted and hundreds of fruits washed. In "successful" marriages, wives are not bothered by their husbands' lack of participation, saying they prefer to keep them out of the kitchen "because of the confusion they create there." There is more than the matter of "confusion" here. The kitchen is female territory and men simply are not welcome in it. When men try to help they are inevitably awkward in a place they know little about, and so this reinforces the view that they should not be in the kitchen. Women are expected to serve their husbands food or tea when and where they require it; they rebel only on those occasions when they are physically exhausted. There are husbands who believe that their wives were placed on this earth in order to serve them, and this belief has become a common remark among Yemeni men.

There are no straightforward practical reasons why men do not do most household tasks. One exception is laundry: religious women claim that husbands will not wash women's clothes because of the fear of pollution from menstrual blood. Indeed, such women do not wash their daughters' undergarments for the same reason: they fear polluting themselves. With respect to other tasks, women say that men perform them so slowly that the wives become frustrated and prefer to take over. During late pregnancy and their children's early years, most men did perform household chores, particularly when their wives worked.[43] As their children grew old enough to help in chores, husbands stopped helping, and it seems that wives expected this. This illustrates that there has not been a redefinition of male roles on this matter of children.[44]

In several families, men use the refusal to do any household chores or marketing as a way of punishing their wives. For example, one Friday Zohara had failed to serve lunch on time; that morning she had mislaid the yeast so the bread was not ready. Her husband, David, became angry and yelled at her. She shouted back that even though she also wanted the bread ready on time, she owed him nothing. He replied that she owed him everything, and in retaliation refused to go marketing for her that day, saying that she could break her back and legs for all he cared. When he stomped out of the kitchen, she complained that he was like a little child who got angry over anything. The quarrel continued over the weekend. On Sunday she went to the market after work, and then, exhausted, to her exercise class, while he studied at the rabbi's house.

In another family, Yona, who held down two jobs, relied on her older daughters to help her in her evening job which involved cleaning the local bank. On the odd occasion when the girls were too busy to help her, her husband had to help, which he did reluctantly after yelling at the daughters for being inconsiderate. One night when one daughter was working overtime in her job and the other two were studying for their high school exams, he refused to help his wife because he wanted to watch a football match on the television. Yona was very angry at him because of this and a long-standing *brogez* (slang: an avoidance relationship resulting from an argument) resulted between all family members. The result was that no one helped her in the bank for several days, which left her working alone virtually eleven hours a day. This particular couple nearly initiated divorce proceedings several times in the course of their marriage because the wife felt that the burden of household maintenance was entirely on her shoulders, but she always relented because she was concerned about the family reputation and the children's upbringing.

While most men are not this inconsiderate, women also try their best not to get into the situation where help can be withdrawn because they know this means more work for themselves. Some women told me they were bothered by their husbands' lack of help, but many of these added that they suppress their anger so that they would not be punished nor their children made to suffer. Men are seen as naturally stubborn and therefore cannot compromise. Women also accept the religious justification for their subordinate position as Bat Zion and Zohara told me, when in the course of a wedding celebration, in a religious household we listened to a rabbi's anecdotes:

> . . . The rabbi is saying that God made woman to help the man, who was bored being alone. This is fitting to say at a wedding because the woman came from the man's rib. Women were not given equal rights because there would be many arguments if they were equal, so God made woman inferior to man.

They went on to say that there was no point in making demands if men were unable to change their behaviour.

By contrast, those wives who are in the labour force and enjoy a relatively compatible relationship with their husbands, deny that there is a division of roles in the home.[45] It is difficult to reconcile this denial with the fact that husbands are not expected to perform household chores. It seems to me that these women have begun to formulate an ideology of mutual help between spouses which has little existence in reality. My following questions to a husband and wife illustrate the ideas behind this contention:

L.G. (to the wife): How do you see the role of women in Judaism?

Wife: There are many differences between men and women–the Bible will tell you why. The woman is the woman and she cannot change her role. But if the husband and wife are compatible, one helps the other. And so there is mutual understanding . . .
L.G. (to the husband): Do you help your wife with the housework?
Husband: Why not, why not? I try to help as much as I can. There are couples where the wife is subordinated. But in our family, thank God, all is common between us. What she says is holy and what I say is holy. Why wouldn't I help her? I am considerate of her. She works harder than a man. If she did not work outside the house maybe I would not help her, but we both work outside. If a child needs changing or washing or something to drink, I help him. What, not watch over one's family? I wish that all Jews would do what I do.

This husband does what he says. Any time that I visited this family, the husband was always working in the yard, and I saw him several times on the bus with parcels from the Tel Aviv market. He does not, however, think that in an ideal world it would be his role to help her any more than it would be her role to work for income. They simply cannot afford for her to stop working, so while she works outside of the home, he helps in it.[46]

Beyond signalling signs of an ideology of mutual help, many wives believe that they and their husbands share in most decision-making, and this is largely because of women's economic contributions. Some feel that they make most of the important decisions, but manipulate their husbands in doing so, putting on a guise of deference to husbands. Men must be humored because they naturally must feel superior, but such women do feel that they are on an equal footing and capable of making and carrying through important decisions.

Finally, husbands do not necessarily view their wives as equals. Men often express the opinion and demonstrate by their behaviour that their wives are meant to serve them; that the husband should curb the mobility of his wife outside the home; that men are clearly superior to women in matters of religion and ritual and that *as males* they are inevitably more intelligent than females. Most wives, if they are tired, however, will tell their husbands to serve themselves; they invariably engage in outside public activities whenever they wish; and they view themselves to be as intelligent as men. Only in matters of religion and ritual are most women prepared to defer readily to their husbands' authority, and such deference is seen as divinely inspired. It seems that husbands rely on a Yemeni model of marital relations while many wives enjoy their Israeli reality.

Domestic and Public Domains in Gadot

In Table 4.2 I identify how the current domestic and public activities of Yemeni Jewish men and women in this study depart from the contention that in capitalist society the domestic domain is primarily delegated to women and the public domain becomes exclusively male.

In Yemen, as I have indicated earlier, women did not go to the market, they did not work in paid employment—although they may have supplemented family income through participation in craft production, they did not have control over their earnings—they had no political rights, and they were not formally educated. On the ideological level, women's activities were viewed exclusively as belonging to the domestic realm. By contrast, it is quite apparent in the above classification that, in Israel, women of the immigrant generation—and even more so their daughters—are not exclusively relegated to the domestic domain; on the contrary, they are quite active outside of it. Some of their activities are shared with their husbands while others are not. In this particular capitalist society, these particular women's lives have not been relegated primarily to the domestic domain.

At the same time, it is true that Yemeni women of the immigrant generation view the domestic world as integral to their responsibilities as mothers and wives. But, unlike in Yemen where mothers-in-law exercised authority over daughters-in-law, and husbands had ultimate authority over children, women in Gadot maintain an interdependent relationship with their husbands and in most cases have more authority over their children than their husbands. Even though during their early years of marriage new wives may have suffered from lack of practical instruction on housekeeping, eventually women's experiences in privatized domestic labour were seen as an improvement over subservience to mothers-in-law and senior sisters-in-law as in Yemen. Nor does life in a nuclear household mean separation from other women. These women spend much of their spare time with friends—not only drinking coffee, but in formal associations and classes oriented to their specific needs and preferences.

Since these women are involved in labour outside of the home that is similar to the labour that they perform in the home, and since they are primarily responsible for housework and childcare, thus carrying women's "double burden," some feminists might argue that this is not liberation at all.[47] But Yemeni Jewish women do not hesitate to claim that they are liberated from their immediate pasts. Most older women now are literate and are active in community activities and organizations. There are even some Yemeni women politicians and entertainers elsewhere in Israel, one of whom, Shoshana Damari, is a national symbol of the successful immigrant. Therefore women have a public role outside their homes through these activities in a world which they define as their own. Among themselves they compete for power and prestige. Furthermore, they explicitly do not wish to engage in formal town politics because this domain is viewed as "corrupt" and as a male world in which they feel they have no place and want no part.[48] However, they are active in expressing their opinions in respect to political parties, school levies, and the provision of day-care centers. While Yemeni Jewish women came to Israel as passive, confused, and dependent immigrants, they now see themselves as active, contributing members of their society.

Compared to life in Yemen, these women enjoy a great deal of freedom. They accept the technological innovations that come with modernization as miraculous and helpful, and although they lament the loss of collective responsibility that was characteristic of life in Yemen, they have no desire to return there. For them, Yemen is remembered as a world of female servitude and seclusion in the domestic domain, and as a place of Jewish suffering in a Muslim nation for 1,500 years.

It is only men of low status who sometimes remark that they would like to return to Yemen, even though they appreciate the freedom which they have as Jews in Israel as compared with the restrictions on Jews in Yemen. For in Yemen, while ultimately subjected to Muslim control, Jewish men had considerable power to direct their extended families and to engage in work which had some meaning for them. In fact, the separation of production from the domestic domain in capitalist society has inevitably meant the alienation of their labour, and I have suggested that this has had considerable repercussions for many of the men. Whereas some contemporary feminists claim that the privatization of domestic life in capitalist society is detrimental for women,[49] this has happened here more to *men*. It is the women who have gained in wealth, in power and in privileges in the home and outside of it since the move to Israel. It becomes quite evident that it would be impossible to talk about the status of these women in their families and their community without analyzing what has happened to their husbands as immigrants in Israel. The transformation of marital relationships has resulted from a combination of husbands' demotion in status in Israeli society, from women's ability to contribute economically to their households and to control their income, and from the increase in self-esteem which women have experienced through extensive participation in public life outside of their homes.

"My Friend Is My Sister"

Rina and Rachel are very dear to each other, having been close friends since they both moved to Gadot in the late 1950s after their marriages. They know each other's every move every day, if not through meeting

TABLE 4.2 Domestic and Public Domains in Israel

	DOMESTIC DOMAIN	
	Women	Men
Socialization of Children	Women are responsible for most child-rearing.	When children are small and wives are in the labour force, husbands help with child-rearing.
	Women are authority figures for their children.	Men who have achieved prestigious economic, political or religious roles are authority figures for their children, while those men who have lost their self-esteem usually fail to be.
Household Chores	Women are responsible for general housework.	Men are responsible for heavy household tasks, such as painting and moving furniture.
Leisure	Leisure time is often spent with other women and men in the household, but primarily with other women.	Leisure time is often spent with other women and men in the household, but primarily with other men.
	Women do homework from adult education courses in the home.	Men study religious texts in the home.

PUBLIC DOMAIN

	Women	Men
Economic Activities	Most women work in paid domestic labour, child-minding and factory work. Women purchase goods in the market. Women usually attend to their own bank accounts and in some cases tend the family's bank account.	Men work in unskilled, semi-skilled or skilled labour. Men purchase goods in the market. Men attend to their own and in some cases to the family's bank account.
Community Activities	Women attend parents' meetings at school, and PTA. Women are involved in the working women's association, the religious women's movement, adult education, exercise classes, sewing and ceramics courses, and choir.	Men attend parents' meetings at school, but less so than women. A minority of men attend adult education classes.
Religious Roles	Women attend the synagogue on holidays and for major rites of passage; they do not lead in formal prayer. Most women attend a lecture on the Portion of the Week led by the rabbi's wife.	Men go to the synagogue several times a week and some attend daily. They are involved in religious study groups after work.
Political Roles	Women vote and have a variety of jural rights in the state. They often attend political meetings and some even go on the campaign trail.	Men vote and have a variety of jural rights in the state. Some men are active in political parties and in workers' committees.

in person, then on the telephone. They attend adult education and exercise classes together; on the Sabbath they meet for coffee and then go to the Portion of the Week sessions, walking there lazily, arm in arm.[50] They never miss the monthly meeting of Na'amat, (the working women's association,) and several times managed to have positions on the board at the same time. Rachel often flees to Rina's home as a break from her domineering husband, and while Rina comforts her, she herself complains about her daughter's improper conduct. They see a historical basis to their friendship: their mothers were born in the same village in Yemen and played together as girls before leaving their villages upon marrying. Rachel and Rina thus feel that they were destined to meet in Gadot and to thrive on each other's company.

Close friendships such as these are common among Yemeni Jewish women, but they also have others outside of a best friend. Friends meet together in large groups particularly on Saturday afternoon, often at the Portion of the Week, and almost always for *ja'ale* (social events named after the foods such as nuts and raisins served at them). At ja'ale they gossip, tell folktales, laugh together, and sometimes mourn together.

A woman's best friend is invariably referred to with a kinship term—my dear sister or my beloved cousin. As one expects kin to help in times of trouble or in cooking and serving during celebrations, so one expects the same of a friend. In fact, many women confided to me that their friends are more important to them than their "real" kin—friends choose each other and thus elect to take on obligations. Kin feel forced to help, but friends want to. Women often contrast the situation remembered for Yemen with that existing in Israel: in Yemen friends were usually woman's relatives by marriage in the household and village of her husband, but in Israel such relatives may have become strangers and hence are not to be trusted. Friends, however, are relations of choice and this element of choice seems to be very important in that it allows a woman to control her own social life and to express her personal preferences.

The majority of women choose Yemeni friends because they share with them a "common language," that is, a common conceptual and cultural framework. Listening carefully, one is aware that friends usually speak a similar dialect of Yemeni Judao-Arabic, originating from the same region of the Yemen. Their husbands often attend the same synagogue; women constantly emphasize the importance of husbands' compatibility if two women wish to become—or remain—friends.

Most women have some non-Yemeni acquaintances, and a few are prepared to admit that they have close friends from Eidot Hamizrah. When women want to legitimate statements particularly in reference to proper conduct or to their economic difficulties in Israeli society, they are prepared to call themselves Mizrahim. By contrast, when a woman wants to disassociate herself or Yemenis from Eidot Hamizrah—for example, when speaking of the higher crime rate that prevails among Iraqis and Moroccans—she will consciously separate herself from Mizrahim. Almost all the women have contacts with other Mizrahi women through work, town activities, in their apartment blocks and through inter-married relatives.[51] Some women report that they value such contacts because they enjoy learning about different cultures and foods. They do not discourage their children from having close friendships with non-Yemenis, but they will discourage them from marrying non-Yemenis—no matter what the cultural origin is. There is, of course, the question of status—Yemenis enjoy relatively high ethnic status in Israel. There is the question of culture—Yemenis openly admit that they want to preserve their cultural traditions. There is also the question of trust—Yemenis find it difficult to trust each other, let alone outsiders. For all these reasons, inter-marriage is discouraged. If their children are to marry outsiders, they prefer Ashkenazim to Mizrahim, both because of Ashkenazi higher status and reputed economic standing.

When women say they have Ashkenazi "friends," they are usually referring to their employers. I rarely saw Ashkenazim in the homes of Yemenis and those few exceptions were invariably next door neighbours. Almost all women who work for Ashkenazi women will personalize the relationship, claiming that the employer-employee relationship is one of *hadadi* (reciprocal) exchanges. These involve childminding or cleaning for money, listening to each other and offering advice, and invitations to rites of passage. In fact, they do not socialize with their employers, except during rites of passage, nor with Ashkenazim generally—unless they have a warm relationship with a Ashkenazi neighbour which is uncommon. Women also come into contact with Ashkenazi women who teach them in adult education courses and invariably they speak highly of them.

On the other hand, there are a number of women who adamantly claim that they have no Ashkenazi friends because they do not share a common language and because Ashkenazim, thinking of Yemenis as barbarians and primitives, therefore snub them. Ashkenazim are often perceived as miserly and dishonest. Several women believe that there is a natural limit on how intimate an Ashkenazi and a Yemeni can become because of cultural differences. It is because of such differences that Yemenis maintain ambivalent feelings towards their employers.

Images of the Ashkenazi Employer

Almost all women of the immigrant generation work or have worked as domestics and child-minders in the homes of middle and upper class

Ashkenazim in surrounding areas. Some of their female employers work outside the home, while others do not. A woman often works for years in the same Ashkenazi household, so that a long-term relationship with the family develops. Women are proud that they help to raise the other woman's children; indeed they often view themselves as irreplaceable members of their employers' households.

There are, of course, many differences between the Yemeni-born woman and her Ashkenazi employer. Besides culture, the most obvious one is class, and here there are sensitive issues. One which is very important to women is whether or not they can turn to their employers for loans. While several women claim that they are too embarrassed to ask for loans and prefer to pay a high rate of interest for bank loans, others say they are discouraged from requesting loans because they perceive Ashkenazim as miserly. By contrast, there are many women who ask for loans and receive them, but this has a significant cost: women who have received loans are afraid to stop working for a woman who lent them money, feeling obligated to them for life.

Yemeni women see "pluses" and "minuses" (their terms) in working for Ashkenazi families. An advantage is the good wage they receive. They are also influenced by their literate and comparatively well-educated Ashkenazi employers to attend adult education courses. They also use what they see as greater participation of Ashkenazi husbands in childcare as weapons against their own husbands when they feel the burdens of working both in paid employment and in housekeeping are too great to bear. As one woman said, "What a lazy and inconsiderate husband I have. My employer's husband, a South African accountant, takes his son to the doctor, which requires him taking time off work."

However, women frequently discuss negative features of Ashkenazi culture. They do not view Ashkenazi women to be as dependable as their Yemeni friends. Although women of the immigrant generation believe that all people in Israel are guided by "self-interest," Mizrahim are less so. Even those employers who give loans are seen as "self-interested" rather than as generous with their money, knowing that a loan will oblige a woman to continue working for her.

Ashkenazim do not have many children (usually two as compared to the four or more among Yemenis) for which Yemeni women pity them. Ashkenazi children like Yemeni food, so their own mothers can never please them. Ashkenazi children might be better educated than Yemeni children, but they are also spoiled by their parents' high standard of living and are often disrespectful to their parents. Ashkenazi daughters always serve in the army (or so the Yemenis believe) and because they are not raised with Yemeni attitudes of proper sexual conduct, a daughter is more likely to bring shame to her family by becoming "ruined" through sexual liaisons.

Very importantly, Ashkenazi employers are secular Jews and since they are secular, they are also profane.

While Yemeni women learn from Ashkenazi women and aspire to part of their lifestyle, they do not want everything that they believe extra money and Western ways bring. So the women select only select features of Ashkenazi culture, such as the importance of formal education for themselves and their children, to bring into their own homes. They do not seem to be bothered by their ambivalent attitudes towards Ashkenazim because they show an awareness of impenetrable barriers between them. In the end, women of the immigrant generation also believe that Yemeni culture is morally and practically superior to Ashkenazi culture.

In sum, Yemeni Jewish women, aware of Ashkenazi women, desire to improve their relative placing in Israeli society, but at the same time, are determined to retain their own cultural identity. Religious practices are extremely important here because religion invariably defined and segregated Jewish life in Yemen; it was an all-encompassing element of economic and political relationships. In Israel, the practice of Yemeni Jewish religious traditions is a focus of identity vis-à-vis other eidot; it also has enormous social and emotional value particularly in the organization of community life, in family rituals, and as a guide to moral behaviour. What is "lost," however, in Israel is the constraining element of religious identity in economic activities and political relationships, for Yemenis anyway. They are now in a Jewish state and have freedoms never experienced by Jews in Yemen: they are free to choose where they live, to work in occupations (such as farming) which were almost exclusively Muslim in Yemen, and to engage in shaping their political present and future. It is noteworthy that the historical "other"—the Arab—is now the minority over whom they have some indirect power.

For Yemeni Jews in Gadot, the Ashkenazim have lost their *Jewish* character, with the important exception of the ultra-Orthodox who are in a class by themselves and who are respected, but seen as "fanatics" by the less doctrinaire Yemenis. The Ashkenazim with whom Yemeni Jewish women have much contact are of a particular sort: they are usually *not* descendants of Jews from the Eastern European *shtetl:* Jews, somewhat like Jews in Yemen, who were segregated from their Christian surroundings and whose lifestyle was defined in opposition to it.[52] The Ashkenazim with whom Yemenis associated derive from an *ethnic* identity: they are urban, cosmopolitan Jews who came from the large cities of Europe and America—Berlin, Paris, London, New York, and Toronto. Being Jewish *is* important, but Judaism (and the practice of its rituals) does not have the significance, in daily life, that it has for Yemeni Jews (and others like them).

So these kind of people provide the secular "other" by which Yemeni Jewish women (and their men to a lesser extent because they have fewer contacts) judge the behaviour of their children, their neighbours, and often, their own behaviour. Yemeni women believe that the lives of those Ashkenazi women are incomplete in respect to their responsibilities as Jewish women in keeping a kosher home, in guiding their relationships with others as defined by Derekh Erets, or in enjoying the rhythm and atmosphere of the Sabbath as Yemenis know it.

Overview

In this chapter we have looked at four of the pivotal personal relationships of Yemeni Jewish women of the immigrant generation: sister-brother, wife-husband, friend-friend, employee-employer. Each has an entirely different character and each portrays part of the complexity in defining and engaging in social relationships in Israeli society. In the relationship of sister and brother, women experience their greatest disappointments in Israel. Having been an irreplaceable source of protection in Yemen, the noble brother has usually been lost to women of the immigrant generation. The bond between a sister and a brother was so strong in Yemen that it seems that the memory—or the idealization—of its emotional and practical importance has brought about an impossible conceptual dilemma. Women judge their brothers by old models which have enormous moral and practical implications; brothers, for their part, have to cope with an Israeli reality where their mothers do not live with them, where their wives have veto power over taking in a desperate sister, where they separate themselves from the shame of a sister's bad marriage in some cases, and where they have no financial motivation (such as the investment of mohar) to enable them to fulfil their traditional duties as protector and provider in times of trouble. When brothers fail them, women do not only say that brothers are "self-interested," thereby contrasting their behaviour with the practice of collective responsibility in Yemen, but, in some cases known to me they even "invent" fraternal obligations among Jews in Yemen—they say that there brothers financially helped their sisters. I have absolutely no evidence that this was in fact the case.

In contrast to this situation, is the relationship between women as friends. Here, in a way that was not fully articulated in Yemen, *women have learned to depend on other women,* most of whom are not relatives by blood or by marriage. In Yemen women hoped to depend on female relatives for emotional support and friendship, but very often they were at loggerheads with mothers- and sisters-in-law and were usually no longer able to maintain regular contact with their own sisters or mothers after marriage. What is fascinating is that in Israel, women will often turn their closest friends into fictive kin, putting onto them the obligations of relatives: helping during celebrations, through emotional ordeals, through troubles with husbands and children, and even providing loans. Women's earning power in Israel has enabled them to loan money, eventually fulfilling for their closest friends the duty, as they define it, of brothers. Unlike in Yemen, women *choose* the women with whom they spend their spare time and these women friends have become an inordinate value. The choosing of friends brings into stark relief, then, women's freedom to decide for themselves in Israel as compared with the constraints that in-laws put on women in Yemen for much of their adult lives. It is particularly in the realm of friendship that there are new social, cultural and emotional models upon which women draw and which they themselves create. Perhaps the underlying factor enabling women to engage so freely, and so regularly, with friends is that they do not have to restrict their interactions to the home or the ritual baths because life in Israel has opened up so many public activities for women.

The relationship of a woman to her Ashkenazi employer is an important one, not only because of its financial rewards, but also because of the ephemeral ways in which the Ashkenazi employer influences her Yemeni domestic over the years. Yemeni women learn new consumer patterns, are impressed with the critical importance of education for women—both for themselves and their Israeli-born daughters—and, in subtle ways and with subtle methods, learn how to stick up for themselves in arguments with their husbands. The Yemeni woman will draw upon her cultural repertoire to adapt to being an employee: as in Yemen, where all of a woman's social ties were face-to-face personal relationships, a woman slowly comes to see her Ashkenazi employer as a friend of sorts, or even, at times, as a relative. She does not view the relationship as a solely instrumental transaction: work for pay. Yet, this interaction is an ethnic one, and one which is not divorced from the ethnic-class realities of Israeli society. As a result, each Yemeni woman has to make decisions about the values of her own culture—that of a Yemeni Jew in Israel—and has to choose which aspects of Ashkenazi culture she does not wish to bring into her home, or which she does not wish her children to bring. In respect to the upbringing of her own children, the exposure to Ashkenazi culture which the Yemeni domestic worker or child-minder gets is critical to whatever understanding she has of the world of the classmates of her own children. Mothers are not as "in the dark" as their daughters like to think.

We paid particular attention to the relationship between spouses, and what we can now see as the paradox attending it. For even though the occupational and economic situations of husbands and wives have undergone radical changes in Israel, changes that have affected their self-images and hence their marital relations, Yemeni Jewish models of gender roles have been upheld to a noteworthy degree. Husbands use old models to define the place of women in society: Women belong in the home. Wives should listen to and serve their husbands. Women should see themselves as mothers first and foremost. Likewise, wives use old models to define and judge the behaviour and duties of their husbands: Husbands should provide economically for their families. Men should be religiously devout. Husbands should discipline the children. How are we to explain this? I suggest that it is on account of being faced with such radical changes, in the thirty years since they left Yemen, that these men and women take refuge in their Yemeni Jewish ways of thinking about the essential duties and attributes of men and women, and on the basis of which they judge each other.

In respect to what husband and wife actually do in Israel, the importance of the change in size and content of the Yemeni Jewish household cannot be underestimated. In Yemen several conjugal families, related through brothers, lived together in one house; the men *together* were responsible for its economic maintenance and the women *together* were responsible for managing it. Soon after the move to Israel, this became a matter for husband and wife alone to handle since the nuclear family household became the norm. So *together* they had to manage, and eventually women have formed a new ideology of mutual help in order to explain conjugal inter-dependence.

There are, however, new ways in which women affect the running of their families and in which they regulate their own behaviour, and, over time, these have come to be seen as part and parcel of women's more varied roles in their families. Related to their husband's loss of prestige and the alienation of husbands' labour, on the one hand, and to their own new-found literacy, paid economic activities, and public involvements on the other, most women are now the primary authority over their children, they have a sense of their own autonomy apart from the control of their husbands, they have freedom of movement outside of their homes, and they see themselves as making an equal and critically necessary contribution to the maintenance of their households. In Yemen, any economic contribution made by women (their reproduction of the labour force, tilling the family fields, tending livestock) was totally un-acknowledged.

Cultural conceptions of high status have changed for Yemeni Jews in Gadot. Here Yemenis may differ from their compatriots who live in ethnically segregated settlements because they have so many more cultural models and socio-economic classes around them in Gadot. In Yemen, a family's status was derived from wealth, learning, and devotion. While a wealthy man might have a more active role in relation to Muslim shaykhs or governors, a learned and devout man could be poor and greatly enjoy the respect of his community. In Israel, while many men of low economic status have chosen to re-create the Yemeni Jewish study sessions of religious texts, the knowledge of who is learned and scholarly is usually kept among those particular men who study together, and a man's religious knowledge does not seem to be a factor that enters into his authority over his wife and children. Most of the "learned" men talked about with reverence by Yemenis in Gadot had, in fact, already died. By contrast, men who have gained considerable public prestige in the religious domain are usually wealthy or have received a formal education in Israel. There is the kind of man who will build a synagogue to honour his father—and such men are economically better off and have powerful personalities. Men who are involved in the religious council usually have had at least high school education, and perhaps have spent some time in a yeshiva. Another avenue to high status is involvement in local politics, whether in the local council or the worker's council and/or labour union.

The small number of men who have achieved positions of high status in Israel, enjoy considerable authority over their children. Also, they invariably have good relationships with their wives who, for their part, tend to be full-time housewives. For these people, the old models of gender relations bear some *reality* in Israel. But most men have not been this fortunate, and wives, with their husbands, have faced considerable difficulties of making ends meet. We have seen how women take on new responsibilities, and bring in a cash income, even as they remain primarily responsible for the housework and childcare; what is particularly revealing about this is the lengths women will go to protect their husbands' already deflated ego and their own sense of a woman's primary devotion to her children. Yet is also true that women draw great strengths from their new activities in Israeli society. Even in the most traditional male domain of all—the practice of religion, women have begun to be active *among themselves,* such as in the Portion of the Week session and seminars run by the Religious Women's Movement. Here is yet another area of life in which they more fully actualize themselves as persons in Israel.

Notes

1. In Yemen, Jews did not have a term for the nuclear family. There they used the Arabic term *bayt* to denote the patronymic group. In Israel, the broad kinship group which includes all paternal relatives is now called hamula, a term

also used by other Mizrahim and Israeli and Palestinian Arabs. I was not able to ascertain why or when Yemenis decided to use this term. Hamula does have some significance for Yemeni born men. It includes all paternal relatives. Its significance lies in the fact that men can expect to rely on members of their "clan" for help in feuds, they may go to them for loans, they would be more likely to form partnerships with paternal relatives than with non-relatives, and together they may try to take control of an economic niche. In Gadot, for example, one clan has complete control of the metal works, another of the auto mechanic shops, and a third, that of the former mayor, has a large number of members in town administration. It is not an important identification for women, however, and for that reason hamula is not discussed in this chapter.

2. For a detailed discussion of kinship terminology in Yemen and Israel, see Gilad 1982.

3. Cf. Firth *et al.* 1969:92.

4. Goitein 1978:21.

5. See Shamgar-Handelman and Belkin (1984) on the use of space in Israeli working class homes.

6. Changes in residence patterns brought about by immigration have numerous implications as we see in *Ginger and Salt*. In immigrant societies where the joint family still functions as a residential and economic unit, sisters-in-law might very well continue to give each other solace—particularly where they *lack* power vis-à-vis their menfolk. This seems to be the case, for example, among some East Asian women in England (Wilson 1978:35).

7. When an elderly woman finds herself in a situation of dependency on her daughter-in-law, this is the reverse of the situation remembered to have existed in Yemen where the elderly mother was the female head of the household. In Gadot, elderly mothers-in-law have lost their power as authority figures since the nuclear household is now the norm and elderly mothers are demoted in status if they are forced to live with a son and his family.

8. Gamlieli 1979:147-149.

9. In the shtetl, a girl's family gave a dowry—transferred to her groom's family—and this is probably because the groom moved to his wife's parents' house, thus his family lost his labour and for this there is some recompense in the form of a dowry.

10. As Lamphere (1986a:267) says of immigrant situations generally: ". . . the place of immigrant men in the local economy will have an important impact on what roles women will play in immigrant families. Thus, women cannot be treated in isolation from men or from the family units of which they are a part."

11. Rosaldo (1974:23-24) originally put the case for the analytical value of using public and domestic domains in relation to gender-related activities and ideologies: ". . . it will be seen that an opposition between 'domestic' and 'public' provides the basis of a structural framework necessary to identify and explore the place of male and female in psychological, cultural, social, and economic aspects of human life. . . . Though this opposition will be more or less salient in different social and ideological systems, it does provide a universal framework for conceptualizing the activities of the sexes. The opposition does

not *determine* cultural stereotypes or asymmetries in the evaluations of the sexes, but rather underlies them, to support a very general (and, for women, often demeaning) identification of women with domestic life and of men with public life . . ."

We will see that women were identified with domestic life in Yemen, but while this is to some extent still an *ideological* truth in Israel, women's activities and their reality is far from being solely domestic. See Yanagisako (1979:193) on the analytical importance of examining "the relationships between change in ideology of family and kinship and change in actual institutional arrangements."

12. On the domestic/pubic debate, see Bujra 1982; Imray and Middleton 1983; Nagata 1985; Quinn 1977; Reiter 1975; Rosaldo 1974, 1980; Sacks 1975; and Sciama 1981.

13. Bujra 1982: 22.

14. Imray and Middleton 1983; Reiter 1975:281; Sciama 1981:90; and Zaretsky 1973.

15. Bujra 1982:25.

16. While in macro-economic terms the character of women's participation in industrial production might be universal in terms of subordination and exploitation, in the domestic sphere of social reproduction, in many developing and industrial societies, women who work in paid employment have great power and authority in the domestic domain no matter how limited their power in the industrial arena may be (P. Cohen 1961:52–54; Lewenhak 1980:244; Makhlouf and Obermeyer 1978:339; Salaff 1981; Salaff and Wong 1982; Tilly and Scott 1978:116; and Touba 1980:59). Moreover, women's participation in production is not simply a reflection of their domestic roles as some writers have suggested (Wajcman 1981:15). A major conclusion of a recent Wenner-Gren conference on the sexual division of labour was summed up by Kelly (1981:272) as follows: "The discussion . . . during the conference led to the conclusion that the division of labour by gender has different meanings depending on its cultural and social contexts. In addition, the activities that women perform are variously defined in terms of the content and the social values attached to them. It cannot be said that women's labour is intrinsically inferior to that of men or that it is universally judged to be so. What confers a differential value upon gender-specific labour is the socially sanctioned rewards bestowed on or denied to groups of men and women."

17. I include economic activities in the domestic sphere because, in Yemen, Jews considered household-based production to be domestic activity. Exceptions to this perception were those occupations which took men out of the home, such as merchants and long-distance traders. In Israel, by contrast, all economic activity is considered to belong to the public domain because production is located outside of the household.

18. Five of thirty-five women married in Yemen.

19. Nine women married first or second cousins.

20. The subject of the continuation, or otherwise, of arranged marriages in immigrant cultures is revealing in what it tells us about particular immigrant communities—whether they are large enough to provide a community with

strong measures of social and family control and a sufficient range of potential spouses; how the host society defines racial and ethnic categories which can act to encourage the maintenance of cultural ways; and whether or not the institution of arranged marriage can prove itself flexible enough to take into account the new demands of the young to refuse a parent's choice of spouse, amongst many other factors. There is tremendous variation cross-culturally. Particularly in the not-so-visible ethnic minorities, parents are often satisfied if their children at least choose as a spouse another Italian, Greek, or Catholic. They are not able to force such choices because they themselves recognize children's freedom to choose, for example, in America; or by contrast, they may even accept "integration" at the level of marriage. A critical factor here is religion: America or Canada might be viewed as essentially Christian nations and thus it is easier for Christian immigrants, whether from the Mediterranean or Eastern Europe, to find their own niche, but one that is not connected to ethnic endogamy. For others, by contrast, who come from societies which are religiously, racially and culturally distinct from the predominantly Christian societies they "join," people may maintain the institution of arranged marriages for numerous reasons: to reestablish ethnic/caste divisions from the old country; to maintain cultural integrity in the new country particularly when facing racial hostility; for young people to prove their devotion and allegiance to their family and community; and so on (Ballard and Ballard 1977:48–50; Bhachu 1986; and Wilson 1978:106–120). These seem to be among the reasons that arranged marriages can withstand the pressures of immigration especially among many Asian groups in England. It is striking, moreover, that among East African Sikhs, in Britain, for example, changes are brought about in the content of arranged marriages that indicate a rise in women's status. Wage earning brides can now contribute financially to their dowries, and this has all sorts of implications for more independence from affinal kin and the right to make important decisions about residence after marriage than was the case in East Africa (Bhachu 1985:164–165).

21. The married children of these older women also feel that they have "modern" marriages. However, they build homes on the backyards or adjoining plots of parents who have detached houses whenever possible for reasons of companionship, convenience to grandmothers who act as childminders, and because it is more prestigious to live in a detached house. In some cases two or three related families who live side-by-side form a domestic group in that they share all domestic labour and meals, but they do maintain separate bank accounts. It seems, then, that if parents and their children are financially able, they will rebuild some attributes of the multiple family household that was characteristic of Jewish life in Yemen.

22. See Chapter 5 for a complete discussion of the family purity rituals.

23. Stevenson 1985:44–46.

24. Cf. Katzir (1976:258) on Yemeni Jewish men on the moshav.

25. Men themselves can suffer from the loss of female relatives: Jamaicans in London may stay with their wives because they have no female relatives to count on in the event of divorce (Foner:1978). Men's suffering from their loss of identity and status in the immigrant context may also lead to domestic violence

(Meintel et al. 1985:36). On the weakening of immigrant fathers' familial authority see Buchanon Stafford 1985; Haddad 1981; and Laguerre 1978.

26. See Amir 1973; Miller 1974; and Shoham 1970b, 1971, 1973, 1976. Such behavioural and psychological side-effects are not simply related to resettlement, but also to the fact that Mizrahi immigrant men were the least employable of all immigrants; hence many suffered from long-term unemployment, and, as well from their relatively lower status as compared with Ashkenazi groups and their dependence upon public institutions (Chouraqui 1973:290-302).

27. When discussing why Yemeni women so readily entered the paid labour force in Israel, one has to keep in mind that other Mizrahi immigrant women of their generation did *not* do so to the same extent. Chouraqui (303) suggests that low education and the demands of their large families prevented Mizrahi women from working outside the home. Yet, Yemeni women, too, were uneducated and had large families, but most have worked in paid labour. In 1960, 26 percent of Mizrahi women were in the labour force, but this figure does not seem so very low when we learn that by 1960 only 52 percent of North African *men* in Israel were in the labour force, the lowest percentage of any immigrant group (Chouraqui:302). In 1953, when larger numbers of North Africans started coming to Israel (very few arrived in the pre-state years), the economy, having already absorbed the Yemenis and the Iraqis into the unskilled labour sectors, was entirely unprepared to receive them. These immigrants did not benefit from a pre-state community like the Yemenis women who forged, through domestic labour, childminding, and office clearing, an economic niche for their own eidah. While Shoham (1973:27-29) argues that the North African Jewish beliefs in the afterlife allow poor people better able to put up with their lot—and thus accept poverty and welfare, neither of which the Yemenis were prepared to do— it is also likely that Yemenis as the "darlings" of the Ashkenazim loosely controlled the domestic labour market and that Ashkenazim preferred to employ them over other Mizrahi immigrant women and men. The plight of North African immigrant women in Israel is seriously understudied so any further suggestions as to why they did not enter the paid labour force in large numbers would be mere speculation.

28. In immigrant situations it is common that employed wives persuade newly-arrived compatriots that women should work in paid employment for the good of their families. For example, see Lamphere's (1986a:273) discussion of this among Columbians in New England.

29. In all, twenty-nine of the thirty-five women in this study worked as domestics, as agricultural labourers, and as factory workers before their marriages.

30. In Chapter 5 there is a detailed discussion about women viewing their involvement in paid labour as an extension of their mothering roles. Prieto (1986:107) summarizes the research on immigrant women which has invariably found that women work outside the home in response to their family's economic needs, not because of any conscious desire for emancipation. Furthermore, they work to enable their children to have a better life, and, for many women, as Gannage (1985:30) aptly puts it, this is the "heart and soul of their struggle" and their ability to put up with their double work day. See also Gannage 1986.

31. In Chapter 1 I stressed the importance of seeing how immigrant women themselves view their situation especially since their self-perceptions might not merge with some feminist interpretations. Even if, objectively, women's position in the new society is one of oppression, misery and subordination, women themselves may view their immigrant lives as considerably better off than in the old country. Foner's (1986) study of Jamaicans in the United States and London, Pessar's (1984) study of Dominicans in New York, and Meintel *et al.* (1985) of Columbians in Montreal, clearly show the discrepancy between the social scientist's evaluation of women's status and the people she studies. These writers, commendably, do not underestimate the importance of giving equal value to women's own evaluations of their position.

This matter, however, is considerably complicated by intra-cultural differences in experience, often based on class status in the old country or differences in the receiving society. Thus, one finds Haitian women in New York who feel degraded because they have gone from high status jobs in Haiti to low status jobs in New York because of lack of American qualifications, racist attitudes, or incompetence in English (Buchanon Stafford 1985:13). If these women had emigrated to Montreal instead, where they could have used their mother tongue (French), they might have been able to retain their high status jobs and to procure even more professional, economic, and social advantages in the immigrant context (Meintel *et al.:*37). Haitians who have gone from not working in Haiti to working in paid labour as migrants in New York, feel this reduces their dependence on men, enables them to fulfill their roles as mothers more effectively because they help the family achieve a higher standard of living, and allows them to invest savings for their old age (Buchanon Stafford:14). For a detailed discussion of the contradictory elements of women's own evaluations as compared with those of the social scientist, see Bhachu 1986:238-239; Brettell and Simon 1986:16-18; Foner 1986; and Nagata 1985:1-4.

32. This is usually called in the literature "the helping syndrome" and is certainly not peculiar to immigrant families (Goody 1985; Epstein 1971; Pitrou 1980; and Prieto 1986). For example, Pitrou (119, 126) has found that while young French middle class women will limit the number of children to one or two, will get more help from husbands in childrearing and will try to re-evaluate motherhood as a woman's privilege in order to have professional careers outside of the home, they still view their income as "contribution pay," of secondary importance to family income. Regardless of how much help women get with child-rearing, part of the reason women see themselves as "helping" their husbands to provide and husbands see themselves as "helping" their wives in the home is because each spouse defines his or her efforts in relation to the essential (or, as Goody[9] says "core") gender role of each other. These cultural notions of duty and responsibility are highly resistant to change (Goody:9-10). Below, I discuss further the ideology of mutual help among Yemenis.

33. It seems that most immigrant men of many cultural backgrounds experience difficulties when their wives go out to work for income. This affects their sense of honour *as defined by life in the old country;* it hurts their ego; it often forces them to participate minimally in child-rearing; it possibly puts their wives and

daughters in physical or sexual danger; and outside work also encourages women to be more independent and outspoken (Buchanon Stafford:16; Lamphere 1986a:273; and Meintel *et al.*:32). Women's entry into wage labour, at first, is probably such a hotly debated issue because immigrant men are not yet certain of their own social position in the new society or whether they can economically provide for their families. If their economic roles have been essential in defining themselves as males, husbands and fathers, then relinquishing exclusive responsibility for financial support of the family is bound to make men feel uneasy about their wives' new earning power.

34. Similarly, for Dominican women in the United States, getting help is a "moral victory," but they do not expect men to take half the burden because this is emasculating (Pessar 1984:91). Eastern European Jewish immigrant women in the United States, while critically important for making ends meet, always maintained a humble acceptance of the male prerogative (Bienstock 1979:175).

35. Or maybe they do not complain specifically about their double work day because it has been the rhythm of their life for so long, and part of the struggle to make ends meet. Gannage (1985:15–28; 1986) relates some gripping evidence of immigrant women's difficulties in juggling the home, their children, and work outside in a foreign environment.

36. Twenty of thirty-five men have not achieved a position of prestige.

37. This happens elsewhere, too. For example, in Haddad's (1981:140) study of Syrian women in Chicago, women's earning power has broken the patriarch's status in the family and, related to this, women have become the disciplinarians of their children. American society itself supports this latter change: schools call in mothers to discipline their children, not fathers, presumably because mothers are thought of as housewives. In the case of the Syrian women who work for income, however, they themselves view their ability to work outside and to discipline their children as an improvement over women's dependence and subjugation in Syria (that is, as an advance beyond the traditional housewife role).

38. It has been found in many studies that the greater the husbands' earnings and status, the less a wife's employment affects the distribution of power in the household (Bahr 1974; Blood and Wolfe 1960; and Scanzoni 1978). Yemeni Jewish couples bear out this assertion inversely: the less a husband earns and the lower his status, the more power his wife has in decision-making and in her authority over the children.

39. The children never mentioned that their father was not intelligent or may have suffered from some sort of personality disorder.

40. There is enormous cross-cultural variety in women's ability to effect changes in the family because of their wage earning power. For some women, changes have been significant in respect to their own autonomy and ability to influence major decisions (Appleyard and Amera 1986; Bhachu 1986; Buchanon Stafford 1985; Fitzpatrick 1971; Foner 1986; Haddad 1981; and Pessar 1984). For others, the changes that have been brought about are usually in respect to those areas directly affected by a woman's employment: childcare and financial decisions rather than getting help with housework or more freedom of movement (Meintel

et al.:33, 34, 40; and Touba 1980:59). It is difficult to explain such differences; it is as though each immigrant context is culturally and economically unique. One cannot even generalize about major regional identifications, as the working patterns—and domestic repercussions that result from these—of South Asian women in Britain clearly demonstrate (Saifullah-Khan 1979:123).

41. Rosman-Brenner 1982. Similar ideas seem to be held by the majority of Israeli men and women, including those in the kibbutz movement, despite popular myths of gender egalitarianism in Israeli society. See Datan 1973; Gerson 1978; Hazleton 1977; Lahav 1977; Rein 1977; Spiro 1980; and Tiger and Shepher 1975.

42. This is not simply a working class syndrome, as discussion of the "helping" ideology points out. It is also firmly rooted in many middle class families as Yoger's (1981) study of Northwestern University faculty members illustrates. There, working women expand their roles by adding new responsibilities rather than by relinquishing old ones. Yoger suggests that this may be to keep tensions at a minimum, tensions that arise through potential conflicts between the demands of the home and the workplace and husbands' and wives' perceptions thereof.

43. In her analysis of the "helping syndrome" among a variety of immigrant women studies, Goody (1985:10) insightfully points out: "There is, of course, a lack of symmetry to a spouse 'helping' in male and female core conjugal roles. For men it is potentially demeaning (to participate in childcare and housework); for women a matter of increased self-respect as well as a source of income. Thus, there is a built-in tendency for men to withdraw from sharing tasks falling within women's core roles. But there is also a tendency for women to continue helping in the male 'provider' role despite the absence of reciprocal help with domestic tasks from the husband. Indeed, the pattern of women's two jobs—waged and domestic—repeatedly found in the studies reported here reflects precisely this imbalance."

44. This is a typical pattern in immigrant families elsewhere (Cf. Appleyard and Amera 1986:224; Meintel *et al:*28 and Pessar 1984:1191). Yet there are reports in the literature where men simply will not help despite a woman's difficulties in juggling all of her responsibilities (see Gannage 1985:23) perhaps because, already feeling humiliation outside the home, they cannot face further humiliation (as they see it to be) in the home (see previous note). It seems, however, it is in this extreme situation, where men do not help at all or are not good spouses otherwise that immigrant women can leave their husbands because they have become accustomed to being economic providers and household managers (see Buchanon Stafford 1985; Foner 1986; Gannage 1985; and Meintel *et al.*:43).

45. Twenty-one of thirty-five wives deny that there was a division of duties in the home. Of these, seventeen work in paid employment, and eighteen enjoy good marital relations. In my observations of these couples, there was a marked correspondence between gender and roles; husbands performed few household chores.

46. This ideology of mutual help is indicated in women's responses to an interview question about their feelings of "equality" in the division of roles between husband and wife. Twenty-eight, or 80 percent, of the thirty-five women

in the research set replied that husbands and wives make equal contributions to household functioning. Seven of eight housewives claimed that they make equal contributions to family functioning through their housework and child-rearing activities. By contrast, six women reported that they contribute *more* than their husbands to family functioning because of their work in paid employment; these women clearly feel that they carry too many burdens. But such responses are clearly in the minority, and most women—whatever they may believe to the contrary—say that there is equality in the division of roles. Most of these couples had been married for at least twenty years. In an American study on "equity in marital roles" at different stages in the family life cycle, it was found that older couples perceived greater equality—"you" and "me" becomes "we"—after years of struggle (Shafer and Keith 1981:359–367). Indeed, this study bears out this contention: younger Yemeni Jewish wives, while clearly receiving more actual "help" in the home from husbands, in fact saw greater inequalities in conjugal duties with too many responsibilities falling on the wife.

47. See Morokvasic 1984:888.

48. Cf. Buchanon Stafford 1985:21.

49. Reiter 1975:281; and Wajcman 1981.

50. The Portion of the Week is the chapter of the Torah that is read in any particular week in the synagogue. In Gadot, the Yemeni rabbi's wife leads a discussion group every Sabbath afternoon to discuss the weekly portion among women. The moral and ethnic significance of this discussion group is discussed in the next chapters.

51. Here "intermarriage" refers to unions of Yemenis with non-Yemeni Jews, not with non-Jews.

52. Zborowsky and Herzog 1970.

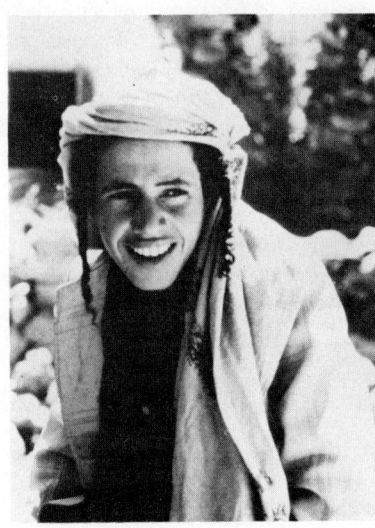
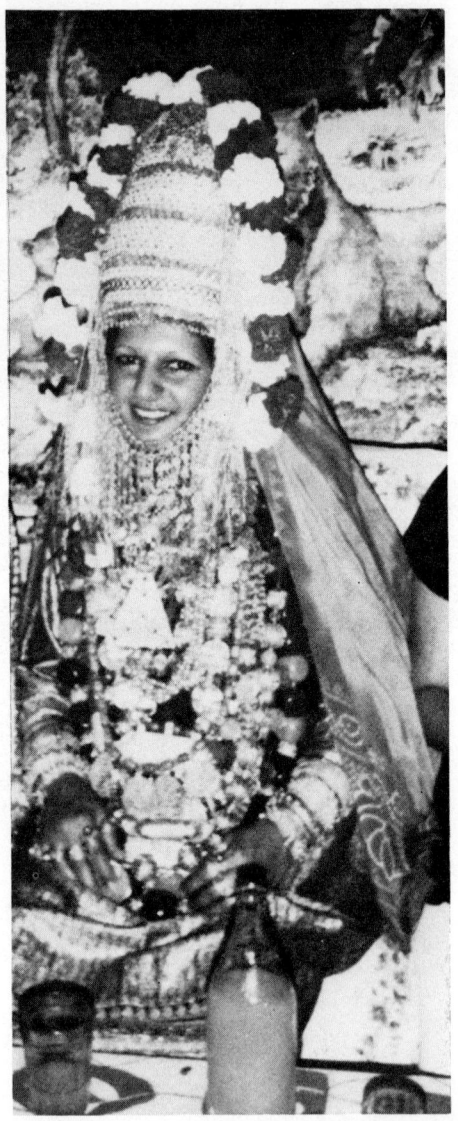

A Yemeni Jewish youth, in Yemen in 1982 (*above*). Photographer: Dr. Unni Wikan. (Photo used by permission of Dr. Wikan.)

The traditional wedding outfit (*right*), once the property of family groups, is now rented for the *hinna* ceremony. The entire outfit, including jewellery, was produced by Jewish artisans.

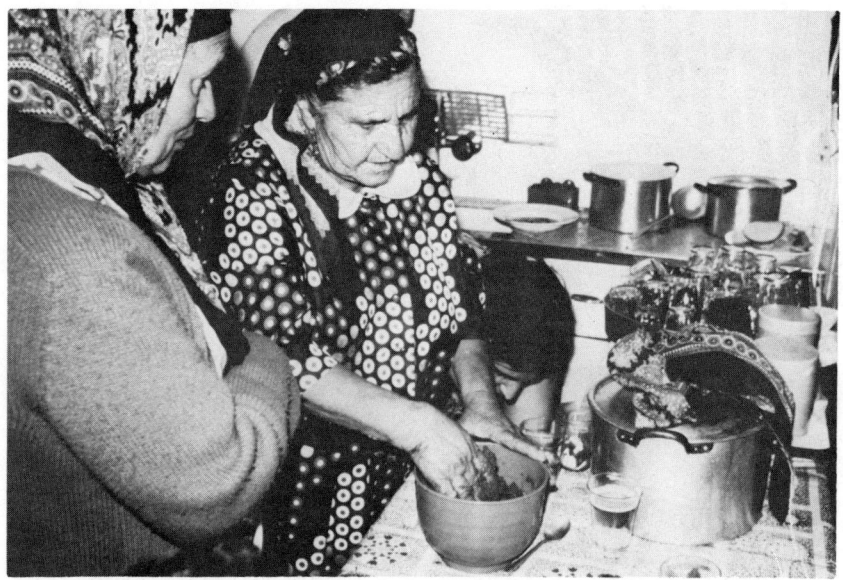

An old mother and grandmother prepare henna, symbolic of fertility and potent in warding off the evil eye.

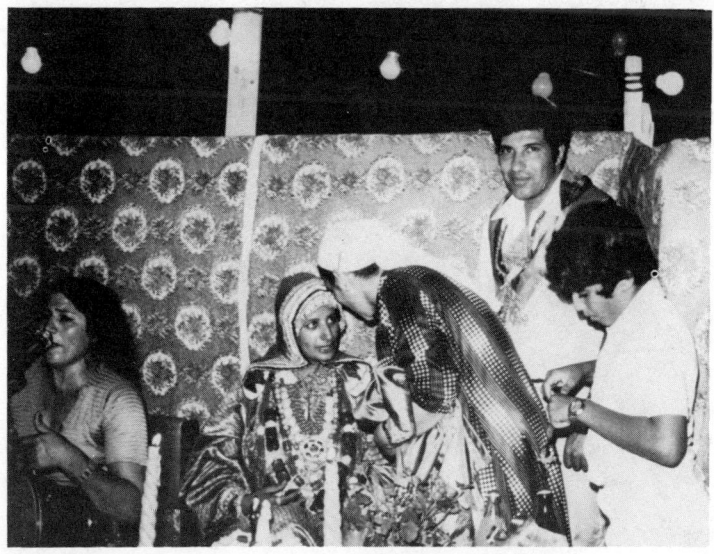

The ritual separation of the bride from her family takes place during the *hinna*, a female-led and female-centered rite of passage.

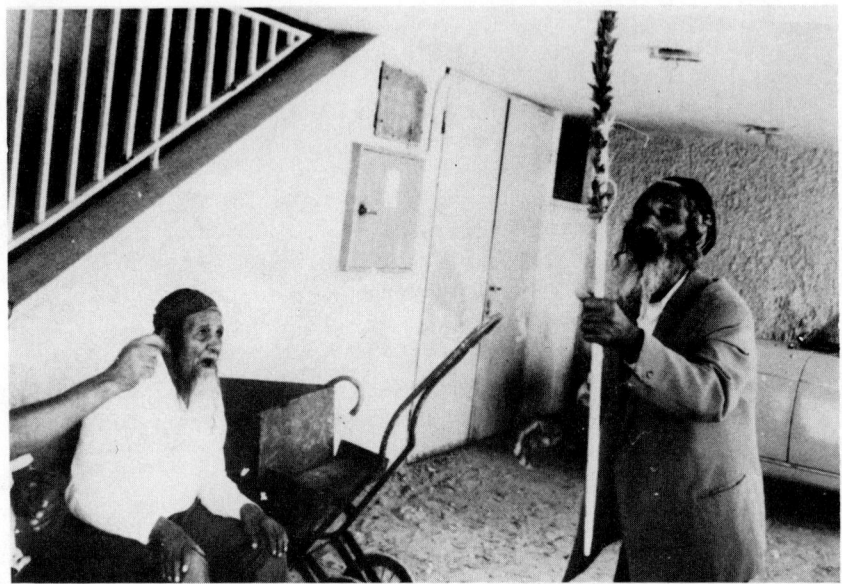

A grandfather born in Yemen chooses the palm branch for his *lulav*, to be used in the synagogue during the harvest holiday of *Sukkot*, the Feast of the Tabernacles.

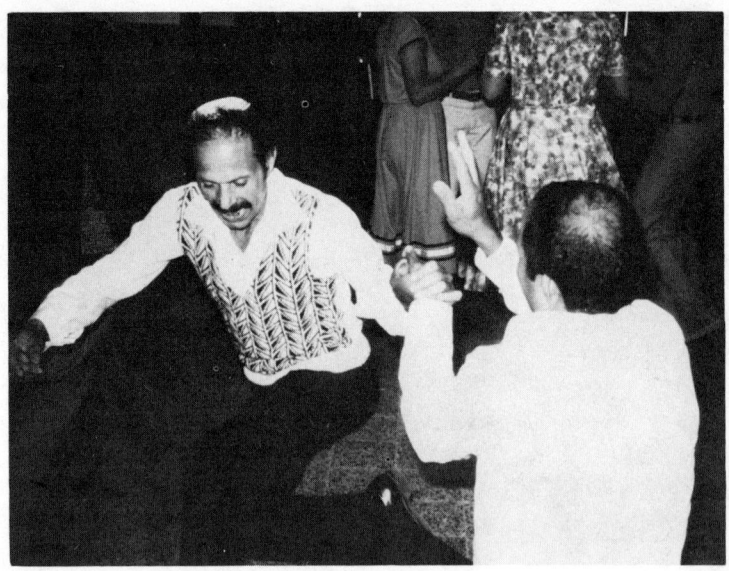

Men of the immigrant generation dancing at a Bar Mitzvah celebration.

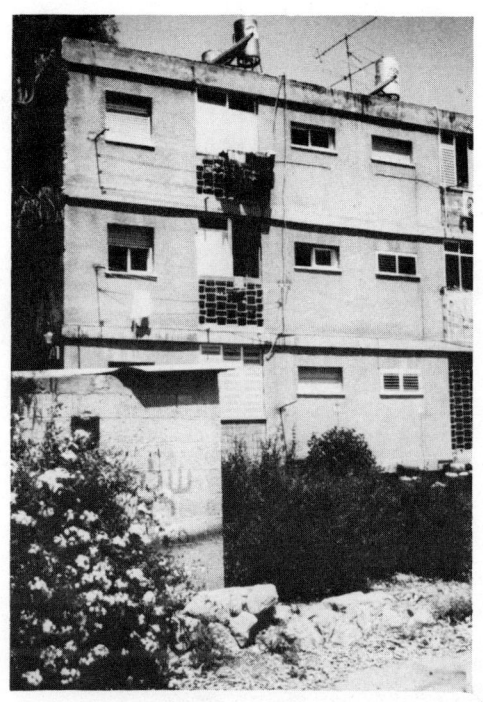

One of Gadot's first apartment buildings. (*left*) Shoes are kept in the cement grids for lack of closet space. At the lower left is the bomb shelter at the back of the building.

New *"vilot"* in Gadot, built by the already-married generation born and educated in Israel. (*below*)

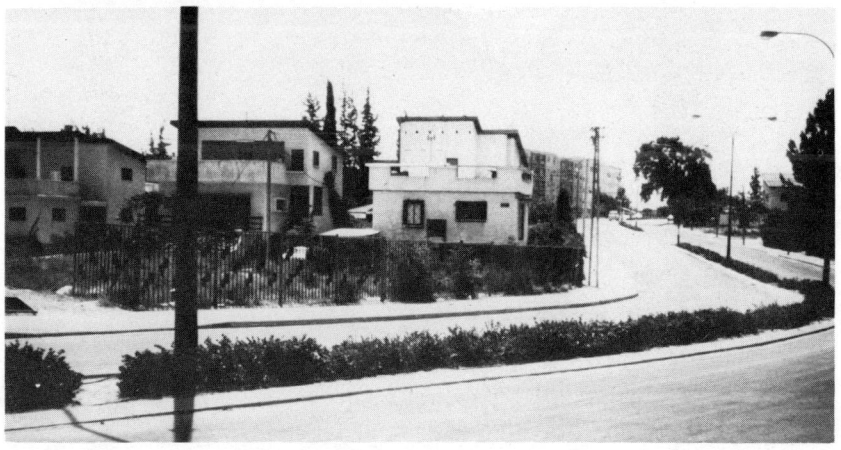

5

Being Female in Transition

> *Middle Eastern women have never had any doubts about their own identities: they were mothers, sisters, daughters, grandmothers, aunts, cousins; they were Muslims, Christians, Jews; they were Armenians, Kurds, Nubians, Berbers. They were Arabs, women. The search for identity has been a Western search, arising as it does out of philosophical ideas about the individual, the single human being, fulfilling itself outside the contexts of family, religion, or ethnic group.*
> —Elizabeth Fernea[1]

Elizabeth Fernea brings here together two states of being: security and crisis. In the first sentence are four different kinds of belonging: family, religion, tribe or ethnic group, and sex. Together these contribute to the formation of "identity," a person's perception of self. For many Middle Eastern women, the knowledge of self-identity and place in the social world has been a source of security. This certainly has been the case for Jewish women in Yemen (or at least as recalled by Yemeni Jewish women now in Israel): they knew who they were, if only on account of lack of options. Nowadays, in Israel, women of the immigrant generation have faced so many crises as part of the long-term immigrant experience, as well as from their families' development, that they do not always present an unambiguous perception of self. Their search for identity *has* been a Western search in that women are often caught between their individual experiences in contemporary Israel and their historical recollection of what had formally comprised Jewish female identity in Yemen. As we have seen, their social and economic activities in Israeli society are dramatically different from those in Yemen; these involvements appear to be complex, confusing, and contradictory because on a daily basis they call into question the traditional notions of female roles among Yemeni Jews.

I am concerned here, as well, with the conceptual distinction of "role" as a definite set of "rules and expectations which are socially defined" and "identity," which introduces a person's perception of self and actual experience.[2] I shall analyze here the social construction of female identity among Yemeni Jewish women through consideration of three critical components: the statuses of daughter and mother, the religious imperatives connected to their biological cycles as women/wives, and their attitudes towards their own sexual experiences. But in trying to relate here women's collective experiences, I shall not forsake individual differences. Identity, after all, is personally negotiated and articulated.

Yemeni Jewish women were brought up to behave as daughter, wife and mother—these were the three important statuses for women of the immigrant generation, as was the case for all the generations before them. Changes from one status to another were marked by rites of passage: hinna and the marriage ceremony marked the transition from daughter to wife. Once a wife, a woman took on the duty to perform taharat hamishpahah, the family purity rituals incumbent on all married women. Once a mother, a woman performed the ritual of seclusion. This is how it was in Yemen and for the first decade or more after moving to Israel.

In Israel, a variety of experiences and ideas shape Yemeni Jewish women's attitudes about being female: (1) As daughters in Israel, their needs have remained subordinate, as in Yemen, to those of their natal families, an experience which has shaped their attitudes towards their own daughters—even though many women emphasize that they wish to treat their daughters differently. (2) Unlike in Yemen, only women who define themselves as "religious" observe the family purity rituals—these rituals and the reasons for their practice shape their perceptions of being female. (3) Attitudes towards sexuality are formed through experiences with their husbands and by gossip exchanged among married women. (4) Ideas about motherhood stress, as before, the primary importance of reproducing the family and of devotion to children; however, women have been forced to make extensive alterations in their perceptions of motherhood because the financial imperative to work in wage labour does not allow them to be full-time mothers and housewives.

Key changes in female identity are not experienced in an isolated Yemeni Jewish culture, rather they occur in the complex secular world of Gadot and the wider Israel. This world strongly influences these women's attitudes towards their parents and husbands, and their own ideas about good mothering. Most notably, the social identities of women have expanded to include their experiences as workers and as participants in public culture, in consequence they allow their daughters freedoms which they never experienced. In sum, their capacity to pass on to their children Yemeni Jewish ways of perceiving women is considerably complicated by their experiences in Israeli society.

The Immigrant Generation as Daughters

We were brought up to observe our religion, to honour our parents, and to speak when spoken to. . . . They put hot pepper on our tongues for saying bad words.
—Hi'a, aged fifty-three

The initial intention of my research, to study contemporary mother and daughter relationships, proved impossible to assess without going back a generation and learning how mothers saw themselves as young daughters, how they perceived their own parents, and how their recollections affected their actions towards their daughters.[3] As one psychologist has found, "It is often due to her own experiences as a daughter that the mother encounters difficulty in rearing her own daughter or feeling comfortable about her ability to do so. . . ."[4] As in many cases the parents of the women were either dead, or living elsewhere in Israel, this discussion is necessarily based on the models which women have built of their parents. I had to probe women's memories and pay attention to conversations in which their parents were discussed.

In Yemen, daughters were the constant companions of their mothers before they married and left to live in their husbands' households. Mothers were responsible for the essential upbringing of daughters, teaching them the domestic and craft skills that were important aspects of becoming good wives and mothers. In addition, they were ultimately responsible for the moral and social training that would make daughters desirable brides. Daughters were trained gradually and informally—most tasks were learned simply through imitating mothers.

Almost all women who spent their early childhood years in Yemen remember their relationships with their mothers as deeply enjoyable, guided by the respect required in Derekh Erets, and thus in accordance with their mothers' wishes.[5] For those who married in Yemen, if the husband lived near-by, an intensive relationship continued, with daughters paying their mothers frequent visits and mothers helping their daughters during childbirth. Many daughters, however, married men living in other towns and saw their mothers infrequently, perhaps only for major rites of passage. Some eventually lived with their mothers again if they returned to their natal families upon divorce or death of a husband. It is recalled that in Yemen young girls were their mothers' most treasured companions, even though women preferred to give birth to boys (their sons would care for them in old age but their daughters left the household upon marriage). Often living under the strict control of their mother-in-law and senior sisters-in-law, a young mother looked to her daughter for love and support. No wonder that when a daughter left to marry, a mother grieved:

> Said the mother of daughters
> "O I wish I would die
> I raised the daughters—
> They were plucked from my garden
> (whilst they were still blooming)."[6]

Daughters, for their part, shared their mothers' sentiments, knowing they would have to leave their families, sometimes for distant lands. A song often sung at the hinna:

> O mother, O father,
> How could you have sold me?
> Sell the flock, sell the cattle
> And the wealth could redeem me.
>
> O my mother who bore me,
> Your heart knows me no more!
> Is it because of the distance
> Or the sons that you since bore?
>
> O the one who bore me,
> If only one roof we could share,
> I would gladly be your maid,
> Your maidservant forever.
>
> If the one who bore me,
> My sobs and cries could hear,
> If you would know your infant's life,
> The one you nursed and reared.
>
> O the one who bore me,
> My heart is burnt and dark
> Like black in ink
> On plain paper
>
> O Sind, O Hind,[7]
> If rainfall at night reaches your ears
> Think not that it is the rain—
> But a river of my tears.
>
> I have sighed a sigh
> Like a camel carrying steel!
> I have killed my own soul,
> To no one can I appeal.
>
> My sigh came up—And shook every bone!

O merciful God,
No one to pity me![8]

This song tells us as much about Yemeni Jewish culture as it does about the grief a daughter feels upon the eve of her marriage; in fact, it places this particular Jewish culture in the wider cultural area of the Middle East and North Africa.[9] Because of the strict adherence to socially defined roles and expectations (in this case the necessity of a daughter's marriage as a component of family honour), the expression of personal desire or ambition is constrained. A mother must deal with her grief of losing her daughter in marriage because marriage is the only acceptable course that a young girl can embark upon. A daughter must accept her own fate because her mother *cannot* be there to protect her against her husband's family. What appears to be a mother's desertion of the daughter, actually enables her to fulfil the position of wife and eventually of mother to which all women must aspire. In Yemen, the joint roles of wife and mother defined a woman's status. Without fulfilling these roles a woman had no social identity; indeed, she was not even seen as a "woman."

In the early years after Yemeni Jewish migration to Israel, there were few dramatic changes in the context of mother-daughter relationships.[10] Yemenis resided among their brethren when they arrived in Israel so it was relatively easy to continue to inculcate in children attitudes of responsibility towards their parents. Women were still locked firmly into the family structure and had little freedom of movement.[11] The youngest girls were sent to school while the older ones went out to work, giving their wages to their fathers to help educate brothers and to provide for the family. On the whole, daughters did not think of doing other than they were requested, and they simply accepted the way in which they were brought up.

For women reared in this milieu in Israel, mothers continued to be regarded as the repository of moral values and proper religious conduct—all of which are prescribed by Derekh Erets:

> Derekh Erets is the most important value. We were brought up to be religious, to maintain our tradition and to accept our roles.
>
> We were raised with religious education, to keep a kosher house in Israel, and to establish a home.
>
> We were raised with Yemeni education: not to gossip, to be modest, to give a hungry man food, not to steal. . . . I appreciate this still today.

Recalling their own childhoods, most women present themselves as dutiful daughters, and often contrast their behaviour as children with that of their own daughters today:

> We had good relationships in Yemen, not like here. There boys lived with their parents until they died. If kids were angry they could be thrown out. Here when children get angry they leave on their own.
>
> One could never be cheeky to parents. You did what they desired; religion required us to do all the things they requested. You could not hurt them. If we disagreed, we did not tell them. Not like today . . .
>
> I understood my mother. A mother is a mother. Now, with this crazy generation, it is something else entirely.

In such recollections of their youth, women often assert that they themselves had always listened to their mothers and followed their advice. These assertions, however, were sometimes contradicted—open opposition to the mother and to the ideals she sought to instil was rarely admitted, but did happen:

> They tried to give us religious upbringing, like in the Yemen. But I never agreed with them. What they said I rejected. I revolted and travelled, but they did not say anything. But they did not want me to go out with boys or sleep in Tel Aviv.

One source of resentment (as we have seen) was that as young girls they were obliged to work to help support their families and to help pay for brothers' education, but little or no financial aid was extended in return to them when they married. They knew that in Yemen girls did not receive financial aid from their families after marriage, but they argued that this should have changed once they themselves began to contribute to raising the family's standard of living. Thus, women have come to realize their own economic input as critical to the consolidation of their natal families after immigration to Israel. This, in part, explains their instrumental view of family obligations: they were forced to invest in their families through their labour power, and on this basis, expected return rewards. Such resentment is most common among older married women whose own husbands have less education and a lower status job than their brothers (whose success is due in some part to their sisters' labour and parents' financial help after their marriage). The contrast between their brothers' success and their own hardships is a constant reminder of their inferior standing as women in their own families. In Israel, they claim, parents should treat sons and daughters equally—but they themselves do not practice what they preach, favouring sons over daughters.

On occasion, women revolted. One, Shoshana, was anxious for more education. She ran away when she was fifteen years old to study and persuaded the principal of a boarding seminary for girls to accept her. Her older brother was sent to fetch her, and she was given no choice but to return home and to go to work in a factory. She fiercely resented doing this while her brothers studied. When her father died, however, she managed to join the army (one of two women who did so) although her mother was violently opposed to this, insisting that she would lose her virginity and hence her honour—which in fact did not happen.

For most women, however, any rebellion against parental expectations was only nominal or quickly undermined. Some women told me that as young girls they had been thwarted by their parents' objections to army service for women. Others disagreed on wider issues. Typical complaints revolved around parental strictness, "tying" girls to the home, and extreme restrictions on their free time; heavy obligations to perform household chores; threats by parents that girls' marriages would be arranged if they were suspected of not conforming to the rules of proper conduct; and demands that they defer to the authority of their brothers. A *minority* of women feel that such experiences have had a liberalizing influence on their own daughters' upbringing:

> I want them to do what they want. I will not tell them to be like me. I want them to observe the Sabbath, but I cannot force them to.

> I want them to learn, to get a profession for their future—not to be like us. We are nothing. We have nothing in our hands.

> No, I no longer want to give them traditional education. The past situation is different from today.

Indeed, as we have seen, most immigrant women who arrived in Israel as young daughters did have experiences unknown to their mothers in Yemen: several years of elementary schooling, possibly involvement in religious youth movements, and, for virtually all, participation in wage labour before their marriages. These women are more likely to express, even if subtly, dissatisfaction with some aspects of their own upbringing than those who either married in Yemen or arrived in Israel in their late teens. For the younger immigrants, the roots of a more complex identity are found in their experiences of their parents' moral philosophies and rigid behavioural expectations, on the one hand, and of the developing standards and greater possibilities for female self-expression in Israel, on the other hand. While daughters born in Israel have considerably more freedom than their immigrant mothers (as we see in the next chapter) the latter, perhaps in the effort to achieve a consistent sense of self-identity, often appear to be dictatorial and domineering to their own daughters as their mothers (and especially their mothers-in-law!) were to them in the old country.

* * *

Mothers in Yemen, and later in Israel, were unable to discuss with daughters intimate subjects, such as menstruation, sexual relations, and romance, no matter how close mothers and daughters were on other issues.[12] Some women joke that, in Yemen, it was believed that ignorance would not breed curiosity or desire to experiment, and so unmarried girls were not informed about sex. If they *were* told, they were ill-informed. Not surprising, then, older women remember first menstruation as a frightening experience, lamenting, even at the time, that their mothers were ashamed or shy to discuss these topics. Even when explanation was imperative, it was often an aunt, grandmother or sister to whom a young girl turned.[13] When I asked why the discussion of intimate matters was taboo, typical responses were:

> We did not speak of intimate things. We were embarrassed. I married twenty-seven years ago and then there was not much to learn. But even if I asked, I did not get an answer. We were told that when we matured, we would understand. Mother and I were ashamed.

> I did not know about my period when I married at the age of eight in Yemen. I cried for my mother who explained to me all the separation rules—by then, as I just said, I was a married woman. It was a terrible story and she was ashamed to tell me . . . really ashamed.

> In Yemen there was shame and we were shy to speak of these topics. I spoke with my aunt and older sister, but not my mother. I was married a year and a half before I got my period—my husband had to wait until then. I was afraid and so ran to the next village to my sister . . .[14]

After the move to Israel, several mothers began to discuss intimate matters with their daughters, fearing that if they did not, daughters might inadvertently lose their virginity in what was considered by them to be a free society. But, more typically, immigrant mothers still kept their immigrant daughters in the dark, and for many of their grown-up daughters—now mothers themselves—this general failure to discuss intimate knowledge remains a source of bitterness. As a result, some Yemeni-born women, now mothers in Israel, have decided to overcome their inhibitions and wish to deal differently with their own daughters. However, the daughters perceive matters otherwise, complaining that discussion of romantic liaisons and physical functions is still taboo.

Despite various criticisms of their parents, the wide majority of mothers see little wrong in the upbringing they received and hope to bring their daughters up in the same way.[15] They believe that mothers are responsible for the inculcation of moral values and fathers for religious values. They want their daughters (and sons) to be imbued with Derekh Erets as they have always defined it.

Relationships with their parents and memories of family life in Yemen are evidently seen as morally superior to those obtaining in contemporary conditions. And while it may be—and indeed probably was—the case that daughters formerly accepted the word of their parents more readily than today, there is an element of idealization here. On the one hand, with so many upsets in ordinary routines, Yemenis of the immigrant generation expect conflicts in the contemporary family. On the other, this was also the case in Yemen. For example, squabbles within the extended family household were undoubtedly frequent, between mother-in-law and daughter-in-law over household chores, between husband and wife,[16] between daughters and their mothers over matches made for them, and so on. Beyond this, feuding between families, often entailing the participation of entire patronymic groups, was common. And men—even kin—argued over styles and interpretations of prayers and biblical texts, with the sacred synagogue as the forum; sometimes such arguments led to the formation of a new synagogue.

Yet, even though arguments occurred within and between families—after all, people do not simply assume "roles" without their own personalities—it does seem certain that women were more emotionally secure in the only statuses available to them as Jewish women in Yemen: daughter, wife, and mother. Conflicts do not seem to have been related to an essential questioning of a woman's duty to herself or to her family—unlike the situation which exists for their Israeli-born daughters. When not telling tales of family feuds and arguments in Yemen, older women frequently assert that in Yemen harmony reigned in the large household, that children had deep respect for their parents, that Derekh Erets guided family life, and that children simply would not dream of questioning parental guidelines. Conflicts in the family more often than not are associated with the move to Israel; while such conflicts may be treated as *normali* (normal), they are regarded as a regrettable (and regretted) part of modern family life. And, as may be seen from the interview responses below, it is secular Israel society which is blamed for mothers' failure to inculcate 'traditional' Jewish values in their children.

To some extent women of the immigrant generation see failure as inevitable in their attempts to raise their daughters properly. The reality is that their daughters have other authority figures, particularly in the school, the army and the university.

> We want to raise them as we were, but in Israel, it is unlikely. We do what we can, but they are influenced by their friends. This is not good. In my opinion, if we lived in a religious area, like B'nei Brak, it would be better because we would not see the secular. It is good when there is one framework for all. . . .
>
> Yes, we want to pass on our values: discipline, respect, to appreciate the eidah. But today that is impossible because their friends and the surroundings corrupt them.
>
> With fervent desire we want to pass on our values. But we cannot raise them as we were raised. They simply do not accept what we say—society and their friends influence them. Maybe it will get better when they marry and have their own children.

Here there is a discrepancy between the parents', and more specifically the mothers', commitment to certain very firmly defined values, and their willingness to allow much greater freedom of movement for the girls than they ever had. On one level mothers look to an idealized past to define the 'proper' way for daughters to behave, but on another level, it seems that in their more tolerant attitudes towards freedom of movement and the importance of educating women, they acknowledge the narrow and restricted character of their own upbringing.

Purification of the Family

Religious women in Israel, as in Yemen, usually practice niddut, the period of ritual separation of husband and wife after the onset of menstruation, and at the end of niddut, immerse themselves in the mikveh, a ritual bath found in all observant Jewish communities. These family purity rituals are fundamentally important because they influence beliefs and practices associated with women's attitudes to their contributions to the Jewish nation, and, indirectly, their ideas about sexuality. While non-observant Jews, including Yemeni women of the Israeli-born generation, argue that the family purity rituals are archaic and barbaric, those who adhere to them vouch for their efficacy, and Yemeni Jewish women are no exception. Let us first see the formal Judaic prescriptions on this matter:

> A woman from whose womb issued a drop of blood, be it ever so small, and whether or not it is her regular period of menstruation, and even if it is the result of an accident, is considered ritually unclean until she counts seven clean days and takes the ritual bath of immersion. Both man and woman who have sexual intercourse after the menstrual flow has begun

incur the penalty of . . . excision (being cut off from their people); and the temporal punishment of caressing one another is flagellation.

It is written (Leviticus 18:19): "And thou shalt not approach a woman in her menstrual uncleanliness; . . ." Because it is written "Thou shalt not approach," it is explained that any kind of approach is forbidden; he should not play with her or indulge in foolery, or even speak words that may lead to sin. But he may be in privacy with her, for since he had already had cohabitation with her and she is also available to him after immersion, his lust will not gain the upper hand, and there is no fear that he would cohabit with her when forbidden.

The husband in that period should not touch her even with his little finger. He is not allowed to eat with her at the same table, unless something separates between his dish and hers. . . . They are not allowed to sleep in the same bed. . . . It is forbidden even when they lie in separate beds, if the beds touch one another. . . .[17]

These rules were explained to me in "folk" form by the Yemeni rabbi's wife, Esther, who was thirty-nine years old in 1981 and the mother of four children. She was sent to Israel in her early childhood as an orphan and was raised in a Sephardi boarding school, where several of her teachers were Yemeni women whose parents had emigrated to Israel during the first waves of Yemeni settlement in Israel from 1882 onwards. She completed both secondary school and a seminary course in nursery school teaching. On both accounts, her educational background and her experiences as an orphan, she stands out among other Yemeni women of her age. In Gadot, right next to her house, she runs a small nursery school which is well attended because of her reputation as a calm and patient childminder.

Esther is ultra-religious, and is the only Yemeni woman I know who covers her head with a wig and the wig with a scarf, a practice usually employed only by a conservative core of Ashkenazi religious women. She began to use this custom when she and her husband lived in B'nei Brak, an ultra-orthodox Ashkenazi section of Tel Aviv, before moving to Gadot. On Saturday afternoon, the Sabbath, she leads a weekly meeting where the Torah Portion of the Week (*pereshat ha'shavua*) is discussed. This meeting, held in a local school, is open to all women in Gadot, but is frequented predominantly by Yemeni women over the age of forty. Older women are more observant of religious rituals than younger women and so are unlikely to be otherwise engaged on a Sabbath afternoon. The meeting is also geared to the specific problems of religious mothers of rebellious teenage children and the difficulties they face in Israel as full-time mothers and workers. Even if younger religious mothers wished to attend, it is unlikely they could because of having to mind their young children. Attendance usually fluctuates between thirty and fifty women.

Esther lectures in detail on her interpretations of the Torah portions, and after an hour or so, opens up a forum for discussion in which mothers can express their point of view. The lessons articulated during the meeting, which always have moral content and seek to interpret proper conduct, quickly spread throughout the Yemeni networks in Gadot. Esther strongly influences the way her listeners conceptualize their world because of her reputation as a sincere and devout woman. She struck me as a person of outstanding integrity and I myself was attracted to the Portion of the Week sessions because, especially, there I was able to learn a lot about female perceptions of Jewish matters in a rhetorical style which I found easy to listen to and interesting in itself.

One of Esther's duties as the rabbi's wife is to inform new brides of their responsibilities as Jewish wives when they attend the mikveh, for their first time, before the marriage ceremony. Thus it is especially appropriate that her version of taharat hamishpahah (family purity rituals) be presented here in some detail. The following text is taken from an interview with Esther conducted on January 27, 1981 (my questions are indented).[18]

> My mother has not yet had reason to, so can you tell me about mikveh and *niddah*?

Yes, I can tell you all about it. A woman must get her period for at least several days a month. This is a woman's sign that she is healthy and the bleeding is controlled by her body. Now, in the Torah there are rules about this. I have my period for seven days. On the seventh day I stop bleeding. During these days it is forbidden for me to eat with my husband. We can eat at the same table, but I cannot serve him. It is forbidden for me to pass something from my hand to his hand. . . . It is forbidden for us to sleep on one bed, one close to the other. It is forbidden for me to kiss him. There is a distance between us, a separation. Now when the seventh day comes I wash myself thoroughly. The next day I check to see if there is any blood. But only seven days later am I really in a closed state [the vagina] and then I go to the mikveh. This is very important.

> Is this separation called niddut?

Yes. It is forbidden to have sexual relations. Why? Because this place [the vagina], the source, it is open. The wise men discovered that, even for them, it is forbidden to have sexual relations between a husband and a wife [at this time]. Why? Because it is like you have a wound in this place. If there was intercourse, it would be rubbed dry. So when a woman is with her period, it is forbidden for her to have relations with her husband.

Does this hurt him, too?

No. This is just for the woman. This place is very delicate, so she has to wait until it gets healthy. For the Ashkenazim, they say a woman gets her period for five days, but the Sephardim want to be sure, so they say for seven days. The seven clean days are connected to everyone. For the Sephardim it is seven and seven. . . . On the fifteenth day she goes to the mikveh.

Now, as for the mikveh. This is a special place and this is not simple water. This is water from the earth and from the rain. The wise men said that only by the water of the mikveh can a woman be purified. This is called taharat hamishpahah. The scientists have discovered, and there is much data on this, that the woman who watches taharat hamishpahah does not get cancer of the womb.[19]

It is hard to believe that these women are without cancer of the womb. How is this so?

Yes, this is true. It is the mind that matters here. Because, first of all, it is her honour. It is good to be separate from her husband for this time because he loves her more. She does not come to him like a cow. If she did, whenever he felt like it. . . . So this way, she is like new every month and she has honour. He appreciates her more. Do you understand? Think of what you see on the street today, the *hutspah* [cheekiness]. There is also an effect on the children. You can see a child on the street who is smart and cute, but his hutspah passes the limit. From where does this hutspah come? It is because his mother did not go to the mikveh.

In the Torah, God did not make man perfect, since the time of Adam and Eve. Things got corrupted and spoiled. Now, what does not get spoiled is the rain because it does not come from the earth. The water is saved in two big barrels and afterwards it is used in the water in the mikveh. . . . These barrels are stored inside the earth to be used when necessary. The rain cannot get spoiled. You see, all gets spoiled in the atmosphere of man because of the snake. The snake spoiled everything. . . . So therefore, the woman cannot be purified at home. The rain water is clean for everything.

Are there blessings that the woman says in the mikveh?

Yes, but each has her own custom. There are all sorts. But there is the blessing that is said inside of the bath. . . . With us, the Sephardim, the woman wears a robe and prays before she goes into the water and then again in the water. The Ashkenazim bless only the inside of the mikveh.

Do you know where these differences in custom come from?

No, but it is interesting. In practice, the Sephardim are more strict. For example, you have seven and seven and by the Ashkenazim, five and seven. This is reality. . . . You see, it depends on the husband. If he is an Ashkenazi, his wife will follow his customs because he is the decision-maker. This is important, to follow your husband and to follow your faith. It is by these practices that we continue on as Jews, on the table [kashrut] and in the family. Heaven forbid, non-Jews are jealous of us because the nation of Israel exists on these rights . . . It all falls on the woman because she is responsible for the table and the family. . . .

Esther's explanation of taharat hamishpahah at first glance stresses the health component—the vagina is a sensitive place which should not be rubbed dry through intercourse. However, there is more than mere hygiene that is in question here. Ultimately, the practice of the family purity rituals is an extremely important obligation for women and one which Esther contends is necessary for the continuation of Judaism. More narrowly, the discipline involved in the family purity rituals demonstrates the virtue of a woman. In Esther's opinion, the consequences of not practising these rituals are grave, affecting one's children who become cheeky and difficult to control. Several times during a Portion of the Week meeting she ventured to comment that women who do not perform the family purity rituals are responsible for all crimes in Israel.

It seems that even though menstruation itself is associated with negative attributes, such as making a woman liable to infection and the belief that a woman is polluted during niddut, it has its positive side as well. Of course, there is the association of the menstrual cycle with the bearing of children and the maximizing of the fertile period of the cycle. But, most importantly, these rituals require tremendous discipline, and, in Esther's view, it is only because of a woman's obligation to purify herself, and hence her family, that the nation of Israel exists today. This is also the case for the observance of the dietary laws which set Jews apart from the Gentile world, women are responsible for their maintenance too. Esther, for her part, expresses these beliefs to her audience at the Portion of the Week, and thus reinforces—and in the case of some women she might initiate for them—the positive aspects of being female in Yemeni Jewish culture. She is not alone in this viewpoint, as an authority on women's position in Jews life attests:

> The Jewish woman is the creator, molder, and guardian of the Jewish home. The family has always been the unit of Jewish existence, and while the man has always been the family's public representative, the woman has been its soul.[20]

For Esther, the observance of taharat hamishpahah portrays women's strength. She does not refer to their weaknesses, as is traditionally thought of when Eve took the apple from the serpent. Rather, she says "the snake" has ruined "the atmosphere of man," not woman. Only those who do not adhere to the rituals of wifehood are weak. The problem, of course, is that in the modern secular world which includes much of Israeli society, there are even religious women who do not practice taharat hamishpahah, as we shall see below.

Esther is atypical of Yemeni Jewish women in Gadot. She is able to see reasons for the practice of the family purity rituals beyond those of hygiene and pollution. And while she avers her ideas to women of her age in Gadot, and these might be grasped at an intellectual level, Yemeni women who perform their ritual duties do so because of their conceptions of pollution and illness. The majority of women who say they are "religious" adhere to taharat hamishpahah and will continue to do so until they attain menopause. Their primary reason for doing so is fear of disease, believing that they are in an unclean state during menstruation. The mikveh purifies them because it is special water from heaven, but the required prayers must be recited in order to become pure again.

There is an omnipresent belief, even among women who do not practice the family purity rituals, that the womb is open to "colds" during menstruation, and that their whole body is dirty at this time. There are women who advise their daughters against using tampons, not only because doing so might affect their virginity, but because the blood must flow right out or one is in a particularly dangerous state. Likewise, because the flow of blood is disrupted during intercourse, women reason that they should not have sexual relations during menstruation.[21]

In Yemen, the prescriptions of taharat hamishpahah were strictly followed. There, as in other religious Jewish communities, the mikveh was a centre of social activity for women where they could meet friends. Therefore, it seems safe to suggest that social pressure, as well as basic hygiene and ritual duty, constrained a woman in Yemen to go to the mikveh, even if she and her husband failed to practice niddut strictly.

In Israel, these prescriptions are not followed all that strictly even by the most observant women in other ritual responsibilities. Some simply do not go to the mikveh, saying that they do not have the time, and a couple even say that they do not see what the mikveh does, believing that it has no symbolic or practical value. One woman, whose mother works at the local mikveh, does not go because it is one of the few really effective ways she can annoy her mother.

In Gadot, as in other towns in Israel, it is less easy for women to know whether friends and acquaintances go to the mikveh or not. Certainly employees in the local mikveh know who attends, but they might assume that religious women who are not attending go to the mikveh in the town where they are employed.

Of the twenty-seven women who work outside the home, fourteen practice the family purity rituals regularly—or so they said during the interview—while thirteen do not. Of the eight women who are not employed, six attend the mikveh. Of the two in this category who do not, one defines herself as "religious" and the other as "secular." Thus, it seems safe to suggest that women who are employed are less likely to attend than those who are not, but since this research set was not compiled randomly, I hesitate to make more than preliminary suggestions on this matter. For example, I do not know whether it is sheer inconvenience that some women do not practice the ritual, or if (as it seems more plausible) it is because of their long-term exposure to the more liberal attitudes about women's ritual duties held by less religious Ashkenazi women.

Employment, however, does seem to be a consideration in the practice of such rituals. It may be because employment offers an extra-familial identity which lessens the importance of women's ritual obligation to herself and her family. Although the anthropological literature is scanty on the subject of *changing* practices with respect to menstrual taboos, one study has directly dealt with this matter. In a study of urban women in Gujarat, India, those who are employed usually to not practice menstrual taboos; only Brahmin women living with their husband's family stay away from the kitchen at this time.[22] Women's attitudes towards other ritual obligations become similarly lax when they are employed, partly because of time constraints, but also because of greater priority being given to the interests of the individual woman rather than her extended family.[23] In fact, in a village in Karnataka State (India), when women can leave the work force because they have become more prosperous, menstrual taboos are elaborated.[24] These kinds of data make one question whether or not women really "believe" in the importance of the taboos, since "belief" seems to shift between having to work for pay and not having to; or if adherence to them is related to prestige: practising the menstrual taboos is an indication of higher economic status in the case of non-Brahmin women and higher ritual status for Brahmins.

Also, unlike in Yemen where women attended the mikveh frequently simply to bathe, in Israel indoor plumbing enables a woman to bathe at home. Indeed, several women perform the mikveh blessings at home because the hours of the public mikveh are inconvenient. Of course, the water in which they immerse themselves is not the fresh rain or spring water that Esther claimed to be an essential element in the purification procedure. And I put this to some women. One of them told me, "It is cleaner in my bathtub than in the mikveh! And it must be because I am the only one who uses it! Also, tell me, did not the bath water come from the rain at one time?" She had a point there—one which arises out of an appreciation of modern plumbing and the circulation of water sources, but halakhah does not have provisions for modern plumbing! What seems to be happening here, is that performing taharat hamishpahah has become a personal choice for women in Gadot, a matter we return to below. By contrast, in Yemen it was enforced partially by social constraints in that other women in the household would know whether or not niddut was being practised; women rarely left their villages and so were expected to attend the mikveh near their homes, like clockwork.

There is another matter here which lies under the surface for those who observe the family purity rituals; it brings us back to the case of Adina, of whom I wrote in the introduction to this book. Adina believed that her own and her children's lives could be destroyed by the "evil eye" because her husband failed to follow the family purity rituals by sexually defiling her before she went to the mikveh. Whereas the rabbi's wife, Esther spoke of the adverse effects on children of women who did not observe niddut, she did not speak of what happened when a husband actually defiled his wife. Adina's dread of what she calls the evil eye is somewhat closer to traditional halakhic indictments that if a man defiles his wife during menstruation the penalty is expulsion from one's people. To some extent this was Adina's fear—for her defilement meant illness, and possibly death for her or her children.

Adina's beliefs, I later learned, after she had recuperated from her trauma, were instilled in her as a young bride in Yemen. In Israel, she did not even think there was a solution to her problem. As I said before, I sent her to the right address, to a Yemeni healer, for the cure. *What is critically important here is the added danger of being female when one no longer has a cultural solution to a serious problem such as defilement.* She was one woman whom I managed, by accident, to observe going through the problem of what seemed to her to be irreversible pollution. It was leading her to hysteria and fears of impending doom.[25] I knew there were others who had the same dreadful experience. Matters pertaining to sexuality are not easily dealt with among many Yemeni Jewish women in Gadot.

Conjugal Duty: Sexual Intercourse

An integral aspect of taharat hamishpahah is the sexual relationship of husband and wife. Only after immersion in the mikveh is a woman "ready" to have sexual relations. Even if a couple has stopped having regular sexual relations, the wife continues to go to the mikveh because her husband might unexpectedly desire intercourse.

The family purity rituals are intended to regulate the desire for sex. Men are forbidden by Jewish law to cohabit with a woman during menstruation because such an act would demonstrate lust. The Jewish code of practice states that intercourse can entail sexual satisfaction, but that it is firmly, and most importantly, related to procreation. It is forbidden for semen to be spilled unnecessarily—the Ganzfried version of the halakhah claims that this is the gravest sin in Judaism because it is equivalent to killing a person.[26] In effect, the "wise men" (according to Esther) have timed the recommencement of sexual relations after niddut to coincide with the phase in the menstrual cycle when a wife is most fertile.[27]

For women of the immigrant generation, virginity was demanded of all respectable brides. During the hinna a bride learned that a blood-stained sheet must publicly be shown the morning after her wedding night, if not right after the new couple entered the marriage bed, as proof of her virginity (as everywhere else in the Middle Eastern world). Most women, however, say that they had no idea of what the act of losing virginity entailed: that is, sexual intercourse.[28] Several women claim that they ran away from their husbands on the wedding night when husbands approached them with, what one woman called, that "hard rock." Others screamed or lay petrified which must have made penetration even more difficult and painful, and such women felt "wounded" for life after defloration. Only later they learned that intercourse is a "normal" activity shared between husband and wife.

Such experiences inevitably shape women's (negative) attitudes towards sex in marriage. Many women still have troubles with sexual relations, particularly since they view intercourse as a means towards procreation, while husbands continue to want intercourse for their own enjoyment. Other women who have decided to stop bearing children at an early age for personal or health reasons, feel that this entails termination of sexual relations. Some unsympathetic husbands find this totally unacceptable: such men believe they should have full discretion to decide when and how a wife's womb should be used and are occasionally violent in pursuing what they feel to be their right. While this is prohibited by Jewish law—a husband must not force sex upon an unwilling wife—this does happen.[29] Several women who do not enjoy sexual intercourse with their husbands are unaware that such a law exists, and when we discussed this issue, they added that they understand why they were not informed (by men who are usually the custodians of the law).

Equally, women sometimes regard the withdrawal of sexual access as a way through which they can retaliate for past traumas. One woman told me that qat makes men "horny" (her choice of words), but that if her husband wants sex, he must get it elsewhere.[30] While this is a way of punishing him for being a bad husband, she feels that it is also a way of not punishing herself after suffering so many bedroom traumas since her wedding night when she had felt her body to be violated.

Most of the women of the immigrant generation, by contrast, regard sexual intercourse as a necessary aspect of their marital and procreative duties, but not one which gives them pleasure.[31] Women often joke with each other, among female friends, that the "place" is simply a hole for men's enjoyment. Equally revealing are their responses—nervous joking— upon hearing about the female "orgasm" from reading or watching movies or when discussing the Talmudic duty of men to satisfy their wives sexually. To such women it seems impossible that female sexual enjoyment is part of Derekh Erets, proper conduct, and most women reject the idea.[32] In Yemeni Jewish folklore, for example, to enjoy sex and to be sexually enticing makes any woman dangerous and suspect of improper conduct. By contrast, as we see in the next chapter, women of the immigrant generation do get excited about the possibility of romance and as they watch love stories on the television, they comment extensively with the use of erotic metaphors. The kind of poetry translated by Caspi also illustrates the passions a female lover (Yemeni Jewish at that) might feel. Here are some excerpts from "O would breast touch breast":

I wish to hold you
And inhale your scent,
To drink the honey
From your tender lips. . . .

What bewildered and confused me?
It is your lips.
O beautiful soul,
My heart melts for you. . . .

Undo the buttons.
Beneath the buttons, precious stones.
Beneath the buttons,
Two emerald breasts. . . .

Two breasts
And a war between them.
Put your hand on them
And calm them. . . .

I open my breasts for you,
For you to squeeze and press,
Woe to you, incapable one,
You came here for naught. . . .

You kissed me once—in turn I kissed you five.
The first one—on the top of your head,
The second—between your eyebrows,
The third—between your lips and teeth,

The fourth—I drowned between your breasts,
The fifth—hush, tell no one.³³

Women's attitudes towards sexual matters have been complicated by exposure to more widely held Israeli attitudes, and this is especially apparent in their reactions to their daughters' sexual transgressions as we shall see in Chapter 7. Yet but a few have altered their views considerably as a result. For example, Badra, a secretary aged forty-two, who considers herself to be completely Westernized, said that on her wedding night she shut her legs to her husband so he had to pry them open, yelling at her all the while that she was frigid. He continues to tell her this, as she lies there like a "wet rag," only submitting to wifely duties. She never realized a woman could enjoy intercourse until she read books and watched movies. She feels that she has adopted a healthier attitude: after blaming herself for being sexually inadequate for the first twenty years of her marriage, she decided that he did not know how to make love to a woman.

Being Female Is Being a Mother

Motherhood is an essential and irreplaceable aspect of female identity in Yemeni Jewish culture. As in Yemen, women's most important responsibilities are in child-rearing and, secondarily, in housekeeping. Mothering is ideally the most valued of all their activities, but after children have been weaned, women spend less and less time with their offspring. Almost all women of the immigrant generation work (or worked) four to eight hours out of the home, plus two hours for travelling to and from jobs. Housework, an essential component of good mothering, involves another three to five hours a day. Many women, particularly those whose children have completed primary education and thus no longer require babysitters, are also active in community affairs such as the working women's association and adult education. In their opinion, these activities contribute to better mothering because experiences in the outside world help them to guide their children. Hence, the actual time women spend with their children is far less than in Yemen where mothers were constantly with their unmarried daughters and later on with their grandchildren. Here I discuss the conflicting imperatives of women's lives: on the one hand, the necessity to work in paid employment, and on the other, the ideal role of full-time mothers.

Women often express feelings of inadequacy concerning the physical and social care and support of small children. Some of these refer to the general problems faced by young working mothers: in the early years of motherhood, many women had found themselves unprepared for aspects of their domestic roles (cooking, cleaning, sewing, and laundry), and many lived in poorly-equipped apartments without modern appliances:

> ... I was not emotionally prepared to be a mother and I did not like housework. Now I thank God that I can wait to iron clothes. I used to think I was an idiot because I could not get it all done, and I would swear at myself. Now it hurts me if I cannot get everything done, but not like before when I was angry with myself.
>
> It was hard at the beginning, to breastfeed and to maintain the house. Slowly one gets used to it, but it was hard.
>
> Now it is fine. But at the beginning when they were little, it seemed impossible to bring them up. We had no washing machine and no oven and lived in one room.

These problems were compounded by the immigrant experience, as well as poverty. We have noted that Yemeni women eventually appreciated the privatization of their household labour, but this did have significant costs. For women who had married in Yemen or soon after arrival in Israel, they quickly had to learn how to manage their own households without their mothers and even their dreaded mothers-in-law, who often lived far away. On first going to work it was often difficult for mothers to find good day care, whether in centres or by private childminders, and the thought of children being minded by "strangers" was often hard to bear. It is with these memories in mind that women, who are now grandmothers, leave the labour force in order to care for grandchildren to whom they feel they can give the time and patience that they did not have for their own children while they were in the labour force.[34]

It is difficult for most mothers everywhere to work full-time and have the responsibilities of the house and childcare, and immigrant mothers face extra difficulty in having to cope with new cultural arrangements for work and childcare. My data were quite clear on this. However, the situation of those mothers born in Israel is quite different. At least half of those we interviewed work in paid employment (the others intend to re-enter the labour force when they find a job or when their children go to school); none expressed any regret at leaving their children either with childminders or in the excellent day care facilities in Gadot. To do so is, for them, the cultural norm. Moreover, many of these women are professionals or white collar workers who enjoy their work for its own value, not viewing it as an extension of their duties as mothers. At the same time, like immigrant women, they know that not to work outside the home would deprive their children of opportunities for social and economic advancement (unless the husband earns a very high income, which is unlikely). Most women born in Israel would not stay at home to be full-time housewives even if they had the choice. As one thirty-one year-old said, "First of all, my duty is to raise my children. Second, it is to clean the house. Third, it is to work outside, and fourth, it is to further my professional education. To be a mother is not only to cook, clean and remain in the house, but also to work and to study." In fact, the only women of the Israeli-born generation who expressed despair and boredom, either during the interview or informal discussions, were all full-time housewives. By contrast, the full-time housewives of the immigrant generation (with only one exception) do not have any regrets, feeling that they are privileged to devote themselves solely to the upbringing of their children.

Many immigrant mothers also feel inadequate because they cannot help their children with their schoolwork and this inadequacy is reinforced each time they see their Ashkenazi employers helping their own children.[35] In fact, teenage children may teach their mothers to read and write. While mothers are appreciative of the time their children devote to such endeavors (recognizing that their children want to help to "advance" them), they are embarrassed: *they* should be teaching their children. In Yemen, literacy was not a component of competent mothering: all females were illiterate. In Israel, even daughters as young as seven may be more literate than their mothers. When immigrant women say, "I should be the teacher of my children," this is based on a model of mother-daughter relationships originating in Yemen where mothers were the primary teachers of their daughters in every sphere of life that mattered: housework, childcare and craft skills. As long as immigrant women maintain the belief that it is they who should be their daughters primary teachers, not school teachers, they will forever feel inadequate. Moreover the recognition of teachers' skills, for which immigrant women hold great admiration, can be painful because it requires mothers to admit that children have other authority figures.

It is precisely because of women's illiteracy or inferior educational achievements that they want their children to complete high school and university. They feel that they must, therefore, work outside the home to provide for their children the best available educational and material goods that their parents could not afford for them. Husbands' incomes are inadequate to reach these goals, so women must bring in an income. Consequently, working in paid employment limits the time they can spend with their children, time that is necessary for good mothering, and even for the performance of household chores.[36]

Work outside the home is an imperative for these women; they do not see that they have any choice. The older they get, the more tired they are from working in and out of the home, and exhaustion causes them to get *atsabim* (nerves) and, as a result, they say, they frequently yell at their children. Yet mothers believe that their children understand the hardships they face as workers (and this belief is substantiated by many of their children) and why they face them.[37] Eventually, work in paid employment became part of a woman's duty towards her family, a sign of her devotion to her children.

Mothers also feel obligated to bring up their children with traditional Yemeni Jewish values, to be the repository of moral values as their mothers were for them. The Jewish commandment "Thou shalt honour they father and mother" is constantly referred to in support of the notion that, in terms of moral training, mothers are always right. Children are to be raised with Derekh Erets, Adam v'Hevrato (collective responsibility), respect for elders and hard work. Inculcating children with these values is seen as a parent's most difficult task because children's experiences outside of the home influence them to reject parental authority:

> . . . My role as a mother is to educate them in what is good and what is evil. I wish they would listen, but society corrupts them.
>
> I see my role as very difficult because the youth of today learn in school to talk back. I am also a widow so this is hard. It is difficult to lead them along the right path. I must have the strength of iron.
>
> It is hard to be a mother, but I have no choice—I am a woman, after all. It is hard because they often do not pay attention to me, telling me that I'm "primitive." I feel that I cannot give them enough good upbringing. The children say that I grew up in Yemen, so I don't know anything. This hurts me.

Even when mothers view their efforts as thwarted by the wider society, they believe that they will pay off when their children marry, have children of their own, and begin to behave "properly" like their mothers. Here, it seems that women have some awareness of the stage they have reached in the development of their families: children in these families are either adolescents or unmarried adults, a typically trying time in family life. Hence, the hardships which mothers see themselves facing result from a variety of factors: working inside and outside the home, questions of their own competence to teach and counsel their children, the perpetuation of the immigrant experience as long as they face new situations which were not part of family life in Yemen, and the stage their family is at in the developmental cycle. The stage in immigrant women's family life in which this research was conducted allows us to question the overwhelming confidence which younger mothers born in Israel report in respect to raising the third generation: of those we interviewed, their children are almost all under the age of ten, and thus have not yet faced the rebellious years of children's adolescence. While they share more with their children by virtue of also having been born in Israel, evidence from other studies suggests that they too will face difficulties when their children are adolescents seeking to assert themselves; there is no reason to believe that younger mothers will not, at some point in their family lives, question their competence in arenas other than those of formal education and religious upbringing.[38]

Rewards for good mothering in the immigrant generation are bestowed by other mothers, especially in terms of respect for those who are self-sacrificing. On countless occasions, I heard women praising other women for being excellent mothers while working outside the home. Efficiency has become a prized attribute: women who work full-time, manage to keep a spotless home, and eventually "marry their children off" are known as *ya'eloot* (efficient) managers of themselves and their households. If a woman does not have to work and has enough money from her husband's income, she is, indeed, in an ideal and much envied situation.

Mothers value other mothers. In general, women are more valued and respected by their husbands, parents and friends when they become mothers. Marriage is the first stage towards becoming an adult woman, but childbirth completes this process. There are some people who believe that a woman is "complete" only when her sons have male children because she knows the family name is being carried on; such thoughts are common among all religious Jews.[39]

Overview

It has been over thirty years since Yemeni Jewish women immigrated to Israel, and yet it is apparent that their past in Yemen reflects considerably on their perceptions of—and the problems with—being female in contemporary Israel. The three crucial statuses of femaleness—daughter, wife, and mother—must be understood in terms of the interaction of Yemeni and Israeli influences which both come into play in daily life. The relative importance of one over the other, or one against the other, is acted out whenever necessary. Let us begin with the status of daughter.

Women of the immigrant generation were daughters in their parents' household until the age of twenty, by which time all women had married. Being a daughter required considerable filial piety and most daughters were obedient to parents. Yet their own experiences, in Israel, as girls outside of the home in elementary school, in the fields or in the factories, gave them a window into being female in ways other than those in which they were raised. No longer were they at the beck and call of their mothers. For they did not spend anywhere nearly as much time at home as girls did in Yemen, even though they still did essentially what parents expected of them. Very importantly, however, life outside the home fuelled their imagination on the personal choices women can make. While their own possibilities were quite limited, there could be new opportunities—in education and in work—for their Israeli-born daughters, and so perceptions of appropriate experiences for females were slowly modified. However, their own models of appropriate behaviour for daughters vis-à-vis themselves as mothers have not changed, because to a large extent "traditional" Yemeni expectations of dutiful daughters are still seen as desirable.

How do we reconcile these apparent contradictions? On the one hand, mothers recognize the restricted character of their own upbringing; on the other, they view themselves as the guardians and disseminators of moral values and proper conduct, expecting their daughters to abide by maternal judgments. Contradictions arise out of the immigrant experience because it is inevitable that old beliefs will clash with new opportunities. Eventually, some sort of synthesis does evolve, a synthesis which apparently makes sense to the immigrant generation, but might not to their Israeli-born children. After some months of great confusion on my part in trying to comprehend how people could constantly portray opposing points of view, I came to realize that they did not consider the contradictions of their beliefs and their daily lives to be problematic. Among people who have a clear, if not always correct, recollection of their past, and who see their present through the mirror of the past, we must learn to accept that they can, and do, live with conflicting beliefs and realities. It is under these conditions that a consistent female identity is impossible to obtain; I had to learn to stop looking for it. To a large extent, so did Yemeni women of the immigrant generation if they wished to cope with the disjunction between ideal *tafkidim* (roles) and reality. While they continue to maintain authoritarian attitudes towards their own children, their behaviour also demonstrates an unusual degree of accommodation of daughters' transgressions. Their accommodation has something to do with their own experiences as young women in Israel: behaviour among other Israeli women was observed and then compared with the expectations for correct female behaviour held by their own parents. Lacking the formal educational and professional achievements of their Ashkenazi employers, and realizing that such achievements are in reach for their own Israeli-born daughters, mothers are forced to come to grips with areas of their own incompetence in Israeli society. This was not a situation faced by Jewish women in Yemen where women were what daughters were to become. While it might be necessary to maintain certain old beliefs in Israel, perhaps for the sake of some historical and psychological continuity with Yemeni Jewish female identity, much has to be put aside if mothers are to have any communication with children whose experiences differ so radically from their own. In fact, it is only when daughters marry, and take on both of the critical statuses of their mothers—wifehood and motherhood—that women of the immigrant generation can match beliefs about proper conduct with their daughters' behaviour towards them; for now the daughters are experiencing for themselves the difficulties incumbent upon married women.

Being a wife in Yemeni Jewish culture carries with it a variety of ritual obligations related to the menstrual cycle. In Israel, it is possible for women not to practise the family purity rituals whereas women simply could not have done so with impunity in Yemen. I have already suggested that the practice of these rituals has become a personal choice for women in Gadot. This element of choice belongs to the expanding roles and options in Israeli society, even for women of the immigrant generation. Once again, and particularly in respect to rituals which older women (for example, mothers-in-law) could easily oversee in Yemen, the residential isolation of the married couple in Gadot allows women not to conform to notions of proper wifely conduct as defined by halakhah or even by the women themselves in respect to their own ideas of cleanliness and hygiene. This brings to the fore questions about "belief" as a *social* phenomenon—when it becomes a matter of personal choice, it is possible not to believe. I often asked myself how women who regard themselves as religious and who were reared in a Yemeni Jewish world could so readily stop practicing some, if not all, of the purity rituals. I am still not sure of the answer, but it does seem to have something to do with the expanding horizons of women in Israel, and in particular with paid employment and how that influences women's attitudes about the activities of mothers in showing devotion towards their children. Perhaps because in Israel women are more actively creating their (economic) destinies than was the case in Yemen, they do not have to look to their own bodies, and indeed to the supernatural, in the same ways as their mothers did, in order to fulfill their important familial and societal contributions as women. Judging by their conduct, it seems that some immigrant women no longer believe in the age-old family purity rituals. They turn to other areas in which to define themselves as female.

As for the women who do continue to practice the family purity rituals, some expose themselves to ritual dangers—for example, when sexual defilement occurs and a woman no longer has a cultural solution. This kind of danger clearly has implications for the formation of female identity in the next generation: what kinds of attitudes do mothers, who have been defiled, pass on to their daughters about themselves as women, about their husbands as men, and about the responsibilities of Jewish wifehood? Women who have not experienced the inconsistency between belief and practice, that is, those who have not experienced defilement, presumably do not face problems on this account, and they may readily accept the notion that Judaism exists today because of women's responsibility towards the table (kashrut) and the family (taharat hamishpahah). However, even their well brought-up daughters may accuse them of being "primitive" for maintaining such attitudes.

It seems to me that it is in the arena of female sexuality that there has been the most continuity between women's experiences in Yemen and their relations with their husbands in Israel. Sexual intercourse is endured because of wifely obligations and the social and biological imperative to procreate. Immigrant women's attitudes regarding their daughters' sexuality do not differ from those of their mothers and grandmothers—pre-marital virginity is equated with honour and there is an inability to recognize daughters as sexual beings. Yet the mothers realize that the secular world of Israeli society holds attitudes drastically different from their own; hence, as I shall show, they make some alterations in their actions towards their daughters.

Notes

1. Fernea 1985:301.
2. Epstein 1978:100–101.
3. Of course there are serious methodological issues in trying to relate what the anthropologist collects as "oral history" to the social and psychological realities of everyday relationships. Whether we are transcribing from tapes or remembering to write down tidbits of information in our journals, it is unlikely that we are ever exact in our interpretations or later in the compilation of collective experiences. For the person who is concerned that anthropology be an exact science, the methodology of the "sociological imagination" as defined by C. Wright Mills (1969), i.e., the intersection of biography, history (including oral tradition), and social structure, will forever prove frustrating and inadequate. Personally, I see anthropology as a humanistic discipline, not as a science, and therefore I have been able to accept my own sociological imagination. This is not to say that I have not experienced difficulties in the writing of *Ginger and Salt* through using extensively "recalled form," that is, people's memories of their own upbringing as well as of Jewish life in Yemen, particularly since personal accounts often prove to be contradictory. I have seen it as my job to sort out the contradictions and to see why they exist (as part of the immigrant experience) and in doing so have tried to convey women's perceptions to the reader inasmuch as this is possible. In this section, on immigrant women as young daughters, I can only present "models" of their relationships with their parents, since, obviously, I was not around to observe them. To ignore people's memories because they are only memories, would be to deny the importance of the emotive and psychological impact of the past on contemporary social life.
4. Caplan 1981:preface.

5. Here there may be an element of idealization of the past. When women say that as daughters they fully enjoyed their relationships with their mothers in Yemen, they may be contrasting their actions as daughters to those of their own daughters in Israel. One only has to read ethnographic accounts of mother-child relationships elsewhere in the larger cultural area to realize the inherent strains in the mother-child relationship. (In particular, see Dwyer 1978:113–124; El Sa'adawi 1980; and Wikan 1982:241–244.) It is likely that women now in Israel do not recall, or choose not to relate, painful experiences of ambivalent feelings concerning their mothers because to do so could undermine their own maternal power in Israel.

6. Caspi 1985:23.

7. O Pakistan, O India: referring to distance.

8. Caspi:73.

9. Barakat (1985:28) has written a seminal article on the traditional and contemporary Arab family, much of which pertains to Jewish families in the Muslim Middle East: "The family is at the centre of social organization in all three Arab patterns of living. . . . The family constitutes the dominant social institution through which persons and groups inherit their religious, social class, and cultural identities. . . . The success or failure of an individual member becomes that of the family as a whole. . . . One's commitment to the family may involve considerable self-denial. Parents, and particularly the mother, deny themselves for the sake of their children. The source of the mother's happiness is the happiness and prosperity of her children. Both children and parents ideally are totally committed to the family itself." There are exceptions to this pattern, but they seem far and few between. Wikan (1982:239) remarks that in Sohar, Oman, a person is seen to have the power to shape the events of one's own life apart from consideration of one's family, and this, Wikan claims, is an exceptional case in the anthropological literature in the Arab world.

10. Of the thirty-five women in this study, five arrived in Israel between the ages of two and four; twenty-two arrived between the ages of five and fourteen; and seven arrived between the ages of 15–25. Four arrived prior to 1948; the only woman who arrived at age two in 1935 lived in an entirely Yemeni area and she received the same kind of upbringing as girls in Yemen.

11. Seven were sent to boarding school. Three of these were orphans; two had particularly problematic relationships with parents; and the remaining two convinced their parents to send them to boarding school because of its educational value.

12. See poem, Chapter 5, section 2.

13. This is common in other cultures where an aunt or grandmother explains bodily functions and the consequences of sexual intercourse to the young girl. For example, in traditional Ga society, the grandmother explains to the girl who has menstruated the "dangers" now attendant on her new situation, how to maintain her self-respect, and how to control herself (Azu 1971:45).

14. Marriage was not consummated until women reached puberty. By contrast, Yemeni Muslim brides do have intercourse even before the onset of menstruation.

15. This includes thirty-one of thirty-five women.

16. Divorce was common in Yemen and, if the problem was not between husband and wife, it could result from her inability to get along with his family.

17. Ganzfried 1963:21-23.

18. The interview was conducted in Hebrew.

19. This point of view is supported by some Jewish medical researches. It is not the mikveh which prevents cancer, but frequent abstention from sexual intercourse. See Meiselman 1978:128.

20. Meiselman:16.

21. According to Meiselman (127) such beliefs would fall into the category of 'folk' theory and do not have a direct relationship to halakhah. But note that Ganzfried uses the term 'unclean' in his interpretation. Although the mikveh is to impart spiritual, not physical cleanliness (*Encyclopedia Judaica*, 11:1534). In both Judaism and Islam, a major intent of the purity rules has to do with cleanliness for prayer (Fischer 1978:205).

22. Wood 1975:49.

23. *op. cit.*:52.

24. Ullrich 1975:67

25. Phyllis Palgi, a clinical anthropologist who has worked extensively with Yemeni Jews, has documented cases in which sexual defilement before a woman has performed the ritual ablutions has led to extreme consequences: spirit possession (Palgi 1978:126; 1983:328). Such women have sometimes ended up in psychiatric wards. Palgi explicitly recognizes the psychological upheavals which might be caused when practices such as the family purity rituals are followed in a less rigidly controlled environment such as Israel. Much of Palgi's work has focused on how the anthropologist can act as a cultural mediator between the two health systems utilized by many Middle Eastern and North African Jews in Israel, that of the traditional healer and the Western physician/psychiatrist.

26. Ganzfried:13-17.

27. As a result of timing the end of niddut with the most fertile time in the monthly cycle, many women get pregnant yearly. In contemporary Israel many resort to abortion as a means of family planning. This is well-documented in Basker's (1980) discussion of the use of abortion for family planning, particularly among Middle Eastern Jewish women. Those among the women whom I interviewed who had undergone repeated abortions viewed pregnancy as an illness and abortion as a cure, as those in Basker's study.

28. Of course this is not the case only among Yemeni Jews. See, for example, Goshen-Gottstein 1966:24-28; Kerr 1958:82; and Wolf 1972:139-140.

29. Again, Palgi (1983:328) suggests that forced intercourse can lead to spirit possession among Yemeni Jews.

30. It is interesting to note that Yemeni Muslim women remark upon the opposite side effects of qat, saying that it reduces men's sexual appetites and potency and prevents men from maintaining an erection (Dorsky:138). Given the fact that qat is a tranquilizer, this is probably true. In the case of my informant, her husband, when "high," probably did ask for sexual relations— thus being rendered "horny"—but since she refused him, she might not be aware of the detrimental effect of qat on male sexual activity.

31. This description of the situation of Yemeni Jewish women is in marked contrast to the data collected by Dorsky (134–139) among Yemeni Muslim women. In 'Amran, new brides are considered to be "normal" if they dislike sexual relations, but eventually they come to enjoy sex and expect their husbands to give them sexual pleasure. In spite of the fact that men (not women) are allowed pre-marital and extra-marital affairs, the situation described by Dorsky is considerably more egalitarian than that described elsewhere in the Muslim Middle East (Dorsky:210; Cf. Vielle 1978). There are a few other reports of female pleasure in sexual relations, such as among the traditional urban housewives in Cairo who expect frequent and lengthy intercourse with their husbands (el Messiri 1978:538), without being seen as "lascivious temptresses," which is how Moroccan women are generally viewed (Dwyer 1978:42; and Maher 1978:119.)

What I find difficult to explain is the difference in attitude and experience described by Yemeni Jewish and Muslim women, who have a lot in common in other matters. Both religions describe menstrual purity rituals, but in the case of Yemeni Jews, the time of abstention from sex (two weeks of every month) is longer and thus the expression of sexual desire (which in itself is culturally ambivalent) is more formally regulated.

32. On the duty of Jewish husbands to satisfy sexually their wives see Ganzfried:15–16. The Yemeni rabbi's wife might have discussed the commentaries on sexual relations in halakhah with women in the Portion of the Week sessions, or the women may have been informed at seminars for religious women in Jerusalem. It is unlikely that they read the halakhah themselves.

33. Caspi 1985:161–165.

34. This experience is reported by the immigrant women workers interviewed by Gannage (1986:57–58, 62): young mothers felt deep regret in having to leave their babies with minders so that they could go out to work; some of these same women leave the labour force in order to mind their grandchildren, in a sense to regain lost joys.

35. Once again, this only belongs to the immigrant experience: mothers born in Israel have received sufficient education to enable them to help their children with their homework. Cf. Abandan-Unat 1982:229.

36. In some immigrant situations, women may even *migrate* in order to earn better incomes, often leaving their children behind, or if taking them, relying on an eldest daughter to act as surrogate mother before she is emotionally ready, and preventing her from attending school (Abandan-Unat 1982:228–229). For some women, migrating alone, even if temporarily, might mean complete estrangement from their children; it is not yet known what effects this will have (Kudat 1982:296).

37. Most of these women had children in high school prior to 1978 when high school education became free of tuition fees.

38. For example, see the following sources in parent-adolescence conflict in the West: Davis 1940; Harris 1969; and Leslie 1973.

39. Ganzfried:6.

6

The Israeli-born Generation: Unmarried Women

Michal is eighteen, has just matriculated from high school, and is anxiously waiting to serve in the Air Force. Zahava is thirty-two, and all she looks forward to is leaving her parents' home in the morning to go to work as a secretary. Michal is just beginning to be pressured to find a husband, while Zahava's family and friends have almost given up hope that she will marry—by this age, she is considered to be an old maid. Both constantly confront dilemmas and questions of emotional and practical importance resulting from being unmarried. Michal wonders how long she can postpone the inevitability of marriage, while Zahava is realizing that if she continues to ward off prospective spouses, she will never marry and, heaven forbid, will remain childless. Michal is beginning to resent her responsibilities in looking after her four younger siblings, but she sighs with relief, knowing that soon she will get a break when she enters the Air Force. Zahava, by contrast, is a dutiful daughter, who relishes her position as oldest child and accepts her familial responsibilities without hesitation; but she too is beginning to feel suffocated by her large and loving family.

What Michal and Zahava have in common, along with their peers, is that they belong to nothing less than a new social category: *ravaka*, (unmarried woman). In Yemen, Jewish women were usually married by the age of twelve and most of those who immigrated to Israel as children married by the age of sixteen, the minimum age for marriage set by the State. As I shall show, the upbringing and educational careers of these younger women are considerably different from their mothers' who grew up in an almost entirely Yemeni Jewish milieu.

Unmarried women in Gadot face special problems. Not only is there no place in their Yemeni parents' world which has no cultural precedent for postponing marriage and children; but nor is there a defined "place" for the unmarried in Israeli society as a whole where the average age of marriage for women is slightly over twenty-one. So the considerable economic and social constraints placed upon them to marry arise not only out of Yemeni culture: the wider society expects women to marry soon after their discharge from the army.

I was originally interested in these women in their status as grown-up daughters vis-à-vis their mothers; several months after beginning field work I realized, when making up a subject index for my journal, that the very fact of their being unmarried warranted intensive study. The issue of marriage is of pressing importance. These women have been reared to regard marriage as a crucial and necessary part of self-esteem and, more importantly, as a duty to their parents and their religion, "to be fruitful and multiply"—to carry on the family line. Nor do the unmarried Yemeni women feel that there is a permanent place for them (and the same is true of their male counterparts) in Israeli society. It seems financially and emotionally impossible to live out adult lives without marriage and children. They are greatly aware that women who never marry are pitied by their friends and families and, as in other cultures, are called "old maids." And from the time they have completed high school, they themselves are constantly reminded of their unmarried status at weddings where everyone says to them *b'korov etzlekh* ("and soon to you"), which they find embarrassing and infuriating at the same time.

For most of these single women over the age of twenty, their childhood friends have already married, and so long-term friendships often end because, as they say, they no longer share a "common language" with married women.[1] Particularly when their married friends become mothers, they are seen to forget about the world "out there" and exclude unmarried women—if only by constantly talking about their children. Ultimately, the wide majority of unmarried women feel that a woman's "natural" destiny is to marry and bear children. To continue friendships with married women—insofar as that is possible—is a constant reminder of what they do not have and, more often then not, do want. In the meantime, they search for other *ravakot*. Yet there is a catch here: while they find comfort in the company of other unmarried women, they can become too "comfortable"; that is, they are less likely to look for spouses although, in the end, they feel they must do so.

This is not to say that these unmarried women have not had boyfriends or even fiances: almost all of them have.[2] When confronted with the possibility of marriage almost all prefer to wait. These women feel that they have enough personal strength and integrity to wait for the "ideal" husband with whom they will enjoy an exciting *and* enduring marriage. In fact three women have called off engagements because they realized that they were getting married for the sake of being married, or to please parents, or for other reasons they deemed inappropriate. They explicitly do not want to repeat the life careers of their mothers who were not well-educated and who had often married through an arranged match, to please their parents, or to escape their families' control. Young women's ideas about good marriages are to some extent a reaction to the often unhappy or non-communicative marriages of their parents as much as they derive from reading women's magazines or watching romantic movies.

For the daughters of the Israeli-born generation, there are short-term alternatives to marriage. These women have the opportunity to attend university which is easier for the unmarried who have more time to study. They are career-oriented and usually committed to their jobs.[3] And they continue to live in their parents' homes where they do not feel as oppressed as their mothers did in their parents' homes. At the same time, marriage is seen as an imperative and most women feel that they should not postpone marriage for too long. They are led to believe, both by their parents and friends through the use of stories of "old maids" that the older they get, the less desirable they will be as brides.[4] The older unmarried women—usually over twenty-five—begin to feel uneasy when they feel they might be too picky about prospective husbands because they are waiting for someone better to come along who might never appear. There is also the fear that as educated and professional women—two factors which afford them the possibility of postponing marriage—they will be undesirable to most Israeli men, regardless of ethnic background, who are generally thought of as chauvinistic, expecting their wives to be less educated than they are themselves and expecting them to put their families before their careers.[5]

While these women are all concerned about marriage, the implications of marriage are treated with some ambivalence. They question whether they will repeat the typical marriage careers of their mothers, carrying too many burdens as full-time workers and as mothers. Will they be able to travel? While living with their parents, they are able to believe that they lead an independent life—paying for their education, travels and pleasures, coming and going as they please, doing what they believe is right for themselves rather than what is right for their parents.

I found myself conducting this study of single women in a different way than I did with their mothers, for in more ways than one I was their peer. The technique of interviewing was clearly out, not because we could not take it seriously, but because my relationship with most of the thirty-three women discussed in this chapter was one of friendship. However, they knew that their stories and our experiences together were recorded in my journal. While I could not possibly feel exactly as they did, I myself was unmarried if in a different cultural context, and for that very reason I was subjected to much of the same kind of public scrutiny as they were. This led to a distinct advantage as a researcher: it was easy to empathize. It was also to my advantage that I was an American—for these Israeli-born women, I was sure to have an open mind so they were able to confide in me rather quickly. I do not feel that I am betraying their trust by writing about them here. They expected that I would do so, and they themselves also felt a need to call attention to their difficulties as ravakot. There were even times when they asked me to record their feelings and experiences in my journal—to be their mouthpiece in a world larger than their own. It was also that world which gave some meaning to their daily troubles: somewhere "out there" it was acceptable to be an adult and to be unmarried.

Going to School— New Opportunities

A critical difference between unmarried women and their mothers of the immigrant generation lies in formal education: in Yemen, Jewish women were illiterate and most of the immigrants in Israel received at most a few years of formal education; for daughters born in Israel education is compulsory up to the ninth grade.[6] Mothers, as we have seen, came to value the formal education of women, desiring that their daughters, as well as their sons, should be well-educated and able to compete for prestigious jobs. Hence, daughters are sent to school for as long as their parents or scholarships can pay the tuition fees, whether this means grades 10–12 or university education. Of the women in this study, all but three completed high school, and half were enrolled in or had completed university courses.

Attending school not only has implications for future employment; values and expectations learned in school are similar to or different from those held to obtain in the home.[7] Important considerations are whether girls attend religious or secular schools, their involvement in extracurricular activities—particularly youth movements—the extent to which they have made friends from different cultural backgrounds, and their perceptions of their teachers' attitudes towards them as Yemenis. Just as we have looked at the effects of the status that immigrant men and women have in the wider society, and the effects of their societal position on their domestic authority and power, so we must learn about children's status in the household and community (that is, the school, army, and workplace) in order to understand the context of parent-child relationships.

Elementary Education

Elementary education in Gadot runs from kindergarten through grade eight. Yemeni parents usually take into account two considerations: the school's reputation and whether the school is religious or secular. The local religious school has a sound academic reputation and is within easy reach of many Yemeni households—in fact, more than half of its pupils are children of Yemeni parents. Half the single women were sent to this school on the grounds that there they would receive proper moral training and schooling which would reinforce religious practices learned in the home. Children who receive at least their elementary education in a religious school are believed to be more respectful and better behaved than those who do not.[8] The local religious school, for example, puts much emphasis on children learning values that Yemeni parents think of as peculiarly Yemeni. This is especially the case for Derekh Erets: on the walls of each classroom are large posters saying *Derekh Erets kadma l'Torah* (proper conduct takes precedence over scholarship). On my visits to this school, parents took pains to make sure that I noticed these dictums.

Of the three secular elementary schools, two enjoy good academic reputations and so the other half of the single women who lived very near to these schools attended them. These schools are to some extent culturally integrated with students of Ashkenazi and Mizrahi descent. The third school, where almost all of the pupils are of North African descent, is said to have lower educational standards and so Yemeni parents living in this school's district undertake to enrol their children elsewhere in Gadot.[9]

Secondary Education

Can you imagine, if I had attended the "convent" [religious secondary school] in Tel Aviv I would never have gone to the army where I learned to think for myself and I would never have enjoyed such freedom and independence. Instead, I would be a "primitive" like my mother.

—A single woman in Gadot

In the Israeli context, attendance at religious or secular secondary schools has important implications for career choices, army participation of women, sexual mores, the future family lives of the students, and the observance of religious practices. In Gadot there is one secular high school (grades nine to twelve) offering both vocational and academic courses of instruction. There is no religious high school in the area so that children attending such schools outside Gadot either board there or must travel an hour to and from school daily.[10] Boys from Yemeni homes are more likely to be sent to religious boarding school than girls who are usually sent to the local high school. Parents reason that boys are more able emotionally to cope with being boarded away from home, that there is still some priority given to the education of boys over girls (boarding schools require more extensive parental funding), and that since boys might choose careers as religious functionaries, they should be prepared for such occupational roles by being given a religious secondary education.[11]

Daughters do not regret having attended religious elementary school, but most of those who did refused to continue on to religious high schools, preferring to attend the local co-educational school. Most simply did not want to travel to and from school, while others did not want to be separated from friends who were going to the local school. When confronted with their daughters' determination, parents were easily persuaded to let daughters study where they wanted, fearing that to force daughters to attend religious school might discourage them from completing high school altogether. Likewise with what they chose to study: although Yemeni mothers of the immigrant generation prefer the "female" professions, such as nursing and teaching, for their daughters, they did not discourage them from studying natural science or business, lest their daughters would leave school if they were not permitted to study what they liked.

Already by the tender age of twelve, children are apparently a force with which to reckon. Recollections about the choice of high school were often preceded with a mother's statement of fear, "I was afraid that . . . she would. . . ." It seems that by the time children were completing elementary education, parents were beginning to realize the limits to their authority over their offspring. Their Israeli-born children, through complete emersion in school and in youth movements, have by the age of twelve been given (by their teachers and counsellors) the tools of persuasion, of arguing for themselves, and, even of empowering themselves vis-à-vis their parents.[12]

Yet parents soon realized that social costs were involved when permitting children to attend secular high school. In some families, parents blame such schools (as well as the army) for destroying the type of family life which they value. Most daughters reflect on the fact that secular schooling taught them values opposed to those of their parents, but, by contrast, they do not regret having acquired new values, particularly those concerning sexual relations and the importance of having careers as well as motherhood, and the ability to decide for oneself.[13] Parents disapprove of secular education because it is co-educational. While they fear for their daughters' chastity once they enter high school, young girls are busy learning new codes of "honour"—particularly those which do not require pre-marital virginity, emphasizing instead solidarity with their friends. Unmarried women were careful to hide friendships with boys during their adolescence, fearing that if their parents knew, they would have been removed from school.[14]

By contrast, the few unmarried women who attended religious high school in Tel Aviv define their honour in remaining chaste,[15] thus supporting parents' opinions that the different values regarding sex which girls learn from peers in secular schools influence their daughters to abandon the ideals of Derekh Erets as related to chastity. Usually parents do not know if their daughters are virgins, but those whose daughters attend religious schools do not worry so much about this, having more trust in their daughters' upbringing.

High school, whether religious or secular, is also a time for making friends from a variety of ethnic backgrounds. The Gadot school is reputed for its successful attempts at "integration": that is, students attend the school from twenty-five different settlements including near-by towns, moshavim, villages and cities, from a variety of economic classes and cultural backgrounds. The values of integration, particularly those concerning equal access to all the school's resources and the mixing of children from a variety of backgrounds in all classes and extra-curricular activities, are not always achieved. Students for their part are skeptical of the school's reputation for successful integration, claiming that teachers systematically discriminate against students from Eidot Hamizrah, encouraging them to study vocations rather than theoretical subjects. Many young women resent the preferential treatment they believe teachers gave to upper-class Ashkenazi students from the neighbouring town of Asher, meaning that such students are given more attention, are invariably streamlined into courses to prepare them for professional careers, and are given extra tutoring when necessary.[16]

At the same time, students from Gadot are pleased to become friends with children from upper class families, claiming that such contacts encourage them to study harder so that they can enter professions which would enable them to make a good living. They do not blame their parents for their inability to provide them with all of the consumer goods that children of wealthy parents receive because they understand that their own parents' educational backgrounds precluded their entry to well-paying professions. Unmarried Yemeni women, in particular, are certain that they can achieve a higher standard of living through their own hard work, if not through marriage. University education is seen as critical for obtaining well-paying and interesting jobs and as a result, many enter academic courses as soon as they are capable of financing higher education.

University Education

While there are young women who remember that their secondary school teachers had encouraged them to study fashion, sewing, or secretarial courses, most did in fact study academic courses which enabled them to attend university. In 1981 half of them either were enrolled in university or had already completed the B.A. Several of these were studying through arrangements with the regular army; having completed conscript duty, they signed a contract which enabled them to continue with their education while working in military jobs. The other women students are funded by their families, part-time jobs, and scholarships from the local council. Single women are pleased with the level of education they have achieved; several contrast their good fortune with the manner in which their mothers had been obliged to work to finance their brothers' education at the expense of their own.

At university young women become friends with Ashkenazi students as they did in high school, but it seems that such friendships are of a different nature. Yemeni women often talk about their new experiences in this Ashkenazi-Western milieu, stressing how important it is to go to the theatre and classical concerts, to broaden one's intellectual horizons and to meet prospective Ashkenazi spouses. Yet their experiences in the university, both in respect to friendships with Ashkenazim and relationships to teachers, are sometimes tainted by feelings that they are discriminated against. They often wonder whether the Ashkenazi men they meet are simply interested in flirting with a pretty Yemeni or if teachers do not encourage them enough because their parents are not literate. Long conversations often betray contradictory experiences, however: the same woman who talks about an episode in which she felt discrimination will talk about another teacher giving her extra attention because she was particularly good at a subject. In both instances, the teacher was Ashkenazi, and it is possible that the women's perceptions reflected reality.

What is clear here is that young women face a variety of attitudes towards them as Yemeni descendants *and* as individuals, and they often consider whether or not their ethnic background will influence the course of new relationships. In the university setting this is of particular importance since the majority of students (and competitors) are children of Ashkenazi parents. When it comes down to it, however, young women insist that in an ideal world they be judged as individuals and not as Yemenis, whether to their advantage or not. While throughout their school years, and even in the army, coming from religious Yemeni homes might have structured their experience, by the time they enter university they see themselves as having obtained liberal values; while they are proud of their ethnic background, they do not want it to either help or hinder them. This is not to say, however, that they always live according to their values. To do so would be naive in the Israeli context where *proteksia* (connections) is often a critical tool and using it through one's ethnic claims is acceptable even if regrettable.

The Army

Army service is the critical starting-off point for the new stage in the life cycle which I have called unmarried adulthood. At this point there is a marked separation of daughter from family as she moves into a totally different milieu. The state then takes over responsibility and control of the young woman who is allowed various freedoms not tolerated in the parental home.

After finishing high school at age eighteen and before entering university, the vast majority of unmarried Yemeni women in Gadot were in the army. The Security Law of 1979 requires men aged eighteen to twenty-nine to do three years of conscript duty and women aged eighteen to twenty-six to do two years, exempting those women who can show reasons of conscience or religious conviction that preclude military service. Unmarried women may be called up for reserve duty until the age of thirty-six, but are usually released from this duty by the age of twenty-four.[17] Married women and mothers are exempt from conscript duty and new women immigrants over the age of twenty usually are not drafted into the army, although they may volunteer. Religious girls who are exempt from service have the option to participate in *Sherut Le'umi* (National Service) for one to two years, where they serve as nurses' aides, teachers and youth group leaders in development towns or poor neighbourhoods. Many girls claim to be religious in order to avoid conscription. Because the religious political parties are opposed to any military service for women, this is a sensitive political issue. As a result the government usually accepts the requests of those women who do not want to serve: only 50 percent of Israeli-born and bred girls serve in the army.

In practice, most conscript duty involves the two years between the ages of eighteen and twenty. Women undergo a six-week course of basic training which includes physical fitness, unarmed combat (self-defence), and how to hold, clean, assemble and fire a gun. With the exception of Nahal participants (the agricultural branch of the army where women serve for two and a half years on kibbutzim), women do not carry arms after completing basic training. On completion of training they are allocated to tasks the army deems appropriate for them, although they have the right to request certain jobs. They are trained "on the job" or in army courses and are rotated at the will of the army. Women soldiers comprise a large segment of the army service staff, working as secretaries, clerks, telephone operators, nurses, teachers, parachute folders, intelligence workers, and so on. Most girls live at home after basic training if their bases are near-by, while others whose bases are far away visit home once a week or fortnight as their leaves permit. Against this background it is possible to relate several features of army service experienced by unmarried Yemeni women in Gadot.

The high level of participation in either the army or National Service for the unmarried women in this study (twenty-nine of thirty-three served) is somewhat unusual for daughters of Yemeni parents. In homogeneous Yemeni neighbourhoods or villages two factors discourage or prevent army service: parents fear for their daughters' chastity and religious schooling which strongly discourage service by women. By contrast, in Gadot, almost all of the unmarried women went to the secular high school, were intensively involved in secular youth movements such as the Girl Scouts or the youth wing of the Labour Party—both movements strongly advocating army service for women—and all of those who served had secular non-Yemeni friends, almost all of whom also served in the army.[18]

About one-third of the women served in Nahal on kibbutzim because their parents believed that the girls would be more closely supervised on kibbutz, despite its reputation for "free love." A minority of women, whose parents initially opposed their army service, threatened to leave home. By the time these women were high school graduates they had learned that parents could be manipulated, by being threatened with leaving home—the second most dishonourable thing an unmarried woman can do, next to losing her virginity before marriage.

As young girls, nearly all of these women anticipated their army service with pleasure. They were excited because the army meant new adventures, love affairs, travel, and new friends. In reality, it also meant two years of hard work and adjusting to life without their families. The women were moved around often during their army service. More often than not they served as support staff, doing menial and tedious tasks which seemed to serve only men. Women clerks were particularly dismayed about the occasional sexual abuse they encountered, considering that it was related to the status of their job. As one woman said, "What was the army for me? Running everywhere as a clerk, and as a clerk, they expected me to run to bed with them as well." Not all sexual experiences in the army are in the category of abuse, however.

Despite some unpleasant encounters and sometimes dreary work, most women would serve in the army again. There they learned the value of independent action and of making their own decisions. Nahal participants, in particular, have only positive comments about their service in the agricultural core; they even encouraged their younger sisters or friends to join the same branch, stressing the importance of comraderie. Seed groups, known as *garinim*, are formed in high school, in the youth movements, or by army recruiters. Usually one enters Nahal with one's school friends and the garin, sometimes numbering 30–40 young people, stays together throughout army service, except for those few who are chosen to become officers. A new soldier knows that she or he will remain with the same group for two or three years and in a rotating pattern of six months in regular army duties, six months on the kibbutz. Good friendships are made and the social life offered on the kibbutz is invariably more exciting than that in the regular branches. A minority remain on the kibbutz and are encouraged to marry in; this was the case for one of the unmarried Yemeni women and for many others from different eidot whom I met over a period of eight years on one kibbutz which customarily took in garinim from Gadot and near-by towns.

An influential aspect of service in Nahal is that each member of the garin is "adopted" by a kibbutz family and a close relationship with the family often continues upon her discharge from the army. Yemeni girls of the Israeli-born generation thus have the chance to observe kibbutz parents and children interacting, usually in harmony. Kibbutz parents are not involved in the direct disciplining of their children who have their own rooms and who have been reared separately from their parents in the children's houses. Thus an important area of concern—learning how to behave—is taken out of parents' hands, placed in the care of the kibbutz system of collective education—and in many families, contributes to a very close parent-child relationship. Young Nahal soldiers observe and participate in families in which authoritarian relationships simply are not seen to exist. This experience might be at the root of some young women's desire to "educate" their "primitive" parents upon returning from their army service on the kibbutz. Parents' behaviour is judged to belong to the Yemeni past; kibbutz "adopted" parents, who are invariably well-educated Ashkenazim, belong to the mainstream of Israeli society, and this is a world which many young women emulate. Hence Yemeni parents face troubles when their daughters return home.

After completing army service, almost all of the young women returning to their parental homes recall that after the freedom they experienced in the army, it was very difficult to adjust to parents' rules. It is indeed a difficult time for all concerned, and parents blame the kibbutz or the army when girls are wayward, meaning they are more independent, more outspoken and more difficult to control than before leaving for the army.

Work

For single women, going out to work is often the highlight of their lives.[19] Even if they are not satisfied with their jobs in some cases, it is unthinkable to be unemployed and supported by one's parents after completing high school, the army or university. They have definite ideas about work appropriate for a "modern" educated woman. While they will work in almost any job, including waitressing or childminding, while pursuing university studies, they draw the line at domestic work which seen as degrading. Such work is acceptable for their mothers who are uneducated, but as educated women, the daughters of dor ha'sponga believe domestic labour is beneath them.

Wages usually range between the equivalent of three to six dollars per hour, a reasonable wage by Israeli standards, and the students are not required to pay income tax.[20] All of the women have their own bank accounts and spend their income on clothes, studies, entertainment, in some cases on cars, and a little is saved for their marriages. Regardless of whether they received secular or religious schooling, working daughters do not contribute their income for household consumption, as their mothers had before them.[21] Only a few daughters who enjoy extremely good relationships with their parents contribute a portion of their income to their families, but this is usually for large purchases such as household appliances. In one case, the daughter had purchased most of the household furniture; this was viewed by her friends, as outright exploitation on the part of her family. More typically, daughters' failure to make substantial economic contributions is the source of considerable conflict, with parents demanding income contributions but lacking the ability to exact them. In fact, during arguments on this matter, daughters often threaten to move out of the house. Clearly these young women are in a much more powerful situation as daughters than their mothers were. In this important respect, Yemeni daughters of the Israeli-born generation are like their Israeli peers, and indeed, parents readily blame the "self-interested" society in which children interact for producing such selfish and ungrateful children.[22] However, in Israel a variety of social services and free education are offered to all citizens. Currently, the public purse is considerably fuller than when Yemeni parents had arrived in the new country, and parents now earn adequate income without necessarily requiring the contributions of their children. In the Yemeni case, daughters seek to legitimate their lack of economic contributions by claiming that this practice prevails in all Israeli households.

The Residential Choice:
Living at Home or Moving Out

Associated with parents' concern over their daughters' chastity, is the question of whether unmarried women remain in the parental home before marriage. If this is not a source of anxiety in one family, it is bound to be in the house next door. Parents and daughters talk about this a lot. Unless a daughter is in the army or living in a university dormitory far from home, she is expected to live with her parents, regardless of her age and financial status. Parents accommodate many breaches of Derekh Erets if only to keep their daughters at home. Any daughter who moves out without parental consent is suspected of improper conduct; it is bad enough if daughters do not marry when they are of age but moving out adds insult to injury.

The majority of single Yemeni women in Gadot live in their parents' homes. For most of those who are religious, moving out is not an issue, and they often joke about secular women saying that they open up whore houses. However, a large number of non-religious women live at home because they respect their parents on this matter.

A key factor in the decision to live at home is fear of loneliness. While in the army women had little opportunity to get lonely because they were busy and always surrounded by people in the barracks and in their jobs. Their lives in both childhood and army service provided lack of privacy and almost no personal space.[23] For women who *want* to remain at home this is not an issue: family life is rarely seen as crowded. Usually they have five or more siblings in the home and while this may create friction—in some families, household warfare—it is also true that siblings are often good pals and socialize together even when they frequently bicker. In fact, most women regard living without a large family as inconceivable.

There are, nevertheless, several women who desperately want to move out but are not prepared to breach relations with their parents. For example, Talia (aged twenty-five) talked a great deal about moving out, but knew that she could not bring herself to do so because her father would accuse her of being dishonourable and her mother, who was emotionally dependent on her, would feel lost. Only if she obtained a teaching post in a distant city could she justify such a move to them.

Parents sometimes go to extremes to persuade their daughters to stay home when they learn that they want to leave. Tamar (aged twenty-four) often spoke about moving out because she found her home situation unbearable, partially because of her younger sister to whom she had not spoken for two years. She also found that as her younger sisters became more involved in school work and their own personal lives she was expected to take on their chores. Because she was very attached to her mother—who had an awful marriage—she felt constrained to remain. After eight months of threatening to leave home, in the midst of a rapidly deteriorating situation, Tamar began to search for an apartment. This action made her parents build another room on to the flat; while publicly the parents claimed that they would have more room for their married children and grandchildren to visit, her mother told me privately that they hoped giving Tamar the extra room would stop her talking about moving. The strategy worked temporarily and Tamar decided to stay at home, locking the door to her new room so that when she was at work her "nosey" sisters would stay out of it. Ultimately, the new room failed to solve the serious troubles she had at home and she moved out several months after I left the field.

In another family, Zahava (aged thirty-two), a religious and a dutiful daughter, decided that leaving Gadot was the only way she could achieve an independent life. Returning from a four-month trip to the United States, where she had learned to exercise her independence, she announced her intention of moving out to her parents whose blessing she expected because she had always demonstrated Derekh Erets and had made extensive economic contributions to the family as a daughter should. A nasty quarrel followed; her parents, fearing scandal, were horrified at the thought of her moving. Her father proclaimed that Zahava would not be permitted to move out of the house before marriage if she were sixty years old. What really hurt Zahava, however, was the fact that her mother whom she had always considered to be her best friend, simply could not side with her, not even privately.

In a third family, Devorah (aged twenty-five) considered moving out because of frequent quarrels with her mother. She planned to move to Tel Aviv with her friend Dahlia, a girl who eventually deserted her elderly mother and became estranged from her family. Devorah wanted to move to Tel Aviv for the night life, to meet "mature" men, and to find new friends. She anticipated difficulty in informing her parents of her intentions—"all hell will break loose," she said, "they may even tell me not to return." If she were to move, it could not be until she was promoted at the bank so that she could easily be transferred to another branch. Another reason for delaying the move, however, appeared uncharacteristic of Devorah who is very confident: having incorporated some of the beliefs of her parents' culture, she really feared living on her own (even though she would be sharing with Dahlia).

Five months after Devorah first expressed her desire to move, I arrived for Friday night dinner to find her and Dahlia scanning apartment ads in the newspaper. Later the next week they began to enquire abut apartments by telephone—right in front of her mother, Zohara, who was then nonchalantly informed that she was leaving home. All hell *did* break loose. Zohara screamed that if her daughter intended to leave she should go at once because they did not want a whore living in their house. She began to cry and said that Devorah, if she left, should never come back for a visit.

Over the next few days, Zohara repeatedly accused Devorah of giving her mother an ulcer and claimed that she would destroy the family reputation. Devorah, regarding her mother's psychosomatic symptoms as no more than a ploy to keep her at home, was not concerned with her family's reputation, at least not as defined by her mother who had not yet joined the modern world. Mother and daughter rarely spoke over the next few weeks, which Devorah thought was better than quarrelling. However, Devorah showed some sensitivity about the brogez (avoidance relationship) when Zohara carried the dispute into Devorah's professional life by going to another bank teller rather than her daughter. This action soon became obvious at the bank and was embarrassing.

Devorah eventually decided to stay at home and buy a car. In doing so she was not complying with her mother's wishes; she simply postponed her move. (In fact, Devorah did not move out before her marriage five years later.) Despite her difficulties at home, she is able to come and go as she pleases and save money, because—her mother claims—she does not help pay the family bills. Devorah's threatened move, however, lessened Zohara's antics about her daughter's misconduct at least temporarily.

These few cases show that parents will use various strategies to persuade their daughters to remain at home—building on a room, threatening to disown the daughter, and feigning illness—but often to no avail. By the time I left the field, eight women of the thirty-three women did not live at home. Five of these left Israel altogether, and were living in Greece, Los Angeles, and New York. Four originally travelled ostensibly to seek adventure, but a major cause for leaving was to avoid a confrontation with their parents. It is interesting to note that emigration is regarded as being more respectable than relocation in Israel.

One of the most unusual women I met in Gadot was Shula (aged twenty-eight). Attractive and cunning, she had worked as a prostitute in Tel Aviv, but lived in her parents' home in Gadot because it was a safe and relatively quiet retreat from her time spent soliciting on the noisy streets of the city. Preferring Americans in the hope that one would take her off to New York, she did meet a client who fell in love with her and with whom she was prepared to go to New York; this plan was "foiled," as she herself said, when he suddenly died of cancer. Shula was determined to leave Gadot and eventually saved enough money to move to New York—where she has two married brothers—and there she continues to work as a prostitute.

Three women left home but stayed in Israel. One of these, Miriam (aged nineteen), the daughter of the local Yemeni rabbi, did not face parental disapproval because she went to live in a religious seminary. She met her fiancé under approved conditions and was married shortly after I left the field. The two other women, however, faced considerable opposition. One was Devorah's friend Dahlia (aged twenty-five) who three years after being discharged from the army, left her elderly widowed mother to live alone in an apartment. While at home Dahlia had never been reprimanded staying out late or not returning home at all, precisely because her mother feared that she would move. Her seven older siblings scolded her for leaving, but she was financially independent and could ignore their advice with impunity. By the time I left the field, nine months after she moved out, she was completely estranged from her family. Dahlia had particular disdain for her upbringing, and resented having to take care of her elderly mother, believing that her married brothers should do so. One brother did take her mother in because she was so frail, but this only aggravated the situation with her brothers who stopped talking to her altogether.

The third woman, Malka (aged twenty-three), lives on a kibbutz in the Golan Heights where she served in Nahal. The second of four children, Malka has been since childhood a strong-willed and independent girl, and under no condition would she return to Gadot because she was committed to kibbutz life. Her parents remain very upset about this because she lives so far away and is, her mother believes, in danger of Palestinian terrorism. The mother also laments the fact that the kibbutz is areligious; hence it is likely that Malka will lose her virginity there, and if she marries, her children may not be raised in a religious manner.

Visits home often prove difficult for Malka. Her mother never fails to accuse her of obtaining her "crazy" ideas from the kibbutz, to which Malka retorts that she was crazier when she lived at home. Malka, for her part, wishes to respect her mother, but finds it difficult because her mother cannot be "rational". The more her mother pesters her, the less she wants to visit home; yet her mother is convinced that if Malka sees how miserable she is without her, she will move back.

To conclude, most women accept the Yemeni expectation that unmarried daughters live at home. Those who consider moving or have moved are able to because their educational, occupational and army careers have provided them with the social and economic tools which enable them to live independent of their families. Hence they take advantage of alternative lifestyles available in Israel, and indeed in the world-at-large. In these social contexts they find they can live as adult unmarried women with identities quite different from those that are deemed proper in Yemeni social circles. Only Dahlia and to a lesser extent Shula became estranged from their families, while the others return to visit home regularly after suffering an initial period of hostility from their parents. There is an important precedent set in those families where daughters do move out and that is that younger daughters find that they can move with less difficulty, knowing that parents are unlikely to disown them if they do.

Changing Notions of Proper Conduct:
New Codes of Honour

A key element of Derekh Erets for Yemenis of the immigrant generation is female pre-marital chastity. Parental assumptions concerning virginity are related to this ideology of honouring others, that is the family before the person, and include the notion of control over women as well as the potential danger of sexual intercourse.[24] The overwhelming majority of mothers of the immigrant generation are opposed to pre-marital sex:[25]

> In my opinion this is not acceptable. I do not say anything today, but I do not like my son and his girlfriend sleeping together. Maybe I am primitive, but I do not care.

> I do not think that this is acceptable. A woman must marry first. In Yemen if a woman was not a virgin she was returned to her parents. So I know that this is not good, and if she is not a virgin, then her husband will call her a *zona* (prostitute). I told my daughters this.

> I am very opposed to this because virginity is a woman's honour. I am the rabbi's wife and so I know whether a pregnancy comes before or after the wedding. Her husband can be cruel to her. Perhaps she gave in to someone else, not just to him. She is cheap in his eyes. . . . In the old days a woman showed her virginity after the wedding by holding out the blood-stained sheet.

Mothers try to inculcate these values in their daughters, leading them to believe that they will suffer familial sanctions, personal guilt, possible madness, "disease of the sex," and deep shame if they deviate from these rules of proper conduct. They emphasize repeatedly that if an unmarried woman is unchaste, she loses the symbol of her honour. Mothers caution their daughters—through the use of gossip and folktales—that if a woman "opens up her legs before marriage," even to the man she marries, her husband will throw it in her face, divorce her and shame her. In the mother's world of her Yemeni friends, she is certainly ashamed if her daughter exhibits improper sexual conduct because she believes that it reflects on her failure to train the girl properly. Moreover, mothers fear for their daughters' emotional well-being, believing that pre-marital sex inevitably causes psychological trauma. They also contend that severe physical effects may result, especially concerning possible impairment of the girl's childbearing capacities from abortions or birth control pills. In this respect their folk beliefs are congruent with Western medical findings: indeed, such "folk" beliefs probably have a basis in medical findings since women who are literate may read about this subject in women's magazines. Since therapeutic abortions and contraceptive pills belong to the Israeli context, mothers have brought these aspects into their lore of reasoning against pre-marital sex. On the occasions when mothers relate the evidence for their beliefs to their daughters, the latter respond by telling their mothers that they are primitive, a response that mothers undoubtedly find hurtful.

Certainly, as I have hinted above, the concern that mothers show over a daughter's virginity is not simply because of the consequences they fear the daughter will suffer. Whereas in Yemen women were conceptualized as integral parts of patronymic groups, in Israel they are seen as the responsibility of nuclear families and the State. This is not the place to discuss mothers' motivations, but an idea that should be seriously considered is that because mothers have lost the security of the Yemeni system of collective responsibility, they feel that they are responsible for their gain or loss of status through their children's actions. Hence they feel anxiety over whether or not they have dutiful and chaste daughters.

Only a few women admit to knowing that their daughters are not virgins and argue that these daughters would not have had pre-marital sex as a result of their own "normal" desires. This refusal to accept the daughters' pre-marital sexuality is interesting in the light of many mothers' expressed opinions about other unmarried women's sexually seductive appearances. Mothers sympathize with the girls in films, appreciate or criticize them, but more often than not, mothers get very excited over the possibility of romance. Therefore, it seems that they are prepared to recognize the sexuality of other women, but not that of their own daughters. This may have something to do with the "newness" of the status of unmarried adult for women of the immigrant generation.

This situation is very complicated for a girl must cope with differing expectations in two worlds. One—that of her parents' generation—teaches that virginity is her honour, and that pre-marital sex demonstrates failure to maintain Derekh Erets. The second—the world outside of her parents' home—presents more problems for the girl because the value of virginity here is ambiguous.

Unmarried Women's Attitudes and Experiences with Pre-Marital Sex

Young non-religious women feel that they should carry themselves with respect and dignity, be discreet and private concerning with whom they make love, and that they should make love only with serious boyfriends. (Only a small minority think that intercourse is a sexual act to be engaged in whenever desired and that it does not matter at what age a girl loses her virginity as long as she is protected against pregnancy.) Both these attitudes, however, represent radically different notions from those to which their mothers adhere, and are caused largely by such young women's participation in secular, ethnically mixed and co-educational schools, in the army, and in the workplace, milieux which contain pressures and expectations for young people to engage in pre-marital sex.

For most women in the study, virginity was not an issue during high school where sexually active girls were considered promiscuous, the subject of gossip, and were thought of as "loose," "butterflies,"or zonot. Almost all young women claim that high school age girls are too emotionally immature to lose their virginity. In secular high school, however, they are given formal sexual education, presented with the biological facts of sexual reproduction and taught how to use contraception.[26] During high school many of these women had boyfriends with whom they experimented but with whom they did not have intercourse. They laugh when recalling awkward moments in their innocence, but remember their earliest sexual experiences as enjoyable. By contrast, several women were very shy during high school and could not imagine kissing boys. They also feared the wrath of their parents, and felt that most boys could not be trusted. Men are often accused of maintaining double standards: men can engage in pre-marital sex but respectable women should not.[27] Women often say that men have no control, and that they are never selective about their partners for intercourse. On this issue the unmarried women share with their mothers similar beliefs about the uncontrollable nature of male sexuality, and sometimes relate in Arabic the expression they learned from their mothers: "A man is like a dog; he will go to every hole."[28]

Ideas about the necessity for pre-marital virginity undergo a radical external change when women enter the army and are confronted with the possibility of pre-marital sex in which the honour of the family is no longer at stake—as long as parents (and parents' friends) do not know. When a girl leaves home her virginity becomes more directly a matter of her own honour and her own concern for her future marriage. Confronted by the possibility of engaging in intercourse on a regular basis, and by the assumptions of female comrades that sexual intercourse is a necessary accompaniment to a valued personal relationship, women began to redefine their honour. To do "it" and not to redefine "it" could result in guilt, shame, and even emotional disaster.

In the army, women are exposed to other notions of honour such as the importance of solidarity with their comrades. The exposure to secular men and women, along with the availability of partners, apparently strongly influences women to enter sexual relations and consequently to redefine their self-respect.[29] Paradoxically, through the consideration of others' (men's) wishes and the different viewpoints of their peers, young women demonstrate part of the prescript of Derekh Erets, but disregard the element which is so important to parents and was previously (as school girls) to themselves—pre-marital chastity. The value of pre-marital sex with boyfriends, which appears to be the norm governing sexual relations for women in secular Israeli society, seems to have been incorporated readily into the viewpoints of many unmarried Yemeni women in Gadot. One should add, however, that five women said that they entered into sexual relationships while in the army because their first partners accused them of being "frigid" or "old maids," and threatened to tarnish their reputations if they did not acquiesce. Soon after such experiences, often including psychological conflicts, women began to redefine the meaning of proper conduct. What is important here is that approval is sought from the army peer group rather than from one's family.[30]

Here, of course, are elements of male control over women: for the minority of girls who felt threatened because their first (or subsequent) partners said that they would tarnish their reputation if they did not acquiesce to sexual advances, they have, in effect, gone from the control of their families to the control of unprincipled men. Some of these men were in a position of authority—as their superiors, even as their officers—and, as young girls having just left home for the first time, they were hardly in a position to defend their rights. This area of male control over females as sexual objects in the army has scarcely been looked at in the sociological literature, but I heard numerous stories in which this was an important, albeit a covert, factor. What becomes evident is that the relating of the story includes not only an account of a physical act, but the sharing of confidential information about sexual advances, with girlfriends who often define such overtures in purely romantic terms, or certainly not in terms in which the female is seen as an "object." There is also the added complication of "prestige," particularly when the lover is himself a well-respected or handsome man, so that girlfriends see the acceptance of advances as honourable.

In these circumstances, and particularly for young women who lose their virginity with young men for whom they do have an emotional attachment, two elements of proper conduct play a part. One is *personal integrity*. In this respect, a girl eventually comes to see herself as responsible for her own sexual actions (rather than for the lack of them)—usually as a result of considerable pressure from her peers (both male and female) to engage in sex. This leads us into the other element: *reputation*. While growing up a girl's reputation (*shem*, or her "name") is connected to that of her family. In the army, her reputation is connected to her actions in a social group of peers, both women and men. In the company of women, she must not be seen promiscuous, and should be known as having sex in an acceptable emotional relationship. In the company of men, the same is true, but individual men may use the threat of tarnishing her reputation if a woman does not submit. Thus, for some women, their "reputation" is subject to male control: having slept with men who said they would not tell anyone, but who did precisely that, the woman may then be with other "dogs" (as they put it) looking for sexual favours.

With few exceptions, the loss of virginity entails some conflicts with women's first partners or subsequent partners. Concerning the actual physical act of intercourse, none of them experienced the traumatic defloration that their mothers were forced to endure. These young women knew what to expect from reading books, sex education, and intimate talks with other women. Most used contraception immediately or promptly obtained it. It seems that the physical effects of defloration and subsequent *sexual* relationships were the least of their worries. Indeed, a few women could not understand what all the fuss was about, pondering why an unbroken hymen could hold such value.[31] After engaging in sexual relations with a man, almost every young woman is concerned about the subsequent relationship she will have. Many stories circulate in which women who make love before marriages are undesirable as brides.[32] As a result, a woman often fears that if she makes love with a man she loves, he will leave her. She also fears that if she does not he will leave her, and so this looks like "damned if you do and damned if you don't" (indirect male control). A woman may try to postpone sexual intercourse for several months in order to gain the respect of a man with whom a woman foresees a long-term relationship, thereby letting him know that she is a serious woman and not to be taken advantage of (indirect female control). Strategies such as this are very common; I myself was instructed never to make love with a man whom I want to marry. Access to the vagina is seen as a "card," that is, a strategy for keeping a man interested. If one holds onto the card, the man might find the woman more desirable. And yet, often women who give such advice do not practice what they preach, afraid that they might be damned if they "don't."

Many Israeli women are not virgins when they marry, obviously do not believe that they will be divorced if they lose their virginity before marriage. Many, however, feel that such loss can cause problems, and, like their mothers, repeat stories of husbands who hold the wife's involvement in pre-marital sex as a weapon against her. Here their mothers' stories are influential.

Very rarely do young women make love with men they claim not to care about. Only a few are able to separate their emotions from the physical act, and even then not on all occasions. Only a few speak of the technical aspects of love making as being important rather than the emotional accompaniment. Even these women, however, refuse to be sexual playmates when they are seriously interested in a man, expecting to be treated as a girlfriend with formal commitments. While there were several women who were more sexually free in the army than after they were discharged, this change was not due simply to moving back home, but because they had become more interested in forging long-term relationships.

Some women have brief affairs without feeling guilty or taken advantage of, but if they are interested in more than an affair they are hesitant to be sexually aggressive because they might appear to be too experienced. I found this perplexing—why were they so guarded with casual relationships when it seemed logical that they would look for easier physical enjoyment with these "passing flings" and be less aggressive with perspective husbands who might consider the number of previous lovers as important? Several women responded directly to this query of mine, admitting that in the back of their minds they know that few of their affairs really are casual or that they are unable to accept them as such.

Almost all the unmarried Yemeni women in Gadot have had several or many boyfriends in their lives and not all of these relationships ended unhappily; nor were most conflicts based on sexual aspects of their relationships. It seems that their fears that a man might leave a woman if she accepts his advances are in reality largely unfounded. One of the few women who believe that a woman's sexual past is unimportant if a man really loves her is herself a virgin. The others think otherwise and though they are willing to enter sexual relations, whenever they do, they wonder if the man will leave them because of this. Most have experienced "one night stands" which they believe justify their fears.

Three patterns present themselves among the young women in Gadot: the first is the acceptance of traditional Yemeni attitudes towards premarital sex. Virginity is retained, although some heavy petting might be experienced. Of the six virgins, five are religious and four of these attended religious high schools. They share to a large extent the belief systems of their parents on most aspects of life, including the association of virginity and honour. In the eyes of their parents they are dutiful daughters, and they do not give their parents reason to suspect otherwise because they dress modestly, come home when their parents tell them to, and, most importantly, treat their parents with respect.

These virgins are somewhat of an extreme in the world outside the Yemeni generations of their parents and grandparents, and the religious school. Although four of them are very young (18–21), the other young women in Gadot refer to them as "old maids" and often joke about them, believing that they are ridiculous for clinging to their virginity. In their view such behaviour is unacceptable.

The second pattern is at the opposite pole and is considered to be improper conduct according to most of the other young women: sexual promiscuity and indiscretion. Only four women fall into this category: one is Shula, the prostitute, who is unacceptable to all the other young women. Another, Anat, works in a shop where her behaviour is highly visible. It was said of her: "What a woman. Her sexuality pours out all over her—in fact, she smells of sex. Why doesn't she cover it up?" Another comment was, "I cannot believe that girl. She walks around in high heels, tight pants, breasts hanging out, flirting all the time, dropping women to speak to men, with whom I am sure she pops into bed." Anat has intercourse with many men and she does not herself find this difficult to contend with. She encounters difficulties only when she is sincerely interested in someone, in which case being considered one of the town's sex objects does not work in her favour. Ironically she married before many of the others: four years after I left the field, she married another clerk from the shop.

The third woman in this category is reputed to be sly and notorious with men—and she, not surprisingly, is Dahlia who left her elderly mother to go live alone. Even her close friend, Anat, cannot accept blatant use of men for material betterment. The fourth, Yardena, who eventually moved to New York, endured a reputation in high school for being a "butterfly" simply because of the way she flirted. She did not lose her virginity until she was in the army where she was in fact, by her own account, a "butterfly." She eventually lost these ways, however, to become more like those who fall in the middle—associating sexual relationships with love.

While these women do not find their own behaviour improper, they are looked upon with disgust by the other single women. They are not thought of as potential wives—others would argue that if a girl "opened up her legs" before marriage too many times, she could not be trusted.[33]

The third pattern is a more moderate route. These women, the majority of those in Gadot (twenty-three of thirty-three) have chosen to lose their virginity, but not to let their parents suspect them of having done so. They are discrete about with whom they make love, when and where, usually doing so only with serious boyfriends. Sometimes these women experience the feelings of guilt which their parents led them to expect, on breaking the rules of Derekh Erets, that is, they dishonoured religion, parents, and the self. This is sometimes the case even when parents do not know that they have been unchaste, so, assuredly, the attitudes with which they were raised have left their mark. By contrast, at least half of these moderate women are comfortable with their activities and most are sorry that their sex lives are constrained by living at home, in a small town, and in a situation where there are few possible boyfriends—all of which contrast to life in the army.

At the same time, for nearly all the women, there remains a belief in Derekh Erets, but it seems that the sexual realm of honour has been separated from the traditional notion. Many of these women are respectful to their parents and try to be helpful. They participate in activities in Gadot, attend family celebrations, regularly visit grandparents, and have respect and consideration for other people. Just the same, ideas of personal honour and proper conduct are in the process of radical change, but the acceptance of the values of what they see as secular Israel has not been an easy process.

Overview

Do children born in Israel complete the process of their parents' immigration? The answer depends upon which perspective one chooses to take: that of the social scientist, relating to the specific context, or that of the actors themselves. Let us consider these three separately.

In the world of comparative sociology, immigrant children and the children of immigrants have begun to attract great attention.[34] In countries such as Britain, Canada, the United States and Israel, the overriding issues of colour prejudice, racism, exploitation of female and child labour, and the perpetuation of inequalities into subsequent generations born in the host countries have caused the notion of immigrant to linger, leading to the term "second generation immigrants." This means that children of widely different cultural and racial backgrounds from those of their "invisible majority" (white) hosts undergo an immigrant experience in which they continue to feel different from, and/or are treated as different by, the dominant culture in which they now live. Without denying the importance of the almost universal prevalence of these issues in the West, I think it is important to consider whether the terms used by social science to describe these social realities actually buttress the very inequalities of which we say we are concerned.

In Israel, research on children of immigrants is especially apparent in the army, the educational system, and in statistical reporting, but it would be considered outrageous if social scientists called such children "second generation immigrants" because it is ideologically incorrect. As it is, the construction of population terminology is a sensitive matter for a lot of people—those who arrived before 1948 are called "veterans" and those who came after are called "immigrants," the latter category being filled largely by Mizrahim. The time period in which a person immigrated to Israel is indeed a matter of prestige—if one fought in the War of Independence, one helped to create the country, or if one stayed in the country during the time of rationing in the 1950s, one is a kind of survivor. Melting pot ideologies (without adequate integration programmes) were intended to do away with the cultural and economic distinctions of time of immigration and country of origin, but as we have seen, this did not happen.

So what do Israeli social scientists call the Israeli-born generation? First of all, *Sabras,* a term reserved only for Jews born in Israel. But further than this, there is the constant interest in parents' country of origin because of the ethno-class relationships which exist in Israeli society. When sociologists are asked if the social gap is diminishing, they are forced to look at the statistical portrait of the Mizrahi generation born in Israel to see if it is catching up to the Sabras of the dominant Ashkenazi culture. But even if they're not asked specifically about this dimension of intra-Jewish relations, sociologists tend to maintain the status quo because they invariably ask the question "What is your eidah" on questionnaires, even when the research subject does not seem to be directly connected to this variable. What this means is that there is a more subtle practice of the notion of "second generation immigrant" in the academic world in Israel today.

The message here is that when asking the question, "Do children complete the immigration process of their parents?," we have to be aware of the ideological and practical significance of the question itself. In the Israeli context, this is a very loaded question, precisely because of ethno-class divisions and ethnic stereotyping. In the context of Israeli society, I shall now address the question of children completing the process of their parents' immigration, the answer arising from the realities of growing up in Gadot.

Growing up in Israel is very similar to growing up elsewhere in the Western world. Formal education up to grade ten is compulsory, but most children complete high school or vocational training, and many go on to study at university level. The fact that there are several educational systems, based upon religious and/or secular curricula is not unusual in the world today. A critical difference, however, is that young people serve in the army, with only religious women and ultra-religious men being exempt from army services.

We have seen much evidence that Yemeni Jewish women of the Israeli-born generation have been able to partake fully in the formal institutions of Israeli youth and young adults. Given the fact that formal Western educational and professional career development were experienced only minimally, if at all, by most Yemeni immigrant parents, it is evident that Israeli-born girls have completed the process of their parents' immigration inasmuch as they fully participate in the major arenas of Israeli society. By all external indicators, these young women can be seen as serious competitors for wealth and privilege in Israeli society, particularly since so many have completed university and have entered professions.

None of this is to say that they have not faced certain obstacles because of their parents' disadvantages as immigrants in Israel, yet these disadvantages have not precluded the Israeli-born generation of Yemenis from achieving educational and occupational success in Israel.[35] Some of this success is due to two factors. One, immigrant mothers worked in paid employment which considerably increased financial resources for the upbringing of their children. The other factor is related to the peculiar nature of Gadot and of its success as an immigrant settlement. The combination of full employment, excellent educational institutions, the stable population base and the covert influence of the wealthy suburb next door promoting upward mobility, among other features, has given the children of Gadot's immigrants a tremendous advantage over those who are generally seen as the "marginal" youth of less successful development towns and lower income urban neighbourhoods: youth who are still seen to be involved in an immigrant experience because they have not yet been able to participate fully as equal and competitive members of the wider (Ashkenazi-Israel) society. It is important to note, however, that while Israeli social scientists have been concerned about the plight of such youth, they seem to blame the cultural backgrounds of Mizrahi parents for the situation of their children; and social scientists are thus not coming to grips with the problems inherent in low socio-economic status, a situation in which the children of many Mizrahi immigrants are the victims. So, while the Israeli-born generation of Yemeni Jews in Gadot are no longer "immigrants" in any recognizable way, this is not necessarily the case for the children of all immigrants in Israel even today, particularly since the indicators of successful "integration" are based on a Western model of achievement.

The evidence suggests, however, a certain paradox: while Gadot's Israeli-born generation can hardly be referred to as "second generation immigrants," as long as young women of Yemeni descent remain unmarried, they insure that their parents continue to have an "immigrant experience." I have suggested above that the immigrant experience can be drawn out for years—indeed, even for a lifetime—if a person's conceptual apparatus is based in the realities of the old country in certain fundamental ways. This is to say that since there is no cultural precedent for the status of unmarried adulthood in Yemeni Jewish culture, finding ways to cope with its existence belongs to the long term process of personal and familial adaptation. The logistics of coping are disclosed in the next chapter.

Once again, this may be the place to bring in the younger Israeli-born mothers in Gadot. They are now rearing a second Israeli-born generation, some in marriages with Jews from cultural backgrounds other than Yemeni. Concerning the families whom I visited often, it took some time for me to identify key aspects of "traditional" Yemeni culture in their family lives. In many ways, with the exception of the colour of their skin, they are indistinguishable from their Ashkenazi peers (and, thus, are very different from their immigrant parents). It is only in religious households (most of the Israeli-born generation in Gadot define themselves as traditional and secular) that some Yemeni Jewish rituals are practised and these almost always pertain to religious observances: diet, family purity rituals, the instruction of sons in Yemeni Jewish religious texts, and the observance of the Sabbath and holidays. Non-religious families have rapidly moved towards the "dominant" Israeli secular culture, although they continue to participate in ethnic gatherings such as hinnot and rites of passage celebrations. However, in respect to child-rearing and health, areas which are still deemed to be women's dominion in the married Israeli-born population, it is possible to find traces of some Yemeni practices.[36]

This brief discussion of the married Israeli-born generation suggests that they do not have an "immigrant experience"; in fact, like their unmarried peers, they are comfortably "Israeli." Yet being Israeli does not mean that a person possesses only one set of cultural characteristics which is seen either as Sabra or Ashkenazi. It usually means that one also has an "ethnic" identity and, possibly, specific cultural characteristics which belong to that identity, along with a deep and all-pervasive identification as an Israeli.

To return to our question, "Do children complete the process of their parents' immigration?" For these Israeli-born Yemenis, the answer would be "yes." The unmarried women of Gadot speak articulately (although sometimes insensitively) about their own parents' immigrant experiences, but any suggestion that they be viewed as "second generation immigrants" would be forcibly (and cogently) dismissed. One feature which makes these young women an unusual subject for anthropological study is the extent to which they are not the "other," that is, they share in significant ways the world view of the researcher. When discussing the ethnic problems of Israeli society, for example, they resort to the same kinds of statistical correlations put forward by Israel's most eminent sociologists. In short, we speak the same language. Here, perhaps, is the soundest proof that to attach to them the title "immigrant" (in terms of a continued sense of strangeness and practical problems) is inappropriate.

Once immigrants from a particular country have established themselves in a new society, they are looked upon as "ethnics," not necessarily by themselves or policy makers, as much as by social scientists. While the concept of *eidahtioot* (ethnicity) is entrenched in Israel, since Jewish society is composed of immigrants, their children and their grandchildren, this is not to say that Jews from over 100 different countries of origin all belong to fully formed ethnic groups; only a sense of difference based upon culture and Diaspora history exists for most people. For the generations born in Israel, ethnic identity is often something rather residual, and, in any event, it is highly situational. This is the case for the young women in Gadot, women whose ethnic consciousness depends upon context.

Being Yemeni is a claim about parents' country-of-origin, what sorts of foods are eaten in the household, the customs used in celebrating Jewish holidays, how they sing and how they dance. As children of Yemeni parents, young women are usually proud of their heritage because this eidah enjoys high prestige in Israeli society. Being Yemeni also means looking like a Yemeni, because of the distinct olive colour, jet black hair, high cheek bones and large brown eyes which mark them off from other Diaspora groups. But such feelings of ethnic pride are coupled with ambivalence about the normative and conceptual conflicts which they experience with their parents. Because their parents were from the Yemen, they also come from a "primitive" background. In Israeli society, the youth conceive of themselves as "modern," holding modern mores and standards of judgement. The debates over the importance of pre-marital chastity and of the residence of unmarried women are just two examples of this; others we consider in the next chapter. In discussions with them, these unmarried women rejected, more often than not, the idea that their upbringing influences them to behave as Yemenis. First and foremost, they consider themselves to be Israeli. Indeed, the younger generation born in Israel do not face the same kinds of conceptual or practical dilemmas faced by their immigrant parents because their recollections of their pasts are not oriented to memories of a Yemen they never lived in, but by the developing standards and expectations of Israeli society. The gap between older parents and their children is not simply one created by "youth culture," as has been said of generation gaps elsewhere in the West, but by a real and pervasive cultural gap between parents and their children who have a completely different orientation to, and experience of, the past. It is to this subject that we turn now.

Notes

1. Most married women of the Israeli-born generation have the same general background as the unmarried women, having roughly the same number of years of education and the same kind of religious-cultural upbringing although half were from towns other than Gadot. Some of these women, particularly those who had served in the army and attended university, also married relatively late

by Israeli standards, that is over the age of twenty-five and had faced similar troubles as their unmarried sisters.

2. Since I left the field in the summer of 1981, sixteen of the thirty-three single women have married.

3. In the United States, while "spinsterhood," whether long or short-term, has generally been a socially recognized (if not a socially desirable category), the opening up of the universities to women in large numbers and women's own commitments to careers have considerably postponed marriage for many women. In the age range 20–24, 36 percent of women were not married in 1960 compared to 28 percent in 1970 in the United States. Popular belief often claims that the use of birth control pills delays marriage because of the new opportunity for "safe sex," or it blames the Women's Liberation Movement. In fact, these factors, along with demographic features, developed together with the enlargement of the *social* category of unmarried women (Bird 1979:27–35).

Israel belongs to the West in terms of its career development patterns, and for the non-religious, the sharing of some general attitudes towards the necessity for marriage (Judaeo-Christian ethic) and, at the same time, the ability to delay it. Yet, for immigrants from pre-industrial societies, delayed marriage is not an acceptable alternative for their daughters and hence unmarried women face more difficulties than those whose parents originate in the Western tradition.

4. In this chapter and the next, particularly in respect to sex and marriage, daughters talk about the stories and gossip which influence their decisions. In the confused context of immigrant cultures, "stories to grow on" are part of a child's life, stories with moral implications related to the way things were done in the old country and to the way things should be done in the new. Kingston's (1975:5) novel of growing up as a Chinese American provocatively questions the value of these stories and she wonders to what they are really related: "Chinese Americans, when you try to understand what things in you are Chinese, how do you separate what is peculiar to childhood, to poverty, insanities, one's family, your mother who marked your growing up with stories, from what is Chinese? What is Chinese tradition and what is the movies?"

5. Older brides, having gained more experience in life, are considered to be more demanding of their husbands. I did not collect evidence which confirmed this belief. But this does appear to be an important theme in "marriage lore" in other cultures. For example, in the quickly changing environment of African towns, women who have had a lengthy education, including training for a career, have passed the normal age of marriage and they become a bad risk in the eyes of potential husbands (Southall 1961:58).

6. Klaff (1977:116) shows that in the early 1960s Yemeni women were the least well-educated in comparison with eleven other country-of-origin groups in Israel (including Turks, Moroccans, Iraqis, Germans and Poles). Hence, the educational achievements of younger Yemeni women in Israel are significantly greater than those of women reared in Yemen and who migrated to Israel.

7. Almost all of the sociological studies of adolescence are concerned with the impact of children's formal education on parental authority (see, for example, White 1977). Seeley (1973:21) aptly criticizes many of these studies as distortions:

they lack "a sense of society and a sense of history." Particularly in immigrant contexts, one must consider the interrelation of power, economic, and ideological structures in order to understand the school experiences of immigrant youth (Allen 1973:53) and their impact on the immigrant family—which is likely undergoing the most dramatic changes of any type of family in a given society (Davis 1939). Fortunately, most anthropological studies of immigrants and their children try to come to grips with precisely these dimensions, and even more recently, have tried to bring to the fore the explicit cultural and racist attitudes of many host societies and their educators (for example, Ballard and Ballard 1977:43–47; Brody 1968; Foner 1978; and Wilson 1978:87–102.)

8. My observations bear this out.

9. In fact, this school is located in the only low-income neighbourhood of Gadot, near the town's centre. The large apartment blocks are subsidized housing for families "blessed with many children," invariably of North African or Turkish origin, where women do not work outside of the home, so the only income is derived from the wages of unskilled husbands and child benefit payments. Given the strong commitment of the local council to good educational facilities, I was always curious about why this school was left to fit the image of a substandard school, related in part to its student population which comes from economically "disadvantaged" (Israeli term) families. I was not able to discover how this was allowed to happen since local politicians and educators were not prepared to discuss the subject.

10. One should note that "boarding schools" in Israel provide an alternative to local public schools for children of all classes since they are heavily subsidized by the government, the religious establishments, and Diaspora charitable organizations. While some are known for their religious character, many boarding schools offer agricultural, vocational, or academic educational streams. Most boarding schools have achieved good reputations and, as socializing institutions, they more than adequately equip their pupils for an independent working life. Some, in fact, are specifically designed for the children of new immigrants, and it can easily be argued that in this context, the boarding school provides the newcomer with a crash course in the values and expectations of Israeli society. See Kahana 1986.

11. Cf. Lewis 1980:21.

12. In concurrence with this study, Jessop's (1981:103) study of parents and adolescents found, particularly on the power dimension in the area of decision-making, that young adolescents begin to seek their independence from the family.

13. Here my data depart from the findings of other studies on the socialization of immigrant youth or Israeli-born children of immigrants in the formal education system. Kahana (1986:28) summarizes the research on this subject, saying that such youth have not internalized the new values imparted to them by their teachers, and, in fact, students' schooling serves to confuse them and create marginality. I am sure this is true in many cases, but, at lease in retrospect, Yemeni young women in Gadot seem to have looked at the choices they had to make as part and parcel of growing up. It may be that the superior educational system in Gadot as a whole, due in large part to its solid economic position

and the influences of the neighbouring upper class suburb, have engendered a different and more positive educational experience and outcome than that known in the more substandard schools in more disadvantaged areas where Mizrahi immigrants predominate (particularly in poor urban neighbourhoods and towns).

14. The importance of this continuous contact with boys from an early age cannot be over-estimated. It is far more difficult to prevent pre-marital sex when contact is continuous from early childhood. In Yemen boys and girls were separated from the time when boys attended school at the age of three. Not sharing the same daily milieu, and living constantly under parental observation enhance the improbability of rules of chastity being broken.

15. Six of the thirty-three unmarried women attended religious secondary schools. Cf. Antonovsky 1980.

16. My discussion with several teachers confirmed these beliefs. Cf. Horowitz 1980; Kahana 1986.

17. Men, both married and unmarried, are called up for reserve duty until the age of fifty-four.

18. Of the twenty-seven women who went to the secular high school in Gadot, twenty-five served in the army. Of the two who did not, one claimed that she was religious to avoid conscription and the other's father prevented her from serving. Of the six women who attended religious schools in Tel Aviv, one served in the army, three in National Service, and two did not serve in either.

19. Nine women are full-time students, three of whom work part-time. The others are in the regular army, either doing conscript duty or as employees of the army, secretarial jobs, teaching, merchandizing, banking, childminding, and for one of these women, prostitution. Of these women, five are also part-time students studying nursing, teaching, accounting, psychology, and biology.

20. Given the high inflation rate, it would be meaningless to report their income in *shekelim*, the Israeli currency.

21. The Yemeni Jewish daughters in Katzir's (1976:244–45) study on the moshav also attended religious schools and the same pattern occurred: "While in the fifties daughters contributed greatly to household labour and in the sixties the working daughters stayed home after work and invested all income in the parents' household, in the late sixties and in the seventies, with mobility, the greater orientation to the towns, the general rise in educational levels of girls, the increase of young women working in the city, and the large numbers of girls in their late teens and early twenties, the contributions of daughters into the household rapidly decreased."

22. In some societies, however, daughters who have received some years of primary and secondary education (and certainly more education than their mothers had received), do contribute their incomes while they live in the parental household. Such contributions seem to depend on the nature of the political economy of these societies: where the family has to provide for most of its social services and parental incomes are entirely inadequate to achieve upward mobility and new consumption patterns, daughters and sons who live in the household contribute their earnings for common consumption. See, for example, Ghana, Azu 1971:107; Morocco, Maher 1978:106; and Hong Kong, Salaff 1981). There

are, apparently, exceptions to this. Wikan (1980:28) reports that in the poorest quarters of Cairo, where poor families must fend for themselves, teenagers who do get jobs spend their incomes on their daily needs and clothing, not making contributions.

23. See Shamgar-Handelman and Belkin (1984) on the utilization of space in large Israeli families.

24. Concepts of honour and shame have been extensively discussed in the anthropological literature. Notable sources are: Campbell 1964; DuBoulay 1974; Dwyer 1978; Herzfeld 1980; Ortner 1978; Peristiany 1965; Pitt-Rivers 1977; Schneider 1971; Wikan 1982; and Wilson 1978.

25. Thirty-three of thirty-five mothers who were interviewed are opposed to pre-marital sex.

26. See Hazleton (1977:125-128) on sexual education courses in Israeli high schools and in the army.

27. For a discussion about the double standards held by Israeli boys respecting ideas about sex, see Antonovsky 1980.

28. Of course the question of who is more in control of sexuality, a man or a woman, differs cross-culturally. For several examples, in Sanani society, it is the women who have "strong sexual impulses which threaten the honour of the male and the integrity of the group," according to Makhlouf (1979:38). In Taroudannt society, men believe that women's sexual passion is uncontrollable, while women "emphasize their own unusual self-control as the element that holds a powerful female sexuality in check" (Dwyer 1978:151). By contrast, the Greek women in Piraeus believe that women control their sexual drive while men's sexual drive is physiologically imperative and cannot be controlled (Hirschon 1978:66-68). Moreover, these data exhibit intra-cultural differences within the Jewish people: folk ideas about sexuality may not be directly related to halakhah, the Jewish code of practice. Halakhah prohibits pre-marital sexual relations for both men and women. It is also prescribed that both should control their sexual desires: a woman must dress modestly so that she will not be pleasing to any man but her husband and a man must not force an unwilling wife to have sexual relations (Feldman 1986:60-80; and Meiselman 1978:116-124.)

29. Adolescents in industrial societies are strongly influenced by their peers to enter sexual relationships. For example, Shah and Zelnick (1981:339-47) found in a nation-wide American study that parents and peers showed very little agreement on ideas about sexual activities, that more young women are influenced by peers who are more permissive than parents, and that adolescent sexual behaviour is consistent with peers. This is not to say, however, that attitudes about sex inculcated during childhood are completely uninfluential once intercourse is experienced, as I show below. For example, Chester and Walker (1980:81) found that when women learned in childhood that sex is unpleasant, they often experience less sexual satisfaction.

30. This section does not discuss Israeli men's views about sex. Hazleton (121) offers an interesting comment which I think has extra validity when men are in the army: "Since their identity as Israelis is strongly linked to their identity as men, the more they can prove themselves stereotypically masculine, the stronger

their Israeli identity becomes. The Israeli man must prove his masculinity time and again; each proof reinforces his sense of national belonging and pride, and his rejection of any 'feminine' qualities within him. His desire for proof is nowhere more explicit than in sexual relations, where it becomes a struggle to master female sexuality, to establish the dominion of the male, and to block this threat to male identity."

31. The main problems that mothers face when trying to impress upon their daughters that this unbroken hymen symbolizes their honour, is that "honour" is now related only to the more ephemeral qualities of reputation and personal integrity. In the Israeli context, it does not have the kind of meaning it had in Yemen, or of which we read in the anthropological literature on honour and shame. That is, virginity has no economic value. Girls are not given in marriage after receipt of mohar: thus there is no property to return if a bride is not found to be a virgin. (Nor do they show a blood stained sheet after the marriage night.) There is little (or less) fear of illegitimate children because of contraception and abortion. Marriages are no longer primarily the joining of two families; free choice of spouse among the generation born in Israel symbolizes that it is now primarily the joining of two individuals. I have yet to hear of a contemporary story in which a girl was really returned to her parents because she was found not to be a virgin upon her marriage. With this in mind, it is easier to understand why some young women in Israel question the fuss made about the importance of pre-marital chastity.

32. Hazleton (134–135) makes much the same point.

33. And yet, by 1986, three of these four women had married.

34. See in particular *New Community,* volumes III, IV and VII. On Asians in Britain: Ballard 1978; Bhatti 1978; Brah 1978; Louden 1978, 1979; and Thompson 1974. On West Indians in Britain: Louden 1978, 1979; Troyna 1979; and Wood 1974. See also Dex 1983; Pryce 1978; Sharpe 1976:229–299; and Wilson 1978.

35. I should note here that I am also thinking of the younger Israeli-born generation mothers who were studied. Like their unmarried sisters, many have also achieved a measure of success, perhaps even more so since they are also married. Of the working mothers, two thirds are in professional or white collar jobs, 20 percent have achieved university degrees, and 28 percent completed twelve years of high school. It is important to note that of the 52 percent of married young women who had only 8–11 years of schooling, most did not grow up in Gadot, but came from entirely Yemeni or Mizrahi moshavim and development towns, thus supporting my contention that girls who grow up in Gadot have more opportunity for formal education.

36. For example, some believe in the evil eye once they have children. Some women use Yemeni spices and pastes particularly when their children are ill. Most women have Yemeni attitudes toward bed-wetting: they believe that when children receive their "common sense," they will stop wetting at night. They are also very permissive with toddlers and pre-school children, unlike the Ashkenazim who are viewed to be over-protective.

7
Proper Conduct and Social Reality: The Immigrant and Israeli-born Generations

Most daughters fail to share their mothers' enthusiasm for early marriage: their primary concern, while continuing to live in the parental home, is to lead an adult life of their own choosing. These daughters chafe against the ideal of absolute parental authority whereby children are expected to be obedient and conform to what is wanted of them. Daughters, these days, have their own ideas about proper conduct which conflict when expectations crystallize in the world that mothers and daughters share—the home—and are made manifest through arguments, debates and interpretations of everyday domestic issues.

Mothers of the immigrant generation had themselves married relatively young by contemporary Israeli standards, between the ages of sixteen and eighteen; a small minority who had married in Yemen had been even younger, between nine and fifteen. After migration to Israel women began marrying later in response to the new rules of the Israeli state, which prohibits marriage before the age of sixteen and because of economic constraints—their labour was needed by the natal family to support it and educate sons. According to the women I interviewed, adolescence did not exist in Yemen, let alone unmarried adulthood—and the women who moved as children to Israel were totally constrained by their natal families.[1] When a daughter married in those days, she put childhood behind her although, as said earlier, it was only by giving birth that she fulfilled her duties as a Jewish woman, to herself and to her natal and conjugal families.

For the immigrant generation, the marriage of a woman's children also bears testimony to her success as a mother—it demonstrates that she has been capable of raising desirable brides and grooms. Children, especially daughters, are not encouraged to wait passively for "luck" to come: by the time a girl reaches eighteen, she is urged to seek out a spouse. As we have seen, arranged marriage is no longer practiced, although members of the immigrant generation were considerably constrained by their parents in their marriage choices. Women of the generation born in Israel, on the other hand, exercise their freedom to meet with men outside the home, and have a wide variety of choices for boyfriends or husbands, many of whom would not meet with their parents' approval. Parents, especially mothers, can do little to ensure the right kind of spouse for their daughters, that is, one who is religious, Yemeni, hard-working, and well-educated. On occasions where mothers suggest that their daughters meet a particular man, daughters' responses are that they will make their own decisions about whom to date. On several occasions, I heard a mother telling her son to arrange a date for his sister, hoping she would listen to her brother if not her mother. This strategy was sometimes successful, but these "blind dates" did not lead to romance or marriage.

Daughters born and educated in Israel have considerable scope for disagreement with their parents and I shall argue that their power to oppose their parents and to construct a lifestyle very different from their mothers' (as unmarried adults) is accountable, at least in part, to the nature of the society their parents joined. If Yemeni Jews had moved to Britain, say, instead of Israel, they might have found themselves having to become heavily involved in their children's marriage choices because the host society would be extremely foreign to them: a society which would see them not only as Jews, but as people of colour. They would probably undergo the same types of problems faced by Asian parents, with their concerns over family honour (and thus honourable marriages) acting strongly to constrain girls' choices, if not to arrange the marriage itself.[2]

For Jewish immigrants and their children, indeed for all Israelis, the subject of intermarriage between eidot is loaded with ideology and prejudice. On the one hand, Israel (for Jews) is a Jewish society, and the statistics on inter-marriage between Jewish eidot have considerable significance when discussing the social gap. This is to say that when the inter-marriage rate goes up (it has been hovering between 17 and 20 percent between Ashkenazim and Mizrahim over the past few years), there is cause for ideological rejoicing because it means that the "exiles" and their children are "integrating" with each other. Yet, the rate of 20 percent is considered by academicians, and popular opinion, to be very low, reinforcing the belief that the cultural and economic gaps between the two dominant ethnic categories are very wide indeed. On the other hand, parents discourage marriage with members of particular eidot; their children often respond by accusing parents of bigotry. In fact the stereotyping of the various eidot is omnipresent among Yemenis and non-Yemenis. In two cases I was told that Yemeni girls found their engagements broken off by men of Polish descent whose parents objected strongly to their sons marrying Yemeni girls—girls who might make good wives, but who were seen to be "primitive" intellectually no matter what standard of education they had achieved. (Nor did the prospective Ashkenazi in-laws want barbaric Yemenis in their families.) Yemeni mothers of the immigrant generation certainly are no better on this account: to marry a Turk is seen as disastrous because they view Turks as drunks, as abusive to their women, totally secular, having bad work habits, and so on. Yet, the marital combination of a Turk and a Yemeni is not rare given the large numbers of both eidot in Gadot. Indeed, there are often serious problems of communication in such marriages, and there were some cases where Yemeni parents stopped speaking with their sons or daughters because of the shame the child had heaped upon them by marrying "down" in this way. Such marriages are not helped by extreme parental disapproval from both sides. Yemeni mothers and fathers are likely to warn their children that marriage with non-Yemenis can bring many problems. And the children, of course, can observe that this is often the case. But daughters born in Israel adamantly claim that they will not be prejudiced in their choice of spouse, as long as he is Jewish and they are "in love," these are reasons enough to marry.

Mothers of children entering their early twenties harp on the theme of marriage constantly, and it is often a source of friction—if not of household warfare—especially between mothers and daughters. With sons it is rather different. Young men in their early twenties, at university, on the point of discharge from the army or barely settled in new jobs, cannot easily afford to "set up house." Parents are usually content for them to wait a while before marriage, especially since they are not overly concerned with their son's honour (that is sex life). However, no such reasons for delay are acceptable in the case of daughters; and even should a woman have a university degree and be in paid employment, it is her future husband who is expected to set up house.

While mothers and adult unmarried daughters are living together in the same home, they endure considerable confrontations—particularly over housework, leisure time, and sexual conduct, and between siblings. Of course, not all households are fraught with tension between the immigrant and Israeli-born generations, and note must be taken here of conditions under which parents and children get along well. It is also noteworthy that mothers and sons do not have the same types of problems as mothers and daughters. Let us start with the conceptual framework which parents use to explain the daily conflicts which beset their families.

Derekh Erets and Interes

When discussing the forces constraining an individual's choices in Israeli society, Yemeni Jews of the immigrant generation say, "What can I do? In Yemen there was Derekh Erets but in Israel there is *interes*." The Israeli-born generation do not use the past in Yemen as a point of reference; instead, they claim "In Israel everyone has interesim (interests)." Parents and children alike joke cynically that only in respect to national security do Jews demonstrate collective concerns rather than individual ones.

For the immigrant generation, Derekh Erets appears to determine an individual's conduct in one's family and community. It requires a person to think of others before oneself, thus it entails the idea of collective responsibility; personal choices should be made in accordance with the wishes of others, particularly parents.[3] It seems, then, that individuality is suppressed as conformity to familial rules is required. In short, Derekh Erets is proper social conduct. Older Yemenis believe that interes is intrinsic to Israeli society. A child becomes *egoisti* because standards of judgement are a reflection of individual concern or of the expectations of the wider society rather than a reflection of the principles of filial responsibility.[4] Children of the Israeli-born generation become self-interested because their experiences in the ethnically-mixed neighbourhood, the school, and the army act to "corrupt" them, detaching them from the values with which they were raised in the home. Interes is seen when children disobey parental rules, when the prescriptions of the Sabbath are ignored; it is behind improper sexual conduct and the avoidance of household chores, and so on. Parents, understandably, associate interes with Israeli society because they do not recall even the remotest possibility of disobeying their parents in the Yemen, and they remember that during their youth in Israel any attempts to rebel against parental rules were quickly dealt with.[5] However, parents' attitudes towards the practice of interes are ambivalent.[6] They strongly recognize that one must be self-interested in order to compete in a capitalist society. (It is likely that their petty-capitalist background in Yemen as artisans and merchants predisposed them to acceptance of the capitalist ethic in Israel even though they had come from a pre-industrial society.) Parents work hard to afford for their children secondary and post-secondary education, viewing higher education as the key to economic security and prestige. But one needs more than formal schooling to gain the necessary social skills which bring about a complete involvement in secular Israeli society; and recognizing this parents also encourage their children to participate in institutions which they themselves view as corrupting influences, namely the youth movement and the army. It seems, in effect, that parents want their children to be Israeli and Yemeni at the same time and to succeed in the world outside the home, but not to discard their heritage, not to forget their values, not to disengage from religious practices, and not to dishonour their parents.

Ironically, parents will sometimes admit (to the anthropologist) they themselves have interesim. Even their concern with filial piety should, in part, be seen in this light: they believe their efforts to help their children obligates the children to take care of them in their old age. However, during the long stage of unmarried adulthood, children often ignore their filial obligations. During this time self-interest wins, but only temporarily. Parents do not fully realize, or are not prepared to admit despite the experiences of other families around them, that married children (*especially* daughters) are more concerned with their parents' needs after they marry than they were in their youth; indeed, after marriage, it is apparent that the Israeli-born generation does believe to some extent in the values with which it was raised in the home.[7]

It is rare to hear Israeli-born daughters employ the concept of Derekh Erets.[8] When they have done something which earns them the parental retort "You have no Derekh Erets," they usually explain their own behaviour by saying that they must assert their own interests. The daughters realize that their actions often conflict with their parents' expectations for them, and they say that they will not be dominated in the way their own mothers had been by their mothers. More often than not, daughters search for appropriate compromises between the conflicting concerns of themselves and their parents. However, the values and norms of Israeli society, as perceived by daughters, still guide them in their choices.

There are concrete areas where Derekh Erets and interes directly confront each other, the most important of which are in housework, the passing of leisure time, and the accommodation of daughters' sexual transgressions. Housework is an essential, and also potentially disruptive, element in the functioning of any household and so deserves special attention. How daughters spend their leisure time says a lot about the quality of their relationships with their parents as does the way in which improper sexual conduct is handled.

Housework: Perennial Problems

In Yemen, Jewish mothers began to teach daughters as young as four light household tasks, not only to help their mothers, but to prepare them to be housekeepers upon marriage. Young girls passed their time playing and helping with housework, and as they grew up they gradually took on the heavier chores, such as gathering firewood and carrying water.

In Gadot, Yemeni daughters also undertake light household chores, such as making beds and dusting, by the age of five. However, they do not do heavy household chores, such as washing floors or hanging laundry, on a daily basis until they finish secondary school. On Friday afternoons, young daughters are expected to help mothers in the extensive cleaning required for the Sabbath. On weekdays, however, girls are expected to study, play, and engage in youth activities, which do not leave much time to help their mothers.

When a girl finishes high school, she is expected to help her mother with all household chores, except cooking the main meals and washing clothes. There is a general division of labour between mothers and daughters, with the heavier tasks progressively falling on daughters as mothers age. Only tasks which require mechanical knowledge are left to brothers and fathers who are also responsible for the occasional jobs of washing windows and shutters, and painting the apartment when required. Routine housework is considered to be "women's work"; while arguments about chores are frequent between mothers and daughters, they occur far less often between husbands and wives, mothers and sons, or fathers and sons because men's involvement in household chores is so limited. Women's work is ideally organized by the mother, but shared between her and her adult unmarried daughters; the ideal is rarely put into practice.

Mothers always do more housework than adult daughters, and most are disappointed that their daughters do not share the burden with them—as they, as daughters, had done with their mothers. Mothers usually rise early, by 5:00 a.m., to cook and launder before they go to work around 7:30 a.m. They wake their daughters before they leave, asking them to do the marketing, to take food out of the oven, to hang out laundry, and so on. Mothers usually arrive home from work at least several hours before their daughters return from work or university, and start preparing the afternoon meal, after which they may take a short nap. Mothers and daughters share in differing proportions the evening chores (when daughters are home); these include cleaning the kitchen, washing floors, and caring for younger children; in most households, mothers toil for two to four hours in the home after work, and daughters one-half to one hour.

Not surprising, in families where mothers and daughters get along well, there is little friction over performing household chores. Daughters help when asked and mothers are tolerant of their "failings." Daughters, in turn, are often prepared to do extra chores to compensate for times when outside work and other activities prevent them from fulfilling their duties at home. For example, when Amalia does not teach or study, her mother prepares the meal while she does the rest of the housework. Her mother praises Amalia for helping, "You have Derekh Erets. As I was a wonderful daughter to my mother, so you are a wonderful daughter to me and your daughter will be to you."

More typically, however, housework is a point of serious conflict—an area where self-interest is expressed *par excellence*. Girls often forget to do tasks mothers have set for them or come home too late to perform them, and quarrels result. Mothers who encourage their daughters to take extra courses or work extra hours, may also reprimand their daughters for not returning immediately from work to help with the chores when they (mothers) are very tired. In effect, mothers defeat their own purpose of ensuring help in the home when they encourage their daughters to experience Israeli society in a way which they themselves were forbidden in their youth. Daughters' rejoinders are hard-hitting, telling their mothers that they should be thankful for whatever help they do get because, in their opinion, housework is the mother's responsibility. Often after arguments, daughters retaliate by refusing to do any housework, including the heavy chores for which they are usually responsible.

On countless occasions mothers in such families asked me if I did not think their daughters were inconsiderate—and self-interested—for not always helping with the chores, and they asked me to speak with them and persuade them to help more.[9] Not once did a mother who was complaining to me mention that she realized her daughter had less time to do chores than she had herself. Although mothers recognize that daughters' work outside the home is tiring, they do not regard it as tiring as their own outside work. Mothers continually complain of their "broken backs" and painful legs (varicose veins) and say they cannot understand how their daughters can act so "sadistically" towards them. To daughters housework is seen as enforced drudgery, and some even say they are tired of "slave labour."

Leisure Time

For both the immigrant and Israeli-born generations days are full of activity: work, studies, housework, visiting friends and families, going to movies, and so on. Yet there is time-off, particularly during the late evenings and, most importantly, on the Sabbath and holidays. Parents expect—or hope—that their grown-up children will display Derekh Erets and spend some of their free hours with them. Among the daughters who spend spare time with their parents are those who define themselves as religious. These girls all enjoy good relationships with their parents who in turn trust their children's judgments which dissipates possible tensions. Such daughters have usually attended religious schools where they have learned their parents' values of Derekh Erets, including respect for elders, the necessity for pre-marital chastity, and to keep the Sabbath Day holy.[10] The Sabbath and holidays are viewed as religious events, not simply as days off. It is a time not only to relax, but to be with one's family; the sanctity of the Sabbath Day reflects the sanctity of the Jewish family. It is on this day, in particular, that religious girls show devotion to their parents.

Occasionally, religious daughters spend the Sabbath with relatives or friends, travelling on Friday morning and returning Saturday after sundown. Often on the Sabbath their friends visit them, and parents do not mind if friends arrive in cars because they realize that to discourage the visiting of secular friends might cause resentment. I found it very pleasant to spend the Sabbath Day with families where both parents and children are religious. There is virtually no arguing, but much eating, drinking, reading, talking, and entertaining of friends and neighbours.

While religious education plays a role in keeping a young unmarried woman in a religious lifestyle, a good relationship between mother and daughter is more important. Religious schooling may help contribute to this relationship through the consistency of values found in school and in Yemeni Jewish homes. Of the six daughters who attended religious elementary and secondary schools, four have continued to be religious. The other two are not and both are suspected of improper conduct by their mothers. From what I could learn, the first indication of abandoning religious ways was their "disappearing" on the Sabbath Day.

One of these two young woman, Rahav, is aged nineteen and the eldest in a family of six children. She studies psychology at Bar Ilan, the religious university. Her mother, Simha, a deeply religious woman, is unlike other women of her age in that she goes to the synagogue to pray every Saturday morning and on all holidays. When I first interviewed Simha, she told me that she was not concerned about Rahav's sexual conduct because she, like all her children, participated in religious "frameworks" in and out of the home. The family always spend the Sabbath together, and during the week often sing and dance.

Several months after the initial interview, Rahav met a secular Polish university student on the bus to Tel Aviv and initiated a romantic relationship with him. As he lived across the street from me, and I often saw them together at his parents' home, Simha soon came to visit me specifically to ask if I had seen Rahav on the Sabbath because she had begun to disappear, presumably with "that Ashkenazi boy." Trying to reassure her, I told Simha that I had seen frequently seen Rahav, sitting on the porch with her boyfriend's parents present. Simha asked me if I would please inform her if I suspected any "immoral" acts, such as driving on the Sabbath or kissing. She believed that her daughter was a "good girl" because Rahav herself had told her mother that she believed it was wrong to make love before marriage. Simha hoped that this boy would not corrupt her.

Simha strongly felt the absence of her daughter on the Sabbath, saying—perhaps to impress me with the necessity of helping her—that the Sabbath atmosphere was ruined. She claimed that until the time of her involvement with this boy, Rahav had been religious. I learned otherwise: Rahav had begun to rebel against parental expectations on returning from her year in Sherut Le'umi in a development town in northern Israel. She and her mother began to argue about her dress— Rahav wanted to wear trousers outside of the home, which is improper attire for a religious girl. This culminated in Simha's cutting up all of her pants. After this episode, Rahav wore skirts to leave the house, changing into trousers on arrival at the university. In fact, on a visit back to the field in March 1982 I met her at her boyfriend's house wearing pants and smoking cigarettes in front of her modestly attired younger sister. It seemed to me that her mother was extremely worried lest Rahav influence the younger children to abandon religious ideals. Other indications of a declining commitment to religious life followed: in 1982 I was informed that Rahav had started travelling on the Sabbath; she also ate bread during Passover—something which even many secular Israeli Jews do not do. She would not, however, forfeit her virginity, despite endless arguments with her boyfriend. Once in the synagogue I asked Simha what she would do if her children became secular, and she laughed, "I will burn them at the stake like witches!"

The second girl who abandoned religion is Michal, eighteen years old and also the eldest (of five children) from a devout family. While believing that she had received a good academic education at her religious secondary school, she rejected religious practices as being incompatible with her ambitions of serving in the air force and becoming a lawyer.[11]

Like Simha, Michal's mother, Ziona, became concerned about her daughter's conduct when she disappeared on the Sabbath Day to visit friends. Ziona complained to me about this, asking me what she had done to deserve her daughter's estrangement from the family. In fact, Michal would spend the Sabbath Day in the home only when I came to visit: we had become quite friendly. Ziona implored me to help reestablish her relationship with her daughter, but was unwilling to tell me why Michal had drifted away from her and the family. Michal eventually told me that it was related to an extremely embarrassing incident at a baby-sitting job some months earlier—an episode I relate below which resulted in Michal's not speaking to her father for over a year.

Michal is an unusual young woman; like all the unmarried women, she is intelligent, but she is also philosophical about her life and the life she intends to live. More so than the other women of the Israeli-born generation, and despite her having just entered the status of ravaka, Michal could predict the consequences of her upbringing and any action she might take. For example, she views her upbringing in a religious home and school as essential to the self-discipline necessary to enable her to complete law school. She also could see that the longer she postponed marriage and the more successful she became as a student and lawyer, the less likely she was to marry. She calculated that she should spend less time with her family in order to learn how to live on her own. Furthermore, she knew that spending less time with her parents would teach them that they would have to pay the consequences—in terms of losing her company and possibly becoming a negative influence on the four younger children—if they continued to pry into her affairs. She recognized that her mother, one of the few full-time housewives in the immigrant generation, did not feel fulfilled in her tasks of looking after her children, despite what Ziona publicly maintained about a woman's ultimate goal. Michal recognized an explicit relationship between honour and chastity, and said to me *before* losing her virginity, "My honour will lie elsewhere, in my successes as a soldier and a professional woman."

Another important feature of Michal's religious and well-respected family is that her father was actually born in Israel to Yemeni parents who had arrived in the 1882 migration. He was formally educated in Israel and has a very well-paid job as an aeronautical engineer, and for this he stands out among his peers. However, despite his position of prestige in the community, he cannot maintain domestic discipline because he works very long hours and thus is rarely home during the week. His wife, who can afford not to work, has sole responsibility for disciplining the children. Ziona, in the "ideal" position as a full-time housewife, wishes to work in paid employment and is studying book-keeping in the hope of getting a job. She told me privately several times that she needs more than just children to fill her life and since in Israel children are self-interested, she better look after herself and find a fulfilling job before they all leave home. What I found fascinating here was that both mother and daughter, while at loggerheads, saw aspects of Yemeni culture—a woman's complete devotion to her family—as inappropriate in the Israeli context.

* * *

In general, young women, regardless of their religious practices, enjoy attending traditional Yemeni celebrations, such as hinnot and special Sabbath gatherings following major celebrations when many friends and relatives gather to eat, tell tales, sing and dance. They enjoy "behaving like Yemenis" in this manner, however, they prefer spending the Sabbath on the beach than with their family and relatives.

Going to the beach on Saturday means travelling by car, which is forbidden by religious parents in accordance with halakhah. The typical pattern for the non-religious girl is that before army service, when she is still largely under parental control, she does not drive, or if she does, she hides this from her parents. Once in the army, children will travel by car on the Sabbath because they are "corrupted" by the secular environment of army life. At first parents become angry and yell at their children, but grown-up children continue to travel with impunity—parental yelling is hardly enough to make them stop driving.[12] Eventually parents stop complaining about travel on the Sabbath because they recognize that their friends' children also drive on the Sabbath and thus their own children are, after all, doing what most young people do. Moreover, they appreciate that young soldiers should enjoy their army leave and this eventually overrides their shame when their children publicly break rules by getting into cars in front of the house early on the Sabbath morning to go to the beach while their fathers walk to the synagogue. Grown-up children, for their part, respect their parents' rules in the home—no one is prepared to ask for the family car on the Sabbath because this is considered too disrespectful. No one smokes in their parents' home on the Sabbath, but some children will turn on lights or the radio after their parents have gone to sleep.

The few non-religious unmarried daughters who enjoy very good relationships with their parents spend the occasional Sabbath in the home because they recognize that their parents enjoy their company. Most "traditional" girls respect their parents' religious lifestyles, so even if they bicker with them, they usually spend holidays at home. By contrast, secular girls spend the least amount of leisure time in the home because they do not feel pressured to be dutiful daughters in this manner.

Young women's self-definitions of religious affiliation—religious, traditional, or secular—are correlated with the quality of the mother-daughter relationship. I have avoided using tables up to now, but Table 7.1 is necessary because it graphically portrays a striking connection.

The thirty-three daughters come from twenty-three families (there are sets of sisters). Nineteen mothers defined themselves as religious, three as traditional and one as secular. We see in this table that when a daughter defines herself as religious, whether she received religious schooling or not, she tends to share a compatible relationship with her mother. Three secular daughters also enjoy good relationships with their mothers, so both religious and non-religious daughters and mothers may share similar values and good relationships. The mothers of these three non-religious daughters themselves are not religious: two define themselves as traditional

TABLE 7.1[13] Daughter's Self-defined Religious Affiliation and Relationship to Her Mother

Relationship to Mother	Religious	Traditional	Secular	Total
Good	4	1	3	8 (24%)
Acceptable	1	4	14	19 (58%)
Poor	0	1	5	6 (18%)
Total	5 (15%)	6 (18%)	22 (67%)	33 (100%)

"Acceptable" means that there are frequent conflicts between mothers and daughters but these are treated as "normal." Yet in comparison to women who have good relationships there are considerably more daily conflicts. Two of these women have relationships which are problematic, but in comparison to the women who have poor relationships with mothers, they fit more neatly into the middle category.

and one as secular. They also happen to be among the most formally educated among the immigrant generation; one had even served in the army. They all have extensive contact with secular Ashkenazim in their jobs—one is a cosmetician with an exclusively Ashkenazi clientele, another is the secretary at the local high school, and the third an office clerk.

These mothers, like their daughters, have had the benefit of nine to twelve years of formal education which has enabled them to achieve high-paying jobs in comparison to others of the immigrant generation. Thus, and critically, their involvement in Israeli society has been of a different nature from the other mothers. It is closer to the experiences of their daughters, and, perhaps, has given them more competence as mothers in the Israeli context. These mothers see themselves as "assimilated" into Israeli culture. Here it might be illuminating to cite what I wrote in my journal after meeting one of these mothers for the first time during an intensive interview:

Impressions: Tzedaka, aged thirty-eight in 1980

> Throughout the entire interview I did not know what to expect from Tzedaka. Some of her answers surprised me, and she knew that. Some answers were typically Yemeni, but I don't think she would admit it. Before I went to interview her, Amalia (my research assistant) told me that Tzedaka has a happy family life, and indeed Tzedaka tried to show me that she does. She told me several times to ask her seventeen-year-old daughter, Riki, who was present about whether or not she (Tzedaka) was telling me the truth. She loves being a mother because she is friends with her children; it is difficult for her to believe she is their mother and not

their friend (she has five children). Indeed, one thing she talked about right in front of her teen-age daughter was her attitude towards pre-marital sex. She said, however, that she herself had enjoyed an intimate relationship with her mother and she could talk about those things. She added that this intimacy of mother-daughter talk is unusual for Yemeni Jews, but she did not know why they were different. She trusts her children; while she is not crazy about pre-marital sex, she asks them to wait until they are at least eighteen and more mature, and to be careful about what they do.

Tzedaka told me that she revolted against her parents (despite her close relationship with her mother) because they wanted her to go to university—unlike other Yemeni families they wanted their daughters not to work, but to study. The family came to Israel in 1945 when Tzedaka was aged three, which she said makes her family different from other Yemenis who came later because the children had the opportunity to get formally educated. She said that she is the black sheep of the family, the least educated with only ten years of education. Her parents expected them to be exceptional, so she revolted against them and stopped studying. Now she is sorry and believes that parents usually know what is best for their children. At the same time, she tries not to demand too much for her children, to believe in their judgement—and never to expect them to do what is asked of them!

Her feelings about being Yemeni were contradictory or ambiguous. First of all she told me that she did not think she could give me a good interview because she is not all that Yemeni, having assimilated into Israel. Yet she cooks Yemeni food, and wants to remember their folklore and traditions. She was quick to observe that had she been raised in the all-Yemeni town of Rosh HaEiyin, she would be more Yemeni because she would not have known another framework. She sees a renaissance of Yemeni culture, a return to roots and wanted to know if I had noticed it. She did not want her children to forget their parents' heritage, but it was most important that they be Israelis first and foremost. . . .

The only "traditional" girl who shares a "poor" relationship with her mother is none other than Rahav who was discussed above. She defines herself as traditional because she continues to relate pre-marital virginity to personal honour, which she herself believes to be a reflection of her religious upbringing. However, she has shown a decreasing commitment to religious values over the years, and this coincides with a deteriorating relationship with her mother, who not only mistrusts her but has tried to punish her for her improper conduct.

It is inescapable to conclude that the sudden break away from home in the army or in Sherut Le'umi contributes to the undermining of the practice of religious precepts, and, in turn, the girl returns home with different expectations from her parents and different preferences for spending her leisure time. However, if a girl does not go to the army, but attends secular post-secondary institutes or travels abroad, that is, if she simply enters an influential secular framework, the same consequences are likely to occur.

Coping with Sexual Conduct

Nothing is so different between the world of the religious Yemeni Jewish household and the secular world of contemporary Israel than the values concerning the proper sexual conduct of adult unmarried women. Outside the home, women who remain virgins by choice are often considered to be "frigid" and are dismissed "old maids." In the home, girls who have sexual relations dishonour themselves and their families, and are sometimes equated with prostitutes. How then, in the light of such contrasting attitudes, do daughters confront their mothers' suspicions and worries about their sexuality and sexual behaviour? For a minority of women who have chosen to commit themselves to religious values, these are non-issues because they and their mothers hold the same values. My interest here, then, is primarily in women who have lost their virginity. Let us begin with how daughters accommodate the concerns of their mothers, followed by how mothers cope with the knowledge of their daughters' sexual conduct.

All daughters know, directly or indirectly, that their mothers are opposed to pre-marital sex.[14] Daughters continually complain about their parents' "ridiculous" expectation that girls remain chaste in "modern" times.[15] Yet, despite the difference of opinion held by mothers of the immigrant generation and their Israeli-born daughters, most unmarried daughters understand the roots of their parents' beliefs, and several even contend that virginity was significant in Yemen because it was yet another way in which men could dominate women. They would relate stories about what happened to unchaste women in Yemen (being stoned, killed, or left to beg) and since their mothers grew up with fears of severe punishment, it is little wonder they worry about their daughters' sexual conduct.

Israeli-born daughters often compare what they consider to be their mothers' archaic beliefs to those of Western Jewish parents. They believe that in Ashkenazi households parents are not opposed to pre-marital sex and that they allow unmarried daughters and sons to sleep with their partners in the parental home. Although there seems to be more open communication about sex in Ashkenazi secular homes, data collected by Israeli sociologists suggest that the differences may not be as great as Yemeni daughters think.[16] It is important, however, that whether such beliefs of liberal Ashkenazi behaviour are true or not, they provide Yemeni daughters with a yardstick by which their parents are judged.

Some mothers and daughters can discuss the daughter's love life— this is usually in cases where the daughters either share the belief system of their parents (that is, in the case of religious girls) or respect their parents' beliefs enough to cover up their improper sexual conduct through the use of "white lies," a form of accommodation for parents' beliefs. Those daughters who want to share intimate knowledge with their mothers resort to the strategy of white lies because this permits them to tell mothers about their private lives while leaving out some sensitive details. For example, Iris tells her mother, Ora, where she is when she stays out all night so that her mother will not worry about her, but when she stays in the apartment of an unmarried man, she quickly adds that she sleeps in his living room, alone on the couch. Her mother believes her and most of Ora's worries concern her younger daughter, Ruth, whom she fears will lose her virginity when she is drunk. However, Ora remains curious about Iris' private life and often tried to eavesdrop when we were speaking in Iris' room. When Ora's presence became obvious, Iris would close the door to her room and then laugh heartily over her mother's efforts to learn about her. On such occasions, she repeatedly emphasized that she must continue to use "white lies" so that her mother would not suspect her of improper conduct and would view her as a *"prima donna."* Another young woman, Malka, said of her mother: "Why upset her? I upset her enough about my political beliefs and my sexual attitudes would shock her. So I simply 'forget' to tell her the details." White lies are seen as a way of reconciling personal freedom with responsibility towards parents, and undoubtedly where daughters are adept at their use, parents worry less about their daughters' conduct.

Some daughters also pretend that they are naive so that their mothers will be less suspicious. They will innocently ask their mothers about how to reject a boyfriend's sexual advance. This embarrasses the mothers, but they try to respond to their daughters' queries, not fully realizing that they are "being had."

By contrast, there are daughters who take no measures to cover up their transgressions of parental rules, often dropping blatant sexual comments in front of their mothers. While Orly is usually considerate of her mother's feelings and uses white lies to ease her suspicions, she and her wayward sister, Anat, sometimes have rather "loose tongues." In one such episode I was shocked over the girls' language at the Sabbath dinner table, albeit in a moment of anger which concluded a week's arguing. Anat asked me about a Canadian male friend of mine whom Orly had platonically befriended. Orly replied, "Go get your own fuck." Anat responded, "I have plenty, thank you." Their parents swore at them in Yemeni Arabic, and no one would translate for me what was said. Their father had told the girls that they would burn in hell, and said that he was going to vomit. He lost his appetite, rose from the table and left the room. Shoshana, their mother, shouted at them for ten minutes about their loss of Derekh Erets, but both girls ignored their parents' protests, not apologizing. An important area of concern here is that, other than verbal demonstrations and the father's leaving the table, the girls were not punished for their bad language. Their brothers remained silent.

Similarly, in another family I observed Rivka's improper conduct flaunted in her mother's face. Rivka was showing me some pictures of her army days. When Hanah, her mother, entered the room and asked to see the pictures Rivka handed them to her mother. When Hanah saw pictures of Rivka half-naked in the kibbutz, she screamed. She told Rivka that a girl must entice a man without relinquishing her honour; if he sees everything before marriage he will not want to marry her. She thought she was adding authenticity to her remarks by attributing them to a "sex doctor." Rivka replied, "So what, it is natural," referring to being photographed and seen in the nude. Later that day Hanah asked me to talk to Rivka about her conduct and explain to her why she misbehaved. Clearly, the daughter's improper conduct concerns not only the fact that she was photographed in the nude, but that she actually showed her mother the evidence of her misconduct.

In these families the mothers know that their daughters engage in improper sexual conduct, but they fail to use any effective sanctions— if, indeed, there are any—to prevent them from doing so. How do other mothers cope with such situations? Nowadays, in Gadot, mothers of the immigrant generation do not disown their daughters should they lose their virginity before marriage; nor do they throw them out of the house after threatening to do so. In view of this situation, it is necessary to ask if there are increasingly tolerant attitudes towards pre-marital sex. Many mothers associate pre-marital chastity with general attitudes towards morality:

> Of course a non-virgin is less moral because she does not respect herself, her parents, or her religion. Furthermore, she is not normal.
>
> Yes, she is less moral. It is important to be a virgin so that one has the trust of one's husband. This is my opinion even if it is not modern. So she should guard her honour. Why? Because if she does not, it is said that she went with many men. They look at her differently. . . . I heard that this is [the same] everywhere.
>
> In my opinion, her value goes down. She is cheap in my eyes. . . .

By contrast, a significant minority of mothers (fourteen of thirty-five), most of whom are very religious, separate morality from the taboo on pre-marital sex.[17] Two ultra-religious women believe that virginity is not connected to morality and that an unchaste girl can continue to be religious. This suggests an increasing tolerance towards unchastity, even though all of these women advocate pre-marital virginity. Two interview responses typical of what seems to be a new trend were:

> The woman is immoral only if she makes herself cheap to every man who asks her. I do not appreciate this. Once in a while, if she really desires a respected man, then I can accept this. But to make herself a prostitute, no. A virgin who gossips and speaks with the evil tongue is more immoral.

> A religious girl can also do this. Virginity and morality are not connected. This can happen to the nicest girl and she can continue to walk the religious path.

In reality, about half of the mothers admit to knowing that their daughters are not virgins, but their behaviour towards them varies considerably. Several mothers attempt to find out about their daughters' activities, viewing everything with curiosity and mistrust. Daughters frequently label such behaviour as "neurotic," and for some other mothers it is, indeed, the cause of psychosomatic illnesses. Other mothers prefer to settle their suspicions simply by asking daughters if they are virgins: daughters reply that they are, but this does not necessarily stop their mothers from worrying about them. Some mothers asked me to find out for them.

There are parents who will actually try to catch their daughters in the act, but these are in the minority. One example of this will suffice: it concerns Michal and her parents and a babysitting incident which took place in October 1980, but which Michal related to me in early April 1981, several months after we met. Her report is taken from my daily journal:

> Michal told me a story which she claimed she could not relate to her friends because they would not understand her good intentions. She has been babysitting for Avigail and Dov, an Ashkenazi couple, for three years, and continued to babysit for Avigail after she and her husband divorced. She considers them close friends . . .

> Avigail took a trip to Europe, so Dov stayed in her house with their daughter. Dov asked Michal to babysit throughout the night so that he would not have to come home. She could sleep in the living room. He told her to ask her mother for permission. She did not think that he wanted to make love to her, so she did not fear asking her mother if she could

babysit throughout the night. When she asked her parents, however, her mother told her that she was absolutely "crazy" and forbade her to sleep there. When Michal arrived to babysit, she repeated this to Dov, and he said that they were naive to think otherwise. She thought that if Dov had asked her parents they might have agreed.

After Dov went out, she went to read in the bedroom because the couch was uncomfortable. Someone banged on the door, and she ran to get it, with her shoes off. It was her parents. They noticed her bare feet immediately and said that if she lost her virginity she would be a prostitute. They assumed that she was waiting for Dov to come home to bed, and that she was not simply reading in the bedroom. There was a big scene and Michal walked out, leaving her parents there to babysit. Dov returned at 2:00 to find her parents there.

Michal was so embarrassed and ashamed that she could not face Dov on the road. She kept saying that the whole episode was a *fashla,* a very embarrassing situation. When she went to visit Avigail, her father followed her to say that he was not allowed to go there any more. She continues to visit Avigail behind their backs . . . she is not of the same "head" as her parents and looks forward to the day when she goes to the army or moves out. Not that they will approve of either event.

Michal told me—and my observations confirm this—that she and her father had not spoken since this incident. Yet her father would buy especially nice clothes for her, which she interpreted as an attempt to buy back her affections. Ziona, her mother, never again mentioned the incident, and she stopped hounding Michal for most misdemeanors, perhaps realizing that to do so caused Michal to become estranged from the family.

The majority of parents, at the level of practice, treat daughters' sexual transgressions with tolerance and accommodation, turning a blind eye. When I discussed this with several mothers, they claimed that Yemenis are different from religious "fanatics" and other Middle Eastern Jews because they are "liberal" in their attitudes towards pre-marital sex, meaning they do not approve of it, but they do not punish their daughters if they engage in it. Such an assertion may be a peculiar characteristic of Yemenis living in Gadot. Several anthropologists who work in homogeneous Yemeni communities have collected cases of infanticide of babies born out-of-wedlock and of severe sanctions imposed on unchaste girls.[18] Only infrequently do such stories circulate in Gadot, which is, in the main, a secular environment and culturally pluralistic, unlike the tightly controlled milieu of an entirely Yemeni settlement.

I discussed above the background of three mothers, two traditional and one secular, who enjoy good relationships with their daughters.

These mothers do not approve of pre-marital sex, but they value an open relationship with daughters on this issue, and do not think that the loss of virginity is, in the words of one woman, "the end of the world." These women discuss the birth control pill with their daughters. It seems that their extensive contact in the non-Yemeni world and their own decisions not to practise many religious precepts may help them in their ability to be understanding of daughters' sexual attitudes and practices. Here are two excerpts from my journal where one woman, Badra, is discussing these issues with her eldest daughter, Penina (aged twenty-one):

> Badra told me that she does not approve of sex before marriage, but one must face facts. Penina was sitting with us through this chat, but she remained silent. Badra does not think that her daughter was on the pill during high school, but went on the pill when she entered the army. She joked that she would not mind if Hagit (aged twenty) went on the pill, if only she would start bringing home boyfriends. She is concerned about Hagit's weight problem and her shyness about meeting men. She does not know what is going on in Hagit's mind and life. Penina added that her sister is somewhat of a mystery. Despite Badra's openness and endeavor to understand her daughters, Hagit is distant to her, but Penina is quite open.
>
> . . . Penina said that she sees her boyfriend too much and wants to see him only once a week. She told me (anthropologist) that she and her mother are always open about sexual relations and her mother directly asks her what she does. Badra told Penina that she would take her to a private doctor to get the pill and would pay for it herself so that this would not appear on her army profile. Badra then said that she feels it is better to be open and know what the girls are doing than not to know. Penina said that it is so nice to be friends with one's mother.

In contrast to the leniency displayed by these non-religious mothers, the others do not discuss sex with their daughters—except to express opposition to it before marriage. However, even these mothers usually manifest flexibility when confronted by their daughters' improper conduct. Several examples are in order here. One mother, Batia often spoke to me of evil young women, that is, those who were unchaste before marriage. Yet it was common knowledge that her oldest daughter, Rina, lived with her boyfriend in Los Angeles.

Closer to Gadot, Batia's next oldest daughter, Tal, was engaged to be married. One Saturday morning during breakfast, Tal's boyfriend walked sleepily out of her bedroom, followed by Tal, in her pajamas, several minutes later. Batia quickly explained to me that his car broke down so he spent the night. She was sure that they did not "do anything." Upon being questioned about this episode, Tal claimed that her mother was so certain that she would marry this boy that she permitted him to stay over frequently. (Batia told me that he slept overnight only once so that I would not spread rumours.) When I asked Tal if they had sexual relations in the bedroom, she replied, "Of course! Are you normal? Could you sleep in the same room with your man and not make love to him?" Batia went to extremes to prevent Tal from dating other men, hanging up the telephone on any man who called for her daughter. Tal believed that her mother could not accept her sleeping with more than one man before marriage, but her mother's actions may simply have been an effort to protect what she thought to be an appropriate match for her daughter.

Of all the cases which I collected, the parents who undoubtedly demonstrated tremendous flexibility over a daughter's improper conduct were the parents of Leah (aged twenty-four) whose child was born out-of-wedlock. Her boyfriend was a criminal, at home on a prison leave when she conceived. The pregnancy was an accident, but a doctor advised her not to have an abortion because he felt that she would have difficulties bringing another pregnancy to term. She decided to marry the father and have the child. The night before the wedding, however, she told a friend that she did not intend to marry him after all because she had decided that she would rather give birth to a "bastard" than to have a criminal for a husband. All of the guests arrived for the wedding but just before proceeding to the canopy for the ceremony, Leah cancelled the wedding. Her parents, deeply religious people, were extremely shocked, and her mother fainted. But they eventually accepted the unwed mother-to-be who continued to live with them during the pregnancy and even after the child was born. The grandmother now cares for the child while Leah is at work. Except for a little malicious gossip about her and the fact that a few people ignore her, no overt sanctions have been imposed on Leah. She continues to work as a secretary in the centre of town, and shows little shame although she is tense. The baby has brought her happiness and she does not regret her birth.

In conclusion, we see that despite mothers' opposition to pre-marital sex, what they actually do about it is a different matter. Punishing their daughters through physical abuse, or throwing them out of the house, can bring the mothers more pain and shame than these responses are worth. I believe they realize this, otherwise their reactions to daughters' improper conduct would be more marked. Moreover, many of their friends are in the same boat; they no longer live in the isolated villages of Yemen or in homogeneous settlements in Israel. They can help cover up their daughters' transgressions simply by ignoring them. For mothers it is a seemingly impossible situation—they fear for their daughters' virtue, and they fear for their own status and reputation in the community. It seems, however, that despite their constant references to the dangers of unchastity, most women of the immigrant generation can cope rather well with their daughters' sexual conduct.

Mothers and Sons[19]

What about boys? In this book they have taken the backstage, not just because our focus is on women, but because it is possible to write about mothers and daughters without reference to their sons, especially since brothers are no longer "noble." That is to say, they are no longer responsible for their sisters' welfare in the case of divorce. There are no good reasons that brothers should be overly concerned with their sisters' pre-marital chastity. Yet, boys obviously have a central place in any family, and mothers of the immigrant generation face specific worries over whether they have filial sons or not.

In Yemen, a woman's life was devoted to preparing her daughter to be a desirable bride and her son to care for her in her old age. In fact, women preferred to give birth to boys rather than girls;[20] After all, daughters left their mothers for their husbands' household upon their marriage. In Yemen mothers indulged their sons, trying to meet all their material wants so that sons would be devoted to them in old age.[21] In contrast to comparatively strict relationships of respect and avoidance with fathers, sons enjoyed their mothers' company, and confided in them as friends. After marriage, sons ideally continued to live in their parents' household or, at least, close by. Thus, even after marriage, sons remained close to their mothers, often to the dismay of their wives, and filial sons took care of their mothers in old age.

This is a somewhat idealized view of mother-son relationships in Yemen, but it provides a powerful model by which mothers of the immigrant generation judge their Israeli-born sons' conduct. In Israel a similar relationship is no longer ensured: sons do not work in their fathers' enterprises and invariably move out upon marriage, if not before. Mothers worry that their married sons will not provide for them in their old age. Of the Israeli-born generation (in this study), the great majority of young men complete secondary education and many study in technical colleges or university. After army service, all work in semi-skilled or skilled occupations, in the regular army as officers, or in white collar professions. In Gadot, most young men are no longer religious, defining themselves as "traditional" Jews, but all spend national and religious holidays with their families, and during holidays they attend the synagogue with their fathers.[22]

* * *

"We treat little boys as if they have no brains of their own," said the mother of young sons. While small boys are raised permissively, as they grow up their behaviour is increasingly controlled and directed towards "becoming a man." Hence, once boys go to school and at least until they reach their Bar Mitzvah age at thirteen, they are constantly told what to do, in what tone of voice to speak, when to ask questions, when to reply, and how to follow orders—in short, to be obedient. When young boys question the authority of their parents or older siblings, a swift rebuke follows and they are often punished for questioning authority.

After their Bar Mitzvah, however, boys are increasingly permitted freedom to do as they please. Religiously confirmed as "men," boys are less easily controlled by their parents, and at the same time, it is expected that as men they will discipline themselves. In the case of the youngest son in a family, even after his Bar Mitzvah, efforts will be made to keep him close to home, and his activities restricted—perhaps because he has so many older siblings telling him what to do. At the same time, the youngest son is more indulged, to ensure his love towards his parents and because they hope that he will care for them in old age—should the other children fail to do so. Also, as the older children are increasingly able to take care of themselves, more attention is given to the younger ones; often more money is available for their education and hobbies.

After boys return from the army, relationships with their mothers are usually warm and respectful.[23] The mother-son relationship appears considerably less problematic than that of mother and daughter precisely because mothers are not terribly concerned about their sons' sexual behaviour or their delaying marriage. Although mothers often tell their sons to act honourably with women, their concern is primarily that he does not get a girl pregnant and be forced into a shameful marriage which would dishonour the family. A few mothers joke about their relief that boys could not get pregnant—they have enough to worry about with their daughters.

It is common for sons to be physically affectionate towards their mothers and hug them in public; this is more readily accepted than the husbands' showing affection to their wives in front of others. Although mothers blush when their sons hug them, they seem very proud of this public display of affection which tells the mother (and others) that her efforts are appreciated and she is loved.

In most families, grown-up sons (married and unmarried) spend many hours discussing personal relationships, politics, household and state economics and other topics with their mothers. They try to explain situations which their mothers find confusing, particularly those having to do with the mother's cultural transition in Israel. Sons may not only tell their mothers that Yemeni thinking is inappropriate, but most will explain patiently why, until their mothers accept—at least overtly—their viewpoints. One example of this "education of primitive parents" is particularly revealing. Nadav, aged twenty-five, told me this story and two days later his mother, Sara, repeated to me exactly the same version of events. The following is taken from my journal:

> After finishing dinner, Nadav walked me [anthropologist] home and we had a long chat about the events surrounding the death of their neighbour's son who had died of cancer at age seventeen. During the funeral procession, many of the old women gossiped about how the mother deserved the death of her son because she had divorced her husband and did not always display Derekh Erets. Her second marriage was to a man with whom she had an affair during her marriage.
>
> Sara told Nadav about the views of the old women, adding that she thinks they might be right, namely, that the mother was being punished for her improper behaviour. Nadav was angry with her for accepting this view, but decided to explain to her rationally why he believed her to be misled, rather than to shout at her that she was "primitive." He had learned by now that Sara could be flexible if he speaks to her in a calm and understanding tone. As Nadav reported to me:
>
> "Why did the old women say bad things about the bereaved mother? Why did they not have pity for her? Because she was divorced . . . I (Nadav) was close to the woman, but not intimately. She told a friend and myself a while back about her circumstances. . . . Until that time we also blamed her for the divorce, but when I heard the whole story, I began to respect her.
>
> "I told my mother that I heard the woman's story. Neither of the two were perfect, but the husband was nervous, crazy, arrogant and sometimes violent. She kept the marriage together until two years ago when her children became old enough to understand their unhappiness. . . . She suffered for years on behalf of her children. Now she is an outcast because they think she drove her husband away. She is not perfect, but she has made sacrifices for her children.
>
> "I explained to my mother that marriage and divorce is one thing, but the death of a child is quite another and nothing can bring the two together. No one deserves to lose a child and only God knows why he was taken in the first place. There are two sides to every story. The couple did not have God's grace, otherwise the marriage would have survived. It is normal for a marriage to break up. I respect this woman because she suffered for her children, and now she will suffer more, the wretched one.

"My mother started crying by the time I was finished and she said that she understood my point and that she would think twice from now on."

There are several points to note concerning this incident. First of all, it is interesting that the old women disapproved of the divorced woman because evidently divorce was generally approved of among Jews in Yemen. Perhaps it was because the woman had an affair with a man during her marriage. Nadav tried to convince his mother that divorce is "normal," that is, it happens, but he did so using an explanation that is grounded in an acceptable cultural framework—by invoking God's grace—and this appealed to his mother's sentiments. He also reminded his mother that she should hear both sides of a story before passing judgement. Secondly, it is significant that Nadav separated cause and effect. The old women's suggestion that the parents' divorce was responsible for the death of the child is an extension of the Yemeni Jewish belief that innocent souls, particularly those of children, are vulnerable to the evil eye and shedim which destroy innocent souls to punish others, in this case the parents. Nadav excluded the possibility of supernatural intervention, arguing that one occurrence was not related to another. Later on I learned that he was able to persuade his mother, who had several miscarriages, that these had not happened because she had behaved improperly.

Nadav and his mother share a very close relationship, nor is this unusual. Like many sons, Nadav confides more about personal affairs with his mother than his father. Mothers, for their part, realize that sons are more intimate with them because fathers are feared and often too judgmental. However, sons do not confide in their mothers about affairs with women, drinking parties, or about their private lives in general.

Sons such as Nadav are seen to be embraced with Derekh Erets. In another family, four young men repeatedly told me how much they loved and respected their mother. They said that she was an excellent mother because everything (meals, laundry, etc.) is prepared on time, she listens to their problems, and she offers advice only when asked. In this family, as in Nadav's, the sons show some acceptance of traditional Yemeni values and these are manifested in their warm and respectful actions towards their parents, in their synagogue attendance on the Sabbath, in their enthusiastic participation in Yemeni celebrations, and in their spending time with their father to read holy scripts—even when they themselves are not particularly devout. This type of behaviour, however, is more noticeable in families where fathers have achieved the respect of the community and retained their authority in the home.

However, there can still be problems over the conduct of sons. For example, the son of one well-respected man who had founded his own synagogue, is a police detective and whose work requires him to work sometimes on the Sabbath. Both parents reprimand him for this practice, and want him to change his job. Despite their disapproval, they are proud of his contribution to the state's security and never fail to tell him so after a major accomplishment. The son says that he likes his job too much to leave it, but he tries to impress on his parents that he does respect them. Indeed, whenever he disagrees with his father or mother, he says, "I respect you because you are my father (or mother). I respect you because you are my elder. But I do not agree with you because . . ."

One problem which causes mothers a great deal of concern and which happens in families where the father has little authority over his children, is that oldest sons do not wish to fulfil the responsibilities assigned to them by parents for disciplining younger children. For example, in Rina's family, Shaul, who is employed by the regular army, refuses to reprimand his younger siblings when he is home on leave, arguing that they should learn to think for themselves. This distresses his mother, who waits for him to come home to help discipline her youngest daughter. Shaul also engages in disrespectful activities in front of his mother—such as sleeping in his bedroom with his Ashkenazi girlfriend; this, in his mother's eyes, profanes the house and, of course, provides a poor example for five younger children. Yet Rina is afraid to complain too much, fearing that he will not visit at all. When mothers discuss these problems, they constantly evoke, as contrast, the respect and devotion of sons in Yemen.

All mothers want their boys to marry, but some regard a son's marriage with ambivalence because they fear losing him to another town or to his wife's family. Usually if sons settle in Gadot they visit their parents frequently; they visit daily if they live next door. Should a married son leave Gadot, it is possible that he visits infrequently and so the fears of some mothers are realized. And, invariably, unless the wife lives next door to her in-laws, a young wife's family is visited more regularly than her husband's whether her parents live in Gadot or not. There is a clear change here from the custom in Yemen: daughters born in Israel are able to maintain close relationships with their parents after their marriage either because they live in the same town or because modern transportation and communication enables them to do so. More importantly, perhaps, sons no longer have the same obligations towards their parents after their marriage, so their wives can pressure them to enter the circle of their own families. Young wives, also, have not gone into marriage upon receipt of mohar and hence they may feel less obligated to their in-laws.

While mothers of the immigrant generation express resentment against their own parents for helping their brothers to settle and not themselves (as indicated earlier) they demonstrate the same pattern towards their own married children. Parents often help newly-married sons to set up house, but not their daughters, still expecting their daughters' husbands' families to do so. I believe that one reason for helping a son financially is to ensure that he will visit them after marriage. Another reason, which is probably not openly discussed, is that helping sons financially to set up their own households will oblige them to help their parents in old age.

Mothers are sad when their sons move out—for whatever reason. One mother, Rachel, was distressed when her son married and went to study in Haifa. While she welcomed marriage, she was upset when he did not visit or forgot to telephone on the Sabbath. Every time she seemed depressed because of this, I reminded her that her son would return to make his home in Gadot, where he was building a house in his parents' yard. Soon her life would be filled with grandchildren. On one occasion, however, after we watched a film on television about children neglecting and leaving parents, she could not be comforted. She said to me, crying the whole time,

> . . . You cannot understand what it is to be a mother, what happens to you when they leave you. . . . Believe me, it was a hard day when Ami left the house after marrying, for both my husband and me. We wanted him to marry and we want the girls to marry, but it is upsetting just the same. When the children are little, they look up to you and there is a lot of joy playing with them. . . . They grow up and troubles begin and eventually they leave you. It is really awful.

Ami, Rachel's son, had not lived in his parents' home for nine years before he married. During this time he had been serving in the regular army. This disturbed Rachel, but not nearly as much as when he married and permanently cleared out his room.

It might be that mothers feel ambivalent about their sons' (and daughters') marriages because the marriage of a child marks the beginning of a new stage in a mother's life. On the one hand, she becomes an in-law and has to learn to cope with new family relationships. On the other, she will soon be a grandmother which usually brings great joy, even if it also indicates that she is getting on in years.

Fears of Old Age

Concern over pending old age is only one facet of the unpredictability of women's relationships with their children in Israel, and in particular with sons. Almost all women express the possibility that no one will care for them in old age. It may be that a documentary series on the abandoned elderly shown over several months on Israeli television created or, at least, intensified this anxiety. Indeed, several daughters told me that their fathers went straight to the bank to open up special accounts for their old age after viewing these documentaries, and some older women discussed the appalling living conditions of the elderly. Perhaps some feared that they too would encounter the same fate.

In fact, such fears are somewhat unrealistic for the women in this study. First of all, unlike some of the subjects of those documentaries, all of the couples will receive pensions which are linked to raises in the cost of living. Secondly, all of them own their homes or apartments, so it is unlikely that they will become homeless. Thirdly, almost all the women live in detached or semi-detached homes, and therefore all have backyards on which houses can be built for their children.[24] If sons or daughters live next door to parents, it seems unlikely that elderly parents will be refused help when it is needed. In such families, that aspect of Yemeni inter-generational relations—mutual help—will continue. For example, grandmothers often do the cooking, while their daughters or daughters-in-law do the heavier task of laundry. By contrast, for those parents who live in apartments or for the few whose children have left Gadot, fears of being left alone after the death of a spouse are somewhat easier to understand. In Israel there is a tendency for children to disperse; they may even leave the country altogether. I knew of several families where at least half the children had emigrated to the United States. In one family, seven of nine children either married and moved to Florida; the remaining two unmarried children intend to emigrate after completing army service. It is possible that their parents will be brought to live with them in Florida, but it is also possible that they may live out their old age without children or grandchildren, and this can mean a great deal of loneliness, hardship, and loss of respect in Yemeni social circles.

Equally, elderly widows living in their married sons' households are not viewed as a desirable part of family life, but as a burden which one sibling has to carry to avoid placing the parent in a home for the elderly. Such elderly widows do not feel welcome and continually complain about how unpleasant their daughters-in-law are to them. This is the reversal of the Yemeni situation where daughters-in-law were subject their mothers-in-law—whatever their moods.

In fact, most of the married children of the women of the immigrant generation have settled in Gadot. Several women even ceased working for income in order to care for their grandchildren when their daughters or daughters-in-law entered the labour force. Women do not take money for this service, but may say that they expect to be looked after in old age. This is not the only motivation for minding grandchildren, however—women feel very useful and happy in doing so, and view it as part of their role as grandmothers. It also indicates that they have achieved enough economic security to stop working in order to enjoy their young grandchildren in a way they could not enjoy with their own children when they re-entered the labour force after each child was weaned. There is little doubt that caring for grandchildren does oblige sons and daughters to look after their mothers and fathers in old age. While trade-offs of this sort were not explicitly expressed during discussions about Yemen, they seem to be more formally negotiated, taking on a transactional character, in Israel—at least, this is what people fear will happen.[25]

I find women's fears about impending doom in old age somewhat enigmatic. There were women who told me that only Ashkenazim have to worry because they believe Ashkenazim throw aged parents into old age homes. Such women insist that among Eidot HaMizrah old people are always cared for by their families. So where do these anxieties originate for other women who express them? First of all, it seems that even if the documentaries on the elderly did not install these fears, they made it easier to articulate such anxieties. Secondly, all these women hear stories of sons failing to adhere to parental expectations—indeed, they feel this keenly when their children are adolescents or ravakim (unmarried adults). Daughters-in-law, however, are viewed as the villains.[26] Thirdly, it seems possible that this is an issue which becomes more salient for women as they pass through the menopause.[27] Fourthly, this may yet be another feature of the long-term immigrant experience. Women who have not yet married off their children or reached retirement age, may have no direct experience of old age in Israel; models of filial duties to elderly parents in Yemen still seem to loom large in their minds. Even so, they know that the Yemeni "reality" of their memories is unlikely to re-establish itself in Israel. They worry about what will take its place. Any attempt at further explanation of concerns on this matter would be merely guesswork on my part because I did not work closely with the grandparent generation, and thus did not learn a lot about their situation as elderly people.

Sibling Relationships

Yemeni Jewish parents hope that the sibling relationship entails mutual help, but, despite mothers' claims that in Israel it is desirable to treat all sons and daughters equally, in practice women try to inculcate the Yemeni system of the older disciplining the younger, and the control of brothers over sisters. In practice, the only families which achieve a system of authority, of the older over the younger, are those in which the father, having achieved a position of prestige in the community, has the self-confidence to enforce his authority in the home. In such cases, the father is able not only to delegate authority to the eldest child, but simply to tell younger children to abide by the wishes of his/her elders. In such families, however, oldest siblings are not necessarily dictatorial; they also help their younger brothers and sisters when they are able.

For example, Ovadia, aged sixty, works in transport, has always earned a good income and, enjoys prestige and respect in the community.[28] He is a patriarch, *par excellence,* expecting his children to follow the paths he has set for them—and to a large extent they do. His wife, Cohava, invariably supports his decisions in regard to their children, and, notwithstanding occasional differences of opinion, his children defer to his wishes.

In this family, all five children get along well. Zahava, the eldest and only daughter, is well-loved by her younger brothers. She helps them with their homework and finances, and babysits for her married brothers whenever necessary. The four boys are respectful of each other and are rarely seen quarrelling. Zahava believes that they are amiable among themselves because they appreciate their traditions; and even though each expresses self-interest, they usually try to be considerate of each other. The family spends every Sabbath and all the holidays together, and Zahava and her brothers often socialize together outside of the home. Indeed, the Yemenis of Gadot praise this family as one "blessed with respectful children"; they represent the Yemeni model of the ideal family.

In most families, however, the father has had some difficulties in adjusting to life in Israel and has not achieved a position of prestige; as I have indicated earlier, such fathers may fail to concern themselves with discipline of children. In these families, mothers look to their older children for help with the younger; this means checking that younger children get up for school, do their chores, adhere to household rules, do their homework, and so on. Mothers expect older children to set good examples for the younger, as well, but in Israel this often proves difficult since children often have other ideas emanating from their own experiences in Israeli society. Furthermore, mothers expect grown-up sons to discipline their sisters, particularly in the realm of sexual conduct— to ensure (somehow) that their sisters are honourable—and in the realm of marriage—to pressure them to marry. It is particularly in these respects that mothers are likely to be disappointed.

Yona moved to Israel in 1948 at the age of eleven, not receiving any formal schooling until she attended adult education classes in Gadot. Her husband, Haim, had been born in Israel to Yemeni parents. His family was so poor that he attended school for only six years when he went to work as a gardener, which remained his occupation. Together they have five children, a son, David, the oldest, and four daughters: Miriam, aged twenty-four, Tamar, aged twenty-three, Bathsheva, aged seventeen, and Sagalit, aged sixteen. Yona and Haim do not enjoy a good marriage because, according to Yona, her husband is lazy and apathetic, spending his free time drinking and watching television. Nor is he interested in disciplining the children. Since the time that Yona decided, after the birth of her youngest child, to take on two jobs, it was necessary for her oldest son to be the disciplinarian of the younger daughters—and he was until he emigrated to London in 1978. Yona firmly adheres to the Yemeni model of sibling relationship based on the authority of the older over the younger children, but the girls do not accept this authority structure now that their brother has left home.

At the same time that David moved to London, the next oldest, Miriam, married and moved to Haifa. She visits the family often, but refuses to participate in the quarrels of her younger sisters because she prefers to have good relationships with all three—and she does. Yona encouraged Tamar, aged twenty in 1978, to become the disciplinarian of her two younger sisters, then aged fifteen and fourteen. Even though it might have seemed simpler to have controlled the girls herself, she said she did not have the time because she had two jobs and began to attend adult education courses.

Yona believes that the troubles in her family began when David left for London. The three younger girls all wanted to contribute to managing the household budget, which had been David's task. Each girl manifested "self-interest" so that when they all sat down to discuss the budget, each wanted money to buy clothes and toiletries rather than to buy items for family use. The mother decided to ask Tamar to budget the finances in order to avoid quarrelling. Since the girls had always respected their eldest brother's authority, Yona assumed that they would respect their sisters—but that proved not to be the case.

Over time, it became clear that Tamar and her next youngest sister, Bathsheva, had not spoken to each other in two years. During the five months in which I visited this family, I never observed the two sisters talking to each other; they were not even willing to leave messages for each other. Yona claims that the brogez began over Bathsheva taking Tamar's clothes without permission, but Tamar maintains that the conflict is more complicated. She believes that she should have the authority to tell Bathsheva how to behave since she is older, and this is expected of her by their mother. However, Bathsheva contends that she is too mature to accept her sister's seniority. Because Bathsheva refused to abide by Tamar's wishes, Tamar does not speak to her. Neither girl seems particularly bothered by this situation, claiming they no longer care for each other. In the meantime, their mother grieves daily over this brogez, and longs for the day when the girls marry and will then be friendly towards each other.

Tamar shares a relatively good relationship with her youngest sister, Sagalit, but she slaps her whenever she misbehaves. Sagalit does not take this passively—she tries to embarrass her mother publicly instead of directly confronting Tamar. She refuses to help her mother with the chores, takes her food in front of guests, and tells her mother to wash her own clothes even when her mother has worked an eleven-hour day. However, when they are not quarrelling, Sagalit seeks advice from Tamar about her boyfriends and they often go shopping together. Bathsheva, for her part, is jealous of their relationship, and often tries to encourage Sagalit to ignore Tamar—she sometimes does.

At the same time, in spite of these conflicts, the three daughters are fond of their mother, taking turns in helping her in her evening job at the local bank. In fact, when she asks the girls to do something for her, they usually listen, but she is absent most of the time. She leaves the management of the household to Tamar because she is so tired, but because Tamar is unsuccessful in getting help from Bathsheva, so she has many chores to do. (This is a main reason why Tamar eventually moved out; she was tired of "slave" labour.)

In this family, the Yemeni model of authority—the older over the younger—has little basis for legitimacy in Israel. The girls' daily activities are not based primarily in the household as was the case in Yemen. Rather they go to work and to school where they are involved with different types of authority; at school, teachers encourage them to speak up for themselves. While Yona's daughters as children were able to accept their brother's authority, as adolescents seeking to assert themselves (while Yona viewed them as requiring guidance), they are not willing to accept the authority of their oldest unmarried sister who had ranked as their equal until the brother left home. The formal authority structure in the family no longer corresponded to the new reality—the younger girls are no longer children but adolescents with their own ideas.[29]

In several families, parents themselves become caught in contradictory expectations because in their natal families in Israel, Yemeni ideals of proper family relations were not followed. For example, in another family where the father usually does not interfere in household battles or in disciplining the children, the mother herself is, despite what she says, confused about who should discipline whom. In Shoshana's family of birth, she was disciplined by her elder brothers (four in all) and sent to work for their benefit. Eventually this subordination of a sister to her brothers, which is typical of the immigrant generation, was turned upside down when she became responsible for the physical care of her aged parents while she and her husband lived with them before moving to Gadot. Shoshana was thus burdened on four fronts for many years: she looked after her brothers, her own small children, her aged parents, and worked full-time. Her husband was having his own difficulties, so she became the only authority figure for her children, but because of the burdens upon her she could not attend to their personal troubles. Her brothers, neglecting their traditional duties, extended little aid. As a result of this eventual inversion of a cultural norm, Shoshana decided to raise her children without gender preferences; in fact, she is particularly fond of one daughter upon whom she relies to maintain domestic discipline when she is unable. Yet, she contradicts herself often, encouraging Natan, her eldest son, to discipline the others, which he usually refuses to do.

Natan, for his part, does not believe that he can influence his siblings, except for the youngest in the family who is the most vulnerable. However, he does tell his sisters, Anat and Orly, to stop being "butterflies" and settle down to marry because he is concerned that the family's reputation is being tarnished by Anat's flaunting of her sexuality and Orly's frequent trips abroad. His efforts are to no avail. Why, rejoins Orly, should she listen to her brother? She argues that he should set an example by settling down himself. As in all the families, the sisters are aware that their maternal uncles often fail to fulfil their mother's expectations for aid and they observe that some young couples do not have any ties with married siblings. They explicitly recognize familial relationships as being guided by self-interest. Nor is there an obvious moral component to unite a sister to her brother, or *vice versa in the Israeli context.* Young women hear stories about the noble brother in Yemen, but they themselves observe that in Israel the noble brother is not so noble.

Israeli-born girls have good reason to disobey the orders of their brothers. Because they often socialize together, the girls know that young men are often involved in activities which are unacceptable to their parents. Girls acquire a great deal of illicit information which could be used to embarrass their brothers in front of their parents. The brothers cannot confront the girls' sexual transgressions more forcibly (other than suggesting that the girls settle down), because they themselves are involved in sexual relationships, in gambling, in snorting cocaine—and they realize that these activities are just as unacceptable as anything their sisters do. Thus these brothers have no virtuous leg to stand on, and while they maintain protective and chauvinistic attitudes towards women, it is possible that there is actually an improvement respecting the "double standards" of which sisters accuse them. It seems that in these circumstances, brothers are unable to punish or reprimand their sisters for activities in which they themselves also participate.[30]

Brothers, too, are involved in the maintenance of a system of "white lies" by which they will present a united front to outsiders. They know that if their sisters are pressured too greatly, they are financially capable of moving out, and they seek to prevent this because they are very concerned about the damage to the family's reputation. Therefore, they often assist in covering up their sisters' transgressions of parental rules. For example, one brother often covers for his sister when she stays away for the night, saying that she sleeps over at his apartment. Brothers often tell their parents that their sisters arrived home shortly after midnight when, in fact, they did not come home until 4:00 a.m.

Almost all families have problems in respect to the desired authority structure among brothers and sisters. Israeli-born children, particularly those who have attended secular schools and have served in the army (especially if in Nahal), derive their models of proper family relationships not only from the social circles of their Yemeni parents, but from friends (and sometimes even army officers), who are neither Yemeni nor religious. Of their friends who come from Ashkenazi middle class families, there are often only one or two children, which perhaps makes for easier parent-child communication than when six or seven children are competing for attention. More importantly, however, in such Ashkenazi families, fathers usually have not suffered from the same kind of immigrant experience as Yemeni men. That is, fathers from Ashkenazi backgrounds usually earn good incomes, have some, if not many, years of Western education, and they are completely comfortable with their (prestigious) place in the ethnic hierarchy of Israeli society. Some Israeli-born Yemeni children told me, with surprise, how their non-Yemeni (invariably Ashkenazi) friends look up to their fathers.

There are two critical reasons that the Ashkenazi families they know appear to be more harmonious: (1) the parental dyad in Ashkenazi families looks to them much stronger than in their own: both parents together discipline their children (unlike in Yemeni families *in Gadot* where mothers usually act alone to discipline their children); and (2) Ashkenazi parents, in these cases, are not religious and so do not judge their children by halakhic imperatives (among Yemenis religious parents often attempt to prescribe halakhic regulations to their non-religious children). So it would look as though Ashkenazi parents have less conflict-ridden relationships with their children.[31] Other cultural factors, however, may be at work here of which Yemeni youth are unaware. For example, when Ashkenazi children *do* disagree with their parents, they may do so when there are no visitors. Whereas Yemeni children, when comfortable around their own friends, will sometimes argue with their parents publicly.

Since in most Yemeni Jewish families in Gadot there is no strong parental dyad, siblings can negotiate parents' demands in their favour; they may even be able to disregard parental wishes with impunity. In spite of the conflict-ridden reality of daily life, Yemeni Jewish parents do not hold a model of parent-child and brother-sister relationships that is open to negotiation—rather they expect that parental authority, or the authority of the oldest child—particularly if it is a boy, should be absolute as it was in Yemen. When mothers complain about these problems, they invariably reminisce about the situation that obtained in Yemen—there, they say, life was simple, there parents were obeyed, and there Derekh Erets prevailed.

Overview

Central to many of the problems discussed in this chapter is the meaning of parenthood for older Yemeni women in Gadot.[32] For the Yemeni-born generation, the parent ideally signifies the embodiment of Derekh Erets, the repository of moral values, and absolute authority over one's children. Will the Israeli children accept this? While children are of pre-school age, this is not so problematic because the child had no choice but to depend on the guidance of parents.[33] However, in Israeli society, social roles are not allocated solely on the basis of kinship and political subordination as they were in Yemen. Rather, children participate in institutions which represent values and norms quite different from those in the home.[34]

What parenthood actually means for many Yemeni-born women is a great deal of frustration and failures to understand why things happen the way they do. The domestic domain is not solely domestic, nor a haven in which parents can be freely Yemeni—it is continually invaded by the wider Israel and its spatial limitations are not as clearly defined as mothers (and fathers) wish them to be. This situation is compounded by their own ambivalent feelings about women's roles: they do not want to be "primitive" or "slaves" as they believe women were in Yemen. And yet, in the home, they are unwilling to give up authority over their children or to redefine sexual codes (sexual codes which their children believe parents are "primitive" for maintaining), and they continually offer strong moral and religious precepts in endeavouring to legitimate their authority. At the same time, when it comes to enforcing the rules which are remembered as having guided parent-child relations in Yemen, or the sanctions which might have been imposed on unchaste girls there, parents are forced to be flexible with their children. They are unwilling to display their children's improper conduct in public. Parents wish to keep children in the home because this is important to the family's reputation, and because their children's companionship and help are dear to them.

Reputation, however, is not the only reason that parents either turn a blind eye, or only verbally reprimand their daughters, when chores do not get done, when there is driving on the Sabbath, or even when girls lose their virginity. There are subtle processes at work which force mothers to question their areas of competence as defined by Yemeni Jews. Being a mother in Israel, for women of the immigrant generation, means that your daughters are well educated, have served in the army (and thus have spent a period of time away from home before marriage), often have a professional presence, and may have travelled the world. There are features of life in Israel, particularly in terms of the opportunities for women, which mothers appreciate and are very proud that their daughters achieve. This is the case even though these same opportunities enable daughters to discard aspects of Yemeni Jewish culture which mothers hold dear. Mothers find it difficult to argue with their daughters on daughters' terms, which are inevitably based on an "Israeli" logic that sometimes escape mothers. In their inability to give credence to their own beliefs and rules, mothers find it necessary to accommodate their daughters' differences of opinion and behaviour.

Mothers' ability to cope, in this particular way, with their daughters' new lifestyles and transgressions, also suggests that they might actually regard their daughters' actions as legitimate in the Israeli context, though they would hesitate to admit this possibility. On the one hand, mothers have also lived a very different kind of life than that known to Jewish women in Yemen, having confronted radical social and economic changes. On the other, their daughters (and sons) are also agents of new attitudes and practices, bringing into the home some essential aspects of what parents see as secular Israel.[35] There are many criteria here of change: language (grammatical Hebrew and contemporary slang); play, including new types of games and children's stories often based on the symbols, heroics, and dramas of contemporary Israeli society (and the wider world as seen on the television); somewhat egalitarian peer groups of girls and boys, sometimes even organized on the socialist pioneering ideology of the left-wing Kibbutz movement, *Hashomer Ha'tzayir*; the values of solidarity with their comrades found in the Scouts, youth movements and the army; the ability to defend one's beliefs (often seen as the "arrogance" of the younger generation Sabra); values of conspicuous consumption; and extremely fashionable dress and cosmetics, and emphasis on creating sexual appeal. While religious mothers, in particular, often look upon these *characteristics* with open approval, they recognize that their *children,* by their conduct, have become an integral part of a new Israeli society. Mothers would not want them to be alienated from their national destiny.

Moreover, Israeli society, in fundamental ways, is also a Jewish society, albeit a very different one from which Jews knew in their isolated communities in Yemen. There are certain paradoxes here: on the one hand, Jewish women knew their place in Yemen, both in their homes and in their political surroundings; they were segregated, as women, from Muslim men and therefore, they did not fear that Muslim society would corrupt their daughters. By contrast, in Israel, they see their daughters as corrupted by a secular, Western society, but this society is composed of Jews. At least, then, their daughters are "corrupted" by other Jewish men and women, and this, I propose, is much more acceptable than if, say, they were living in another Western country where the Gentiles are the ones doing the corrupting and where inter-religious marriages would pose a great threat. I believe that mothers' fundamental wish is that their children will not face the same kinds of difficulties they themselves faced as immigrants. Mothers and fathers worked to achieve "integration" for their children. The price they paid for "integration" has been heavy: children do not see their Yemeni heritage as integral to who they are (at least not while they are single); they discard both Yemeni and religious Jewish practices; they disregard their parents' authority; and they may delay marriage.[36]

Finally, another factor allows parents to accept, at least on the surface, their daughters' transgressions: the softening of community surveillance. Not living in a tightly bound, segregated Yemeni Jewish community, provides enormous scope for manoeuvre. Children's transgressions are often dealt with inside of the household, sometimes meaning that they are not dealt with at all. The critical eye of others is not so readily apparent, certainly not like in the introspective Jewish villages of Yemen. "Gossip" does abound—it is the stuff that lies at the centre of women's conversations—but people carefully choose what to relate. The relaxing of community surveillance even allows *mothers* to "get away with" breaches of religious imperatives: for example, on the Sabbath Eve, after sundown, when their husbands are away at the synagogue, women often watch the Arabic language romance movies of which they are fond. They do this even though it breaks a Sabbath injunction (because it requires using electricity) and a woman has a younger child stand watch for the father who will shortly return from the synagogue. When he comes into sight, the television is turned off, and the husband never knows (or turns a blind eye himself) that his wife has, in fact, profaned the Sabbath. In the privacy of one's nuclear family and nuclear home, a lot of breeches of proper conduct may occur with impunity.

Notes

1. H. Cohen (1973:152) says of Jews in Yemen: "The parents were interested in bringing their children speedily to the stage where they would leave childhood behind, and the child for his part tried to resemble a grown-up by learning to sit quietly, without moving. . . . The kind of education that the Jewish child received, added to the influence of Muslim suppression, undoubtedly had an

effect on the formation of his character, and he generally grew up an obedient individual."

2. See Chapter 4, note 20; Ballard 1978; Ballard and Ballard 1977; Bhachu 1986; Brah 1979; and Wilson 1978:106–120; and on the children of West Indians in Britain, see Sharpe 1976:240–249.

3. An interesting idea to consider is that the ideology of Derekh Erets belongs to the practice of parenthood. Parental expectations that children should take into account others' opinions and not act on their own is common cross-culturally, but by no means universal. For example, since parents sacrifice for their children, parents in working class Turin expect reciprocal self-denial (Pearlin 1974:45).

4. In general, cultures experiencing significant social changes due to the penetration of capital and the consequent increases in material consumption, also face serious difficulties with their youth. Turinese parents, for example, see their children being influenced by strange and new values which belong to materialism, contributing to their children's "moral erosion" and movement away from proper conceptions of right and wrong (Pearlin: 37–39).

5. Even though not using the terms "proper conduct" and "self-interest" to judge children's behaviour, it seems that this distinction is a feature common to many immigrant situations, particularly when children are educated entirely in the host society. Indian and Pakistani families in a Western Canadian city look at dating and romantic love with horror, attributing children's desire for these to the "corrupting influences" of "Western culture" and the media. All evils—youthful rebellion, pre-marital sex, weak family ties, common-law marriages, and lack of respect for the elders—are related to this (Wakil et al. 1981:939). Arab Americans often say that their children are "lost to America" (Elkholy 1976:171). Even in rigidly controlled immigrant communities (those set off by a combination of racial and cultural-religious features seem to be more able to control their offspring because the host society excludes them), where children do accept many family values, such children will nevertheless ask for explicit rationales as they have been taught to in school. South Asian parents do not like this: while they may be sympathetic to children's aspirations, they fear the gossip and critical comment of their ethnic community (Ballard 1979:110–116).

6. Turinese parents also express ambivalence. While they lament the negative effects of materialism on their children, they believe it is important that children should have more opportunities to compete with the bourgeoisie. But this does not mean that children should be "independent" from the family unit, on the contrary, parents want a great deal of control so that they can protect family honour and their daughters' chastity (Pearlin:29–48). Like with the Yemenis, it is difficult to achieve a sense of balance between conflicting expectations, those of the family, and the parents' and children's conflicting interpretations of the wider society.

7. See Gilad 1982, Chapter 8 for a complete composition on this point. Data from Israel shows close ties between the generations (Katz and Gurevitch 1976:34).

8. I did hear this term used more often among younger married women (aged 20–34) who were themselves religious, but never among young women (married or unmarried) who were not religious.

9. I always found myself in an ethical dilemma when mothers asked me for my opinion of their daughters' behaviour, particularly on housework. I honestly said that I was not very helpful in my own mother's house, without saying why. However, I know from my own experience that refusing to do chores is a form of rebellion to parental rules, and that young daughters often do not like to take orders when they are beginning to express themselves as individuals. Moreover, arguments with one's mother over housework might not really have much to do with the mother, but with the daughter's own troubles within herself and with her world; a mother is an easy target on which a daughter can take out her frustrations, often with impunity. Yet I felt it would have been culturally inappropriate to psychologize in this manner with these mothers; I simply agreed that their daughters were self-interested.

10. Of the five women who are religious, all enjoy warm and amiable relationships with their mothers; four of these attended religious secondary schools.

11. Michel did both. She eventually completed law school in 1986.

12. It was often my feeling that parents were not so upset that their children were breaking Sabbath or parental rules, but because they knew that the freedom to drive meant the freedom to spend the Sabbath elsewhere rather than at home.

13. An explanation of the formation of categories in this table is in order. As I said at the beginning of Chapter 6, I did not formally interview the unmarried women. However, I did ask each one about the extent of their religious observances. The evaluation of relationships with their mothers as "good," "acceptable" or "poor" was based on a combination of numerous discussions with mothers and daughters about their relationships and my observations. This table was formed about a year after I left the field, so it necessarily reflects my retrospective evaluations. I considered factors such as frequency, type and significance of conflict; the extent to which daughters helped with housework and childcare; whether or not mother and daughter socialized and shopped together; the terms of affection (or lack thereof) that they used to refer to each other; and their friends' opinions of their relationships.

14. Direct statements include "guard your honour" or "keep away from the boys," phrases also used by some working class mothers in England who say that they will tell their daughters about sex, but these phrases provide the content of the instruction (Kerr 1958:73). In a previous note (Chapter 5, note 13), I drew attention to the cross-cultural commonality of mothers and daughters not discussing, on the whole, sex and menstruation. This is not a phenomenon which belongs solely to "traditional" cultures, as Walters and Walters (1980:814–815) point out: mothers in America generally do not discuss sex with their daughters. Whether the reasons are "shyness" (Kerr:73), the belief that discussion could invite experimentation (for example, believed by Yemeni Jews and Cubans in America, Boone 1980:256), the belief that husbands should provide instruction (Boone 1980), or underlying discomfort of a psycho-sexual sort which is rarely brought out into the open, the taboo on "intimate" conversation about sex seems to be a little researched topic. Caplan (1981) presents some cogent psychological interpretations of mother-daughter taboos on sexual discussion and

physical affection; and she relates these, in part, to unconscious fears of homosexual behaviour. I would hesitate, however, to relate her analysis to the data that I collected in Gadot because this was a realm which one could not easily pry into (outside of the psychologist's office, that is).

15. In secular Israel where sexual purity is not an important value and where young people are expected to meet and pursue one another (Antonovsky 1980; Peres *et al.* 1980:476). it is not surprising that the Israeli-born generation feels this way. However, this is not necessarily a common complaint among children of immigrants elsewhere in the West. For example, it seems that Asian (Indian and Pakistani) children, whether they are in Canada or England, do not view their parents' or community's expectations about arranged marriage—family honour and pre-marital chastity required for both—as primitive, although serious breaches of conduct may occur (but these seem to re-enforce the necessity to abide by parents' wishes) (Saifullah-Khan 1979; Wakil *et al.* 1981; and Wilson 1978:103-120). Once again the factors which encourage children to follow the wishes of their parents seem to be related to their own cultural community's ways of maintaining their integrity of identity (on East African Sikhs in England, see Bhachu 1985:99), of maintaining the economic subjugation of women, of maintaining links with the "old country," and not least, of the host society's attempts to maintain firm boundaries based on race, culture, and class. West Indian black girls, by contrast, often do question their parents' competence to direct their sexuality, yet, they too are excluded from "British society" by race and class. They seem to be more able to question their parents and to question the strongly held value of pre-marital chastity. This may be because the match between values and practice was not consistently maintained in the West Indies (partly resulting from colonialist impingement on family norms, and because unwed mothers often do find acceptance in their families [Sharpe:240-249]).

16. In a discussion with sociologist Lea Handelman, she claimed that most secular Ashkenazi parents do not discuss sexual matters freely with their children or permit intercourse among unmarried partners in the house. By contrast, Antonovsky's (1980:94) research indicates that there is some discussion of these issues: "Those older boys and older modern (Ashkenazi) girls who discuss their concerns and problems with their parents report higher rates of intercourse than those who talk with their parents less frequently. The responses of the older girls from traditional families support the prediction that more communication is related to lower rates of coitus."

17. A methodological note is in order here: It is possible that in response to the question of whether or not non-virgins are moral, women might have thought that I was not a virgin and thus were not willing to insult me by saying that non-virgins are immoral. The women who knew me well did not hesitate to tell me if they thought that non-virgins were immoral, nor did they suspect me of improper conduct as women whom I interviewed on meeting them for the first time might well have done.

18. See Palgi 1975.

19. It is beyond the scope of this book to discuss fathers and sons. Very briefly, sons are considerably better educated than their fathers, and work in

more skilled occupations. Relationships of avoidance and respect are generally typical of father-son relationships, although a minority of sons do not respect their fathers at all and have, accordingly, moved out of the parental house. Unmarried sons who live in the parental home do not hand their incomes over to their fathers as in Yemen, but make token financial contributions towards paying bills. It is understood that a son must save money to set up his own household, so the father stays silent on this issue.

20. While some mothers of the immigrant generation still believe it is more important to give birth to boys than to girls, this is no longer the case for the Israeli-born. Young mothers want a son to carry on the family name, but girls are equally welcome. In Kouvetaris' (1976:178) study of Greek American families, he found that the preference for boys over girls in America changes because: (1) no dowry is given upon marriage (girls are no longer an economic liability); (2) girls incorporated Greek ideals and norms more readily than boys; (3) girls are more attached to their parents; and (4) daughters, not sons, look after elderly parents. In Israel, young mothers see themselves as devoted to their elderly parents as well, but yet another reason to welcome girls as much as boys may concern fears about their sons' military careers: sons face combat and are, therefore, much more likely to be killed than daughters.

21. For other reasons for maternal preferences for male children see *inter alia* Ammar (1954:95-96); DuBoulay (1974:106); Granqvist (1950); and Mynttie (1978:226).

22. The fact that these Israeli-born men are no longer strictly observant is atypical among Yemenis. In homogeneous settlements they are much more likely to be religious; Lewis (1980:16-17) reports that with the exception of army-age boys, all Israeli-born men continue to be religious in the development town where he worked outside of Haifa. There Yemenis maintain a culturally homogeneous ethnic community, unlike the culturally diverse, secular environment which characterizes Gadot.

23. In only two families did I observe sons who were disrespectful to their mothers.

24. Twenty-seven of thirty-five women lived in such homes rather than in apartment flats, admittedly a rather high number. It does indicate, however, that Yemenis preferred to live in what began as two-room semi-detached homes rather than apartments so that rooms could be built on as needed, like in Yemen. Most homes have been enlarged to four or five rooms.

25. The fear of who will care for aged parents may be especially prevalent in situations of social change, particularly when married children set up their own households upon their marriage and may live far away from parents. Pearlin (35-36) writes that economic insecurity encourages Italian parents to nurture family solidarity, so that children will look after their aged parents: "Old age is anticipated with some anxiety because of its economic uncertainties and adult children are expected to maintain an obligation for the care of their parents. This obligation isn't solely moral; it can assume the nature of a calculated exchange." However, we must beware of idealizing the situation of the elderly in preindustrial societies, as Foner's (1984:194-201) critique of modernization

theory points out, stressing that it is too easy to take a "before and after" approach to problems such as these.

26. The viewpoint of the daughter-in-law is often opposite to that held to obtain in such stories. Several young married women said that their husbands want nothing to do with their "primitive" parents or they no longer wished to expose their children to the conservative atmosphere in their parents' home. These women claimed that they try in vain to encourage their husbands to develop better relationships with their parents.

27. I did not learn enough about menopause in the field. Perhaps because of my own youth, it was a subject to which I simply was not sensitive. Also I realized only late in field work that the issue of care in old age is an important concern to many women. I cannot explain why; old age did not appear in my subject index until I had been in the field for ten months. See Datan *et al.* 1981 for an informative study of women in middle-age in five Israeli ethnic groups, and Brown and Kerns 1985 for cross-cultural studies on this topic.

28. While I found that in families where the father had achieved a position of prestige, there was harmony in the family, this was not the case if the mother had achieved a position of prestige in the community. The wide majority of mothers in the immigrant generation are well-respected and well-liked; their efforts of working outside the home and attending adult education courses are widely appreciated in Yemeni women's circles. Most of them, however, have difficulties with their adolescent and older unmarried daughters.

29. Cf. Harris (1969:182) on the age-related aspect of the family authority system.

30. Brothers are no longer guardians of their sisters' honour. It might be that if brothers were still to receive mohar upon the marriage of their sisters, which means that virginity would still be a critical agent in the mohar transaction, brothers might be more energetic about overseeing their sisters' activity. The generation born in Israel does not discuss mohar, except on the odd occasion when they refer to their grandmothers "being bought" in Yemen upon their marriages.

31. I am in no way suggesting that *religious* Ashkenazi parents have worse relationships with their children than the secular. If their children are also religious, presumably they share good relationships like the religious Yemeni mothers and daughters in this study. I am merely making a comment about the importance of the commenserability of values: since most Israeli-born Yemeni children in Gadot do not grasp their parents' religious precepts of way of life, inevitably there are conflicts.

32. See R. and R. Rapoport and Strelitz 1977 on the difficulties and attributes of parenting in industrial societies.

33. To what extent children's experiences in day-care centres affect the long-term parent-child relationship is a scarcely researched subject, but it may in fact have some influence.

34. Harris (1969:180) has found: "Where most social roles are allocated on the basis of kinship, there will be no sharp transition to be made when the child's sphere of interaction extends beyond the nuclear family. Where, however,

this is not the case the child will be confronted with sources of authority which rival the authority of the family itself. The more plural the society and the more individuated the family, the great chance of the values transmitted by that authority being inconsistent with those of the family. . . ."

35. In Elkholy's (1976) study of Arab American youth and their parents, he cites Warner: ". . . the child, not the parent, becomes the transmitting agent of social change."

36. Here, I am referring to the attitudes of parents who have non-religious children only, although even the religious ones think their children should have more regard for *Yemeni* ways during their infrequent arguments. Of course parents do not feel this way all the time, particularly on those occasions when their unmarried children attend the synagogue (on holidays particularly) or hinnot. Lewis (1980) writes of the flowering of Yemeni ethnicity in Israel, claiming that the young have gone back to their roots, particularly in respect to music, dance, and food, but also that they generally share the values of their parents. He writes of this as a country-wide phenomenon, but the people that he studied lived in a relatively homogeneous ethnic enclave. Gadot's Yemeni population is at the opposite extreme. In the next chapter, I will return to Lewis' contentions about the strengthening of Yemeni ethnicity, but I will maintain, more strongly than he, that it is a State supported movement more so than a grassroots one.

8

The Immigrant Experience

In this final chapter I am concerned with aspects of the Yemeni Jews' experience which distinguish them as an immigrant group, both with reference to Israel as a receiving society, and in relation to other immigrant groups within Israel. My discussion begins at the broadest level looking specifically at what differentiates Israel from other Western receiving countries in the world today. I then go to the specific case of Yemeni Jews in Israel where I am concerned with the unique characteristics of the Yemeni Jewish migration, its contribution to Israeli society, and the symbolic construction of the general ethnic identity of Yemeni Jews today. However, I also bring to light certain intra-ethnic differences among Yemenis, concluding that there are significant differences within the immigrant group and among its Israeli-born descendants. Finally, I am concerned with the anthropological lessons which have been generated through the specific study of Yemeni Jews in Gadot, critically commenting upon the general issues associated with the study of immigrant women in general, particularly feminist scholarship and modernization theory.

In a special way, *Ginger and Salt* is a study of a people over time and in place. The historical condition of Jews in Yemen has left its mark on each facet of Yemeni Jewish life in Israel, even thirty years after migration. Although on occasion I have used the ethnographic record to falsify or support the contemporary claims of Yemeni Jews in Gadot, I have been primarily concerned with their perception of the significance of images of social life associated with their home of exile. The nostalgia for, and idealization of, the past might suggest that Yemeni Jews envision Yemen as the "mother country," but, and this is one of their outstanding features as an immigrant group in the world-at-large: it is Israel, the receiving society, that is their "mother country." This paradox has had many implications for their involvement in, and criticism of, Israeli society as they experience it.

As a study over time, *Ginger and Salt* began with a depiction of Jewish social structure in Yemen, and throughout the book, I have described how models of the past have been used by the Yemenis to judge and interpret the realities of their new lifestyle in Israel. I also described the period of immigration itself, the problems faced by new immigrants in the early years after immigration, and issues of status and behaviour associated with the developmental cycle of families in both Yemen and Israel. While Yemeni Jews, as immigrants, confronted dramatically new ways of organizing family and community life, I have nowhere suggested that the social transitions in the immigrant experience were made only during the immediate years after migration. Rather, it was the long-term immigrant experience that caught my attention. I have therefore suggested that as long as people face new situations not belonging to their original cultural and cognitive maps, they are likely to continue to have an immigrant experience. Images and norms are not static, however. They are continually adjusted, or are newly conceived, to comprehend the challenges, disappointments, and opportunities of Israeli society. Yemeni Jews of the immigrant generation would hardly call themselves "immigrants" today; they see themselves as "veterans" compared to the new immigrants who still come daily through Israel's open gates of entry to Jews. Yet, they do see themselves as an eidah, as a people with a common past and a distinctive place in the social fabric of Israeli society.

As a study in place, this work has been concerned more specifically with the place of Jews in Yemen, the existence of Jews in Israel and the unique setting of Gadot in the suburban fringe of metropolitan Tel Aviv. To reiterate briefly, Gadot is outstanding among other immigrant settlements because of its fully employed population, its good educational system, its ability to keep the younger generation in the town, its vibrant political culture, and, particularly, its extremely diverse population who do not maintain ethnically segregated neighbourhoods. As a result of all these factors, the Yemeni Jews of Gadot are both similar to, and fundamentally different from, Yemeni Jews who have settled in many other areas of Israel.[1]

Israel as a Receiving Society

There is no denying the importance of official policy, or the lack of official policy, in influencing the nature of immigration streams. At the very least, centering on immigration policy makes us attentive to important variations in these streams— the extent to which they are legal or clandestine, predominated by single or married migrants, by men or women, by workers or dependents. . . .
—Caroline Brettell and Rita Simon[2]

The most salient features of Israel's immigration policy are that it is inclusive—towards Jews—and exclusive—towards non-Jews.[3] The Law of Return (described briefly in Chapter 3) permitted free access to Israel of all Jews, regardless of class, culture, or country-of-origin. This law was enacted for practical and ideological reasons. On the one hand, with the declaration of statehood, many Jews had to flee Arab lands and there were thousands of Holocaust survivors awaiting refuge. The Law of Return enabled the opening of the immigration gates which had been strictly controlled throughout the British mandate. On the other hand, Israel was created as a state for the Jews, and so an open immigration policy was ideologically necessary. Moreover, the practical consolidation of the Zionist dream required a much larger Jewish population than that which existed when statehood was declared. Population growth was thus encouraged through an unrestricted immigration policy for Jews.

As an exclusive immigration policy, non-Jews, including former residents of Palestine, have considerable difficulty in immigrating to Israel even though the country does provide for naturalization procedures. The particularistic nature of the immigration policy is an example of a fundamental contradiction in Israeli society: Israel is a *Jewish* state, but in its Declaration of Independence it also envisions itself as a *democratic* state. One out of every six Israelis is not a Jew, but an Arab, and Arabs are not granted the same kinds of immigration rights as do Jews. All of this might seem tangential to the women of *Ginger and Salt,* but this context is critical to an understanding of a transference of "cultural other" from Arab to Jew. Firstly, they have gone from Jewish encapsulation as a minority in Yemeni Arab society, to a political economy in which Jews are a majority. Secondly, they need not have much interaction with the Arab minority: the actions and ideas of other Jews, many of whom were also immigrants like themselves, provide the focal points of reference for Yemeni Jews in Israel.

The implications of Israel as a Jewish state are important on other levels as well, further differentiating Israel from the other major receiving countries of the West.[4] For example, even though many countries of the West become havens for some refugees, their immigration policies are intricately involved with their requirements for labour. While the need for labour was a factor in the early immigration of Yemeni Jews to Palestine, the *raison d'etre* of Israeli immigration policy is ideological, not one related to the capitalist labour market—even though the outcome has in fact helped develop the economic infrastructure of the Jewish state. Israel is, above all, a place of refuge for Jews and its immigration policy is designed around the fulfillment of a national destiny, of a new Jewish state in an ancient land. Marxists might argue otherwise, particularly since the open immigration policy enabled the importation of what was to become the Jewish working class, but the sources of working class immigrants have largely been dried up: they are not a renewable resource. There are ethnic-class distinctions in Israeli society, but as individuals better themselves economically, it is not other Jewish migrants who take their place at the lower rungs of the working class ladder, but Arabs. Since the early 1970s, Jewish immigrants have tended to be from the Western and Soviet middle classes, and their entry is not refused on the grounds that other Israelis can perform their jobs—an argument used in the United States and Canada to keep the middle class jobs for resident North Americans, and the lower class jobs, seen as undesirable to many Americans, for poorly educated migrants. Nor does Israel have a temporary migrant work force, female or male, which has characterized the immigrant communities of many Western European countries.[5] Nor does Israel maintain discriminatory policies towards female immigrants; while some female immigrants who are household heads might not be defined as such, this does not prevent them from having equal access to language training, skills upgrading, or formal education as is the case in some other countries.[6] Above all, this is because in Israel women have rights as *Jewish* immigrants which override the fact of gender.

On another level, Israel as a receiving society differs significantly from other Western nations because as a Jewish state, it offers to new immigrants full-fledged citizenship, something that Jews lacked in the Diaspora either because they viewed themselves as a people in exile or because of discriminatory laws and practices. In principle, Jewishness provides the gateway to immediate access to all social institutions, including the armed services.[7] Thus, in 1948, some new immigrants went directly from the boat to the war zone. Perhaps the ultimate proof of Israel's distinction in this respect is that Israelis do not question the loyalty to the state of new immigrants. For example, Lebanese or Syrian or Egyptian Jews would not be put into re-location camps during times of war with Israel's neighbours as Japanese Americans were during the second world war. While eidah figures prominently in daily interaction and in the macro socio-economic inequalities of Jewish Israeli society, there is a perceived common enemy—the Arabs—who cause submersion of internal differences. This fact in the building of nationhood, as an ongoing feature of social and political relations, is of considerable importance for the reception immigrants receive in the Old-New Land.

Nearly every country in the world has, at some time in its history, incorporated foreign-born populations and may have, even at the same time, dispersed some of its own. Few contemporary nations, however, are viewed as essentially "immigrant societies," based upon the hard work and creative energies of newcomers. It is ironic that several of these nations—the United States, Canada, and Israel—have systematically been involved in the politics of displacement of indigenous peoples (native

Indians, Inuit, and Palestinian Arabs). Thus the founding ideologies of these nations have simultaneously taken into consideration and omitted from consideration peoples displaced from their native soil.

I believe that the original (Ashkenazi) melting pot policy (mizug hagaluyot) has to be understood within this context—the forming of a new Jewish nation, however loosely defined, occurred during the period of fighting for the life and legitimation of the nation, a time in which political and military efforts were being extended to displace some (not all) Palestinian Arabs who had been living, for some time, in the ancient land of Israel. The melting pot policy looked in these three directions: to the Arab "other," to the "absorption" of new, largely Mizrahi, immigrants, and to the nation-states of Europe and North America which supported the formation of Israel as a state for the Jews.

The policy of kibbutz hagaluyot, the Ingathering of the Exiles, legislated by the Law of Return, was the blood correlative of the melting pot idea. No Jew would be excluded, yet every Jew was to become the spitting image of the courageous, forthcoming, Western-educated and Western-oriented "veteran" Israeli; in this image—to borrow an old metaphor—the Ashkenazi establishment wanted to create "the new Jew." In Chapter 3 I described why the melting pot policy was transformed into a cultural mosaic, but I did not discuss a relevant feature: in the long-term, the divisive potential of the Jewish religion has contributed to the cultural and political heterogeneity (even among Ashkenazim) of modern Israel. The "secular," albeit devoutly nationalistic, cadres of the Ashkenazi policy-makers seemed to have missed the crucial significance of religious faith in the lives of many Jews, perhaps because many of these Ashkenazim, or their parents, had fled the introspective religious world of the shtetl. While many new immigrants ceased to practise religious rituals on a daily basis, many others did not. The cleavages between the secular and religious, and also within the religious camp itself, are of just as great (if not greater) consequence for the temper and character of the Israeli state as are the ethnic origins (with consequences of class differences) of its Jewish citizens.[8]

Nonetheless, it is appropriate to conclude this section by emphasizing, once again, the importance of the Ingathering of the Exiles, the distinctiveness of the different eidot, and the Yemenis in particular. After the declaration of statehood (let alone during the Holocaust), entire Jewish communities were dismantled, and so Israel became the permanent home of some communities transplanted almost in their entirety, such as Libya, Iraq, and Yemen.[9] Almost every eidah has its peculiar saga of immigration and each makes its particular contribution to the new Israel, whether it originated in the West or the East. Not all, however, share the prominent ethnic platform, rich in symbolism, of the Yemenis who have been highly visible in Israel's historical development since the beginning of the new Jewish settlement in Palestine in 1881, and who have come to have a special role in the implementation of the official policy of cultural pluralism.

Yemeni Jewish Ethnicity and the Israeli State

Basically two kinds of explanations for women's presence in migratory movements are generally put forward, depending on the author's basic approach: most often, female migration is explained in terms of individual motives and personal drives. Seldom is it interpreted in terms of structural factors and social forces that are seen either as incorporating these individual motivations or are mentioned independently from them.

—Mirjana Morokvasic[10]

Where a researcher's "basic approach" is the extended case method or the collection of life histories, it may be difficult to relate individual experiences to a structure of population movement. On the other hand, general statements about the socio-economic features of women in migration, whether originating in the mother country and/or beginning life anew in the host country, seem woefully inadequate when trying to understand the tragedies and triumphs of the migrant story. Ideally, the anthropologist can reach a synthesis of these two approaches, and this has been my aim.

While my approach as a field worker was to rely on intensive interviews, extended case studies and participant-observation, I realized that the Yemeni Jews of Gadot had a history before my arrival and would continue to create a history after my departure. Their history, in fact, led me never to ask the question which leads to the individualistic interpretation of migration movements: "why did you migrate?"[11] The reasons for Yemeni Jewish migration to Israel were already well-documented in the historical literature; it becomes readily apparent that this migration was a truly collective phenomenon, having ingredients of a traditional labour migration and unique characteristics as a Jewish refugee movement (even though several thousand Jews remained in Yemen). This is not to say that individuals do not have their own stories of departure, virtually everyone does, remembering, in particular, those family members who died of disease and malnutrition on the long trek to the transit camps in Aden. Everyone recalls the pain of leaving their homes and villages, their Muslim neighbours, their possessions and their workshops. In their own words, "We left everything." Yet, it is still possible to generalize about these individual experiences, to understand them in terms of the social structure of both Jewish place in Yemen and Jewish longing (across time) for Zion.

The vast majority of Jews in Asia and Africa, like their (now annihilated) cousins in Eastern Europe, were desperately poor and set apart as Jews. The Yemeni story is no exception, and, as I have noted in Chapter 2, Jews lived a precarious existence there. Three features of their lives pushed them to make the long trip to Palestine in pre-state times. Two were their tenuous economic position and their political troubles as a persecuted minority. The economic push is a factor which Yemeni Jews have in common with other labour migrations. Jewish migration to Palestine was foreseen as a betterment of the lot of the Jewish artisan and his family, and I have described that on this account many Yemeni Jewish men initially met disappointment in Palestine. The political factor, being a persecuted minority, they have in common with other refugee movements. The third feature which brought them out of Yemen to a *particular* land, Palestine and then Israel, was a nascent Zionism: the belief that one day they would be free in a reconstituted Jewish commonwealth. The events of the late 19th and 20th centuries enabled this to happen. First, Ottoman control over Yemen and Palestine during the turn of the century opened up immigration channels for Jews, a migration movement which continued illegally when Yemen once again was ruled by the Zaydis and Palestine ruled by the British. Second, there was the creation of a new Jewish settlement in Palestine in which Yemeni Jews played no small part.

The major movement of Yemeni Jews during Operation Magic Carpet (1948–1950) was entirely a refugee movement. Jews did not leave their homes because of dreams of economic betterment in the Promised Land: the wealthy left as well as the poor. Nor did they leave only because of a national vision of the new Jewish commonwealth, although I am certain that most people saw their ascent to Zion in this light. Rather, they were forced to leave because of a transnational conflict, the Israeli-Arab war of 1948, better known (in Israeli circles) as the War of Independence. In response to that war, the story goes, Imam Ahmed permitted the Jews to emigrate. If the Jews of Yemen had not faced the periodic extreme persecutions and had not been so isolated as a Jewish group from other Jews, they might not have left. It took some time, for example, for the Jews of Morocco to come to Palestine, and obviously, the Jews of America find they can live in relative ease and prosperity as Jews in America. For the Jews of Yemen, once they arrived in Israel, there was, and is, no going back; in this sense, they also formed a refugee movement, men and women alike.

For the pre-state immigrants, Palestine, as a political entity, was not a "host society" in any ordinary sense of the term. Jewish settlement had its own quasi-state apparatus—political, economic, educational, and paramilitary—and its own ideological plans. But there was also a Palestinian Arab society, and Ottoman, followed by British rulers. I have argued that the Jewish settlement authorities, while not offering much in the way of practical assistance after arrival in Palestine, did encourage the immigration to Israel to help create an indigenous Jewish working class. It is likely that some Jews emigrated from Yemen in response to pleas such as those by the Zionist delegate Yavnieli (see Chapter 2, Note 32), and to some of these immigrants practical assistance, including cash, was extended to enable them to reach Palestine. The peculiar history of Yemeni Jews, together with their physical contributions to the new Jewish settlement in Palestine, are critical to an understanding of their prestigious ethnic profile in Israel today.

Yemeni Jewish men helped to build roads, construct buildings, and till fields. They also participated in the paramilitary organizations. Women also worked in the fields to help provide for their families, but their major contribution, undoubtedly, was in the reproduction of the labour force: they bore many children (desperately needed by the up and coming Jewish state; even so, this factor is generally omitted in discussions of Yemeni Jewish contributions to the foundation of Israel). At the same time, Yemeni Jews contributed to the creation of a national material and symbolic culture through folklore, dance, music, food and crafts:

> From early in the twentieth century until the 1980s, Yemenite Jews have played a role in the thought and the arts of the Palestinian and Israeli public which is far out of proportion to their numbers. . . . the Yemeni Jews and their culture offered just what the new artists of Palestine and Israel were looking for: an authentically Jewish tradition, apparently very ancient, rooted in the Middle East and the desert. . . . If secular socialist administrators and organizers had problems with some aspects of Yemenite behavior [sic] and culture, and some Ashkenazi rabbis and religious teachers were unable to appreciate Yemenite religious tradition, artists, romantics, those in search of national roots for a new and truly Jewish art, seized upon and supported the arts of the Yemenites.[12]

I turn now to two implications of what might be called state-controlled ethnicity. One is the power of the state to redefine a people's cultural institutions; specifically in regard to gender roles, marriage customs, and occupation. The other is more abstract: the use by the state of "Yemeni" as a symbol of a policy of enlightened cultural pluralism, together with the use to which Yemenis themselves put this situation.

The policy of cultural pluralism, which began to gain currency in the early 1970s, appears to demonstrate a tolerance for the diverse cultural ways of the eidot. Perhaps its most important contribution is that this policy, combined with political pressure from Eidot HaMizrah leaders, has put the history of Jews from Asia and Africa onto the curriculum of Israeli primary and secondary schools; until recently "History of the Jews" meant the study of the Bible and European Jews.[13] The idea of cultural pluralism, however, falls far short of general acceptance of divergent forms of Judaism (for example, the present day controversy over the Jewishness of the Ethiopian Jews). It is a policy that deals primarily with what its critics have called "folklore," that is, the emphasis is on dress, food, dance, drama, and the arts. The promotion of entertainment and the arts is designed to take our attention away from the more serious problems of the ethnic-class relations of Israeli society; the perspective of cultural pluralism does not re-legislate the myriad of (Diaspora Jewish) norms and customs which were outlawed in Israel. This is not to call for a return to child marriage or to political rights only for men: I merely maintain that as a policy "cultural pluralism" is arbitrarily defined and, more importantly, it does not give back to peoples their particular cultural orientations. Israel looks West, not to the Levant.[14]

In reality, the Ashkenazi fear that the new state would become "Levantanized" probably provided the basis for outlawing many practices which immigrants like the Yemenis brought with them to Israel. In effect, the outlawing of polygamy, child-marriages, and other norms, along with the granting of political equality under *secular* law to women, dramatically challenged the authority of Yemeni men over their wives and daughters. Only in the area of family law, which is under the auspices of the Rabbinate, do men still have the legal prerogative over their wives. Thus the state seriously controlled and confined Yemeni ethnicity through the redefinition of marriage arrangements and gender roles, granting women more power relative to their men and children more power relative to their parents. These were amongst the reasons why Yemeni men faced more difficulties in facing the practical and conceptual challenges of the new society: their own areas of control over their families were serious undermined by the Israeli state. Many men, particularly in low status jobs, found haven in reconstructing traditional male study groups and visiting sessions. They managed their loss of control over their wives and children by encapsulating themselves outside some family responsibilities. It is usually only the few men who have achieved a position of status and prestige in the wider society—with the aid of Israeli formal education leading to better paying jobs and their own forceful personalities—who manage to maintain some authority over their children.

Women of the immigrant generation have no desire to go back to the old ways of Yemen in the areas of arranged marriage, mohar, polygamy, and restrictions on their movement outside of the home, seeing such customs as indicators of their subjugation as women. Once again, it is only those men who have suffered in the long term from their ambivalent relationship with "Israeli society" who sometimes remark that "it was a lot better in the old days" (in Yemen).

On another level, as I have argued above, the Yemeni eidah has a symbolic and practical role in state-controlled ethnicity. Since the state has already outlawed the more "primitive" customs of the Yemeni Jewish Diaspora, it has been able to play on the important Yemeni contribution to the building of the state, both on the ground and in its *culture,* to show that it, the state, does not discriminate. As the "darlings of the Ashkenazim" and as economically successful immigrants (due to women, as well as men, working for income)—when compared with the rest of the all-encompassing category of Eidot HaMizrah—the Yemenis are lauded by the state as a prosperous immigrant group.

I agree with Herbert Lewis that Yemenis readily rise to the occasion when asked to perform for the state, whether the performance is directed to its citizens or to its visiting philanthropists from the Diaspora.[15] They do so because their high public profile sets them apart from other eidot from Asia and Africa who have not earned such a prestigious reputation. Their participation in public events also affirms that their heritage is worth maintaining. Hence, they function as a symbol for the state of its successful cultural policy, and as a symbol for themselves as an eidah with a distinctive and special contribution to the history of the Jewish people and the creation of the new Jewish state.

All of this is by way of background in the endeavour to understand another peculiarity of Yemeni Jews in Israel; and that is their constant daily recall of their past in Yemen.[16] This has been a theme throughout the book: Under what circumstances do people use old rituals, beliefs, and models in new contexts? Although it happens in other immigrant groups elsewhere in the world—particularly where colour, race, religion and culture serve to differentiate people from the majority host society—chronic reference to the past is not common to all Jewish immigrants in Israel, whether they derive from the broad categories of Ashkenazi or Mizrahi. Discussions with other anthropologists of Israel, as well as my own experience, have led me to believe that the all-pervasive idealization of and reference to the past—to its rituals and beliefs—does not exist among Holocaust survivors, Moroccans, Libyans, and others. This may be because of repulsive and painful memories of their countries-of-origin (in the case of survivors) or because of low ethnic status in Israel in the case of some Asian-African groups.

At first, wondering why the Yemeni-born generation in Gadot continually refers to their past, I thought in terms of what was wrong with life in Israel. In this regard, I could look to the evidence that life in

Israel remains confusing and full of contradictions for the immigrant generation, and I have contended that many men have faced these dilemmas less successfully than women. But this is also true of other immigrant groups in Israel. Now I have rephrased the question to ask what is "right" for Yemenis in Israel that might lead them to refer to their past so regularly. There may be an answer along these lines: since Yemenis function as the symbol of the successful (Mizrahi) immigrant on a national level, their identity as Yemenis, regardless of what they practice in terms of their original culture, remains very significant for the immigrant generation. The "state" pressures Yemenis to be Yemenis. Their idealization of the past, and their constant reference to it, becomes a part of the "politics of minority ethnicity," a positive statement about their ethnic status in Israel.[17] That is, they separate themselves from other Eidot HaMizrah who, in many respects, are closest to themselves. At the same time, they affirm their cultural integrity and contribution to the state to the ephemeral "dominant culture," Ashkenazi Israel, and to their Israeli-born children.

There is a certain irony here, that the frequent use of Yemen as mother country imagery (not literally as "mother country") is related to the social and ethnic status of Yemenis of the immigrant generation in Israel. In Yemen, Zion (ancient Israel) was the "mother country": the belief that one day Jews would settle in the mother country, Zion, kept Yemeni Jews alive as a people in the face of extreme adversity. In Yemen and Israel, then, mother country imagery functioned/functions similarly for Yemeni Jews, keeping a distinctive sense of identity alive.

And yet, in Gadot, the Israeli-born generation ceases to use mother-country imagery—except to explain the behaviour of its immigrant parents. By contrast, the mother country imagery of Zion served its purpose through 2,000 years of exile.

I am not suggesting that the Israeli-born generation will cease to have an ethnic identity since they do not often use Yemen as a point of reference. Several sociologists have clearly illustrated that third and fourth generation descendants of immigrants in the United States continue to practise some cultural forms of their countries-of-origin, even if they are fundamentally altered to fit life in America.[18] Yet, in the case of many American-born "ethnics," there is the possibility of return to the mother country of parents or great-grandparents, either for a visit or even permanently. The return visit can serve to maintain a distinctive identity in the United States (or elsewhere) and give reason for remaining in the United States.[19] In the Yemeni Jewish case, there is *no* return and this may have something to do with the lack of orientation to Yemen among the Israeli-born. Participating in various Yemeni cultural events does not necessarily mean that the Israeli-born will have an image of the Jewish place in Yemen that is socially relevant to their attitudes and behaviour in Israel.

In the home, use of "mother country imagery" is highly selective, used under particular circumstances. It is most apparent during arguments and debates with wayward children about proper conduct. It is also used to describe areas of change relevant to the working and public lives of women. It is used by men to lament the loss of control over their labour and of their positions as teachers of their sons. And it is used by the Israeli-born generation to explain the habits and values of their parents. Thousands of sentences in ordinary conversation begin with *"B'Teman* (in Yemen). . . ."

The use of Yemen, as a mother country imagery, is seen not only in reference to the Jewish cultural "Others" of Israeli society whether German, French, Iraqi or Tunisian—but as part of the personal politics of one's own familial relationships. With children, in particular, the reference to the way things were done in Yemen is supposed to lend power and strength to parental prescriptions. This strategy often backfires, however, since children draw their legitimacy from Israeli society as they see it.

Since I have argued that the Yemeni Jewish past continues to have an important place in the conceptual organization of the immigrant generation, one may then ask if there is a Yemeni ethnic revival taking place in Israel today as Herbert Lewis claims.[20] Lewis believes that the maintenance of ethnically segregated neighbourhoods, with the synagogue as a main focus of identification and activity, re-affirms Yemeni ethnic identity, even among the Israeli-born. Moreover, updated forms of Yemeni music, dance, and drama groups flourish on a national scale, such as exhibitions, concerts, conferences, ethnic retreats, elaborate hinnot, and other "ethnic" activities. Lewis sees this re-emergence of cultural identity and practices as a grassroots movement, although he mentions that state institutions, specifically the Ministry of Culture and Education and the Histadrut, support these endeavors with encouragement and financial support as part of its policy of cultural pluralism. He claims that Yemenis, more than any other eidah, are prepared to meet the challenges both of their heritage and their Israeli identity—and on the latter account have generally not supported ethnic parties.

Perhaps because I studied Yemenis in an extremely culturally diverse milieux, and Lewis studied a community which was ethnically segregated and concerned about that it remain so, I am more skeptical than he about the ethnic revival as a grassroots movement. First of all, I am not convinced that the reproduction of material culture (or cultures) has critical implications for behaviour in the home or on the street. Secondly, I believe that Yemeni willingness to participate in this revival—and this means the Israeli-born generations—is related to the conscious desire to separate themselves from association with Eidot HaMizrah in the hot ethnic climate of present day Israel. Thirdly, after discussions with Yemenis in Gadot who are active in the national arena and with colleagues who work for the Ministry of Education, I have come to believe that the reproduction of Yemeni Jewish cultural forms is a feature of state-controlled (and largely generated) ethnicity. Israeli politicians, out of necessity, have had to adopt a policy of cultural pluralism. Yemenis, because of their long identification with Jewish settlement in Palestine and perhaps, as Lewis claims, because their *male* folklore and ritual dramas are based on *Jewish* religious themes, almost always figure as the eidah to support when the government and the Histadrut (a quasi-governmental institution) are trying to demonstrate enlightened "pluralism." I believe that some Yemenis are aware of this. For example, upon return from one of these ethnic retreats, women spoke of the Histadrut officials—Ashkenazi—who used the weekend as a ready political platform. In an effort to lure the "ethnics" back to voting for the Labour Party, the officials spoke of the end of the days of discrimination, the beginning of cultural recognition, the "class" interests of Yemeni domestic labourers and road workers, and the education of the Israeli-born generation. Women who were present at the retreat were angry because what was supposed to be a peaceful weekend with friends from all over the country had been turned into a (party) political occasion. Yet, they also realized that they were no longer the passive immigrants that characterized their social station in Israel during the early 1950s. Women, as well as men, argued openly with the Histadrut officials, claiming that their votes could not be bought with promises for a better life like in the old days. One Gadot woman who took the platform maintained,

> I have made it in this country by my own sweat. And now, blessed be the Lord, I rest easily. My house is large, my fridge is full, my children (without the evil eye) are healthy. Only my grandchildren have yet to be born! What do you know of discrimination? In the end, we made our own future.

Before leaving this discussion of Yemeni ethnicity and the Israeli state, I turn to intra-Yemeni differences in Israel. Parminder Bhachu concludes her study of East African Sikhs in England with a statement about diversity among minorities—in respect to culture, class, responses to migration—and she warns against generalizations.[21] An overview of the anthropological studies of Yemeni Jews in Israel points to the same conclusions.[22] The differences in the data collected by Yael Katzir on a moshav in the early 1970s, by Herbert Lewis in an ethnic urban neighbourhood in the mid-1970s, and my study of Yemenis in Gadot during 1980–81 do not result from differences in "theoretical" perspective. Rather they result from three very different kinds of settlement and from a focus on the effects of resettlement on both women and men in the case of Katzir and myself, and only on men by Lewis.[23]

Lewis' study of Kiryat Eliahu, a small city outside of Haifa, has a Yemeni population of 1,300, about 5 percent of the town's residents. Approximately 90 percent of the Yemenis live in one area of town where the original Yemeni residents had settled. Lewis portrays these Yemenis as a reflection of their national stereotype: they are seen as hard working, willing to take any job (menial jobs are not considered shameful by them), religiously devout (they send their children to religious elementary and secondary schools), and they are "contented with little" (which they themselves see as a primary value). Thus Yemeni homes do not have wallpaper, there is a lack of ornaments, the furniture is old and worn, and so, like in Yemen, the rooms are bare. The Yemenis of this town consider the chase after modernity and conspicuous consumption as frivolous. They save and invest their money in their children's education and property. With the exception of adolescent young men who might not go to synagogue, the youth apparently do not question their parents: "parents are honored because it is a tenet of Judaism, but Judaism continues to be respected and practiced in part because of respect and concern for parents. . . ."[24] Fathers (of the Israeli-born generation) continue to have the joy of teaching their young sons religious texts. The Yemeni family, the eidah, and the synagogue serve to reinforce the maintenance of Yemeni values and customs.

Katzir's study of the effects of resettlement on the status and self-image of Yemeni Jewish women in a moshav outside Jerusalem stands somewhere between Lewis' study and my own in Gadot. On the moshav, men have formal political power as household heads, they have their own constellation of activities and they continue to have a strong belief in the values of the old country. Men of the immigrant generation, who comprise the moshav farming households, are somewhat segregated from the society-at-large since they live and work on the farm. Like the Yemeni men of Gadot, these men have lost authority over their children, in part because they do not have an understanding of their children's experiences outside the moshav, whether in school or the workplace. Women, by contrast, were eager to become economically active in the new society, to raise the standard of living of their households, to educate their children, and, in Katzir's words, they "wanted to escape from their past economic subordination and vulnerability in Yemen."[25] Women developed a lucrative retail trade in eggs which they sold in the Jerusalem market and to the private homes of the (Mizrahi) middle class in Jerusalem.

Through this activity, which fits in well with their daily round of responsibilities in housework and childcare, women have a cash income, some of which is spent on groceries, and much of which is spent on the purchase of consumer goods. Women, through their large network and long-term contacts with middle class housewives incorporated what Katzir calls the "middle class housewife model" as their own. This model requires withdrawal from the labour force when it became economically feasible—working women are perceived to be from households of lower economic status, so withdrawal from the labour force indicates economic security. The women, on account of their much greater "integration" into Israeli society than the men, brought new values of material consumption and spending patterns into their homes. Thus, mothers give their children pocket money when fathers do not deem it necessary, and because of mothers' exposure to the more liberal and "modern" ways of their middle class "friends" (clientele), they are more understanding of their children than are fathers. Katzir views women as well as the Israeli-born children as the agents of social change in the moshav. She does not, however, report the extensive kinds of conflicts between mothers and daughters that I encountered in Gadot. The lack of generational conflict may have something to do with the constraints of moshav life, which is culturally and physically distant from the city, and the tightly-knit ethnic community, the fact that few girls went to the army having had only religious schooling and that they marry around the age of twenty as they are expected to—an avenue of mobility out of the moshav.

Lewis, at least in two articles on the Yemenis of Kiryat Eliahu, does not refer to women, except to tell us that the immigrant generation works as domestics and the Israeli-born women aim to be teachers (some may work as domestics while achieving that goal in the university).[26] As a result, we learn of a Yemeni ethnic community bound to the solidary social circles of men. Since Katzir and I both found that women's involvement in Israeli society has had important implications for their relationships with their children, for their ability to produce a cash income and hence to redefine their economic role, and for their own community involvements, it is difficult to believe that the women of Kiryat Eliahu have not introduced cultural changes into their own homes.

A critical difference between Lewis' study and my own is that the men have different concerns about their relative economic and ethnic status in Israeli society. Lewis' Yemenis are proud of their contributions to the state, they do not seem to mind that they perform low status jobs with low incomes, and they enjoy the reconstituted Yemeni social and religious activities. It seems that the tightly-knit ethnic neighbourhood is somewhat responsible for these attitudes: they take refuge in each other, without (Jewish) ethnic "others" looking on. The situation in

Gadot is different in kind. While some men took jobs as unskilled labourers because they had no choice, they now complain about this, referring to the time in Yemen when they were artisans and well-respected for their crafts. Men who have not achieved a position of prestige in the community find a haven in their study groups and qat sessions, as I have indicated earlier, but to the exclusion of everything else that is "Israeli." They are envious of Yemeni men who have succeeded in local politics or in achieving other positions of leadership; this is a situation aggravated by the fact that most of their neighbours in Gadot are not Yemeni and next door to Gadot is Asher, one of Israel's wealthiest communities. So Yemeni men in Gadot are constantly reminded of who they are (or who they are not) in Israeli society, no matter who they once were. Their children look to Israel, not to the eidah, for indications of proper conduct and social status. Men in Gadot, moreover, seem to have suffered from the fact that their wives work for income—this has affected their sense of honour and their image of providers for their families, something not mentioned by Lewis. What is perhaps most revealing in the differences between these two groups of men, is that Gadot men did not speak (at least not to me) of the value of "contentment with little" which Lewis emphasises is central to the Yemeni world view.[27] Indeed, the homes of almost all Yemenis in Gadot have all the modern conveniences, many have wallpaper, all have relatively new living room furniture and dining room sets, that is, they do engage in conspicuous consumption. Their married children sometimes even procure the advice of interior decorators!

This brief comparison of intra-ethnic differences among Yemenis in Israel also leads to the conclusion that the Israeli state has impinged upon Yemeni Jewish culture in different ways depending upon local context. Yemeni Jews have become part of Israeli society in dramatically different ways. Another case in point is how young married couples are, on the whole, no longer religious in Gadot but still devoutly religious in Kiryat Eliahu. In Gadot, for the Israeli-born, belonging to the Yemeni eidah is not the enveloping identification it is in Kiryat Eliahu. For the Yemenis of Gadot, their town is much more open society and this, perhaps, has allowed for more possibilities of self-expression and social change than in the introspective and "closed" ethnic neighbourhood of Kiryat Eliahu.

Issues in the Anthropological Study of the Immigrant Experience

Ginger and Salt brings to the forefront several anthropological issues in the study of migration, the family, and modernization. These issues include: (1) the simple to complex society continuum; (2) the unidimensional nature of "norms"; (3) the shift from extended to nuclear families associated with modernization; and (4) the necessity for the anthropological study of the immigrant experience over time. In this section I comment upon each of these features, but first I would like to mention the contribution of *Ginger and Salt* to feminist scholarship.

Ginger and Salt is, above all, an ethnographic portrait of Yemeni-born immigrants and their Israeli-born children; comparisons with other cultures have been placed in footnotes so as not to interrupt the narrative flow of the text. By and large, the studies of migrant situations to which I have referred are involved in a theoretical tension between the feminist perspective of the authors (a necessary corrective to the strong male-bias which prevailed until recently in immigrant studies), and the familial and societal positions as viewed by immigrants themselves.[28] In this book, I have approached women in terms of their status in the community and the Israeli state, their participation in wage labour and the repercussions this has had in domestic politics, the recognition of gender as of great consequence in the immigrant experience, and the changes in their self-image in Israeli society. If this is to be called a feminist perspective because the focus has been women-centred, then so be it. However, if *Ginger and Salt* has a contribution to make to feminist scholarship, it derives from the viewpoint of the individual women, who do not see themselves as the downtrodden of Israeli society. I conclude that the more data we collect from the contemporary ethnographic scene, the more likelihood that the universal, and ideologically-generated, claims of some feminists will have to be modified.

I had my own lessons to learn in this regard through my field experience. Before going to the field, I was active in the Women's Movement. As a result, I was interested in the status of Yemeni women as domestic workers and their exploitation in the division of labour of Israeli society. I was concerned about their separate and "subordinate" position in the Jewish religion. I was appalled by the conditions of their double work day. However, I was also given strong warning by a senior (male) colleague, that my role in the field, especially the first time around, was not that of social critic or political advocate, but to learn another culture from its own perspective. I followed his advice and eventually I saw things differently, learning of a variety of perspectives among the women studied. The opinions held by younger women closely resembled my own, but their mothers' viewpoints clearly did not. In describing the lives of both generations, I have endeavoured not to privilege one point of view over another, recognizing that the multiplicity of values belongs to the complex social and cultural life of Yemeni Jewish women in Gadot. The anthropology of women has provided the cross-cultural framework, both immigrant and Middle Eastern, in this study of Yemeni Jewish women. However, the anthropological questions which arose during field work and after my departure belonged not to a specific anthropology of women but to anthropology in general. It seemed, at first, that the social life of Gadot did not fit into the analytical frameworks of traditional social anthropology. Gadot, like Israel, is, above all, a developing society, not a "developed" one. The lives of Yemenis, and their children, reflected a field of constantly changing social relations.

* * *

First, it becomes clear from a detailed ethnographic account of Yemeni Jews' past in Yemen and their settlement in Israel, that it would be erroneous to view their immigrant experience as a movement from a simple to a complex society. This is a characterization often made in the study of the migration of "third world" peoples to "first world" nations, particularly in the absence of a comprehensive description of life in the sending society. It is true that differences in the level of technology are readily observable: the Yemenis, for example, were literally flown by airplane out of the fifteenth century into the twentieth. Yet, the Yemeni Jews like most of today's immigrants, come from a highly complex, stratified society in Yemen and moved into an equally—but differently—complex, stratified society in Israel. The receiving society is not seen as the one which must make changes, however: the host society expects newcomers to make modifications in some of their own cultural attitudes and practices so that they can "adapt" to their new homes.[29]

Yemen, as a sending society, can hardly be labelled as "simple" in its social or political organization. Arab Muslim society itself is a plural society, highly differentiated along the lines of Muslim sect, tribe, and region, with extreme disparities between the ruling and peasant classes. Jews were often found in the middle of the country's political turmoil and their status as d'himmi changed in kind depending on whether Yemen's rulers were Zay'di Muslims or the more tolerant Ottoman Turks. Even relations within the Jewish communities were highly complex, particularly since there was no overall centralized Jewish authority, although the rabbinical courts in San'a endeavored to fulfil this role on occasion. Rather, Jewish relations were characterized by extensive economic competition in the Jewish artisan class, competition which required frequent migrations of Jews between towns and villages all over Yemen. The world of women was invariably affected by the insecure position of Jews within the Yemeni state and by their own migrations, within Yemen, with their menfolk. Yet, like Muslim women, they were forbidden to have a public profile and it seems that their lot was characterized by a marked degree of lack of choice—not that Jewish men were much better off.

Israel manifests complexities of a different nature; Yemeni Jews in Israel participate in numerous kinds of relationships—some which appear only in stereotypical images, others of which belong to daily interaction. Thus, their formal political relations with Arabs have switched to one in which Jews are dominant. Of more direct consequence to their daily lives, Yemeni Jews in Gadot are concerned about intra-Jewish relations, particularly about the (perceived) religious versus secular norms and institutions which have enormous implications for their relationships with their Israeli-born children. By and large, religious Ashkenazim do not come into frequent contact with Yemenis in Gadot, but they are people whom Yemenis generally admire. By contrast, Yemeni women have extensive contact with their Ashkenazi employers, their own adult education teachers, the teachers of their children, their children's friends, and their own Ashkenazi neighbours. Perceptions of Ashkenazi female culture have become a yardstick by which Yemeni women measure their own behaviour and that of their children, but I have suggested that their perceptions are not based on a tradition-to-modernity continuum. That is, Yemeni women do not accept a total Ashkenazi package, rejecting values such as the trend towards secular Judaism, the move to smaller families, the acceptability of pre-marital sex, and so on. But they do have other aspirations which probably originated in an "Ashkenazi" (that is, Western European) context and yet have become their own: for example, higher education, entry of women into the professions, control over their own income, and for some women, cessation of the practice of family purity rituals.

Yemeni Jews in Israel are also engaged in class relations, and these are related both to the symbolic content of their relationships with Ashkenazim, and their images of themselves as middle class as compared with less fortunate people in general. Yemeni men and women of the immigrant generation fulfil unskilled and skilled labour positions, and they see this as a natural, if not a regrettable aspect of their inferior skills in Israel. Yet, their low income jobs have not prevented them from upward mobility in Israel, as is evidenced by their economic security and their own children's successes. Indeed, almost all women, when asked to which class they belong, define themselves as "middle class" even though they fulfil traditionally working class positions. They point to their comfortable homes and their ability to support their large families as evidence of a middle class standard of living. They may not take trips to Europe like the Ashkenazi middle class, but they do save their income, investing it in (besides their homes) their children's education and in helping to purchase apartments for their newly married children. Their married children (both in the skilled and white collar professions), however, belong to the stereotypical middle class: they *do* vacation in Europe.

Not least, parents and children in Israel live separately in a plurality of worlds. They come together in the home, where their disparate and varied experiences in the work place, friendship circles, and schools or army meet and confront each other. The home itself, then, is a microcosm of the diversity and complexity of Israeli society. The two worlds of Yemen and Israel are not really comparable, even if Yemeni Jews themselves make comparisons daily. In sociological perspective, Yemen and Israel exist in two different political, economic and technological epochs. Yemeni Jews have not gone from a simple to a complex society, but from one form of complex relations to another. However, the Yemeni Jewish historical experience of flexibility is seen as the predecessor for their ability to modify their culture and behaviour to meet the constraints and approach the challenges of Israeli society.

Ginger and Salt is also a story about contradictions and how people cope with them. These themes belong to the question concerning what makes for the ability to accommodate conflicting imperatives—those dictated by the past and those that belong to the present. I have suggested that contradiction has become a "normal" part of the routine cognitive efforts and social actions of the immigrant generation, but less so for their children who have grown up with the ways of Israeli society. The constant flow of contradiction, however, does not necessarily belong to the accepted wisdom of anthropological notions of culture. What becomes strikingly clear in the study of the long-term immigrant experience is that parents and children do not share the same culture even while they live together: they have different expectations, sentiments, interpretations, and even customs. Furthermore, in the study of individual people, it becomes evident that not all immigrants have had the same kinds of experiences in Israeli society. Of the many families I knew in Gadot, I never found a "typical" one although Yemeni Jews of the immigrant generation certainly have definite models of the ideal family. The type of person a woman is, or becomes, depends on her experiences in her natal family (with her siblings as well as with her parents), the character of the town or village in which she was raised, her level of education, her experiences in the army, her husband's character and social position (in the case of married women), as well as upon the specificities of her individual personality: her intelligence, flexibility, capacity for understanding the needs of others, and so on.

Belonging to the complex character of Israeli society are not only the transnational dispute, the ethnic-class distinctions, the religious-secular rifts, the ideological rainbow, but also the influences of cultural and social norms of the West and Middle East. These make for a situation in which many different points of view and expectations for behaviour exist simultaneously. Therefore, Yemeni Jews and their children cannot be expected to have an intact belief system; it would be a misleading premise, for a people in flux, to think that they do or will. However, since for Jews Israel is a Jewish society, the toss up of norms—and the ability to choose from among them—is made somewhat easier for Yemeni Jews, and leads to their abilities to accommodate conflicting imperatives. What results is the situational use of norms, very much in the way anthropologists speak of the situational use of ethnicity. That is, people can pick and choose, and they do. On the one hand, there are a set of norms belonging to a wide gamut of possibilities for action in Israeli society. On the other hand, and related to the plurality of norms, there are alternatives to each norm. It is particularly during times of crisis that choices must be made. Thus the long crisis period for Yemeni parents of their daughters' unmarried adulthood is possible because from the ages of eighteen to twenty-three (beyond that *most* Israelis worry about their marriages and are expected to marry), there is an unmarried culture in Israel. During this stage, and during adolescence, Israeli-born children are very adept at reversing the normative expectations of their parents. They manage to do so very successfully, even if causing painful reactions, because there is a normative framework among their peers which provides a place for them.

We must make the distinction between norms and individual action. People do not just act according to their "status," their stage in the life cycle, or according to the expectations of their cultural group. They act in response to their own peculiar and unique set of life circumstances. The result for "society" is enormous diversity, and, for Yemeni parents, in a society where the amount of normative choices are far greater than in Yemen, some confusion. The possibilities are endless, and we have seen the scope for the modification of Yemeni Jewish culture and for the creation of the new culture(s) of Israeli-born children. Thus there are parents who admit that they too have interesim while expecting their children to demonstrate Derekh Erets. Michal taxes her mother's tolerance by saying that she will model nude just to provoke an argument and get a reaction. By contrast, Nadav patiently explains to his mother why her Yemeni Jewish thinking is inappropriate in respect to the early death of a child, but offers the explanation in a culturally appropriate framework. Zahava, after thirty-two years of exemplary filial behaviour, decides to move out of the house and this threatens her father's honour. Adina practises an ancient ritual and takes considerable psychological risks since she does not have the knowledge of the cure for defilement (ginger and salt) since this knowledge has also been lost through the immigrant experience. Devorah, as an unmarried woman, was an extremely wayward daughter, but now (in 1988) three years after her marriage, she and her mother get along so well that she is considering buying the apartment across the hallway. Now that she has entered a new status—marriage—she can behave differently *if she chooses*.

The conclusion is that "norms" are alive and changing and part of the individual's cognition. Norms exist inside a person (through learning and observing) as well as out there, in what we call "society." The norms of Israeli society are many and diverse; they act as references for conduct and decisions, but they do not have the power to determine behaviour.

The existence of contradictory norms and values generates a broad range of possible courses of action. For women of the immigrant generation, their ability to choose from among these has probably contributed to their feelings of autonomy in Israel. In this regard, they are free to make political party choices, to remain in the paid labour force, to invent an entirely new leisure and educational life, amongst other features which do not belong to some of their "ideal" perceptions of the past in Yemen. In these respects, the alternatives available to women in Israel have worked to their benefit, in their opinion anyway.

Yet, also belonging to the contradictory elements of life in Israel are actions which Yemeni women find inappropriate, whether for their own peers or their children. Thus, older married women who cease to be devoutly religious or are not devoted first and foremost to the upbringing of their children, are severely criticized by their friends and acquaintances. It is acceptable that Jews and women are free in Israel, but they should not be *that* free. Furthermore, the price to pay for living with the contradictory alternatives can be heavy: while their Israeli-born children are busy creating for themselves a new lifestyle, parents are watching, often confused and hurt by the courses of action chosen by their children. When parents, especially mothers, stop just watching and start responding to their children's choices, household warfare sometimes results. As for the children, they are not really acting totally on their own as self-interested individuals—as mothers claim—but are interacting in accordance with the values of their own peers who strongly influence their choices.

Some contradictions are reconcilable, others are not. For example, mothers reconcile their activity in the labour force as part of their new duties to their families in Israel, even though outside work takes away from the time they spend in rearing their children which is supposed to be the primary occupation of women in Yemeni Jewish culture. By contrast, they cannot reconcile their often inconsistent responses to their children's behaviour such as encouraging their daughters to have a night life and then yelling at them when they don't come home to do the chores. Mothers say that is their prerogative to be dictatorial because they are mothers, no matter how inconsistent they are. This belief, however, stands in a vacuum, because non-religious children simply do not accept this dictum.

Daughters have their own problems with reconciling their often contradictory beliefs and behaviour. Their activities in sexual relationships often do not mesh with the strategies they believe women should use to keep their men. The lack of fit between action and belief does cause emotional dilemmas for some young women. Furthermore, they realize that the more professional and experienced they become in their occupations the less desirable they will be as brides to "chauvinist" Israeli men. Yet they continue to strive for excitement and "advancement." Israeli-born daughters are more wont to think about the effects of their actions than are their mothers; in fact, daughters realize this when accusing their mothers for being "irrational" when mothers are contradictory or inconsistent. What daughters label as "irrational," I would call confused, and I have suggested that a good deal of confusion results in the long-term immigrant experience when the cultural and cognitive frameworks of the old country continue to have influence in the radically different social conditions of the new.

Even if not always apparent, *Ginger and Salt* concerns how ideas associated with being female change—some ideas associated with being female have changed or are still evolving, and others—such as the strength in the belief for the necessity to marry and the gender models which older women have of their own marriage roles—have not changed to any remarkable degree. It is inevitable to conclude that the myriad of norms, customs, and beliefs that women of the immigrant generation confronted after moving to Israel, first as young girls and later as married women, provided them with the tools to change their perceptions of femaleness. With respect to their attitudes about their own reproductive cycles, as evidenced in the fact that the practice of the family purity rituals has become a personal choice for women in Gadot, I have suggested that since women are more actively creating their own social and economic destinies in Israel than was the case in Yemen, they are no longer forced to look to their own bodies to fulfil their important familial and societal contributions as women. Although some women may suggest that they are primarily responsible for housework and childcare, and even that they are (ideologically) subordinate to their husbands, it is evident in their actions that women rarely fulfil the image of the submissive female which characterized their descriptions of the life of women in Yemen.

Moreover, in the Jewish context of Israeli society, women of the immigrant generation can enjoy—or regret—the toss up of norms. Not least of these are the close friendships they build with other women their own age, relationships of choice and of complete equality, a feature of female relations not remembered to exist in Yemen. All their pivotal personal relationships have changed in Israel, and this reflects that they have more identities, more statuses, than those of daughter, sister, wife and mother as was the case in Yemen. They are also friends and paid workers, and have their own special talents by which to define their femaleness. Within all of these possibilities for involvement in society, a consistent female identity is impossible to obtain, particularly since women hold on to contradictory models. Yet, it is living with these contradictions, I have argued, that permit women of the immigrant generation to function as well as they do.

Ginger and Salt, like other recent studies of immigrant families, calls into question the assumption—belonging to modernization—that the shift in residence patterns and household composition (from extended to nuclear) leads to the breakdown of the extended family. Before starting field work, I was led to believe that since the nuclear household rapidly (and by lack of choice) became the norm in Israeli society for all new immigrants, there could emerge a complete breakdown of the extended family. This feature was highlighted in the early studies of immigrant settlement in Israel, during the first years after immigration. Moreover, Israel was viewed as a "modern" society, where the extended family household had no place. The immigrant family (from the Asian and African continents) dramatically confronts this change to the nuclear household upon arrival.

I have demonstrated in *Ginger and Salt,* that the change in household composition and residence patterns (no longer necessarily patrilocal) has had enormous implications for the Yemeni Jewish family. The mother-in-law, no longer head of a large household of sons and their wives and children, has lost her authority over daughters-in-law. The father has lost control over the earning power of his sons. Household labour became privatized with one woman alone being responsible for chores, until her children became old enough to help. With the nuclearization of the household the conjugal pair became interdependent, the noble brother began to disregard his "traditional" responsibilities to his sisters, the family became able to cover-up the transgressions of Derekh Erets of their children, and women gained power and control over their own lives and income. Some of these changes are seen as positive and others as negative by Yemeni Jews.

Despite these modifications to the Yemeni Jewish family, the long-term study of a migrant group reveals a re-constitution of extended family relations, although not necessarily reflecting the filial and fraternal obligations remembered to exist in Yemen. Indeed, during the first years after settlement it appeared that the extended family itself did break down, not just the extended family household, because immigrants in the process of establishing themselves did not have the time or the means to keep up with their relatives in many cases. But, once having consolidated themselves in Israel, a variety of patterns began to emerge. Obviously Yemeni Jews (or other groups) did not discuss exactly what form their new extended family relations would take. Rather, patterns took shape which responded to the constraints of Israeli society, particularly in respect to the distance one lived from kin, the desire to carry on with the customs of rites of passage from the old country, financial and housing constraints, and the general norm of strong relations between at least the grandparent and parent-child generations in the society-at-large. Some extended family patterns are discussed here, but not all people engage in them or do so to the same degree. There is considerable scope for involvement with kin for most people, however.

1. Visiting relatives is a common way of spending leisure time and holidays. People try to visit close kin, that is, brothers, sisters, aunts, uncles, and first cousins, at least during major rites of passage and funerals, no matter where they live in the country. Whether or not they actually attend the ceremony, most men and women will make contributions in cash, if not in kind, to help pay for the celebrations or rituals.

2. Hamula: Some men of the immigrant generation are more likely to form business partnerships with members of the same the patronymic group than with non-kin. Thus, Gadot metal works are controlled by two hamulot. In Gadot, six of twelve Yemeni synagogues are known as "private synagogues" because the membership is related through blood, thus providing a regular forum for social and religious activity for the (male) members of the hamula. Several hamulot in town have managed to live in close proximity; one of these has forty-four male heads of household, while another has thirty-three. In fact, in Gadot, at least nine hamulot are identified by Yemeni Jews, and thus it becomes clear that for the members of these patronymic groups, extensive contact with relatives is possible.

3. As a study over time, *Ginger and Salt* reveals a new form of extended family residential proximity in respect to the three generations of grandparent, parent and child. I have previously referred to the fact that many Israeli-born children, now married, build their homes on the backyard or side lots of their parents' houses. They do so because they prefer to own detached homes than to live in apartment blocks, and because it is more prestigious, let alone more spacious, to own one's own home. The effect of this housing pattern has been instrumental in re-constituting an extended family domestic group, although one that does not completely resemble the Yemeni form. Thus, women have their own households and each household has its own purse. However, many goods and services are exchanged; children have frequent contact with

grandparents—who may be instrumental in passing on Yemeni Jewish identity to the second generation of Israeli-born; grandmothers act as childminders; many meals are eaten together; laundry is often shared between the two women, and so on. Either a son or a daughter may build a house on the parents' yard, it is usually the first children to marry who endeavour to do so. In several cases in Gadot several brothers and sisters have constructed homes large enough for three or four families, separated into housing units for their conjugal families. This type of building activity began around 1970 in Gadot, with the marriages of the Israeli-born or bred, and continues today wherever the parental generation owns a private or a semi-detached home. A study of residence patterns among new immigrants in the early 1950s probably could not have predicted that this residence pattern would emerge.

4. Friendship is a relationship that is usually not conceived of in "family" terms. Friends fill numerous affective and instrumental functions in Gadot, and it would be difficult to conceive of life without them. While friendship between families may end with the death of its original members, for the living, the value of friends can be as important as kin. Friends in Gadot, some of whom are not even Yemeni, are conceived of in family terms, even referred to with kinship terms. Hence, if we stretch our imagination we may view friendship as an "as if" extended family relationship. For women, in particular, friendship is a relationship of free choice, and thus has a crucial place in their self-perceptions as freer individuals in Israel. In at least several cases known to me, intimate ties with friends have taken priority over extended family activity. This is particularly likely to happen where there had been previous hardship or scandal in the kin group.

These data evidently suggest that extensive extended family relations can be re-constituted over time in the immigrant context.[30] The patterns which I have briefly outlined here do not belong solely to Yemeni Jews, however. For example, it is also common in Gadot, and elsewhere, for Ashkenazi (whether German, Polish, or Czechoslovakian) children to build on their parents' yards. These data make one question whether the Israeli sociology of immigrants in the early 1950s was conducted by people who accepted—and themselves aspired to—ideal type notions of the nuclear family in "modern society," disregarding the reality that the Israeli Jewish family, whether from the West or East or born in Israel, is steeped in the modified traditions of larger kin groups.

The fourth lesson of *Ginger and Salt* is that the study of the immigrant experience should preferably take place over time, not just at a moment in time. *Ginger and Salt* clearly shows that the immigrant experience does not belong only to the first few crisis years immediately after migration and during resettlement in a new country. The immigrant experience over time includes cognitive dissonance, and the chronic separation and merging of a diversity of cultural norms based upon Jewish life in Yemen, the place of Yemeni Jews in the cultural milieux of the Middle East, the influences of "Western" lifestyles, of "Ashkenazi" values, of the wider Jewish religion, and, not least, of the developing standards and expectations of Israeli society—whatever these may be. As a study over time, *Ginger and Salt* demonstrates that people from the same migrant culture "adapt" differently depending upon location of resettlement, the number of years of formal education achieved in the receiving society, the type of schooling (religious or secular) received by native-born children, and the person's gender—men and women have had different experiences and different things to gain, lose or change over the years in comparison to where they began in Yemen.

The life cycle of the family has also been a concern of this study: the immigrant experience will manifest different characteristics depending upon the stage any particular family has reached in its life cycle, including the families of people who came to Israel as young children and for whom Yemen does hold important value and reference. I have suggested that the period of adolescence and unmarried adulthood has been particularly difficult to cope with for parents who had immigrated to Israel during 1948–50, even thirty years after their emigration from Yemen, since these stages in the life cycle have no cultural precedence for Yemeni Jews. Many of these difficulties—in respect to the conduct and aspirations of Israeli-born children—fade away into the past as well, once children marry and their mothers become grandmothers. Grandmothers simply do not have the same kinds of troubles with their married daughters as they did before their daughters married. Many aspects of the immigrant experience seem to draw to a close with grandparenthood, although cultural ways and ethnic identity are still critically important to the social organization and conceptual frameworks in which they live. Grandparents consciously endeavor to ensure that their grandchildren, the second Israeli-born generation, have a knowledge of the customs, traditions, and values of the Yemeni Jewish heritage. That generation has yet to be studied.

I am certainly not suggesting that immigrants should be studied only when a native-born generation reaches maturity in the new country so that we can learn more about the immigrant experience. On the contrary, the study of *new* immigrant families and their children is critical to increase an understanding of the host culture attitudes towards strangers in their midst and to better ensure relevant, culturally aware, and fair social and immigration policies. I do maintain, however, that the experience of new immigrants, in the process of establishing themselves should be seen in proper perspective: in terms of their past, their migration experience, their present circumstances, and the knowledge that things will inevitably change in the future.

Epilogue

Nothing in this study suggests that Yemenis of future generations will be ashamed of their heritage, and they may very well maintain a positive identification with it. However, there is much more to an ethnic community and to eidah than that. Given the trend towards secular Judaism and an Israeli identity, which I so often observed among younger married women in Gadot, I do not believe that a Yemeni Jewish culture, with any community strength, has a hope of surviving several generations in Israel, at least not in such a culturally diverse place as Gadot. The separate life paths of Amalia, Hagar, Zahava, Dorit, and Devorah are suggestive in this respect.

It is now January 1987. Amalia, who was my research assistant in the field, married last year at the age of 30 to a secular Ashkenazi from "a good family." They live in a neighbourhood of Asher, next to Gadot. She has taken leave of absence from her jobs as a high school sociology teacher and counsellor in order to complete her M.A. thesis in sociology. She is expecting her first child, and is very content, particularly after having suffered through a long-term relationship with an American Israeli of whom her parents strongly disapproved. Amalia's younger sister, Hagar, became a world traveller, having spent two years abroad after leaving the army. She lived with her English (non-Jewish) boyfriend for a while and worked at odd jobs to support herself. Upon returning to Israel, she worked in security at the international airport and continued to have a "bohemian" lifestyle even while living in her parents' home. In spite of her reputation as the family "astronaut" because of her travels, moodiness and rebellions, Hagar has begun to study in Haifa in the preparatory year for university. According to Amalia, Hagar has "returned to earth," becoming more serious and concerned about her future.

Zahava, the oldest unmarried woman I knew in Gadot, is now 39 and still unmarried. She lives in her own apartment, which she purchased last year, in Tel Aviv. After years of working for the same firm, she changed jobs to liven up her life. She remains a devoted member of her family. Three of her four brothers are married; two have built a large duplex in her parents back yard, next to the synagogue her father built some years ago to honour his own father.

Dorit lives permanently in West Germany, where she met her non-Jewish German husband, and they married in 1984. He is a life insurance agent and she works in a stylish boutique. She claims that her parents have been kind to them, despite his being non-Jewish, but this may be because he has announced that he intends to convert to Judaism. Dorit's older sister, Devorah, married a non-Yemeni Israeli Jew in 1985, after years of explorations and enjoying the "good life." Devorah gave birth to her first child in 1986 and continues to work in the local bank. As I mentioned briefly above in the discussion of norms, Devorah now shares a very good relationship with her mother, after eleven years of constant conflicts while she was a *ravaka*. Dorit and Devorah's oldest brother has also been married for several years, and their second to youngest brother has a serious girlfriend; the youngest boy is now in the army. For a period of twelve years their mother, Zohara, suffered through the trauma of having four adult unmarried children. For Zohara, life is now incomparably easier and more enjoyable than during those tumultuous times.

These five women all carry a Yemeni consciousness, but they will not sustain a Yemeni Jewish community. There will surely be many others like them in the next generations.

Notes

1. There is a rich literature on Israeli immigrant communities which, in some respects, also illustrate some of the points made in *Ginger and Salt*. However, the majority of these studies have been conducted by men and are about men, or, in the attitudinal surveys, have not considered gender as a unit of analysis. Nor has their concern been specifically with the family, but rather with the micro-politics of nation-building, cultural adaptations to moshav or development town life, and the religious and symbolic life of (male) immigrants (see bibliography for sources). Studies which are directly relevant to Yemeni Jewish women, particularly those by Phyllis Palgi and Yael Katzir, have been referred to. Unfortunately I did not have available to me Shalva Weil's Ph.D. thesis on the Indian Jewish family in Lod. There are studies in Hebrew of which I may be unaware, but the findings of one study which will be published in Hebrew and should be particularly relevant was conducted by Rachel Rosen of the Hebrew University on Moroccan moshav women, particularly on their notions of purity and danger, and honour and shame. Also, Rachel Kimor's M.A. thesis (in Hebrew) on the elaborate use of menstrual taboos in the maintenance of Samaritan ethnic identity is relevant.

2. Brettell and Simon 1986:6.

3. It might be worth recalling that the pre-state Yishuv, Jewish settlement in Palestine, actively assisted both outside Palestine and on its beaches, in the clandestine migration of Jews to Israel. British immigration policy towards Jews heavily restricted their entry, thus forcing many Jews back to Europe, eventually to die in the death camps. With this background in mind, it is easier to understand the immediate enactment of the Law of Return after the declaration of statehood.

4. Bernstein and Swirski (1982) have aptly criticized the Eisenstadt school of sociology (as exemplified in the *Absorption of Immigrants* [1953]) for viewing the pre-state Ashkenazi establishment as a "receiving society" like that of Britain

or America, where the immigrants have to do all the adapting, not the host society. She points out that during the early years of statehood, Israel itself was a new society, in the process of modernizing. It was not a fully developed state in any sense of the word, but rather a developing state. Therefore the tremendous number of immigrants (from Asia and Africa) had the potential to transform (and indeed have done so in important respects) the host society.

5. Of course, one could conceivably argue that as a capitalist country Israel does not need a migrant work force because since 1967, it has had a ready supply of cheap labour from the West Bank and Gaza. Moreover, if peace comes to the region, it may one day get a real migrant work force from other Arab countries. I remember well when on a visit to Egypt in 1981, an Egyptian man told me that he was pleased about the peace with Israel because he heard that he could earn a good wage in Tel Aviv and therefore send remittances home. He was considering a temporary migration. One should also note that there is a temporary labour force on the kibbutz where Jewish and non-Jewish young adults volunteer their labour in exchange for room, board, minimal pocket money, and, not least, the kibbutz experience.

6. For example, Canada admits most women into the country as the dependents of men, whether they are or not. This restricted their access to language courses which until 1985 were subsidized only for the household head, invariably designated as a man, unless the family itself could pay for the lessons. Furthermore, when brought in as dependents on the husband's entry permit, if he is deported, the wife is also subject to deportation (Boyd 1986:47).

7. This is not to say that there is agreement on "Who is a Jew," a controversy which has besieged the state since its inception, particularly since the authorities who decide who is a Jew—the Rabbinate and the secular Supreme Court—frequently do not agree on this matter.

8. Shortly after writing this, I came across a book review by Nissim Rejwan (1986) in the *Jerusalem Post,* which began with: "The grave nature of the cleavage between religious and secular Jews in Israeli society is acknowledged now even by the optimistic. Earlier this year, Professor Asher Arian, a prominent Tel Aviv University political scientist, warned that the inability to find a conciliatory formula for their co-existence 'presents a greater danger to Israeli democracy.' He added that, while the ethnic division, acute as it may be, 'is likely to resolve itself in the long run or to re-emerge in the more familiar guise of social class conflict, the religious cleavage, in contrast, is likely to persist.'"

9. Some people were left behind or stayed behind by choice, but this differs from country to country. While there are several thousand Jews in North Yemen, in Alexandria, Egypt, Jews can no longer form a minyan for a congregation because there are not even ten adult men in the Jewish community. Many of the Egyptian Jews, however, emigrated to France and Canada.

10. Morokvasic 1983:28.
11. See Morokvasic 28.
12. H. Lewis 1982:19
13. I agree with Loeb (1985:213) and A. Lewis (1985:151) that the term "Oriental" or Eidot HaMizrah has little explanatory value. I also recognize the

original use of the term Oriental as an ethnocentric one designed by early Ashkenazi settlers to refer to the indigenous Jewish population in Palestine (A. Lewis:143). As A. Lewis claims, "Oriental" is a phantom of Israeli (principally Ashkenazi) explanations for Jewish inequalities in Israel. If possible, one should refer to specific countries-of-origin.

In this discussion I use the term Mizrahi to refer to Jews from the Asian and African continents in comparison with that other major and probably more culturally meaningful, category, Ashkenazi. Throughout *Ginger and Salt,* I have generally used the terms Ashkenazi and Mizrahi (or Eidot HaMizrah) only in the contexts which Yemenis in Gadot do. This present discussion is more general, however, and I use these terms in the lack of another general term to refer to immigrants from the Asian-African continents as a *conceptual* set of people.

14. Similar criticisms have been levied at "multicultural" policies in other countries. In Canada, for example, multiculturalism, with its stress on "heritage" languages (for example, Chinese, Italian, and Polish) and material culture does not deal with incipient racism among the invisible majority population. In Britain, multicultural programmes on the BBC, such as "Asian Magazine" or "Ebony," speak to ethnic constituents, giving their social and cultural interests some time on the tube. However, these programmes are not usually watched by the white British public, and I have heard comments that they are too soft in their commentaries on the British (white) population's racial attitudes. It is as if Enoch Powell's speech on prohibiting further immigration haunts the cultural "Others" of British society, lending to a deep down fear that one day they may be deported if they speak out (Lloyd-Jones 1981).

15. Lewis 1982.

16. Cf. Loeb (1985) who analyzed the imagery of the past among Jews from Habban, an isolated desert town in South Yemen.

17. Gold and Paine 1985.

18. Amongst them are Gans 1962; and Glazer and Moynihan 1965.

19. See Dunziger's (1983) study of immigrants in Newfoundland in which she illustrates how visits to the country-of-origin reinforce the decision to migrate.

20. Lewis 1982.

21. Bhachu 1985:74.

22. I will refer in this discussion only to Katzir's (1976) study and Lewis' (1985), since Palgi's work with Yemenis is not based on a community study and Cohen's (1961) is dated, although it is a critical contribution to the ethnographic record on Yemenis in Israel.

23. This finding lends support to the general criticisms of migration studies which do not use gender as a unit of analysis. I am in strong disagreement with Leeds (1976) who believes gender is not a proper focus in the study of migration.

24. Lewis 1985:227.

25. Katzir:253.

26. Lewis 1982, 1985.

27. Lewis 1985:225.

28. Particularly relevant here, see: Gannage 1986; Morokovasic 1984; Pessar 1984; Safa 1984; and Wilson 1978; and the edited volumes of Gilad and Meintel 1985; Phizacklea 1983; Seller 1981; and Simon and Brettell 1985.

29. The social effects that immigrant people have on the societies they join is a sparsely researched subject; yet here it is clear that applied research is sorely needed in many countries, especially in places like the urban neighbourhoods of Britain where racial conflicts show evidence of white British difficulties in their own "absorption" of immigrants.

30. The social and economic implications of the joint family household and the extended family have been particularly well-documented for Asian groups in Britain where the maintenance of the joint household is usually viewed either as an exploitative institution of women, or as their haven in British society, depending on the perspective of the author. Among British-born Asians, however, the nuclear family household is becoming increasingly the norm, although extensive contact with kin is maintained. Even in the tightly controlled ethnic neighbourhood communities among South Asians, there is a "way out" provided by the more "liberal" (that is, individual comes first) norms of British society, as is clearly shown in Shan's (1985) gripping autobiography, a story about her attempts to free herself from the grips of her husband and her obligations towards her extended family.

Glossary

Adam v'Hevrato. Man and his social world (collective responsibility).
Aliyah. The term used to denote the immigration of Jews to Palestine/Israel; literally: ascent.
Anglo-Saxim. Jews from English speaking countries.
Aqil. Wise man.
Ashkenazi. (Pl. Ashkenazim) originally referring to Jews of Franco-Germany including Poland. In this study I use the term Ashkenazi to refer to Jews of European, American or South African origin or descent, with the exception of Jews from the Balkans.
Atsabim. Nerves; usually referring to being angry or nervous.
Bar Mitzvah. (Pl. *Bar Mitzvot*) a rite of passage in which a male on his thirteenth birthday is religiously confirmed as an adult.
Bat. Daughter (*bati:* my daughter).
Bayit. House, home.
Bayt. (Arabic; pl. *buyut*) house, home; patronymic group.
Bayti. Domestic.
B'korov etzlekh. And soon to you.
B'nei Akiva. The national religious youth movement.
B'nei mishpahah. Cognates; sons of the family.
Brit. Male circumcision ceremony.
Brogez. (Slang) an avoidance relationship resulting from an argument.
Dati. (Pl. *datiyim*) a religious Jew.
Derekh Erets. Literally "way of the world"; proper conduct; etiquette.
D'himmi. (Arabic) the legal status of Jews under Islam, meaning "protected foreigner."
D'or ha'sponga. The floor mop generation; referring to Yemeni women of the immigrant generation who work as domestic labourers.
Egoisti. Egoistic.
Eidah. (Pl. *eidot*) community; ethnic group.
Eidahtioot. Ethnicity.
Eidot HaMizrah. Literally "the Eastern communities," referring to Jews of Middle Eastern, North African and Asian origin or descent; also known as Orientals or Easterners. Some are of Sephardi background because they adhere to customs which originated in medieval Spain.
Fashla. (Arabic) embarrassment or shame resulting from an unexpected happening; bad performance; failure.
Feministi. (Adj.) feminist.

Garin. (Pl. *garinim*) seed groups, comprising a basic unit in Nahal, the agricultural corps of the army.
Get. A Jewish writ of divorce.
Hadadi. Reciprocal.
Halakhah. (Adj.: *halakhic*) the Jewish code of practice; religious law.
Hamula. (Pl. *hamulot*) patronymic group (in the Jewish Yemeni context in Israel); slang for "mob."
Hiloni. (Pl. *hilonim*) a secular Jew.
Hinna. (Pl. *hinnot*) henna; the traditional ceremony held to teach the bride how to be a wife and to separate her from her natal family. In Yemen the hinna lasted for one week and was performed only by women. In Israel the hinna is held two nights before the wedding. If the parents of the bride and groom are from the same region in Yemen, a *hinna* is held separately for each. If the parents are from different regions in Yemen, one *hinna* is held for both bride and groom to symbolize the joining of the two regions. *Hinna* is put on the fingers of the bride and groom to ward off the evil eye, to wish good luck, and to encourage fertility.
Histadrut. General Federation of Labour; Israel's major trade union.
Hustpah. Nerve; a better English translation might be "cheeky." A person who manifests *hustpah* is cheeky, arrogant, or outrageous.
Interes. (Pl. *interesim*) interest; self-interest.
Ja'ale. (Arabic) nuts, raisins, dried fruits.
Jizya. Poll-tax levied on Jews in Yemen and elsewhere in Islamic states.
Kashrut. The Jewish dietary laws.
Ketuba. Marriage contract.
Kibbutz. Collective farm.
Kibbutz hagaluyot. The ingathering of the exiles.
Krovei mishpahah. All consanguines and affines; relatives of the family.
Labrioot. To your health; be healthy.
Ma'abarot. Temporary immigrant camps of the sort offered to new immigrants in Israel during the 1950s.
Ma'almeh. (Jewish dialect of Yemeni Arabic) school for Jewish boys in Yemen.
Mesorati. (Pl. *mesoratiyim*) a traditional Jew, neither fully secular nor fully religious.
Mezuzah. Parchment scroll in container attached to the door post of Jewish homes.
Mikveh. Ritual bath.
Mishpahah. Family.
Miskena. (Pl. *miskenot*) female wretched one; poor one.
Mitzvah. (Pl. *mitzvot*) good deeds; religious commandments and imperatives.
Mizrahi. (Pl. *Mizrahim*) literally "Easterner." This term is often used by Israelis to refer to a person from *Eidot HaMizrah*.
Mizug hagaluyot. Mixing of the exiles (denoting "melting pot," an ultimate goal of Zionist ideology).
Mohar. Bridewealth, brideprice.
Mohel. Man who performs the act of circumcision of a Jewish male.

Mori. The teacher of boys in the *ma'lameh*.
Moshav. (Pl. *moshavim*) smallholders co-operative village.
Moshava. (Pl. *moshavot*) a mixed community, having both urban and rural attributes. The original *moshavot* were farming villages set up on a non-co-operative basis. Several of the early moshavot were Rehovot, Rishon Letzion and Petah Tikva.
Na'amat. The working women's association.
Nargila. Water pipe.
Nedunia. (Hebrew) dowry.
Niddah: A menstruant woman.
Niddut. The period of ritual separation of husband and wife for twelve or fourteen days after the onset of menses lasting until the wife performs the ritual of immersion in the *mikveh*.
Normali. Normal.
Pereshat ha'shavua. The Torah's Portion of the Week; a section of the Torah is read each week in the synagogue.
Proteksia. "Connections;" nepotistic use of contacts for personal benefit and for cutting corners.
Qat. (*Catha edulis Forsk*) a leafy green plant with a slight valium content.
Ravaka. (Pl. *ravakot*; masculine: *ravak*) adult unmarried woman.
Sabra. Jews born in Israel. (It is the name of a desert fruit.).
Shaykh. (Arabic) tribal leaders.
Shed. (Pl. *shedim*) evil spirit.
Shekel. (Pl. *shekelim*) the Israeli currency.
Shem. Name; reputation.
Sherut Leumi. National Service, a period of state service usually lasting for one year.
Shtetl. The Eastern and Central European Jewish village.
Tafkid. (Pl. *tafkidim*) role.
Taharat hamishpahah. The family purity rituals.
Ya'eloot. Efficient.
Yeshiva. Ultra-religious school.
Yishuv. Jewish settlement in Palestine.
Zona. (Pl. *zonot*) prostitute or whore. It is also used in a context that implies that someone is very selfish or inconsiderate.

Bibliography

Abadan-Unat, Nermin
1982 "The Effect of International Labour Migration Women's Roles: The Turkish Case" in Cigdern Kagitcibasi, ed., *Sex Roles, Family and Community in Turkey*. Bloomington: Indiana University Press, pp. 207-234.

Abir, Mordochai
1974 "International Commerce and Yemen's Jewry, 15th-19th Century." Jerusalem: Ben Zvi Institute. Draft only.

Ahroni, Reuben
1986 *Yemenite Jewry: Origins, Culture and Literature*. Bloomington: Indiana University Press.

Albrecht, S. L., H. Bahr and B. Chadwick
1979 "Changing Family and Sex Roles: An Assessment of Age Differences" in *Journal of Marriage and the Family*, 41(1):41-50.

Alcalay, Reuben
1965 *The Complete Hebrew-English Dictionary*. Jerusalem: Massadah.

Allen, Sheila
1973 "Some Theoretical Problems in the Study of Youth" in Harry Silverstein, ed., *The Sociology of Youth, Evolution and Revolution*. New York: Macmillan Publishing Co., pp. 51-61.

Allman J., ed.
1978 *Women's Status and Fertility in the Muslim World*. London: Praeger Publishers.

Amir, M.
1973 "The Epidemiology of Drug Abuse in Israel" in *Israel Annals of Psychiatry and Related Disciplines*, XI:219-270.

Amir, Y.
1973 "The Effects of Inter-ethnic Contact on Friendship Choices in the Military." *Journal of Cross-Cultural Psychology*, 4(3):361-373.

Ammar, Hamed
1954 *Growing Up in an Egyptian Village*. London: Routledge and Kegan Paul.

Andezian, Sossie
1986 "Women's roles in Organizing Symbolic Life: Algerian Female Immigrants in France" in Rita Simon and Caroline Brettell, eds., *International Migration:*

The Female Experience. Totawa, New Jersey: Rowman and Allanheld, pp. 254–266.

Andezian, Sossie and Jocelyn Streiff
1982 "Transpositions and Reinterpretations of the Traditional Female Role in an Immigrant Situation" in UNESCO *Living in Two Cultures: The Socio-Cultural Situation of Migrant Workers and their Families.* UNESCO. Aldershot: Gower, pp. 308–317.

Anthias, Floya
1983 "Sexual Divisions and Ethnic Adaptation: The Case of Greek-Cypriot Women" in Annie Phizacklea, ed., *One Way Ticket: Migration and Female Labour.* London: Routledge and Kegan Paul, pp. 73–94.

Antonovksy, Helen
1980 *Adolescent Sexuality.* Lexington, Massachusetts: Lexington Books.

Appleyard, Reginald and Anna Amera
1986 "Post War Immigration of Greek Women to Australia: A Longitudinal Study" in Simon and Brettell, *International Migration: The Female Experience,* pp. 215–228.

Aronoff, Myron
1973a "Ritual Rebellion and Assertion in an Israeli Town" in *Jewish Journal of Sociology,* 15(1):79–105.
1973b "The Politics of Religion in an Israeli New Town" in *Eastern Anthropologist,* 26(2):145.
1973c "Development Towns in Israel" in M. Curtis and M. Chertoff, eds., *Israel: Social Structure and Change.* New Brunswick, New Jersey: Transaction Books, pp. 27–46.
1974a "Political Change in Israel: The Case of a New Town" in *Political Science Quarterly,* 69(3):613.
1974b *Frontiertown: The Politics of Community Building in Israel.* Manchester: Manchester University Press.

Avineri, Shlomo
1973 "Israel: Two Nations?" in Curtis and Chertoff, *Israel: Social Structure and Change* pp. 281–307.

Azu, Diana
1971 *The Ga Family and Social Change.* Cambridge, England: African Studies Centre.

Bahr, Stephen
1974 "Effects on Family Power and Division of Labour in the Family" in Lois Hoffman and F. Ivan Nye, eds., *Working Mothers.* San Francisco: Jossey-Bass.

Baldwin, Elaine
1972 *Differentiation and Co-operation in an Israeli Veteran Co-operative Village.* Manchester: Manchester University Press.

Bibliography

Ballard, Catherine
1978 "Arranged Marriages in the British Context" in *New Community*, VI(3):181-96.
1979 "Conflict, Continuity and Change: Second Generation South Asians" in V. Saifullah-Khan, ed., *Minority Families in Britain*. London: Macmillan, pp. 109-29.

Ballard, Roger and Catherine Ballard
1977 "The Sikhs: The Development of South Asian Settlements in Britain" in James L. Watson, ed. *Between Two Cultures: Migrants and Minorities in Britain*. Oxford: Basil Blackwell, pp. 21-56.

Barakat, Halim
1985 "The Arab Family and the Challenge of Social Transformation" in E. Fernea, ed. *Women and the Family in the Middle East*. Austin: University of Texas Press, pp. 27-48.

Barer, Shlomo
1953 *The Magic Carpet*. London: Secker and Warberg.

Bar-Yosef, Rivkah
1968 "De-socialization and Re-socialization: The Adjustment of Immigrants" in *International Migration Review*, 2(3):27-43.

Basker, Eileen
1980 *Belief Systems, Cultural Milieu and Reproductive Behaviour: Women Seeking Abortions in a Hospital in Israel*. Ph.D. Hebrew University of Jerusalem.

Baum, Charlotte, Paula Hyman and Sonya Michal
1981 "Pearls Around the Neck, a Stone Upon the Heart: Becoming an American Lady" in Maxime Seller, ed., *Immigrant Women*. Philadelphia: Temple University Press, pp. 140-45.

Beck, L., and N. Keddie, eds.
1978 *Women in the Muslim World*. Cambridge, Massachusetts: Harvard University Press.

Bellos, Susan
1978 "A Poverty of Prospects" in *Jerusalem Post*, March 28, 1978, p. 12.

Ben-Rafael, Eliezer
1982 *The Emergence of Ethnicity: Cultural Groups and Social Conflict in Israel*. Westport, Connecticut: Greenwood.

Berdichevsky, Norman
1980 "The Persistence of the Yemeni Quarter in an Israeli Town" in Ernest Krausz, ed., *Studies in Israeli Society, Vol 1., Migration, Ethnicity and Community*. New Brunswick, New Jersey: Transaction Books.

Berler, Alexander
1970 *New Towns in Israel*. Jerusalem: Israel University Press.

Berler, A. and S. Shaked
1966 *Twenty-five Development Towns in Israel.* Israel: Ministry of Housing.

Bernstein, Deborah
1976 *Contradictions and Protest in the Process of Nation-Building: the Black Panthers of Israel 1971-72.* Ph.D. University of Sussex.

Bernstein, Deborah and Shlomo Swirski
1982 "The Rapid Economic Development of Israel and the Emergence of the Ethnic Division of Labour" in *British Journal of Sociology,* 33(1):64-85.

Bhachu, Parminder
1985 *Twice Migrants: East African Sikh Settlers in Britain.* London: Tavistock.
1986 "Work, Dowry, and Marriage Among East African Sikh Women in the United Kingdom" in Simon and Brettell, *International Migration: The Female Experience,* pp. 229-240.

Bhatti, F.M.
1978 "Young Pakistanis in Britain: Educational Needs and Problems" in *New Community,* VII(3):406-414.

Bienstock, Beverly
1974 "The Changing Image of the American Jewish Mother" in V. Tufte and B. Myeroff, eds., *Changing Images of the Family.* New Haven, Connecticut: Yale University Press, pp. 173-191.

Bird, Caroline
1979 "Women Should Stay Single" in J. Gipson Wells, ed., *Marriage and the Family,* 2nd Edition. New York, Macmillan, pp. 27-35.

Block, Harriet
1976 "Changing Domestic Roles among Polish Immigrant Women" in *Anthropological Quarterly,* 49(1):3-10.

Blood, Robert and Donald Wolfe
1960 *Husbands and Wives: The Dynamic of Married Living.* New York: Free Press.

Boone, Margaret
1980 "The Uses of Traditional Concepts in the Development of New Urban Roles" in E. Bourguignon, ed., *A World of Women.* New York: Praeger Publishers, pp. 235-270.

Bott, Elizabeth
1955 "Urban Families: Conjugal Roles and Social Networks" in J. Friedl and N. Chrisman, eds., *City Ways, a Selective Reader in Urban Anthropology.* New York: Thomas Y. Cromwell, 1975, pp. 139-186.

Boyd, Monica
1986 "Immigrant Women in Canada" in Simon and Brettell, *International Migration: The Female Experience,* pp. 45-61.

Brah, Avtar
1978 "South Asian Teenagers in Southall: Their Perceptions of Marriage, Family and Ethnicity Identity" in *New Community*, VI(3):197-206.

Brauer, Eric
1934 *Ethnologie der Jemenitschen Juden*. Heidelberg: Winters. In German.

Brettell, Caroline B. and Rita J. Simon
1986 "Immigrant Women: An Introduction" in Simon and Brettell, *International Migration: The Female Experience*, 3-20.

Brody, Eugene, ed.
1968 *Minority Group Adolescents in the United States*. Baltimore: The Williams and Wilkins Co.

Brouwer, Lenie and Marijke Priester
1983 "Living in Between: Turkish Women in Their Homeland and in the Netherlands" in Phizacklea, *One Way Ticket*, pp. 113-130.

Brown, Judith and Virginia Kerns, eds.
1985 *In Her Prime: A New View of Middle Aged Women*. South Hadley, Massachusettes: Bergin and Garvey Publishers.

Buchanon Stafford, Susan
1985 "Haitian Emigrant Women: A Cultural Perspective" in *Anthropologica*, 27(1).

Bujra, Janet
1982 "Introductory: Female Solidarity and the Sexual Division of Labour" in Pat Caplin and Janet Bujra, eds., *Women United, Women Divided*. Bloomington, Indiana: Indiana University Press, pp. 13-45.

Campbell, John
1964 *Honour, Family and Patronage*. Oxford: Oxford University Press.

Caplan, Paula
1981 *Barriers Between Women*. Jamaica, New York: Spectrum Publications.

Caspi, Mishael
1985 *Daughters of Yemen*. Berkeley: University of California Press.

Central Bureau of Statistics, Jerusalem
1961 *Census of Population and Housing*.
1972 *Census of Population and Housing, #1, Demographic Characteristics of the Population-Part III*. (Composition of Population in Localities and Statistical Areas).
1980a *Local Authorities in Israel 1978/1979 Physical Data*, Special Series #636.
1980b *Statistical Abstract of Israel, #31*.

Chester, R. and C. Walker
1980 "Sexual Experience and Attitudes of British Women" in W. Armytage *et al.*, eds., *Changing Patterns of Sexual Behaviour*. London: Academic Press, pp. 71-92.

Chouraqui, Andre
1973 *Between East and West: A History of the Jews of North Africa.* New York: Atheneum.

Cohen, Erik
1970 "Development Towns: the Social Dynamics of 'Planted' Communities in Israel" in S. Eisenstadt *et al.*, eds., *Integration and Development in Israel.* Jerusalem: Israel Universities Press, pp. 587–618.
1972 "The Black Panthers of Israeli Society" in *Jewish Journal of Sociology,* 14(1):93–104.

Cohen, Ezra
1980 *Yitseat Teman.* Israel: Ben-Non Press. In Hebrew.

Cohen, Hayyim
1973 *The Jews of the Middle East, 1860–1972.* Jerusalem: Israel Universities Press.

Cohen, Percy
1961 *Leadership and Politics Amongst Israeli Yemenis.* Ph.D. University of London.
1967 "Israel's Ethnic Problem" in *Jewish Journal of Sociology,* 9:100–107.
1968 "Ethnic Group Differences in Israel" in *Race,* 9:303–310.

Comay, Y. and A. Kirschenbaum
1973 "The Israeli New Town: an Experiment at Population Redistribution" in *Economic Development and Cultural Change,* 22:124–134.

Conger, John
1977 *Adolescence and Youth: Psychological Development in a Changing World.* New York: Harper and Row. Second Edition.

Curtis, M., and M. Chertoff, eds.
1973 *Israel: Social Structure and Change.* New Brunswick, New Jersey: Transaction Books.

Dahnbany-Miraglia, Dina
1975 "Verbal Protective Behaviour among Yemeni Jews." Working Papers in Yiddish and East European Jews Studies, #13. New York: Max Weinreich Center for Advanced Jewish Studies of the YIVO Institute for Jewish Research.

Datan, Nancy
1973 "Your Daughters Shall Prophesy: Ancient and Contemporary Perspectives on the Women of Israel" in Curtis and Chertoff *Israel: Social Structure and Change,* pp. 379–388.

Datan, N., A. Antonovsky and B. Maoz
1981 *A Time to Reap: the Middle Age of Women in Five Israeli Sub-Cultures.* Baltimore, Maryland: John Hopkins University Press.

Davis, Kingsley
1940 "The Sociology of Parent-Youth Conflict" in R. Coser, ed., *The Family: Its Structures and Functions.* New York: Macmillan, 1974, pp. 446–459.

Deshen, Shlomo
1965 "A Case of Breakdown of Modernization in an Israeli Immigrant Community" in *Jewish Journal of Sociology*, 7(1):63-91.
1966 "Conflict and Social Change: The Case of an Israeli Village" in *Sociologia Ruralis*, 7:31-35.
1970 *Immigrant Voters in Israel: Parties and Congregations in a Local Election Campaign*. Manchester: Manchester University Press.
1974 "Political Ethnicity and Cultural Ethnicity in Israel During the 1960s" in A. Cohen, ed., *Urban Ethnicity*. London: Tavistock, pp. 281-309.

Deshen, Shlomo and Moshe Shokeid
1974 *The Predicament of the Homecoming*. Ithaca: Cornell University Press.

de Souza, Alfred, ed.
1975 *Women in Contemporary India: Traditional Images and Changing Roles*. Delhi: Manohar.

de Vaux, Roland
1965 *Ancient Israel: Volume I: Social Institutions*. New York: McGraw-Hill.

Dex, Shirley
1983 "The Second Generation: West Indian Female School Leavers" in Phizacklea, *One Way Ticket* pp. 552-40.

Dorsky, Susan
1986 *Women of Amran*. Salt Lake City: University of Utah Press.

DuBoulay, Juliet
1974 *Portrait of a Greek Mountain Village*. Oxford: Clarendon Press.

Dunziger, Janet
1983 *A Comparative Study of Narrative Accounts of Visits Home Drawn From the Immigrant Ethnic Community in St. John's, Newfoundland*. Memorial University, M.A. Folklore.

Dwyer, Daisy
1978 *Images and Self-Images: Male and Female in Morocco*. New York: Columbia University Press.

Eisenstadt, Shmuel
1954 *The Absorption of Immigrants*. London: Routledge and Kegan Paul.
1967 *Israeli Society*. London: Widenfeld and Nicolson.

Elkholy, Abbo
1976 "The Arab American Family" in Charles Mindel and R. Habenstein, eds., *Ethnic Families in America: Patterns and Variations*. New York: Elsevier, pp. 150-167.

el-Messiri, Sawsan
1978 "Self-Images of Traditional Urban Women in Cairo" in Beck and Keddie, *Women in the Muslim World*, pp. 522-540.

Elon, Amos
1973 "The Black Panthers of Israel" in Donald Gelfand and Russell Lee, eds., *Ethnic Conflicts and Power: A Cross-National Perspective.* New York: John Wiley and Sons, pp. 173–178.

El Sa'adawi, Nawal
1980 *The Hidden Face of Eve: Women in the Arab World.* London: Zed Press.

Encyclopedia Judaica
1971 "Yemen" in Vol. #16:739–760.
1971 "*Mikveh*" in Vol. 11.
1971 "*Niddut*" in Vol. 12.

Epstein, A. L.
1978 *Ethos and Identity.* London: Tavistock.

Epstein, C. F.
1971 "Law Partners and Marital Partners: Strains in the Dual-career Family Enterprise" in *Human Relations,* 24(6):549–564.

Etzioni-Halevy, Eva
1977 *Political Culture in Israel.* New York: Praeger Publishers.

Fein, Leonard
1968 *Politics in Israel.* Boston: Little, Brown and Company.

Feldman, David
1978 *Marital Relations, Birth Control and Abortion in Jewish Law.* New York: Schocken Books.

Fernea, Elizabeth
1969 *Guests of the Shaikh.* New York: Anchor Books.
1976 *A Street in Marrakech.* New York: Anchor Books.

Fernea, Elizabeth, ed.
1985 *Women and the Family in the Middle East: New Voices of Change.* Austin: University of Texas Press, pp. 301–302.

Firth, Raymond, Jane Hubert and Anthony Forge
1969 *Families and Their Relatives, Kinship in a Middle-class Sector of London: An Anthropological Study.* London: Routledge and Kegan Paul.

Fischar, Lucy
1981 "Transitions in the Mother-Daughter Relationship" in *Journal of Marriage and the Family,* 43(3):613–622.

Fischer, Michael
1978 "On Changing the Concept and Position of Persian Women" in Beck and Keddie, *Women in the Muslim World,* pp. 189–215.

Fitzpatrick, Joseph
1976 "The Puerto-Rican Family" in Mindel and Habenstein, *Ethnic Families in America.* pp. 192–218.

Foner, Nancy
1978 *Jamaica Farewell: Jamaican Immigrants in London.* Berkeley: University of California Press.
1984 *Ages in Conflict: A Cross-Cultural Perspective on Inequality Between Old and Young.* New York: Columbia University Press.
1986 "Sex Roles and Sensibilities: Jamaican Women in New York and London" in Simon and Brettell, *International Migration: The Female Experience*, pp. 133–151.

Friedlander, D. and C. Goldscheider
1979 *The Population of Israel.* New York: Columbia University Press.

Friedl, Ernestine
1962 *Vasilika: A Village in Modern Greece.* New York: Holt, Rinehart and Winston.

Friendly, Alfred
1972 "Israel's Oriental Immigrants and Druze, Report #2." Minority Rights Group (London).

Gamlieli, Nissim
1979 *Arabic Love Songs of Yemenite Jewish Women.* Tel Aviv. In Hebrew.

Gannage, Charlene
1985 "Haven or Heartache: Immigrant Women Workers in the Household" in *Anthropologica*, 27(1).
1986 *Double Day, Double Bind: Women Garment Workers.* Toronto: The Women's Press.

Gans, Herbert
1962 *The Urban Villagers.* New York: The Free Press.

Ganzfried, Solomon
1963 *Code of Jewish Law.* New York: Hebrew Publishing Company.

Gerholm, T.
1977 *Market, Mosque and Mafraj.* Stockholm Studies in Social Anthropology, 5.

Gerson, Menachem
1978 *Family, Women and Socialization in the Kibbutz.* Lexington, Massachusetts: Lexington books.

Gilad, Lisa
1982 *Yemeni Jewish Women: The Changing Family in an Israeli New Town.* Ph.D. University of Cambridge, England.

Gilad, Lisa and Deirdre Meintel, eds.
1985 *Female Migrants in the Work Force: Domestic Repercussions.* Special Issue. *Anthropologica*, 27(1).

Glazer, Nathan and Daniel Moynihan
1963 *Beyond the Melting Pot.* Boston: MIT Press.

Goitein, Shlomo
1947 *Tales from the Land of Sheba*. New York: Schocken Books.
1953 "Jewish Education in Yemen as an Archetype of Traditional Jewish Education" in C. Frankenstein, ed., *Between Past and Future*. Jerusalem: Henrietta Szold Foundation.
1955 "Portrait of a Yemenite Weavers' Village" in *Jewish Social Studies*, 17:3-26.
1964 *Jews and Arabs: Their Contacts Throughout the Ages*. New York: Schocken Books.
1969 "The Jews in Yemen" in A. J. Arberry, ed., *Religion in the Middle East, Volume 1*. Cambridge: Cambridge University Press, pp. 226-234.
1978 *A Mediterranean Society, Volume III. The Family*. Berkeley, University of California Press.

Gold, Gerald and Robert Paine
1984 "Introduction" in Gerald Gold, ed., *Minorities and Mother Country Imagery*. St. John's: ISER Books, pp. 1-16.

Goldberg, Harvey
1972 *Cave Dwellers and Citrus Growers*. Cambridge: Cambridge University Press.

Goody, Esther
1985 "Introduction" in *Anthropologica*, Volume 27(1).

Gonzalez, Nancie
1973 "Multiple Migratory Experiences of Dominican Women" in *Anthropological Quarterly*, 49(1):36-44.

Goshen-Gottstein, Esther
1966 *Marriage and First Pregnancy*. London: Tavistock.

Granqvist, H.
1931 *Marriage Conditions in a Palestinian Village*. Helsingfors: Commentationes Humanarum Litterarum.
1950 *Child Problems among the Arabs*. Helsingfors: Soderstrom and Company.

Haddad, Safia
1981 "Syrian Women in Chicago: New Responsibilities . . . New Skills" in Maxime Seller, ed. *Immigrant Women*. Philadelphia: Temple University Press. pp. 136-139.

Harris, C.
1969 *The Family*. London: George Allen and Unwin Ltd.

Hazleton, Lesley
1977 *Israeli Women: Reality Behind the Myths*. New York: Simon and Schuster.

Heller, Celia
1973 "The Emerging Consciousness of the Ethnic Problem in Israel" in Curtis and Chertoff, *Israel Social Structure and Change*, pp. 313-333.

Herzfield, Michael
1980 "Honour and Shame: Problems in the Comparative Analysis of Moral Systems" in *Man*, 15(2):339-351.

Hess Buechler, Judith-Maria
1976 "Something Funny Happened on the Way to the Agora: A Comparison of Bolivian and Spanish Galician Female Migrants" in *Anthropological Quarterly*, 49(1):36-44.

Hirschon, Renee
1978 "Open Body, Closed Space: The Transformation of Female Sexuality" in S. Ardener, ed., *Defining Females: The Nature of Women in Society*. London: Croom Helm, pp. 66-88.

Horowitz, Tamar
1980 "Integration and the Social Gap" in *Jerusalem Quarterly*, 15:134-142.

Imray, Linda and Middleton, Audry
1983 "Public and Private: Making the Boundaries" in E. Garmarnikow *et al.*, eds., *The Public and the Private*. London: Heineman, pp. 12-27.

Jessop, Dorothy Jones
1981 "Family Relationships as Viewed by Parents and Adolescents: A Specification" in *Journal of Marriage and the Family*, 43(1):95-104.

Jiggets, J. Ida
1957 *A Study in the Absorption and Integration of the Yemenite Jew in the State of Israel*. Ed.D. New York University. Ann Arbor: Xerox University Microfilms.

Johnson, Colleen
1982 "Sibling Solidarity: Its Origins and Functioning in Italian American Families" in *Journal of Marriage and the Family*, 44(1):156-167.

Kahane, Reuven
1986 "Informal Agencies of Socialization and the Integration of Immigrant Youth into Society: An Example from Israel" in *International Migration Review*, XX(1):21-39.

Katz, Elihu and Michael Gurevitch
1976 *The Secularization of Leisure: Culture and Communication in Israel*. Cambridge, Massachusetts: Harvard University Press.

Katzir, Yael
1976 *The Effects of Resettlement on the Status and Role of Yemeni Jewish Women: The Case of Ramat Oranim, Israel*. Ph.D. University of California, Berkeley. Ann Arbor: Xerox University Microfilms.

Kelly, Maria
1981 "Development and the Sexual Division of Labour: An Introduction" in *Signs: Journal of Women in Culture and Society*, 7(2):268-278.

Kennedy, J., J. Teague, and L. Fairbanks
1980 "Qat Use in North Yemen and the Problem of Addiction: A Study in Medical Anthropology" in *Culture, Medicine, and Psychiatry*, 4:311–344.

Kerr, Madelaine
1958 *The People of Ship Street.* London: Routledge and Kegan Paul.

Kingston, Maxime Hong
1978 *The Women Warrior.* London: Penguin.

Klaff, Vivian
1973 "Ethnic Segregation in Israel" in *Demography*, 10(2):161–184.
1977 "Residence and Integration in Israel: A Mosaic of Segregated Peoples" in *Ethnicity*, 4:103–121.

Kourvetaris, George
1976 "The Greek American Family" in Mindel and Habenstein, *Ethnic Families in America,* pp. 168–191.

Kramer, Sydelle and Jenny Masur, eds.
1976 *Jewish Grandmothers.* Boston: Beacon Press.

Krausz, Ernest
1972 "The Making of a Community: The Ethnic Factor." Published by The Anglo-Israel Association, London, Pamphlet No. 34.

Kudat, Ayse
1982 "Personal, Familial, and Societal Impacts of Turkish Women's Migration to Europe" in UNESCO *Living in Two Cultures,* pp. 292–304.

Laguerre, Michel
1978 "Ticouloute and His Kinfolk: The Study of a Haitian Extended Family" in D. Shimkin, E. Shimkin, and D. Frate, eds., *The Extended Family in Black Societies.* The Hague: Mouton, pp. 410–446.

Lahav, Pnina
1977 "Raising the Status of Women Through Law: The Case of Israel" in *Signs: Journal of Women in Culture and Society,* 3(1):193–210.

Lamphere, Louise
1986a "Working Mothers and Family Strategies: Portuguese and Columbian Women in a New England Community" in Simon and Brettell, *International Migration: The Female Experience,* pp. 226–285.
1986b "From Working Daughters to Working Mothers; Production and Reproduction in an Industrial Community" in *American Ethnologist,* 13(1):118–130.

Lancaster, William
1981 *The Rwala Bedouin Today.* Cambridge: Cambridge University Press.

Leeds, Anthony
1976 "Women in the Migratory process: A Reductionist Outlook" in Phizacklea, *One Way Ticket,* pp. 13–32.

Leslie, Gerald
1973 *The Family in Social Context.* New York: Oxford University Press. Second Edition.

Lewando-Hundt, Gillian
1978 *Women's Power and Settlement: The Effect of Settlement on the Position of Negev Bedouin Women.* M. Phil., University of Edinburgh.

Lewenhak, Sheila
1980 *Women and Work.* Glasgow: William Collins and Sons Ltd.

Lewis, Arnold
1985 "Phantom Ethnicity: 'Oriental Jews in Israeli Society'" in Alex Weingrod, ed., *Studies in Israeli Ethnicity, After the Ingathering.* Glasgow: Gordon and Breach Science Publishers, pp. 133–58.

Lewis, Herbert
1980 "Ethnicity, Culture and Adaptation among Yemenites in a Heterogeneous Community." Paper presented at Ben Gurion University Conference on Israeli Ethnicity, June 16–19, 1980. Unedited Version.
1982 "The Maintenance and Flowering of Yemenite Jewish Ethnicity in Israel." Unpublished.
1985 "Ethnicity, Culture, and Adaptation among Yemenites in a Heterogeneous Community" in Weingrod, *Studies in Israeli Ethnicity,* pp. 217–236.

Lipset, Seymour Martin
1973 "The Israeli Dilemma" in Curtis and Chertoff, *Israel: Social Structure and Change,* pp. 349–363.

Lissak, Moshe
1973 "Pluralism in Israeli Society" in Curtis and Chertoff, *Israel: Social Structure and Change,* pp. 363–369.

Lloyd-Jones, David
1981 "The Art of Enoch Powell: The Rhetorical Structure of a Speech on Immigration" in Robert Paine, ed., *Politically Speaking: Cross-Cultural Studies of Rhetoric.* Philadelphia: ISHI; St. John's: Institute of Social and Economic Research, pp. 87–112.

Loeb, Lawrence, D.
1985 "Folk Models of Habbani Ethnic Identity" in Weingrod, *Studies in Israeli Ethnicity,* pp. 201–16.

Lopata, H., ed.
1980 *Research in the Interweave of Social Roles, Vol. 1.* Greenwich, Connecticut: JAI Press.

Louden, Delroy
1978 "Self-Esteem and Locus of Control: Some Findings on Immigrant Adolescents in Britain" in *New Community,* VI(3):218–234.
1979 "Adolescents under Stress: Some Case Studies" in *New Community,* III(3):415–421.

Lutfiyya, A.
1970 "The Family" in A. Lutfiyya and C. Churchill, eds., *Readings in Arab Middle Eastern Societies and Cultures*. The Hague: Moutin and Co., pp. 504–525.

Maher, Vanessa
1974 *Women and Property in Morocco*. Cambridge: Cambridge University Press.
1978 "Women and Social Change in Morocco" in Beck and Keddie, *Women in the Muslim World*, pp. 100–123.

Makhlouf, Carla
1979 *Changing Veils, Women and Modernization in North Yemen*. London: Croom Helm.

Makhlouf, Carla and G. Obermeyer
1978 "Women and Social Change in Urban North Yemen" in Allman, ed., *Women's Status and Fertility in the Muslim World*, pp. 333)348.

Mars, Leonard
1980 *The Village and the State: Administration, Ethnicity, and Politics in an Immigrant Town*. London: Routledge and Kegan Paul.

Marx, Emmanuel
1976 *The Social Context of Violent Behaviour: A Social Anthropological Study in an Immigrant Town*. London: Routledge and Kegan Paul.

Matras, Judah
1973 "Israel's New Frontier: The Urban Periphery" in Curtis and Chertoff, *Israel: Social Structure and Change*, pp. 3–14.

Meintel, Deirdre, Micheline Labelle and Genevieve Turcotte
1985 "Migration, Wage Labour and Domestic Relationships: Immigrant Women Workers in Montreal." *Anthropologica*, 27(1).

Meiselman, Moshe
1978 *Jewish Women in Jewish Law*. New York: Yeshiva University Press.

Mernissi, Fatima
1975 *Beyond the Veil: Male-Female Dynamics in a Modern Muslim Society*. New York: John Wiley and Sons.

Miller, Lewis
1971 "The Epidemiology of Drug Abuse in Israel" in *Israel Annals of Psychiatry and Related Disciplines*, 9:3–10.

Mills, C. Wright
1969 *The Sociological Imagination*. New York: Oxford University Press.

Mindel, Charles and R. Habenstein, eds.
1976 *Ethnic Families in America: Patterns and Variations*. New York: Elsevier.

Morokvasic, Mirjana
1983 "Women in Migration: Beyond the Reductionist Outlook" in Phizacklea, *One Way Ticket* 13–32.

1984 "Birds of Passage are Also Women" in *International Migration Review,* 18(4):886–907.

Mundy, Martha
1979 "Women's Inheritance of Land in Highland Yemen" in *Arabian Studies,* 5:161–187.
1981 *Land and Family in a Yemeni Village.* Ph.D. University of Cambridge.

Myntti, Cynthia
1978 "Changing Roles in Five Beirut Households" in Allman, *Women's Status and Fertility in the Muslim World,* pp. 270–288.

Nagata, Judith
1974 "What is a Malay?" in *American Ethnologist,* 1(3):331–350.
1985 "Conclusions" in *Anthropologica,* 27(1).

Nelson, C.
1974 "Public and Private Politics: Women in the Middle Eastern World" in *American Ethnologist,* 1:551–564.

Ortner, Sherry
1978 "The Virgin and the State" in *Feminist Studies,* 4(3):19–36.

Pack, Howard
1973 "Income Distribution and Economic Development: The Case of Israel" in Curtis and Chertoff, *Israel: Social Structure and Change,* pp. 175–198.

Palgi, Phyllis
1975 "Discontinuity in the Female Role within the Traditional Family in Modern Society: A Case of Infanticide" in J. Anthony, ed., *Children in Society.* New York: Wiley Press.
1978 "Persistent Traditional Yemenite Ways of Dealing with Stress in Israel" in *Mental Health and Society,* 5(3–4):113–140.
1983 "Mental Health, Traditional Beliefs and the Moral Order Among Yemenite Jews in Israel" in Lola Romanucci-Ross, D. Moerman, and L. Tancredi, eds., *The Anthropology of Medicine: From Culture to Method.* New York: Praeger, pp. 319–335.

Patai, Raphael
1970a "The Middle East as a Culture Area" in Lutfiyya and Churchill, *Readings in Arab Middle Eastern Societies and Cultures,* pp. 187–204.
1970b *Israel Between East and West.* Westport, Connecticut: Greenwood Publishing Company. Second Edition.

Pearlin, Leonard
1974 *Class, Context and Family Relations, A Cross National Study.* Boston: Little, Brown and Co.

Peleg, J. and S. Peleg
1977 "The Ethnic Factor in Politics: The Mobilization Model and the Case of Israel" in *Ethnicity,* 4:177–187.

Peres, Yochanon
1971 "Ethnic Relations in Israel" in *American Journal of Sociology*, 75:1021–1047.

Peres, Y., L. Meisels and R. Frank
1980 "Commercial Matchmaking in Modern Israel: A Case of Dubious Rationality" in *Journal of Comparative Family Studies*, XI(4):475–484.

Peres, Y. and R. Schrift
1978 "Intermarriage and Interethnic Relations: A Comparative Study" in *Ethnic and Racial Studies*, 1(4):428–450.

Peristiany, J. ed.
1965 *Honour and Shame: The Values of Mediterranean Society*. London: Weidenfeld and Nicolson.

Pessar, Patricia
1984 "The Linkage Between the Household and the Work Place of Dominican Women in the United States" in *International Migration Review*, 18(4):1188–1211.

Peters, Emyrs
1978 "The Status of Women in Four Middle Eastern Communities" in Beck and Keddie, *Women in the Muslim World*, pp. 311–350.

Phizacklea, Annie, ed.
1983 *One Way Ticket: Migration and Female Labour*. London: Routledge and Kegan Paul.

Pitrou, Agnes
1980 "The Status of Women in French Families: Change or Stability in Patterns and Practices?" in H. Lopata, ed., *Research in the Interweave of Social Roles, Vol. 1*. Greenwich, Connecticut: JAI Press, pp. 119–138.

Pitt-Rivers, Julian
1977 *The Fate of Schechem or the Politics of Sex*. Cambridge: Cambridge University Press.

Prieto, Yolanda
1986 "Cuban Women and Work in the United States: A New Jersey Case Study" in Simon and Brettell, *International Migration: The Female Experience*, pp. 95–112.

Pryce, Kenneth
1978 "Lifestyles of West Indians in Britain: A Study of Bristol" in *New Community*, VI(3):207–217.

Quinn, Naomi 1977
"Anthropological Studies of Women's Status" in *Annual Review of Anthropology*, 6:181–225.

Rapoport, Rhona and Robert, and Z. Strelitz
1977 *Fathers, Mothers and Others*. London: Routledge and Kegan Paul.

Ratzhabi, Yehuda
1978 "Jewish Yemen" in J. Rappel, ed., *From the East and the West: Eastern Jewish Communities—Heritage and Culture.* Jerusalem: Ministry of Defence, pp. 205-282. In Hebrew.

Rein, Natalie
1980 *Daughters of Rachel: Women in Israel.* Middlesex: Penguin.

Reiter, Rayna
1975 "Men and Women in the South of France" in R. Reiter, ed., *Toward an Anthropology of Women.* New York: Monthly Review Press, pp. 252-282.

Reiter, R., ed.
1975 *Toward an Anthropology of Women.* New York: Monthly Review Press.

Rejwan, Nissim
1968 "The Communal Front" in I. Naamani, D. Rudavksy and A. Katsch, eds., *Israel: Politics and Philosophy.* New York: Behrman House, pp. 284-291.
1971 "From 'Mixing' to Participation: Social Implications of the Rise of Israeli Black Panthers" in *New Middle East,* May, pp. 20-24.
1986 "Pluralism and Cant." Book Review, *The Jerusalem Post International Edition.* December 27, 1986, p. 18.

Remba, Oded
1973 "Income Inequality in Israel" in Curtis and Chertoff, *Israel: Social Structure and Change,* pp. 199-215.

Rosaldo, M.
1974 "Women, Culture and Society: A Theoretical Overview" in M. Rosaldo and L. Lamphere, eds., *Women, Culture and Society.* Stanford: Stanford University Press, pp. 97-112.
1980 "The Use and Abuse of Anthropology: Reflections on Feminism and Cross-Cultural Understanding" in *Signs: Journal of Women in Culture and Society,* 5(3):389-417.

Rosman-Brenner, J.
1982 "Another Look at Jewish Women and Feminism." Unpublished paper delivered at the International Interdisciplinary Congress on Women, Haifa, Israel, January 1, 1982.

Sacks, Karen
1975 "Engels Revisited: Women, the Organization of Production, and Private Property" in Reiter, *Toward an Anthropology of Women,* pp. 211-234.

Safa, Helen
1984 "Female Employment and the Social Reproduction of the Puerto Rican Working Class" in *International Migration Review,* 18(4):1168-1187.

Saifullah-Khan, Verity
1976 "Purdah in the British Situation" in D. Barker and S. Allen *Dependence and Exploitation in Work and Marriage.* London: Longman, pp. 224-245.

1977 "The Pakistanis; Mirpuri Villagers at Home and in Bradford" in Watson, *Between Two Cultures,* pp. 57–89.
1979 "Work and Network: South Asian Women in London" in Sandra Wallman, ed., *Ethnicity at Work.* London: MacMillan, pp. 115–134.

Salaff, Janet
1981 *Working Daughters of Hong Kong.* Cambridge: Cambridge University Press.

Salaff, Janet and Aline Wong
1982 "Women, Work and the Family Under Conditions of Rapid Industrialization." Working Paper Series, No. 30A. Structural Analysis Program, University of Toronto.

Scanzoni, John
1978 *Sex Roles, Women's Work, and Marital Conflict.* Lexington: Lexington Books.

Schechtman, Joseph
1952 "The Repatriation of Yemenite Jewry" in *Jewish Social Studies,* 14(1):209–224.
1961 *On the Wings of Eagles.* New York: T. Yoseloff.

Schmidt, Dana
1968 *Yemen: The Unknown War.* London: Bodley Head.

Schneider, J.
1971 "Of Vigilence and Virgins: Honour, Shame and Access to Resources on Mediterranean Societies" in *Ethnology,* 10:1–24.

Sciama, Lidia
1981 "The Problem of Privacy in Mediterranean Anthropology" in Shirley Ardner, ed., *Women and Space: Ground Rules and Social Maps.* London: Croom Helm, pp. 89–110.

Scott, Hugh
1942 *In the High Yemen.* London: John Murray.

Seeley, John
1973 "Adolescence: The Management of Emancipation in History and Life History" in Silverstein, *The Sociology of Youth,* pp. 21–27.

Seller, Maxine, ed.
1981 *Immigrant Women.* Philadelphia: Temple University Press.

Shafer, R. B. and P. M. Keith
1981 "Equity in Marital Roles Across the Family Life Cycle" in *Journal of Marriage and the Family,* 43(2):359–367.

Shah, F. and M. Zelnick
1981 "Parent and Peer Influence on Sexual Behaviour, Contraceptive Use, and Pregnancy, Experience of Young Women" in *Journal of Marriage and the Family,* 43(2):339–347.

Shama, Avraham and Mark Iris
1977 *Immigration Without Integration: Third World Jews in Israel.* Cambridge, Massachusetts: Schenkman Publishing Company.

Shamgar-Handelman, Lea and Ruth Belkin
1984 "They Won't Stay Home Forever: Patterns of Home Space Allocation" in *Urban Anthropology*, 13(1):117–144.

Shan, Sharan-Jeet
1985 *In My Own Name.* London: The Women's Press.

Shapiro, Ovadia, ed.
1971 *Rural Settlements of New Immigrants in Israel.* Jerusalem: Keter Publishing House.

Sharpe, Sue
1976 *'Just Like a Girl', How Girls Learn to be Women.* Middlesex: Penguin.

Shoham, Schlomo
1973a "Migration and Crime in Israel: A Research Proposal" in S. Shoham, ed., *Israel Studies in Criminology, Vol.2.* Jerusalem: Jerusalem Academic Press, pp. 21–33.

Shoham, Schlomo, ed.
1970a *The Mark of Cain.* Jerusalem: Israel Universities Press.
1970b, 1971, 1973b, 1976 Israel Studies in Criminology. Tel Aviv: Gomeh Publishing House (1970) and Jerusalem: Jerusalem Academic Press.

Shokeid, Moshe
1971 *The Dual Heritage.* Manchester: Manchester University Press.

Shuval, Judith
1963 *Immigrants on the Threshold.* New York: Atherton Press.

Silverstein, Harry, ed.
1973 *The Sociology of Youth, Evolution and Revolution.* New York: Macmillan Publishing Co.

Simon, Rita and Caroline Brettell, eds.
1986 *International Migration: The Female Experience.* Totawa, New Jersey: Rowman and Allanheld, pp. 254–266.

Simon, Rita and Margo Deley
1984 "The Work Experience of Undocumented Mexican Women Migrants in Los Angeles" in *International Migration Review*, 18(4):1212–1229.

Smith, M. Estellie
1976 "Networks and Migration Settlement: Cherchez La Femme" in *Anthropological Quarterly*, 49(1):20–27.

Smooha, Sammy
1978 *Israel: Pluralism and Conflict.* London: Routledge and Kegan Paul.

Smooha, S. and Y. Peres
1975 "The Dynamics of Ethnic Inequalities: The Case of Israel" in *Social Dynamics*, 1:63–97.

Southall, Aidan
1961 "Introduction" to A. Southall, ed., *Social Change in Modern Africa*. London: Oxford University Press.

Spector, Johanna
1960 "Bridal Songs and Ceremonies from San'a, Yemen" in R. Patai, ed., *Studies in Biblical and Jewish Folklore*. Bloomington: Indiana University Press, pp. 255–289.

Spiegel, E.
1968 *New Towns in Israel*. Struttgart: Karl Krumer Verlag.

Spilerman, Seymour and Jack Habib
1974 *Development Towns in Israel: The Role of Community in Creating Ethnic Disparities in Labour Force Characteristics*. Madison: University of Wisconsin Press.

Spiro, M.
1980 *Gender and Culture*. New York: Schocken Books.

Stillman, Yedida
1981 "Attitudes Towards Women in Traditional Near Eastern Societies" in S. Morag, I. Ben-Ami, and N. Stillman, eds., *Studies in Judaism and Islam*. Jerusalem: The Magnes Press, The Hebrew University, pp. 345–360.

Stevenson, Thomas
1985 *Social Change in a Yemeni Highlands Town*. Salt Lake City: University of Utah Press.

Stone, Karen
1983 "Motherhood and Waged Work: West Indian, Asian and White Mothers Compared" in Phizacklea *One Way Ticket*, pp. 54–72.

Thomas, D.L., V. Gecas, A. Weigert, and E. Rooney
1974 *Family Socialization and the Adolescent*. Lexington, Massachusettes: Lexington Books, pp. 63–156.

Thompson, Marcus
1974 "The Second Generation: Punjabi or English?" in *New Community*, III(3):242–248.

Tiger, Lioner and Joseph Shepher
1975 *Women in the Kibbutz*. Middlesex: Penguin.

Tilly, Louise and Joan Scott
1978 *Women, Work and Family*. New York: Holt, Rinehart and Winston.

Tobi, Yosef
1974 "The Authority of the Jewish Community of San'a Over the Other Communities of Yemen." Jerusalem: Ben Zvi Institute. Draft only.

Tobi, Yosef, ed.
1976 *Legacy of the Jews of Yemen*. Jerusalem: Ahuva Press. In Hebrew.

Toledano, Henry
1973 "Time to Stir the Melting Pot" in Curtis and Chertoff, *Israel: Social Structure and Change*, pp. 333–349.

Touba, J. R.
1980 "Sex Segregation and Women's Role in the Economic System: The Case of Iran" in Lopata, *Research in the Interweave of Social Roles*, pp 51–98.

Troyna, Barry
1979 "Differential Commitment to Ethnic Identity by Black Youths in Britain" in *New Community*, VII(3):406–414.

Ullrich, Helen
1975 "Etiquette among Women in Karnataka: Forms of Address in the Village and Family" in de Souza, *Women in Contemporary India*, pp. 54–72.

UNESCO
1982 *Living in Two Cultures: The Socio-Cultural Situation of Migrant Workers and their Families*. UNESCO. Aldershot: Gower.

Vielle, Paul
1978 "Iranian Women in Family, Alliance and Sexual Politics" in Beck and Keddie, *Women in the Muslim World*, pp. 451–472.

Wajcman, Judy
1981 "Work and the Family: Who Gets the 'Best of Both Worlds'?" in the Cambridge Women's Study Group, eds., *Women in Society*. London: Virago Press.

Wakil, S. P., C.M. Siddique and F. A. Wakil
1981 "Between Two Cultures: A Study on Socialization of Children of Immigrants" in *Journal of Marriage and the Family*, 43(4):929–940.

Walters, J. and L. H. Walters
1980 "Parent-child Relationships: A Review, 1970–1979" in *Journal of Marriage and the Family*, 42(4):807–822.

Watson, James L., ed.
1977 *Between Two Cultures: Migrants and Minorities in Britain*. Oxford: Basil Blackwell.

Weingrod, Alex
1962 "Administered Communities: Some Characteristics of New Immigrant Villages in Israel" in *Economic Development and Cultural Change*, 11(1):69–86.
1965 *Israel: Group Relations in a New Society*. London: Pall Mall Publications.
1966 *Reluctant Pioneers: Village Development in Israel*. Ithaca: Cornell University Press.

1971 "'Stable' and 'Unstable' Village Development" in Ovadia Shapiro, ed., *Rural Settlements of New Immigrants in Israel*, pp. 171-188.

Weingrod, Alex, ed.
1975 *Studies in Israeli Ethnicity, After the Ingathering*. Glasgow: Gordon and Breach Science Publishers.

Weintraub, Dov
1971 *Immigration and Social Change; Agricultural Settlement of New Immigrants in Israel*. Manchester: Manchester University Press.

Weir, Shelagh
1985 *Qat in Yemen: Consumption and Social Change*. London: British Museum Publications Limited.

Weller, Leonard
1974 *Sociology in Israel*. Westport, Connecticut: Greenwood Press.

White, Graham
1977 *Socialization*. London: Longman.

Wikan, Unni
1980 *Life Among the Poor in Cairo*. London: Tavistock.
1982 *Behind the Veil in Arabia: Women in Oman*. Baltimore: Johns Hopkins University Press.

Willner, Dorothy
1965 "Politics and Change in Israel: The Case of Land Settlement" in *Human Organization*, 24:65-72.
1969 *Nation-Building and Community in Israel*. Princeton: Princeton University Press.

Wilson, Amrit
1978 *Finding a Voice: Asian Women in Britain*. London: Virago.

Wolf, Margery
1972 *Women and the Family in Rural Taiwan*. Stanford: Stanford University Press.

Wood, Marjorie
1975 "Employment and Family Change: A Study of Middle Class Women in Urban Gujarat" in de Souza *Women in Contemporary India*, pp. 37-53.

Yanagisako, Sylvia
1979 "Family and Household: The Analysis of Domestic Groups" in *Annual Review of Anthropology*, 8:161-205.

"Yemen's Jews Send Out Call for Help"
1982 *Jerusalem Post*, February 16, 1982.

Yoger, Sara
1981 "Do Professional Women Have Egalitarian Marital Relationships?" in *Journal of Marriage and the Family*, 43(4):865-872.

Young, M. and P. Willmott
1957 *Family and Kinship in East London*. Middlesex: Penguin.

Zaretsky, E.
1973 "Capitalism, the Family and Personal Life" in *Socialist Revolution*, 13-14:69-125; 15:19-70.

Zborowksy, Mark and Elizabeth Herzog
1970 *Life is With People*. New York: Schocken Books.

Zimmels, H.
1958 *Ashkenazim and Sephardim*. London: Oxford University Press.

Index

Accommodation
  of conflicting imperatives, 3, 230–233
  of sexual conduct, 182–189
  See also Control, parental
Adolescence, 3, 127, 128, 163(n7), 164(n12), 169, 199, 231, 237
Alienation of labour, 81, 90
Ambivalence, 71, 72, 87, 137, 162, 172, 193, 194, 202, 205(n6)
Army, 143–146, 159, 172, 179, 181–182, 201
Arranged marriage, 93–94(n20), 170, 207(n1)
  in Israel, 62–63, 111, 219
  in Yemen, 18, 63
  See also Marriage
Asher, 30, 49, 141, 226
Ashkenazi(m), 38, 43, 46, 47, 49, 59, 117, 139, 182, 201, 207(n15), 229, 241(n13)
  education, 48, 141
  employers, 86–88, 89, 126, 129
  friends, 85
  neighbours, 35
  women and work, 69
Authority, 57, 196–202
  brother's, 111
  husband's, 76
  mother's, 56, 61, 72, 80, 90
  mother-in-law's, 66, 80, 92(n7)
  parental, 2, 37, 74, 127, 140, 163(n7), 169
  patriarchal, 69, 91, 192, 193, 219
  teacher's, 113, 126
Avoidance relationship, 78, 149, 198–199, 208(n19)

Black Panthers, 5

Chastity, 3, 141, 144, 146, 151, 154, 162, 178, 184, 205(n6). *See also* Virginity
Chauvinism, 137, 200
Childbirth, 21, 128
Childminding, 34, 125

Chores, 77, 80, 111, 126, 173–175, 199.
  See also Division of labour
Class, 96(n31), 223
  and ethnicity, 5, 48, 89, 141, 219
Class development, 45, 68
Collective responsibility, 15, 88, 127, 152
Community, 34
Community surveillance, 204
Conjugal relations, 90–91, 114, 116, 117, 121–124, 130–131
  domestic/public distinction, 61–62, 64–65(table), 80–81, 82–83(table)
  See also Arranged marriage; Defilement; Division of labour; Employment, of women; Family purity rituals; Hinna; Labour history; Marriage; Sexuality; Sexual relations
Contraception, 151, 155, 163(n3), 167(n31), 187
Contradiction, 129, 142, 199, 213, 221, 230–234
Control, 11
  income, 21, 75
  male, 14, 16, 155, 167(n30), 222
  parental, 147–149, 179
Councils
  local, 30, 31, 91, 142
  religious, 32, 68
  worker's, 32, 68, 91
Cultural pluralism, 46, 218, 219, 220, 222, 223

Daily routine
  in Israel, 76–77, 174
  in Yemen, 22
Day care, 34, 125
Decision-making, 76, 79, 97(n38), 117–118, 164(n12)
Defilement, 120, 121, 130–131, 133(n25).
  See also Family purity rituals
Derekh Eretz, 15, 57, 58, 88, 107, 109, 113, 123, 127, 141, 147, 151, 154, 157, 158, 172–173, 175, 184, 192, 202, 205(n3), 231. *See also* Proper conduct

Index

Developmental cycle, 127, 128, 194, 237
Development towns, 45, 160
Discrimination, 14, 49, 52, 220, 223. *See also* Prejudice
Division of labour, 76, 77, 78, 79. *See also* Gender roles
Divorce, 19, 22, 27, 54, 56, 57, 78, 132(n16), 155, 192
Domestic domain
   in Israel, 61, 82(table), 92(n11)
   in Yemen, 64, 71, 76, 80
Domestic group, 94(n21), 235
Domestic labour, 69, 80, 146
Double burden, 72, 76, 80, 86, 95(n30), 125, 126, 127, 175
Double standards, 153, 200
Dowry, 59, 92

Eastern Jews. *See* Mizrahim
Education
   adult, 37, 86
   boarding school, 132, 139–140, 164
   elementary, 111, 128
   and ethnic origin, 47–48
   financial aid, 58–60, 110
   literacy, 80, 90, 126
   religious schooling, 139, 140, 144, 156, 165(nn 18, 21), 175–176
   secular schooling, 139, 140, 144, 159, 165(n18), 201
   and upward mobility, 70, 71
   of women, 71
   See also Feminist scholarship
Eidah, 46, 159, 212, 214, 220, 224, 238
Employment, 33, 34, 68, 83(table)
   effects of, 2, 95(n27)
   and ethnic origin, 47
   in Gadot, 30, 33
   and loans, 86, 88
   in Palestine, 24
   of research set, 36–37
   of women, 69, 70, 71
Ethnic differentiation, 34, 201
Ethnic interaction, 35, 84, 85, 86–87, 120, 142, 145, 171, 229
Ethnicity, 46, 49, 142, 161, 210(n36), 216–226
Evil eye, 1, 17, 19, 23, 74, 121, 167(n36), 192
Evil spirits, 15, 192
Exploitation of women. *See* Women, subordination to men

Family, 53, 132(n9), 165(n22), 224
   extended, 36, 55–58, 67, 234–236, 242(n30)
   nuclear, 67
Family conflict
   in Israel, 146–149, 150, 171, 175–178, 232
   in Yemen, 113
Family purity rituals, 1, 19–20, 67, 106, 114–121, 130, 131, 133(nn 25, 27), 134(n31)
Family relationships
   brothers, 55, 60
   cousins, 57
   father-son, 207–208(n19)
   mother-daughter, 42, 107–114, 126, 128–129, 171–189, 202–204, 206(n14)
   mother-son, 171, 189–196
   siblings, 196–202
   sister-brother, 54–60, 69, 88
   sisters, 55
   See also Family roles
Family roles, 76, 174
   in Yemen, 18, 53, 106–107
   See also Family relationships; Gender roles
Family size, 377
Feminist scholarship, 7, 61, 81, 96(n31), 227–228
Field work
   choice of, 3–6
   methodology, 38–43, 131(n3), 137–138
Filial piety, 128, 189, 196. *See also* Derekh Eretz
Friendship
   immigrant generation, 81, 84–86, 88–89, 123, 225, 233–234
   Israeli-born, 136, 140–141

Gadot, 30–35
   Ashkenazim in, 5
   cultural diversity, 2, 29, 40, 49, 186, 212, 238
   development of, 5, 160
   schools, 31, 33, 164(n13)
   Yemenis in, 34–35
Gender ideology, 16, 61, 71, 77, 78, 79, 91, 93(n16), 96(n32), 98(nn 41, 42, 43), 98–99(n46), 233. *See also* Family roles
Gender preferences, 107, 200, 208
Gender roles, 2, 8, 21, 23, 86, 90–91, 96(n32), 98(n45), 202, 219, 225
   in Yemen, 203–204
   See also Family relationships; Segregation; Women
Gossip, 106, 151, 163(n4), 185, 188, 204
Grandmothers, 34, 195, 196
Grandparents, 237

Halakhah, 16, 37, 76, 120, 122, 130, 134(n32), 166(n28), 179, 201
Hamulot. *See* Patronymic groups
Hinna, 19, 66–67, 106
Histadrut, 32
Honour, 3, 63, 70, 96(n33), 109, 117, 131, 140–141, 152–158, 167(n31), 171, 178, 184, 205(n6), 226
Host society, 8, 94(n20), 96(n31), 158, 164(n7), 170, 211, 212–216, 237, 239(n4), 240(n4)
Israel as, 203–204
Household, 50
composition in Israel, 26, 56, 60, 90
composition in Yemen, 16–17
Housewives, 126, 178
Housework. *See* Chores
Housing, 24, 29–30, 195

Identity, 2, 106, 109, 111, 120, 150, 234
ethnic, 2, 9, 47, 48, 87, 161–162, 207(n15), 221–222, 237
female, 53, 105–106, 118, 129–130
gender, 65
male, 166–167(n30)
Immigrant experience, 105, 125, 127, 158, 160–161, 196, 212–242
Israeli studies, 239(n1)
See also Immigrants; Women, and the immigrant experience
Immigrants
absorption of, 45
Asian, 92(n6), 94(n20), 97(n40), 170, 205(n5), 207(n15), 242(n30)
Jamaican, 94(n25)
Jewish, to Israel, 44–45
second generation, 158, 160–161
See also Immigrant experience; Israel, immigration to; Mizrahim, as immigrants; Refugees; under Women; Yemeni Jews, emigration
Immigration policy, 212–214
Improper conduct, 147, 149, 151, 157, 183–188, 200–202
Income, 126, 223
differentials, 47–48
India, 120
Individualism, 15. *See also* Self-interest
In-laws
brother-in-law, 20, 55, 58
daughter-in-law, 195–196, 209(n26)
mother-in-law, 20–21, 54, 60, 62, 67, 89, 107
sister-in-law, 20, 56, 62, 67, 89, 107
Integration, 2, 31, 49, 94(n20), 139, 160, 170, 204–205
Interes. *See* Self-interest

Intermarriage, 63, 99(n51), 170–171
Intimacy, 112, 187, 132(n13), 206(n14)
Islam, 13–14, 16, 63. *See also* Muslims
Israel
immigration to, 27–28(nn 32, 33), 44
sociology of, 5
See also Host society

Jewish law. *See* Halakhah
Judaism, 13, 15, 33, 87, 122, 131, 219, 224. *See also* Halakhah

Kashrut, 32, 131
Kibbutz, 144–145

Labour history, 69–71, 95(n27)
Labour power, 110
Law of Return, 44, 213, 215, 239(n3)
Leadership, 14, 34, 224. *See also* Control; Power relations
Low status, 75, 81, 90, 95(n26), 110, 160, 225

Ma'abarot, 25–26, 34, 44
Marital conflict, 56–57, 77–78
Marriage, 13, 60, 66, 109, 128, 136–137, 169, 197
age, 63, 135–136, 169
ceremony, 106
courtship, 66
early years, 67–68
endogamy, 63, 94(n20)
engagement, 136, 171
modern marriage, 62, 94(n21)
polygamy, 17, 219
polygyny, 26
wedding ceremony, 19–20
See also Arranged marriage; Conjugal relations; Divorce; Hinna; Unmarried Women
Marriage contract, 18
Masculinity, 72, 166(n30), 167(n30)
Mayor, 31–32, 34, 57, 68, 92
Mediation, 57
Melting pot, 45, 159, 215. *See also* Integration
Menopause, 196, 209(n27)
Menstruation, 1, 18, 20, 112, 114–118, 121
Middle Eastern Jews. *See* Mizrahim
Migration
study of, 228–236
and women, 7
Mikveh, 1, 20, 32, 89, 114, 116–117, 119, 133(n19)
Minorities, 43, 87, 94(n20), 217, 223

Mizrahim, 43, 46–47, 85, 159, 240–241(n13)
 education, 48
 ethnic profile, 6
 as immigrants, 5, 44–45, 95(n26), 165(n13)
 Israeli-born, 49
Mohar, 19, 27, 54, 60, 88, 193, 209(n30)
Moroccans, 46
Moshav, 4, 45, 224–225
Mother country, 211, 216, 221–222
Motherhood, 106, 124–128, 180
 Israeli-born, 125–126, 160–161
Muslims, 14–16, 204
 women, 134(n31)
 Zaydis, 24

Nahal, 143–145, 150, 201
National Service, 143–144, 181
Nation-building, 46, 68, 214
North African Jews. *See* Mizrahim

Old age, 22, 194–196, 209(n27)
Old maid, 135–137, 154, 156
Operation Magic Carpet, 25, 217. *See also* Yemeni Jews, emigration
Ottoman Empire, 24

Parenthood, 202, 205(n3)
Passover, 4
Pathology, 69
Patronymic groups, 16, 35, 91, 113, 152, 235
Political roles, 81(table)
Politics, 25
Pollution, 119
Population terminology, 158, 241(n13)
 immigrants, 148, 212
 Sabras, 159, 203
 veterans, 44, 158, 212
Power relations, 55–56, 68, 72, 75, 81, 87–88, 93(n16), 97(nn 33, 37, 38), 140, 164(n7), 219, 234
Prejudice, 46, 170. *See also* Discrimination
Prestige, 70, 72, 76, 80, 90, 120, 162, 196, 219, 226
Privacy, 55, 147, 204
Proper conduct, 15, 86, 116, 130, 154, 158, 169, 205(n3). *See also* Derekh Eretz
Public clerk, 32, 50
Public domain, 61, 74, 76, 80, 83(table), 92(n11), 93(n17), 106

Qat, 13, 36, 74, 122, 133(n30), 226

Rebellion, 1, 83, 206(n9)
Receiving society. *See* Host society
Refugees, 25, 213, 216–217
Religious observance, 37, 87, 91, 161
 and mother-daughter relationships, 79, 180–181
Religious roles, 83(table)
Reputation, 57–58, 78, 149, 154, 189, 200, 202, 220
Resettlement, 69, 236
Ritual baths. *See* Mikveh
Roles, 105, 109, 113, 129

Sabbath, 30, 88, 99(n50), 115, 176–177
Second generation immigrants. *See* Immigrants, second generation
Segregation, 31, 49
Self-esteem, 36, 64, 68, 83, 136
Self-image, 90
Self-interest, 58, 86, 88, 146, 172–173, 175, 197–198, 200, 205(n5), 231
Sephardim, 51, 117. *See also* Mizrahim
Settlement authorities, 25, 44, 218
Sexual abuse, 144
Sexual intercourse, 18–19, 122–124, 133(n19), 151, 154, 155
Sexuality
 female, 106
 female attitudes toward, 122, 123, 124, 131
 and self-control, 153, 166(n28)
 See also Defilement; Family purity rituals; Motherhood; Sexual relations, pre-marital; Unmarried women; Virginity
Sexual relations
 family discussion about, 112
 pre-marital, 3, 152–158, 165(n14), 182–188
 Yemeni Muslim women, 134(n31)
 See also Conjugal relations; Sexuality
Shame, 3, 20, 70, 87–88, 151, 153, 171, 179
Shtetl, 87, 92(n9), 215
Social activities, 36, 75, 82(table), 84
Social gap, 46, 159
Social organizations, 47
Social welfare, 31
Standard of living, 48
Stereotypes, 46, 49, 85, 93(n11), 159, 171, 224
Synagogue, 32–33, 35–36, 113, 222, 235
Syrian immigrants, 97(n37)

Taharat hamishpahah. *See* Family purity rituals

Torah, 15, 115–116, 117
Turks
  in business, 34
  and intermarriage, 171
  and religion, 50

Unchastity. *See* Chastity; Sexual relations
Unmarried adulthood, 2, 127, 169, 173, 178, 231, 237
Unmarried women, 2, 3, 42, 135–138, 182
  army service, 143–145, 181–182
  education, 138–142
  residence, 146–150, 162
  work, 145–146
  See also Family conflict; Family relationships; Sexuality; Sexual relations
Upbringing, 15, 78, 80, 89, 111, 113, 114, 129, 141, 157, 162, 178, 181
  discipline, 197–198
  obedience, 128, 204(n1)

Values, 2, 37, 44, 66, 89, 109, 114, 127–129, 140, 142, 151, 158, 164(n13), 172, 175, 181, 202, 209(n32), 225–226
Virginity, 112, 119, 122, 131, 150–157, 167(n31), 185, 209(n30). *See also* Chastity; Sexual relations

Wage labour, 78, 97(n33), 111. *See also* Employment
Widowhood, 36
Women
  economic roles, 71
  illiteracy, 15, 71
  and the immigrant experience, 6–9
  in Israel, 3
  Middle Eastern, 105
  and migration, 7
  subordination to men, 66, 76, 78, 93(n16), 199
  in Yemen, 3
  See also Education; Employment; Gender roles; Motherhood; Sexuality; Sexual relations; Unmarried women; Virginity; Widowhood
Working class, 25

Yemen, 13
  economic roles, 63(table)
  family relationships, 18, 21
  household chores, 64(table)
  Jewish settlement, 13–14
  leisure, 64(table)
  political roles, 65(table)
  religious roles, 65(table)
  socialization of children, 64(table)
  See also Yemeni Jews
Yemeni Jews
  communal organization, 14
  education, 14
  emigration, 23–25
  ethnic profile, 6, 34
  homogeneous settlements, 49, 51, 91, 144, 188, 208(n22), 222–226
  legal status, 14
  spiritual life, 15
Youth groups, 32, 111, 140, 172

Zionism, 25, 44–45, 47–48, 213